Open Distributed Systems

Selected Titles from The Artech House
Telecommunications and Networking Library

Vinton G. Cerf, Series Editor

For further information on these and other Artech House titles, contact:

Artech House
685 Canton Street
Norwood, MA 02062
617-769-9750
Fax: 617-769-6334
Telex: 951-659
email: artech@world.std.com

Artech House
Portland House, Stag Place
London SW1E 5XA England
+44 (0)171-973-8077
Fax: +44 (0)171 630 0166
Telex: 951-659
email: bookco@artech.demon.co.uk

Open Distributed Systems

Jon Crowcroft
University College London

Artech House
Boston • London

First published in the UK in 1995 by UCL Press.

UCL Press Limited
University College London
Gower Street
London WC1E 6BT

The name of University College London (UCL) is a registered
trade mark used by UCL Press with the consent of the owner.

Published in 1995 in the United States by

Artech House, Inc.
685 Canton Street
Norwood, MA 02062
USA

Library of Congress Cataloging-in-Publication Data

Crowcroft, Jon.
    Open distributed systems / Jon Crowcroft.
        p.   cm.
    Includes bibliographical references and index.
    ISBN 0-89006-839-9 (alk. paper)
    1. Electronic data processing—Distributed processing.   I. Title.
QA76.9.DSC79   1996
004'.36—dc20   95-48909
                                                                              CIP

Printed and bound in Great Britain.

Contents

10   Distributed file systems   297
with Nermeen Ismail, University College London

11   Load balancing   315
with S. Hailes, University College London

12   Future lessons and challenges   355

Preface

This book is an introduction to open distributed systems. It covers the principles of distributed systems and their application to standards. Particular emphasis is placed on novel applications in the areas of multimedia and load sharing, both as an integral part of these systems and as examples of complex distributed applications.

Theme and purpose
Systems are distributed for either or both of two main reasons:
1. An organization and its information systems may be inherently distributed and, in connecting its systems into a seamless whole, a distributed system appears.
2. An organization may take inherently centralized information processing systems and distribute them to achieve higher reliability, availability, safety or performance, or all of these.

A distributed system consists of a number of components, which are themselves computer systems. The components are connected by some communications medium, usually a sophisticated network. Applications execute by using a number of processes in different component systems. These processes communicate and interact to achieve productive work within the application. A distributed system has a number of advantages over a single computer system:
- It can be more fault-tolerant. It can be designed so that if one component of the system fails then the others will continue to work. Such a system will provide useful work in the face of quite a large number of failures in individual component systems.
- It is more flexible. A distributed system can be made up from a number of different components. Some of these components may be specialized for a specific task, others may be general-purpose.
- It is easier to extend. More processing, storage or other power can be obtained by increasing the number of components.
- It is easier to upgrade. When a single large computer system becomes obsolete all of it has to be replaced in a costly and disruptive operation. A distributed system may be upgraded in increments by replacing individual components without a major disruption or a large cash injection.

Distributed systems also introduce several problems not encountered in centralized systems:
- They are significantly more complex.
- They introduce problems of synchronization between processes.
- They introduce problems of maintaining consistency of data.
- In general, there is no longer a central management entity in control of the whole system.

Approach

The object-oriented (OO) paradigm is well suited for both description and implementation of distributed systems. The advantages of such an approach are in increased decomposition of systems into modules (refinement), and in data abstraction. Since standards are emerging based on these techniques, this book uses this paradigm implicitly throughout, and explicitly in places.

Object-oriented models

Object-oriented models appear in many aspects of computer science: system design, programming, etc. The essence of an object-oriented approach is that concepts, ideas, processes, or data, or combinations of these, are grouped together into a capsule called an "object". An object supports a number of interfaces with which it communicates with other objects. In a programming analogy, an interface is like the declaration of a procedure or function. Thus an interface can be supported by one or more actual implementations or definitions. In an object-oriented model the implementations behind interfaces are called "methods" or "operations".

Objects provide us with a effective way of encapsulating things so that we can use them in other parts of the model. The interface describes exactly how to use the object. In a true object model everything is an object; however, going too far down this road enables us to describe anything recursively and thus we end up explaining nothing. We will use the object concept to build up a model of a distributed system; the model will then show us what types of object interaction we will need to support. The re-usability of objects, and refinement through inheritance, makes systems more open, since they can support diversity, but permits comprehension of diverse systems into one. The first part of this book describes mechanisms needed to build up a distributed system. Just because we are using an object-oriented approach, to make our descriptions consistent and related, does not mean that we must build an object-oriented distributed system. The reader must distinguish between a tool used to put across ideas and a tool used to design and build a system. It is possible to use object-oriented languages and object-oriented support systems to build a distributed system. However, it is just as possible to program and use a distributed system in assembler code if required.

Open distributed systems

The main purpose behind this text is to introduce the reader to a special category of distributed systems: that of open distributed systems. A number of experimental distributed systems have been built in universities and research laboratories. Each of these was developed to demonstrate different concepts and consequently each has a number of strengths and weaknesses. However, it is not possible to take the strong parts from each system and put them together to make a really good distributed system. This is because the individual components of the systems were designed and built to work only with other components of the local system. This book is *not* about distributed operating systems.

An open distributed system is made up of components that may be obtained from a number of different sources, which together work as a single distributed system. In 1988 the International Standards Organization (ISO) began work on preparing standards for open distributed processing (ODP). These standards have now largely been completed, and define the interfaces and protocols to be used in the various components of an open distributed system. The first task of the group working on the ODP standards was to define a reference model from which individual standards would be identified. The material used in this book is designed to enable the reader to understand the ODP standards and to see how they all fit together. However, this is not a book about the ODP standards, but a book containing the background technical knowledge about distributed systems necessary to understand and interpret the standards.

The ODP standards are intended to provide the framework within which distributed applications may be built and executed. This is an application-oriented view. However, the standards will use a large number of system-oriented mechanisms to support the applications, and hence a lot of the material in this text is system-oriented. In order to include as much material as possible on distributed systems we have assumed that the reader will be familiar with a number of other technical areas. These include an understanding of communications architectures such as the open systems interconnection architecture or the US Department of Defense internet architecture, together with some understanding of centralized operating systems architectures. It is also helpful to have some familiarity with high-level programming abstractions, such as object-oriented programming or the abstract data type methodology. The text includes references to other books, papers, and journals; these are intended to provide background reading where such familiarity is assumed.

Distributed operating systems

The ODP standards, and this text, assume a model where distributed applications are running in multiple processes in multiple computers linked by communications. The application programmer will be supported by a programming environment and run-time system that will make many aspects of distribution in the system transparent. For instance, the programmer may not have to worry about where the parts of the application are running, which can all be taken care of, if required; this is called location transparency.

There is another approach to supporting applications in a distributed system, namely by using a distributed operating system. On every computer system with an operating system the OS provides an interface which the programs use to obtain services, such as input and output.

In a distributed operating system this interface is enhanced so that a program may be run on any computer in the distributed system and can access data on any other computer. The operating system provides data, execution and location transparency, often through an extended naming scheme. The advantage of a distributed operating system is that is uses an interface below that of the application program. This means the existing programming environments may be used, the programmer may use the system with little or no extra training, and in some cases existing software may be used. The disadvantage is that a number of problems are left for the programmer and user to handle, for instance concurrency; and because of the advantage above, programmers are given little support for this. Essentially, the distributed operating system dictates the policies of distribution for all aspects of programming. This means that the programmer is not able to use the distributed functionality in an application-specific way to optimize a solution.

Another major disadvantage is that the distributed system is tied to a style of operating system interface. There are lots of different operating systems today, to meet different requirements (real or imaginary); there is no reason why future distributed systems will not need different operating system interfaces. Consequently it is not possible to build a truly heterogeneous open distributed system by building it on top of a homogeneous distributed operating system.

The ODP model provides an application interface to the distributed system. This interface is extremely simple and is concerned with aspects of distribution only. The application may still be run on any local operating system that is appropriate.

The ODP model does include the use of distributed operating systems, but would require any particular type of distributed operating system to interwork with other types through ODP and also with non-distributed operating systems. The applications would see no difference.[1] One popular implementor's specification for some parts of ODP is the Common Object Request Broker Architecture (CORBA). This is covered in Chapter 7.

A model for open distributed systems

This section introduces the model being developed in the ISO ODP committee which will act as a reference model, in a similar manner to the way the Open Systems Interconnection (OSI) reference model was used to develop the OSI services and protocols.

To understand why a reference model is important it is necessary to understand a little about the way standards are made and used. When a new technical area is identified for standardization the experts are brought together to define the area. This results in a consensus of the general model applicable to the technical area. The general model describes all possible systems that could be built. An analysis of the general model will identify a number of components and interfaces between components. A series of design decisions are then made in choosing interfaces and components which will form the basis of a reference model. The reference model will prescribe all possible open systems in the technical area, which is a subset of all possible systems. The open systems will contain the identified components and will use the identified interfaces between the components. The functionality of the components, and their relationships, are set out in the reference model.

---

1. It might be argued that by the time complete transparency functions have been provided to support distributed applications, ODP would itself be just a distributed operating system in another guise!

The interfaces represent the next step for standardization. Each interface becomes a specific standard. Work on the interfaces will be carried out in parallel to complete a set of standards. In the process of producing the standards a number of choices will be made in the design of the interfaces, which will further constrain the set of possible open systems. When the standards are completed they will represent a set of conformance rules such that any system supporting the standards will be a conformant system in the technical area.

The standards process is a progressive elimination of all possible systems down to a set of conformant systems. Each step involves making design decisions; and, just as important, areas of design freedom for the next stage are identified. Eventually, design freedoms are left at the end of the standards process; these represent aspects of the systems which are not essential for interworking and are areas that can then be used by manufacturers to make unique products and by end-users to create specific systems.

The reference model is not part of the standard that describes conformant systems; therefore it is not a standard that systems can claim conformance to. The purpose of the reference model is to translate the general model of the technical area into a framework which will enable its standardization. Once the individual standards have been identified and their relationships established, work on them can proceed in parallel. This enables a technical area to be standardized in the fastest possible way.

In some cases the standards will define the products almost completely, as tends to be the case in OSI, where the communications design freedoms are very small. In other cases, such as management and security, the standards allow considerable design freedoms at a number of stages, and where decisions are made they are constrained to those aspects of interworking. Security and management have a big impact on the internal working of components and systems. The standards have a role to ensure that interworking can take place, and that when all the design freedoms have been taken up in an end-user system then that system will be secure and manageable, as required by the end-user. Whereas OSI standards can specify the full details for communications, it is not possible for a security or management standard to fully specify a secure or manageable system

Of course, one cannot mention standards without quoting the line attributed to Grace Hopper: "The great thing about standards is that there are so many to choose from".

Intended usage

This book is intended to provide a self-contained text on open distributed processing. We assume that the reader has a basic knowledge of programming, operating systems and the facilities provided by low-level communications architectures. Knowledge of distributed operating systems or applications is not required, since the text introduces many of the concepts that they have in common with open distributed systems.

The text is partly based on material taught in a specialist Masters course in

Distributed Systems, and partly on material taught in several commercial courses, as well as the author's own research. It should therefore be suitable for the third year of an undergraduate course, for postgraduate students, or for those in industry working with standards and distributed systems.

Each chapter covers a different aspect of the technology and each is presented in a different way. There are many aspects to these systems, and many valid approaches. Our publisher would throw up his hands in horror if we attempted to show all approaches to all aspects. The advantage of this approach is that most chapters can be read independently. For example, the chapter on formal methods can easily be omitted at a first read. Also, the chapters on examples of distributed system problems are each independent of the other. The penultimate chapter is presented at a greater level of detail, and the final chapter is deliberately contentious.

Organization

The book is loosely organized in two parts: the first part covers the theory of distributed systems, the second half contains three special examples of distributed systems. The first example shows how a multimedia conferencing system can be *built* as a distributed application, the second how a management system can be *modelled* as a distributed application. Management of a distributed system is a complex embedded system and requires handles in all parts of the system. stresses our architectural design is multimedia conferencing. The final example will show how a distributed file system has been built as an example user application. Chapter 11 is about a more complex problem, that of load balancing in distributed systems, and is aimed at the research-minded reader. The last chapter is a discussion of some of the problems that are considered unsolved or worthy of further research in distributed systems.

Acknowledgements

Thanks are due to Rob Cole, Graham Knight, Steve Hailes, Ian Wakeman, James Cowan, Mark Handley, Atanu Ghosh, Alina da Cruz, Nermeen Ismail and Dave Lewis for many an evening's lively discussion. Thanks to Nigel Edwards from Hewlett-Packard and ANSA. Thanks to George Michaelson, Andrew Campbell, Paul Barker and Steve Kille for standardizationalism. We also enjoyed the presence for many years of the Reality Checkpoint on Parker's Piece.

For Chapter 7, we wish to acknowledge Mike Beasley of ICL Ltd and ANSA for providing me with some of the code examples and for his painstaking comments on early drafts of this work. Comments of and conversations with Andrew Herbert, Chris Mayers and Andrew Watson of APM Ltd. and ANSA were extremely helpful. Finally we wish to thank James de Raeve and Paul Tanner of X/Open for providing information on X/Open's work on conformance testing for CORBA.

CHAPTER 1

What are open distributed systems and what are they for?

1.1 Introduction

We all want to communicate. Individuals communicate to achieve their day-to-day desires and requirements. Organizations communicate about their business goals.

Communication is built round the common goals of an organization. The organization develops a vocabulary to name the objects that concern it, together with a language appropriate to describing the relations between these objects, the actions that may be performed on these objects, and the methods (ways) in which these actions may be carried out. The objectives behind communication are many. A party may desire to communicate a command or wish to another, or may wish to elicit information from another.

In almost all enterprises (see for example Fig. 1.1), there is some degree of geographic distribution of the components of the system, and some requirement for communication between these parts. Communication may require complex rules to overcome the limitations of distant communication. These rules will deal with the problems of limited expressiveness of remote communication. Distant communication incurs limitations such as restrictions on speed (rate) and latency

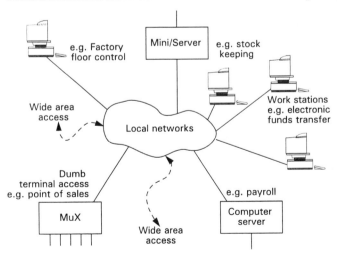

Figure 1.1 Distributed system.

1

(delay) of information transfer, and increased chance of errors. The need for low-level rules for communication is dealt with in more detail in Chapter 5.

The range of human communication mechanisms extends from face-to-face communication, including one-to-one and one-to-many, through telephone calls, the slower medium of letters, and the more rapid equivalent of facsimile. These mechanisms are all reflected in the ways that computers are used to communicate.

Computers may be used to share visualizations of data through real-time graphics, to exchange textual information in real time or to communicate offline using store-and-forward messaging systems. Programs may communicate in similar ways to those that users do using such programmed facilities.

As well as geographical distribution, in almost all enterprises there is some degree of autonomy of the components of the system. Different parts of an organization will have different ways of communicating, internally and externally. This will be for reasons of efficiency and expressiveness. Efficiency may dictate that locally understood vocabularies are used in some places (for example, doctors and pharmacists use specialist terms). Different parts of the organization will have no interest in the detailed operations of each other, so summaries and reports will be exchanged that hide detail. Autonomy and heterogeneity are natural consequences of the growth and evolution of any large-scale organization. Scale leads to diversity. It also leads to problems with systems modelled around 100% availability. In large systems there are always faults and error conditions.

Just as natural languages are used differently by different specialists (and indeed by ordinary people when speaking or writing), so different computer users have different computing approaches and different distribution requirements. Accounts, stock control, points of sale, factory automation, real-time control systems, electronic funds-transfer systems and many other applications will all have very different internal structures.

The implications of all these points are that distributed computing is required, and that it must allow a degree of autonomy for the separate systems, as in Figure 1.2. This autonomy combined with the ability to communicate freely with other systems is what is partly meant by *open distributed systems*. The openness is a requirement of the autonomy of different users to acquire, install and operate different appropriate systems while maintaining consistent distribution mechanisms across all users' systems.[1]

Computing systems are used in a wide variety of organizations, for a wide variety of reasons. These reasons can be analysed from a number of *viewpoints* as explained in the following section. Many of these ideas were developed under the UK Alvey Project, ANSA ("Advanced Network Systems Architecture") (APM 1989, 1992, Herbert 1994) and were then elaborated by the EC Esprit Project ISA ("Integrated Systems Architecture"). The work has been taken up by the

---

1. The difference between what is available commercially and what is described here can be summed up by paraphrasing the famous question and answer of Gandhi's concerning Western Civilization: "What do you think of distributed systems?" "I think they would be a jolly good idea."

Figure 1.2 Open distributed system.

International Standards Organization under the Open Distributed Processing Working Group.

1.2 The viewpoints

The open distributed processing (ODP) reference model work has identified five viewpoints which may be used to examine a distributed system. These viewpoints are tools to help with the analysis of a distributed system. Different groups of people from different backgrounds are involved in specifying, building, using and running a distributed system.

The viewpoints represent those perspectives of the distributed system that are important to the different groups of people involved in the system. Each group sees some aspects in great detail, but other parts are described only vaguely as they are not important to that group. For instance, the users of the system will want to know a lot about what the system does in terms of using information and producing useful results; they will not be interested in exactly which CPU model, or disk drive, or even disk sector, they are using to achieve their work. On the other hand, the operations manager will be very concerned about CPU utilization, disk blocking, and sharing hardware resources, but will not be very interested in what the distributed system is actually doing in terms of the input and the results.

The five viewpoints are not meant to represent five layers; however, they do have some relationship, in that we can see how refining one viewpoint may well lead to another. Viewpoints are not in and of themselves refinements or part of any particular development methodology. All viewpoints are always valid. The viewpoints will overlap; there are no distinct boundaries.

The viewpoints are just perspectives on an underlying model, or actual system. If there were no underlying model then the perspectives would become disjoint. When used in the context of an underlying model then each perspective (viewpoint description) is different in the concepts that it brings into focus as important and in the concepts that are hidden or ignored. Each perspective will represent a different level of abstraction of the system. These are illustrated in Table 1.1. A number of projects have contributed to the way these ideas may be projected onto distributed systems in five ways. Who uses which viewpoint is shown in Table 1.2.

Table 1.1 Framework of abstractions document.

Viewpoint	Discipline	Areas of concern	What is specified
Enterprise	Management Economics Social sciences	Human & social issues Management & finance Legal concerns	Requirements
Information	Data models Knowledge Representation	Information models Information flow Information structure	Conceptual design & specifications
Computation	Software engineering	Application & process design & development (concurrency models, Abstract Data Types, distributed algorithms)	Design & development
Engineering	Operating systems Database systems Communication systems	Distributed system infrastructure Application support Transparencies – naming, building, etc.	Infrastructure building blocks
Technology	End-products of relevant disciplines	Technology	Technology

Table 1.2 Viewpoint users.

Viewpoint	User
Enterprise	Management
Information	Information management specialists
Computational	Application programmers
Engineering	Operating system and communications specialists
Technology	Implementation and maintenance staff

Enterprise

This projection describes how computing systems and the distribution of computing resources match the objectives and organization of the enterprise. It shows what the system's function is within the enterprise, rather than how it functions.

Note that "enterprise" represents any human endeavour in a social context. It does not just mean a business company, but might be a trade association, a charity, a standards group, a community of interest, anything that requires interaction and computerization. In this viewpoint, distribution is inherent, but largely transparent.

Information

This projection identifies the information used within the organization. It shows where the information is used, and in which ways it is processed. It indicates the meaning of the information within the system to its users.

An information model reflects the real world, for instance a stock record should be matched by actual stock on shelves, as accounting information is matched by money in the bank. Workflow analysis is often used to derive the information model implicit in an organization.

The information projection does not just contain the information requirements and models of the enterprise, but also the information requirements of the distributed system. For security, access-control information must be kept, and this can be described from this viewpoint. Obviously the access-control information will select the enterprise model for access control, but is part of the information needed within the distributed system. Thus, there are two components of the information viewpoint: information requirements for the enterprise, and for the distribution itself. Distribution is usually taken for granted in this viewpoint, so it is inherent and transparent.

Computational

This projection shows how the applications may be structured so that they are independent of the computer systems and networks on which they run. It produces a computational model for how information and its processing are represented, how applications are specified, and how separate applications are linked and interfaced. This viewpoint would include any inherent distribution and parallelism in the application.

The importance of this viewpoint is that it represents the capabilities of the distributed system to the applications programmer. In particular, it enables the programmer to invoke all the transparencies that are required from a distributed system (see below). Alternatively, of course, the programmer can ignore the transparencies and handle distribution directly. So in this viewpoint distribution can be transparent, or it can be made explicit.

Engineering

This projection relates the underlying components of a distributed system to the applications. It is here that such issues as performance, reliability and availability are decided.

This is the viewpoint where distribution is explicit, and must be handled. For instance, replication mechanisms might be introduced to increase reliability. Different mechanisms would be selected based on engineering tradeoffs concerning cost, performance and availability constraints.

Technology

The technology projection maps the distributed system onto the processing nodes and communications infrastructure that form the hardware and software base. Distribution is not part of this viewpoint.

 Reality checkpoint   The open distributed processing model is still undergoing evolution. What is presented in this book is not meant to reflect the ODP community's model at all, but this author's extraction of those points that were found useful and were reasonably complete at the time of writing.

1.3 Transparencies

A transparency is some aspect of the distributed system that is hidden from the user (programmer, system developer, user or application program). A transparency is provided by including some set of mechanisms in the distributed system at a layer below the interface where the transparency is required. A number of basic transparencies have been defined for a distributed system. It is important to realize that not all of these are appropriate for every system or are available at the same level of interface. In fact, all transparencies have an associated cost, and it is extremely important for the distributed system implementor to be aware of this. Much of the text of this book describes engineering solutions to archiving these transparencies and attempts to outline the cost of the solutions. It is a matter for much research how the costs of implementing multiple transparencies interact. This is part of current research in how to reduce operating system and communications stack overheads through such approaches as application layer framing and integrated layer processing (Clark & Tennenhouse 1990). The transparencies are listed below.

Access transparency

There should be no apparent difference between local and remote access methods. In other words, explicit communication may be hidden. For instance, from a user's point of view, access to a remote service such as a printer should be identical with access to a local printer. From a programmer's point of view, the access method to a remote object may be identical to accessing a local object of the same class.

This transparency has two parts:
1. Keeping a syntactical or mechanical consistency between distributed and non-distributed access.
2. Keeping the same semantics. Because the semantics of remote access are more complex, particularly as regards failure modes, this means that the local access should be a subset. Remote access will not always look like local access in that certain facilities may not be reasonable to support (for example, global exhaustive searching of a distributed system for a single object may be unreasonable in terms of network traffic).

Location transparency

The details of the topology of the system should be of no concern to the user. The location of an object in the system may not be visible to the user or programmer. This differs from access transparency in that both the naming and access methods may be the same. Names may give no hint as to location.

Concurrency transparency

Users and applications should be able to access shared data or objects without interference with each other. This requires very complex mechanisms in a distributed system, since there exists true concurrency rather than the simulated concurrency of a central system. For example, a distributed printing service must provide the same atomic access per file as a central system so that printout is not randomly interleaved.

Replication transparency
If the system provides replication (for availability or performance reasons) it should not concern the user. As for all transparencies, we include the applications programmer as a user.

Fault transparency
If software or hardware failures occur, these should be hidden from the user. This can be difficult to provide in a distributed system, since partial failure of the communications subsystem is possible, and this may not be reported. As far as possible, fault transparency will be provided by mechanisms that relate to access transparency. However, when the faults are inherent in the distributed nature of the system, then access transparency may not be maintained. The mechanisms that allow a system to hide faults may result in changes to access mechanisms (e.g. access to reliable objects may be different from access to simple objects). In a software system, especially a networked one, it is often hard to tell the difference between a failed and a slow-running process or processor. This distinction is hidden or made visible here.

Migration transparency
If objects (processes or data) migrate (to provide better performance, or reliability, or to hide differences between hosts), this should be hidden from the user.

Performance transparency
The configuration of the system should not be apparent to the user in terms of performance. This may require complex resource-management mechanisms. It may not be possible at all in cases where resources are only accessible via low-performance networks.

Scaling transparency
A system should be able to grow without affecting application algorithms. Graceful growth and evolution is an important requirement for most enterprises. A system should also be capable of scaling down to small environments where required, and be space- and/or time-efficient as required.

The transparencies are only one group of *properties* of an open distributed system. The other groups are obligations and persistence.
Obligations are drawn from the properties of cooperation. These are "contractual" in the object-oriented programming sense. The behaviour of applications or objects can be evaluated against precise specifications. Obligations include:

Quality of service
In a similar sense to the QoS terminology used in telecommunications, we may assign a set of values to various parameters of open distributed system services, such as availability and performance.

Policy
A set of prescriptive requirements may be imposed on the system to exclude certain behaviours merely for policy reasons. For instance, some particular set of users may be disallowed from access to some services at certain times. *Constraints* are similar to policies but apply to the behaviour of particular objects in the system, rather than to behaviour of the system as a whole.

These obligations are not implemented as objects themselves, but may be imposed by some objects within the system.

Persistence
Persistence is the notion of activity versus passivity. In conventional systems, the ideas of process and data express activity and passivity respectively. In an open distributed system, the notion is less well defined since objects may be seen as passive relative to some parts of the system (e.g. a migration object would see other objects as passive, while clients of these objects after they have migrated would see them as active).

The reader may ask what freedom is left for the systems or applications programmer when there are so many descriptive and prescriptive properties. That is exactly the strength of the open distributed systems approach:

The specification of the system will lead directly through object modelling to the choice of engineering and other tradeoffs available to the programmer. Prescriptive properties rule out those not available. Descriptive properties give choice – for example between failure transparency and access transparency constrained by a cost policy.

The first seven chapters of this book discuss the design of the mechanisms needed to support these transparencies and describe some of the engineering costs involved in implementations of these mechanisms.

The rest of this chapter outlines the distinction between operating system and application service support, and then provides an overview of the object-oriented approach to structuring modules in open distributed systems. Much of the material is presented from the engineering viewpoint.

1.4 Central operating system services
Central operating systems traditionally provide a *virtual machine* which has a unified view of various peripherals. Typically these are implemented as structured views of data (as in file systems and databases) and processes (running programs).

Two alternative views of an operating system are:
- *A communications system*
  It allows the sharing of resources such as filestore and CPU between users. It allows multiple users of multiple files and processes.
- *A resource manager*
  It controls a number of simple devices and adds functionality by sequencing access and providing protection mechanisms to prevent disorderly use.

Operating systems evolved to provide more convenient access to computing resources, and also to provide more efficient use of those resources. For convenience, a standard interface to the virtual machine is provided. For efficiency and convenience, multi-tasking is provided.

Multi-tasking provides the programmer with the illusion of concurrency on single-processor architectures. This illusion greatly simplifies the design of programs handling streams of input and output to and from different devices (sources and sinks). Neither the operating system nor the applications programmer can know in advance which events will occur in what order. It is much more natural to model separate sources and sinks as being handled by separate processes. Thus we can identify a set of base objects that exist in the virtual machine (see Fig. 1.3).

- users
- processes (which may be divided into various levels of threads of control)
- filestore (usually provided as a uniform view of input/output devices, with a base set of methods and some refinements for special-case devices)

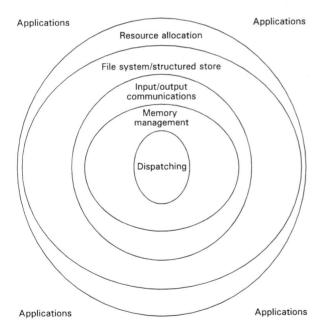

Figure 1.3 Operating system components.

- communications channels

Furthermore, we can identify a set of base operations on these objects such as:

- create/destroy (user/process/file/directory/channel)
- initialize (user/process/file/directory/channel)
- identify/authenticate a user/process/file
- change permissions for user/process/file/channel
- send/receive data to/from file/channel
- control device

1.4.1 System interfaces

An operating system supports a virtual machine by providing a standard system interface. At the immediate interface to the operating system, this is typically provided as one or more *monitors*.

A monitor is a collection of procedures that may be executed by a collection of concurrent processes. It protects its internal data from the users, and is a mechanism for synchronizing access to the resources the procedures use. Since only the monitor can access its private data, it automatically provides mutual exclusion between customer processes. Entry to the monitor by one process excludes entry by others. This is described further in Chapter 2.

In this sense, the operating system is very like a collection of objects accessed by standard methods. The operating system monitor is a single monolithic monitor, which protects not only private data but also privileged instructions. Usually, hardware support is required to secure access to this kind of monitor (via system "traps"). However, modern languages and compiler support mean that this is less necessary.

These procedures in an operating system monitor are usually divided into those to do with file access, those to do with process manipulation, and those to do with inter-process communication (IPC). Inter-process communication (Fig. 1.4) can be provided in several ways:

- shared memory
- message passing
- streams/pipes/named pipes
- FIFO buffers
- remote procedure call

We can further classify the IPC mechanisms into the broad classes:

- reliable
- unreliable

Reliable communication channels fail only with the end-system (e.g. if a central computer bus fails, usually the entire machine (stable storage/memory/CPU access) fails). Unreliable channels exhibit various different types of fault. Messages may be lost, reordered, duplicated, changed to apparently correct but different messages and even created as if from nowhere by the channel; all of these problems may have to be overcome by the IPC mechanism.

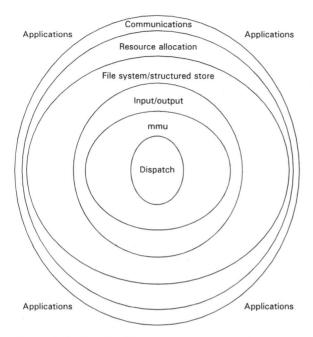

Figure 1.4 Distributed operating system services.

We can also classify IPC mechanisms by when the association between one process and another is made. (This is orthogonal to the issue of reliability.)

Connection binding
This can be further refined by seeing whether the inter-process association is at compile time, link time or run time. Many systems (typically message passing) have no notion of connectedness.

Independent messages
This can be refined by the strength of synchronization involved in sending and/or receiving a message.

1.4.2 Distributed operating systems

Distributed operating systems extend the notion of a virtual machine over a number of interconnected computers or hosts. Note that the user/programmer still has the illusion of working on a single system. All the issues of concurrency and distribution are completely hidden by the virtual machine, and the user/programmer is not at liberty to exploit them (nor should be hindered by them!).

Distributed operating systems (Fig. 1.5) are often broadly classified into two extremes of a spectrum:

- *Loosely coupled systems*
  Components are workstations, LAN, servers; e.g. V-System, BSD Unix.

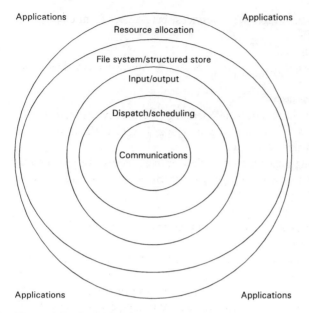

Figure 1.5 Distributed operating system.

- *Tightly coupled systems*

  Components are processors, memory, bus, I/O; e.g. Meiko Compute Surface.

Often this classification is really a reflection of the reliability and performance of the communications subsystem. Frequently, shared memory systems are regarded as more tightly coupled than message passing systems.

Another way of looking at these classifications is to think of tightly coupled systems as *dependent*, and loosely coupled systems as *independent*, where the dependency is in terms of system availability in the face of failure of some single host. In tightly coupled systems, it is reasonable to consider shared memory (or at least hierarchical cache mechanisms) as a communications mechanism. In loosely coupled systems, only message passing can be considered.

Distributed systems have been around since the early 1970s. Examples of early distributed systems include the Xerox Distributed Filesystem and Grapevine, Cedar, the Cambridge Distributed System, the UCLA Locks System, the Newcastle Connection, the CMU Accent System (Vice and Virtue), and the MIT Argus System. More recent distributed systems include Apollo Domain, BSD Unix and Sun RPC, YP+NFS, Vrije University Amoeba, Cambridge Mayflower, Standard V-System, CMU MACH System, the Berkeley Sprite System, and ATT Bell Labs Plan 9; these are discussed informally in the final chapter of this book. They can be categorized as follows.

- *Network operating systems*

  These are conventional centralized operating systems with networking facilities added as operating system services, but distinct from other (I/O) services; e.g. 4.xBSD Unix.

- *Distributed operating systems*
  These systems allow a distributed set of processors to appear as a single system; e.g. MACH.
- *Distributed human access*
  A set of systems running centralized operating system services are made to appear as a single system to the human user; e.g. OS + X Windows.
- *Distributed file systems*
  Rather than providing a global human view of the systems, we provide the systems with a global view of storage, and therefore any programs too with the same view; e.g. Unix + NFS.
- *Distributed processing environments*
  The axis of distribution is the processor rather than terminal/window I/O or the storage system; e.g. V-System/Amoeba.

In practice, the most widespread systems are those combining distributed file access and distributed human access. The workstation/fileserver/compute-server model has evolved in the last ten years, mainly because of the costs of LAN access. It has enough performance to provide realistic remote disk/file access and memory/bitmap display, with costs dropping low enough to make window-based software realistic on the desktop.

Slowly, some more useful distributed tools are emerging: Since distributed systems have existed mainly in a research and development environment, there has been some work on tools to help with software development in a distributed environment. These include:

- automated software distribution (BSD rdist)
- shared views of data (single editor, multiple reviewers!), conferencing
- generation of multiple executables for different architectures from a single program-source development tree (including multiple source-code revisions control trees).
- distributed make facilities (ability to compile independent source files separately and automatically on multiple workstations)

Enslow's classic classification (1978) uses three axes of distribution:

- *Processors*
  Any interesting distributed system has processing capability in more than one place.
- *Control*
  The programs that make up the system have components in more than one processor. Another way of saying this is that the thread of control crosses more than one address space.
- *Data*
  The data required for a given task are located at more than one place – perhaps replicated for reliability reasons, or partitioned for performance reasons.

If we apply these models to the systems above, we can see the choices made in the distribution of services. Distribution of services is rather different from distribution of the operating system itself. In some systems (e.g. Sun NFS/Newcastle Connection) an operating system service (file access) has been distributed from within the operating system. In others (e.g. printing), the service has been distributed above (outside) the operating system. To provide this distribution, a number of communication mechanisms are required, and these are overviewed in the next section.

1.5 Communications support

When considering why we need specialized communications software, and how it will differ from existing applications and systems software, we must consider the hierarchy, consisting of:

- what the user wants to communicate
- what the operating system provides for communications support
- what the medium provides in terms of basic communication

1.5.1 Users

By "users" we mean, ultimately, human computer users, but also include a wide class of application programs. The kind of things users wish to communicate cover a wide spectrum, as shown in Table 1.3.

Table 1.3 Spectrum of communications.

Traditional	Established	Modern
Analogue voice	Terminal access	Window-based graphics terminal
Telex	File transfer	Shared files/file access
TV	Electronic mail	Conferencing/multimedial mail
Mail order	Remote job entry	Load sharing/replication services

1.5.2 Operating system facilities

Most OS support is for some form of communication and sharing of devices, and so has some facilities for building protocols. However, conventional device support usually assumes that devices are accessed over a local bus, and so are almost error free and with delays similar to memory-access latencies. Also, sharing of devices is by access, being only via a device driver, and is therefore easily achieved.

The system safely separates users from each other, and protects devices from aberrant behaviour of users' processes by restricting access through system calls. Within the kernel, or in a real time system, the structuring is rather different, with closer cooperation between processes or threads of control, less protection, and the assumption that the programmer is more expert.

1.5.3 Operating system support

For reliability, flow control and other communication support functions, we need to use agreed protocols. Some systems go one step further, and agree meta-protocols, with which they negotiate which protocols to use. What is a protocol? First and foremost, it is a set of agreed rules on what is meant by each unit of data exchanged, i.e. it is the encoding or agreed meaning for bits/bytes/words exchanged. Examples of such rules are:

- the use of English in international diplomacy
- the use of particular dictionaries for Scrabble
- the use of the ASCII code for characters stored in computers

The way in which a data item is represented in a host depends on the language used to describe the object, the compiler and the hardware base. In heterogeneous systems, all three of these may vary across machines. Thus a common base is needed for describing objects ("abstract syntax") and for exchanging them over the network ("concrete syntax"). This same language can be used to describe the control information in protocols as well. It is sometimes also known as "external data representation". Rules for protocols, as with a human conversation, are a set of agreements for structuring communication between parties. Examples of such structurings are:

- *The client/server model*
  An example of this is request response (remote procedure call).
- *The master/slave model*
  Examples of this are printer servers (e.g. PostScript printers) which have significant processing power, but are complete slaves to a master machine.
- *The peer/peer model*
  Examples of this include such applications as distributed directories.

There are many others.

To make conversations, or lectures, possible, we have some rules or protocols. Examples of such structures are:

- question and answer
- the monologue (broadcast)
- the conversation
- a cry for help, directed to a certain group of listeners (multicast)
- an order and an acknowledgement

You should note that each end point of a communication session is autonomous, that is, parties can decide to stop or start talking at any time they wish, or to interrupt another party, and so on. This is concurrency, and is what makes the design and implementation of protocols difficult.

Here is an example of some (pretend) protocol behaviour to illustrate various aspects of communication in a very common place situation.

```
User Jones: "Can I talk to Smith, please?"
Operator to Jones: "Yes, hold the line a moment."
Operator to Smith: "I have a Jones on the line: will you accept
```

```
the call?"
Smith to Operator: "Yes."
Operator to Jones: "Go ahead, Jones."
Jones to Smith: "Hi there, about this contract..."
Smith to Jones: "Oh, you want Hilary for that..."
```

This illustrates the problems of :
- location
- addressing
- structure of communication
- use of agents/servers for assistance

These protocols are often implemented within an operating system. However, we must distinguish between the protocol and the service. The next section discusses the idea of service, and *behavioural equivalence* of services. This is discussed further in Chapters 5 and 6. Lastly, there must be a set of rules for how to solve problems of communication. These we address next.

1.6 Open communications

Open communications are distinguished from other communication paradigms by the separation of the idea of *service* from the idea of *protocol*. A protocol implements a required service. How the protocol works is of no concern to the user, so long as it meets the requirement. This is in keeping with the ODP notion of transparencies. We can separate service requirements into two main components:
- type of service
- quality of service

The type of service defines the semantics provided by the underlying protocol. Thus we might define:
- messaging
- request/response
- streams

and so forth.

The quality of service defines the *reliability* and *performance* of the underlying protocol. Thus we might define:
- reliable messaging
- best-attempt messaging

and so on.

We can refine type of service further to include the semantics of the actual service interface. This can be
- synchronous or asynchronous
- blocking or non-blocking

We can also refine the notion of type of service for services like messaging and request/response:
- at most once

- at least once
- exactly once

The communications model has implications for the relationship between the communicating end points. For instance, a very common way of structuring distributed programs is the *client/server* model. Typically, this would employ the request/response communications model. Other models include:

- a master/slave model, usually implemented when some central system controls subsidiary distributed components (e.g. in monitoring and control systems)
- a peer relationship, where all systems are both clients and servers

1.7 Open distributed systems

Open distributed systems differ from distributed operating systems in a fundamental way: the support for distributed *applications* is provided by each host in an open way. There is *middleware* between the simple communications facilities that each host provides and the application. This layer ensures a high degree of independence between the underlying system and applications. In this way, the distributed system programmer may provide a *different* virtual machine depending on the requirements of the application in question. Each host's operating system must be supplemented with the toolset adequate for the set of distributed applications that are required for that host to participate. The full toolset is not required – the application programmer picks and chooses appropriate tools. This has major advantages over monolithic distributed operating systems in terms of performance, management and scalability. Distributed OS provide a common interface to the application regardless of the physical platform, thus supporting homogeneity for the application programmer.

1.8 Objects as a modelling concept

The object model derives from the discipline of software engineering: the unit of modularization appropriate for a system is derived from the data structures appropriate for its implementation. This is highly appropriate in distributed systems since it is immediately apparent that one level of modularization is defined by the address space of each machine in the system (see Ch. 11, especially §11.4). For type safety and consistency of the system, objects are implementations of abstract data types (ADT) (i.e. there is an algebra of the types in the system which can be checked). In a distributed system, it will be necessary to extend this concept to include the notion of temporal ordering of operations and also the order of failures.

1.8.1 A worked example

We shall now consider a real-world example of ADT/class/object derivation, namely a remote printer/spooler. First we must identify what we print: usually a file, which is a vector of bytes. This may be refined by noting that different printers accept different kinds of file, such as text only, or PostScript. This means we refine both the type of file and to define a new type for printer which was opaque previously. Then we identify some useful operations (using the American convention: # is "number of"):

1. add "file" to printer queue – succeeds, returns q#, or fails
2. remove q# from queue – succeeds, returns ok, or q# not in queue
3. list queue

This has introduced the idea that the printer is spooled, and that there is an abstract data type "queue". The ADT would define q as an ordered set of files (size/ byte array and type) + q#s, with operations typically defined as follows:

• adding to q appends the set
• removing checks q# is in the queue set and removes it

If the initial queue is empty, q# can have a maximum size, so add can fail.

The class "printer" now has an internal private type, queue, and some public operations, add, remove and list. This is implemented as an object, the set of code that implements the type and operations, with an interface. A number of these may be instantiated (brought to life) as server processes in a system with different parameters (such as printer type). We can see how this can easily be refined to add printer usage accounting per user, for example. This example will be expanded in Chapter 2 and then used in Chapter 3 to illustrate concurrent access and how list (= read) can be concurrent, while add/remove (= write) cannot.[2]

Storage for objects (the data structures and code that implements them) should be automatically allocated and deallocated as appropriate. Modules/objects are just higher-level types than the base types of the language that implements them – this is the *class/superclass* relationship. A class describes something that either extends an existing class or else limits the functionality of an existing class – this is called *refinement*.

Operations (methods) used within a program can refer to objects of more than one type - the meaning of the operation is determined by each implementation in the class, (e.g. append can add a file to a printer queue or add a block to a file). This is called *polymorphism* and implies that *dynamic binding* of operations to instances of objects can happen. We shall see that this is very appropriate in distributed systems.

Finally, it should be feasible to define new classes that can refine more than a single previous class. This is called *multiple inheritance*. For instance, when implementing a calendar, a programmer should be able to draw on existing modules/classes for a simple algebra of time, on an existing implementation of a simple windowing system, on an existing spreadsheet object, and so on.

The notion of transparency described at the beginning of this chapter is one justification for the object-oriented approach. The mechanisms that implement the transparencies are base methods in the base classes in the system. Once these

---

2. We must stress again that an ADT is *not* the same as an object. An object implements a class which may implement an ADT, but needs checking/testing in the normal fashion.

have been identified, the programmer can choose whether or not to use them and can combine them through multiple inheritance to form any appropriate class of system. Further justifications include:

- The object-oriented methodology is to increase software re-usability.
- A collection of methods determines the object class (or type). In a distributed system, this can help identify a given object uniquely. Clearly, it is helpful to distinguish service types, even just so that clients don't start talking to a tape drive when what they really want is a printer. However, the strong typing implied by this approach can be taken further towards helping the programmer with conformance. We shall look at formal approaches in Chapter 5.
- This in turn aids clear design and implementation of a system.

The implementation of the object is accessed by a collection of methods only, and there are several mechanisms used to implement *invocation* of a method. Typically *message passing* is used in centralized object-oriented systems. This is also the case in distributed systems.

One process sends a message to another. Once the primitive send operation has been completed, the sender is unaware of the fate of the message. At some later stage, the receiver may issue a receive operation, or not. It may fail. For example, in the Smalltalk programming environment, sending the message " +1" to "2" results in "3". Note, though, that there is no implied "returned" result, and even if there were it might be that there is no strict interleaving of method messages and result messages. In practice, the level of granularity of objects in a distributed system will be larger than that of centralized object-oriented systems.

In distributed systems, remote procedure call (also called "remote operations") has been used most commonly as the primitive communicating mechanism of choice.

A process in one address space executes a procedure in another address space. Apart from access to "global" variables, the procedure call is synchronous, exactly as a normal (local) procedure call is. The fine detail of an implementation *hides* the various mechanisms that implement some of the transparencies, such as:

- concurrent access control for consistency
- replication for fault tolerance
- migration for performance and heterogeneity of machines
- scaling

This is discussed further in Chapters 2 and 3.

The task for the programmer given a specification is to define an object that meets this specification. There are then several steps in the process of building a service:

- In the process of designing the object, the programmer may call on existing methods/types.
- It may be that this object is so similar to previous types of objects that it may be a subclass, and inherit all their methods.

- The service that the object will provide is defined in an interface. This will be the set of public types and procedures/methods available on the object.
- The interface is compiled, and linked with the code that implements the private methods the service requires.
- This may then be linked with a variety of existing system objects to provide different performance/reliability functionality.
- This is then executed to provide the service. This service is an interface to an instance of the class the object was drawn from.

Example

Here we present an example of the use of the object-oriented approach applied to a parts database for some fictitious automotive company (Fig. 1.6).

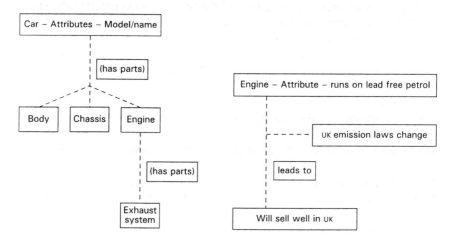

Figure 1.6 Enterprise views.   **Figure 1.7** Alternative views.

A collection of different access operations might be designed for such a database, depending on the user. The distributor and manufacturer may need highly reliable (but perhaps not completely consistent) access. The accounts department might require complete consistency in any data but not have any performance constraints. So, associated with the views of the data are methods for accessing them (this is different from the conventional relational database, where the methods are part of the database implementation, not part of the data or relations). An alternative view might be from marketer's system, as in Figure 1.7.

The relevant data may be distributed in a number of different systems, in databases acquired from different suppliers. The users may need to access the data with different toolsets. For instance, the automotive designer may wish to access the chassis/body information from within a CAD/CAM system. The legal department may wish to access the exhaust system information from a legal database access system.

A complete specification would address details as small as printing of correct forms for invoicing for a part, or for printing legal certificates of roadworthiness, and so forth.

How can we decompose the design of the access system to unify the optimal amount of the subsystem so that software effort is not too great? The answer lies in the way that the object-oriented approach allows us to abstract modules from the requirements and identify common subsystems/modules/objects by the processes of refinement and inheritance.

1.8.2 Objects and processes

Objects and processes are often confused in the literature. An instance of an implementation of an object *may* be a process (in the Unix sense of the word). However, there is no real reason to prevent the implementor programming many objects in a single process. From the other extreme, at some level (view), a collection of processes may implement a single object. However, in distributed systems we have true concurrency and separate address spaces between different machines. In this case, it may be wise to implement objects as processes.

Reasons include:

- robustness
- performance
- availability

This notion is discussed at greater length in Chapters 2 and 3.

1.8.3 Objects and distribution

There will exist some base set of methods and types in any object-oriented system. Usually this will include:

- creation (constructors in C++)
- destruction (destructors)
- initialization

In an open distributed system, we will wish to augment this list. We may include:

- location (adding name to directory)
- performance (adding statistics retrieval methods to the base class – these may be operations for invoking statistics or for event reporting)
- availability (adding probe/loopback/echo methods)
- replication methods
- migration methods

These will be the base set of methods that form the toolset the application programmer draws from when addressing the transparencies required which in themselves derive from the viewpoints described at the beginning of this chapter. The published interface for these methods allows prototyping by the applications programmer, and thus facilitates distributed application building and has several desirable side effects such as change control (new versions can coexist, since the version can be made part of the interface specification). An object may have multiple interfaces, of course. This can be for administrative reasons, or else simply to separate management, service and access control, for example. Finally, an interface might contain public state variables visible outside the object. This can be used so that information can be lodged in an interface and be available to the object at successive invocations of methods. This can support a "whiteboard" style of communication between objects. This set of base methods and their implementation and typical use are described further in Chapter 7.

There are many problems still to be solved in distributed systems. Most of these stem from scaling. The advantages of incremental growth and fault tolerance may be outweighed by disadvantages of communications costs replication of effort (operating system and application software being required at many sites instead of one or a few, distributed authentication, etc.).

1.9 Summary

In Chapter 1 we have evolved a view of open distributed systems that is more subtle than simple distributed services or distributed operating systems. We have introduced the ideas of properties and design freedoms of open distributed systems, which enable the systems designer and implementor to identify the objects required in a system from its specification, and to make engineering and other choices in the design and implementation.

Few computing services (from the computational viewpoint) inherently require distribution from the computational point of view alone. Indeed, only those highly fault-tolerant algorithms usually employed for actually managing a network itself (e.g. routeing algorithms, fault isolation algorithms) are themselves distributed.

However, it is clear that the other viewpoints (enterprise and informational) give us justifications for distribution of services. Computing facilities, personnel and information may already exist at more than one site. Engineering reasons may constrain some facilities to exist closer to one facility than another (e.g. oilwell monitoring closer to the well than to the magnate's office).

We have argued that open distributed systems with publicly available interfaces are the correct approach to building solutions to these types of problems.

1.10 Exercises

1. Identify the major components, interfaces and operations for a distributed system for voting in a medium-sized country.
2. Identify the major components, interfaces and operations of a system for providing online route information for drivers of rented cars. How might this need to be changed (enhanced) if used by emergency rescue teams?
3. Select the interfaces and operations for a system for online submission of students' work for assessment by teachers. How should this be modified if it allows online storage and return of grades?
4. Identify the system modules in a distributed system to handle vehicle regis-

tration:

(a) for the police,

(b) for a car rental company,

(c) for the domestic car buyer.

5. Imagine two estate agencies with several offices each. If they were to combine forces and pass information concerning properties and prospective clients, how might their internal and external interactions be distributed? Explain how this is reflected in the viewpoints: enterprise, information, computational, engineering and technology; and what special requirements might arise for transparencies: access, location, concurrency, fault, migration, performance and scaling.

CHAPTER 2

Modules, communication and concurrency

2.1 Introduction

In this chapter we look at modularity in distributed systems. As we said in Chapter 1, systems are distributed for two basic reasons: either components of the system are distributed because of inherent organizational reasons, or else they are distributed explicitly by the implementors for reasons of performance. In either case, the components represent modules that need to communicate, since at the very least they occupy different address spaces. This means that we must move data from one module to another by some inter-process communications mechanism if we want to coordinate computation. The modules are inherently concurrent, that is to say they reside on separate processors which are not explicitly coupled in their execution. It is the programmer's task to provide any such coordination if it is needed. We normally refer to these modules as *processes* or *tasks*. They are run on systems just like any other jobs, which means they must be installed, scheduled, and so forth.

Before communication can take place, there must be mechanisms to provide a way of finding the right module on the right computer. Then the appropriate inter-process communication mechanism must be selected. Finally, any rules that constrain when we can and cannot communicate between modules must be respected. Ideally, to make the task for the programmer easier, all of these mechanisms are provided as simple extensions of the same mechanisms that are present within a single computer system. In the context of the viewpoints presented in Chapter 1, access, location and concurrency transparency for the distributed application fall into the engineering and computational viewpoints. These mechanisms are the most well understood of distributed systems.

For example, processes that implement services that provide access to distributed organizational information or technology are usually named hierarchically, and accessed through remote procedure call. Often, concurrency control is not required. Sometimes, replicated servers are provided to increase performance, sometimes through lightweight processes or *threads* which allow a programmer finer-grain control over concurrency, performance and scheduling than conventional processes. On the other hand, programs that have been distributed for reasons of performance or availability often employ message passing as a communications mechanism, and may use a private naming system.

2.2 Addressing, naming and routeing

In order to discuss access and location transparency, we need to understand how objects are named, addressed and reached within a distributed system. The classic definitions of these three terms are due to Shoch & Hupp (1982):

- A name distinguishes one object in a distributed system from another.
- Its address tells us where an object is.
- A route is how to get to an object from elsewhere.

In a distributed system, access transparency means that we must *hide* the distribution from the application somehow. However, often hiding only goes as far as the access mechanism (e.g. remote procedural), and the distribution may be apparent from the *name*. Examples of distribution being obvious from the name are common in distributed programs such as electronic mail and some distributed file systems (e.g. names for remote files in many PC network file-sharing systems include the remote fileserver name). However, in a distributed system many objects may have the same name (sometimes deliberately as in groups, sometimes by accident); and an object may have many names. Choosing unique names in a large distributed system is a hard problem, which some argue it doesn't even make sense to try to solve.

To access an object, we must derive first an address, and then a route to that address, from its name. Addressing and routeing are the mechanisms that hide the distribution from the application. Names often become addresses and vice versa as you move through different levels of abstraction in the system: as an example, here are the mappings from name to address at the application level and network level, and then from name to address from the Internet level to the local-area-network level:

```
waffle.cs.ucl.ac.uk -> 128.16.8.88 -> 8:0:20:c:14:e1
```

(!) Reality Checkpoint   Names, addresses and routes are so often confused that one might be forgiven for saying one person's name is another person's address. The reason for the confusion is partly the multiplicity of contexts these words are used in, but also partly that, although the design requirements are clear, the functions are often mixed up in implementation or in presentation to a human user. In the author's experience, the easiest way to understand the model given here is to map it to one particular implementation (be it the postal service, the telephone system, the Internet or some other) and thereafter think of all new systems encountered in terms of that!

2.2.1 Worked example of name spaces

As a way of considering naming and access transparency let us consider user file-system naming configurations that could be employed for a campus distributed system based on the Unix file-path naming convention. Chapter 10 will discuss distributed file systems at greater length. For now, let us ignore the distribution mechanisms (as indeed we should when designing a transparent naming scheme).

We make the following initial assumptions (in no significant order):

- None of the systems has a practical limit to file-system tree depth.
- A file system cannot span more than a single physical device.
- File systems appear as subtrees starting at any point from the root of the tree downwards, i.e. where they are "mounted".

Our goals include the following points:

- The distributed file system allows remote file systems to be mounted as if they are local.
- It is possible to create pointers to files and directories so that they can appear elsewhere.
- User names are administered globally. For each name there is a password entry, possibly accessed through a nameserver which identifies that user and their home directory.
- A user generally will have only a single "home directory" (the root of their own file tree), which will be physically located on a single file system.
- We have to provide as much robustness and location transparency as possible. The view of the file system should if possible be the same from wherever the user logs in. A user should be able to continue work even if the usual workstation is not available.
- We may want some number of special users with special privileges.
- By default, all accounts will be unreadable by others. We will want "shareware" accounts, as well as accounts for teachers to "test" the environment (i.e. with the same paths/views as ordinary users). We have to choose whether we use an Access Control List mechanism (each user with access permissions entered in a list associated with each file/directory) or a group mechanism (each file with group ownership, each user in some number of groups).

There are at least three approaches to how users see their home directories in the file-system tree, and to providing some reasonable naming scheme:

The opaque approach

The file-system tree is the same from all machines, but the location of the files (i.e. the fileserver name) is explicit. A typical pathname for a home directory might be

`/cs/research/aproject/aserver/janedoe`

More generally, the campus file tree could have paths like

`/campus/dept/deptorganization/servername/janedoe`

where `dept` = department name (e.g. `chem`), `deptorganization` = department organization (e.g. `1styr`) and `servername` = departmental (or shared) cluster server machine name (or central machine name).

27

The flat approach

This is illustrated in Figure 2.1. All users' directories are mounted file stores. They appear on all machines as:

`/users/userfred`

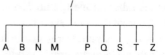

Flat naming tree – remote systems appear at the same level as local ones

Figure 2.1   The flat naming approach.

The subjective or prefixing approach

This is illustrated in Figure 2.2. Here we have:

`/users/groupofusers/userfred`

where the group of users is logically grouped on some particular server(s).[1]

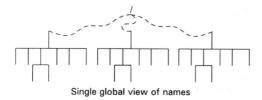

Single global view of names

Figure 2.2   The global naming approach.

Probably, there will be some central machine with a number of large disks and a number of partitions on each. This machine will act as a main fileserver, storing the bulk of common data/systems, and possibly providing sink for backup and source for software distribution. (Note: many medium-size systems still do not allow "striping" of a file system over multiple disks. The only advantage is performance of large systems; the disadvantages are many, and include consistency problems and reliability – see Ch. 3).

In our example, we choose to have user filestores on "cluster servers" situated in a large department with local users predominating. Workstations will not normally have any user filestore on at all, though they may well have disks to store commonly used system files or to cache files while in use. We must accommodate autonomy within the system; there may already be existing distributed file systems in several departments with existing naming (hierarchy) strategies.

So we have a set of file systems, many on the central machine, several on each cluster server. We have a set of users, who may have their home directory on the central machine or on a cluster server or a "third party" server (existing department's). You can view this as the hardware tree:

- the network
- the fileservers

---

1. Note that any one case may be simulated (on a distributed Unix system) from the other two, using symbolic links.

- the disks on the file servers
- the partitions on the disks

Somehow, we have to resolve/map/ match this tree to the user's view(s). The view from any server (central or cluster) is illustrated in Figure 2.3.

The fact that any remote mounted filestore that is not part of the actual path to a given user's filestore is always one level away from the ../.. path (*upwards* through the lines in the file-system hierarchy) to root means that machine failures are nor-

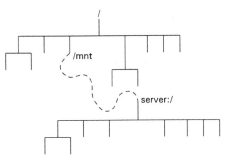

Hierarchical, subjective naming tree

Figure 2.3 File system naming hierarchy.

mally hidden from users (i.e. reading the path to locate a file does not hang – so long as it is implemented as a trace back through the tree, rather than top down on each file system from the root). Note that there are three levels at which a remote mount may occur:

- One, the "highest", represents a departmental filestore. This will allow departments to "own" cluster server filestores or include their own fileservers in the scheme.
- One represents a project or suborganization of a department. This allows projects in departments to act like departments.
- The lowest represents users being spread across more than one machine even within a departmental project. This allows groups of users to spread their home-directories/work-areas over several machines (e.g. librarians who take more file space than a single machine could offer, or medical people who require more reliability than achievable from a single fileserver). In this case, we would have to employ pointers when the user's file space requirements exceeded a single drive.

There will be a lot of symbolic links as the system grows – this may be easily managed if remote systems are only made visible (mounted) on demand, and any required links created for the duration of usage. To accommodate non-flat existing filestores, we might have pseudo-users at the same level as users on supported filestores, which are actually mount points for these whole foreign systems (e.g. /users/cs). In all these cases, distributed access and naming are consistent with local access. However, the naming can hide the distribution or not. It is an engineering choice whether to do this.

2.3 Concurrent systems

Concurrency is the property of a system that more than one thing is (apparently) happening at the same time. In the software world, we commonly find three types of concurrency:

- Fake concurrency can be provided by a multiprogramming environment or operating system. This exists down to the level of interrupts and up through system calls to concurrent programming environments. Although processes appear to run concurrently, the use of a single processor ensures that this is not really so.

- Real concurrency can exist in a tightly coupled multiprocessor environment. This is of less interest to us here, as communication in such an environment is generally provided by hardware, and such devices are special-purpose (e.g. graph reduction machines for functional languages, distributed array processes, etc.).

- Real concurrency can exist in a loosely coupled distributed system. It is this third that is our main concern.

There are three challenges with concurrent systems:

- *Scheduling*
  This is concerned with when and how concurrent tasks can make appropriate use of shared system resources such as CPU, I/O and memory.

- *Synchronization*
  This is concerned with the relative ordering of events between related threads of control in the system. For instance, a process cannot extract a character from a buffer until a user has typed one in. More generally, when a resource or object is common or shared, then an arbitrary interleaving of accesses to it can lead to unpredictable results.

- *Communication*
  When two processes or threads of control synchronize, they usually wish to exchange information. There are many different techniques for exchanging information, such as shared memory, message passing, remote procedure call, and rendezvous.

What distinguishes distributed systems from parallel systems? First, communication is characteristically much more expensive between distributed processes than between parallel ones. This usually rules out models based on simulated shared memory. Secondly, hardware in a distributed system is generally fault tolerant. The network may partition, processing nodes fail, and yet a distributed algorithm may successfully complete. Note that this is only a potential for greater reliability. The economics of disk prices versus processor and network prices meant that many so-called distributed file systems that evolved in the 1980s were less reliable than centralized ones, since the separation of application/client from server/disk via a network simply introduced more points of failure than a centralized system would have.[2]

2.3.1 Time sequence diagrams

A useful tool for showing the structure of sequences of events and exchange of information is the time sequence diagram as in Figure 2.4. Where the continuous

---

2. Leading to Lamport's famous definition of a distributed system: "A distributed system is one in which a machine which you never knew existed can stop you getting your work done."

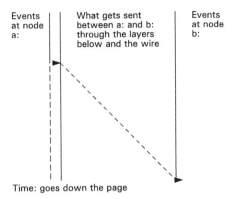

Figure 2.4 A time sequence diagram.

line is active and the dotted line is idle/blocked. We shall use these diagrams informally to explain various synchronization and IPC mechanisms.

2.4 Interleaving and true parallelism

2.4.1 Interleaving

Because of the unpredictable nature of the real-world input to a system – the non-deterministic order of events – it is far cleaner to model the system behaviours as a set of (cooperating) processes/tasks/threads, each of which deals with an appropriate stream of events. This can then be implemented using co-routines or multiprocessing. We then view the system as if these tasks actually run concurrently.

We shall give examples of the range of unexpected events that might be about to occur in the interfaces for a simple workstation with the real world. A user may be about to click on a mouse button. On the other hand they may decide to go and have a lemonade. In contrast, a request may have been issued to a disk controller to read a certain block (or to a network controller to receive a packet). A simple disk or network may bound accurately the time to complete this action. More sophisticated hardware may sort requests and act on them in an unexpected order.

2.4.2 Atomicity

What actually happens in a single system is that event-handling processes/tasks are interleaved. This means that at any point in execution, one task could stop and then another run. There will be some indivisible (atomic) unit of execution that cannot be suspended. Without special software to allow the programmer to control when task pre-emption happens, this unit of execution can be at the level of a single instruction.

2.4.3 Scheduling

Preemption is a common method of scheduling in time-sharing systems. Any process may be suspended at an apparently arbitrary moment to allow some other

31

process to run. This is often to achieve a "fair share" of processing time. In pre-emptive operating systems, the granularity of interleaving may be as small as a single instruction. Run-to-completion is more common in monolithic or embedded systems. Each process runs until it has completed the current task, and then voluntarily hands control back to a scheduler which decides which process to run next. In run-to-completion real-time systems, the granularity of interleaving will be decided by the programmer. In a distributed system, there is real concurrency, whether we want it or not. This brings special problems:

- In a central system, at least one component is immune from the concurrency: the dispatcher or scheduler. In a distributed system, the scheduler function itself is distributed.
- Partial failure of a system is possible. This aspect of distribution makes programming particularly hard. Because of the lack of tight coupling of components, there is a lack of information (or immediate information) under partial failure. Explicit mechanisms, such as probes and timeout mechanisms, must be added by the distributed systems programmer to account for this.

2.5 Shared resources – problems with concurrency

What are the special programming problems in systems with interleaving or distributed concurrency? First, whether we have an interleaved system or a real distributed system, we have to protect critical regions of code. These are sections of code that may alter the value of shared variables. Because of concurrency, it is possible for incorrect values to arise, where the sequence of operations on these variables is not carefully controlled. This is discussed further in Chapter 3. Secondly, we have to control ownership of resources. A number of incorrect behaviours can result from incorrect sequences of resource allocation. These are:

- deadlock
- livelock
- lack of fairness

2.5.1 Deadlock

The order of required resources for the order of execution of two or more tasks is such that neither can proceed, as in Table 2.1. Going back to the example of the printer spooler: Add "file" to printer queue – succeeds, returns q#, or fails. Remove q# from queue – succeeds, returns ok, or q# not in queue. If A grabs the spool area to add something to the queue, while B grabs the queue to delete something, then A and B will deadlock waiting for the other resource. We will see in Chapter 3 how transactions can help with this synchronization problem.

Table 2.1 Deadlock.

Process A	Process B
Has object b	Has object a
Needs object a	Needs object b

2.5.2 Livelock

In Figure 2.5, process A and process B grab resources in a sensible order and coordinate, but unfortunately they spend the entire time exchanging resources and not using them.

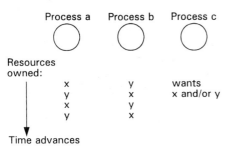

Figure 2.5 Livelock.

2.5.3 Fairness

A resource-greedy process can mean that other processes do not get access to an object as often as necessary– an example of this often occurs in operating systems that over-prioritize a diskette drive, so that terminal access is radically slowed down when the diskette is running. Distributed systems involve another resource that must be shared fairly – the network.

Reasoning about the number of possible orderings of events in distributed or centralized concurrent systems is simply not feasible in the same as way as for sequential programs. Instead, formal mathematically founded systems now exist for defining and checking the behaviour of such systems of distributed concurrent tasks – for example:

- Milner's CCS (calculus of communicating systems) (Milner 1989)
- Hoare's CSP (Communicating Sequential Processes) (Hoare 1985). (These are really formal languages for describing concurrent behaviour, but have an axiomatic basis which allow properties to be derived, such as whether a particular system meets some specification.)
- LOTOS (Language of Temporal Ordering Semantics) (ISO 1989a). The OSI LOTOS language is closely based on CCS.
- Estelle languages (ISO 1989b)
- temporal logic (a logic based on operators such as "eventually", "until", etc.)

Some of these are introduced in Chapter 5. It must be noted here, though, that while it is attractive in principle that one may be able to build provably correct distributed systems one day, recent application in real large systems has been of limited success, and as a result, industrial application of formal approaches only advances in small steps.

ⓘ   Reality Checkpoint   The work of operating systems designers has meant that most application programmers have managed to avoid dealing with

33

concurrency. Unfortunately, distributed systems remove that luxury. Distributed systems inherently require the programmer to be intimately aware of concurrent programming problems and techniques, no matter how hard distributed systems designers may have struggled to avoid this so far.

2.6 Mutual exclusion

Here we show an example of concurrent access by two processes ("threads", "active objects" and other terms are commonly used) to illustrate how inconsistencies arise if we permit arbitrary sequences of accesses to shared resources. Consider the parts database we introduced in Chapter 1. If two customer sites wished to order a part from some particular warehouse, the sequence of operations each would execute might be as in Figure 2.6.

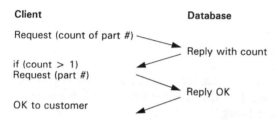

Client   **Database**

Request (count of part #)

Reply with count

if (count > 1)
Request (part #)

Reply OK

OK to customer

Figure 2.6   Mutual exclusion.

Now the problem is that the database is shared, and if two clients access the data in an arbitrarily interleaved sequence of operations, the data become inconsistent, or the client gets inconsistent replies. In the next chapter, we will see how transactions are used as the general mechanism to hide these kinds of problems through the notion of *atomic actions*.

2.7 Consumers, producers and critical regions

Using the paradigm of layering for modularization, we have a natural model for building communications protocols where a service is provided by a layer to a layer above. Layering is described in more detail in Chapter 6. There are only three external interfaces to a protocol layer: lower-layer input events, upper-layer request events and timer events. Corresponding to these are requests from this layer to the layer below, and indications (usually implemented as events) from this layer to the layer above. There are internal events (e.g. timers) and control events (e.g. network resets, user aborts, etc.). We have modelled a layer as a set of cooperating tasks, processes, threads of control or whatever, which are essentially concurrent. Although this concurrency is usually fictional (i.e. interleaved execution by a single processor, rather than a multiprocessor), it is convenient for designing and implementing protocols – a thread for each stream of events is easier to program than a calculated polling loop. This is discussed in more detail in Chapter 6.

Having chosen to implement most protocols as a set of cooperating concurrent threads of control, we are left with the problem that the cooperation is often by means of shared memory. This leads to one main problem, and subsequently to a set of safe structures that can be employed to avoid the problem:

- Each thread within a layer (protocol) that deals with events from a layer above is a consumer of those events, but a producer for events of the layer below (usually as a result).
- Each thread within a layer dealing with events from the layer below is a consumer of those events, and generally produces events for the layer above as a result.
- Thus, through many layers, we have a chain of producers from the top down to the bottom, and another chain of producers from bottom to top. Each chain of producers is matched by a chain of consumers.
- All of this is to ensure lack of deadlock, although it cannot ensure fairness, lack of livelock, etc.
- It is intuitively obvious that the system makes flow control reasonably easy to implement.

This chain of producers and consumers is almost always bidirectional. In other words, each producer is also a consumer of events and information in the other direction. This is illustrated in Figures 2.7, 2.8, 2.9 and 2.10.

```
-- 1/2 of Printer Spooler System
--      Consumer of User events, Producer of Network requests ...

    for(ever)
    {
        sleep(user-q-event);

        prev = spl-printeruser()
        print-request = deq(user-q);
        spl-restore(prev)

        -- make up some printer requests
        -- printrequest made from print-request

        prev = spl-printer()
        startprintergoing(q, printrequest)
        spl-restore(prev)

        wakeup(thatprinter);

    }
```

Figure 2.7 Producer consumer chain – user to net.

```
--  1/2 of Printer - NS1
--      Consumer of printer events

   for(ever)
   {
       sleep(thatprinter);

       ...
   }
```

Figure 2.8 Producer consumer chain – consumer.

```
Some explanations:

- sleep - waits (suspends this task/process/thread) till some
other task wakes us up with appropriate event).

- wakeup - wakeup any task sleeping for this event.

- spl-? - set priority level to exclude any tasks from waking up who
need this level of access.

- spl-x - restore all previous priority levels.

- que - add a buffer/packet to a queue for another process to.

- dequeue - remove a buffer from a queue.

-- - is a comment
```

Figure 2.9 Producer consumer chain – key.

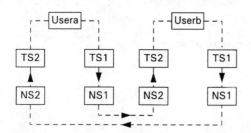

Figure 2.10 Flow of information in producer–consumer chain.

Figure 2.10 shows a full system from one host (user) to another; we have a chain of production and consumption that contains at least eight tasks.

The mutual exclusion plus synchronization prevents inconsistency or deadlock across the entire system. However, it is possible for a producer to produce more than a consumer can handle at any point in this system, as we have no model for flow control. Flow control of resources is usually achieved by counting the numbers of buffers being queued and dequeued at each producer/consumer boundary, and bounding this number (i.e. stopping production when we have queued some given number of events for a consumer who has not yet managed them. Of course, the same relationship between a process "above" another process exists for "peer" processes across the network.

2.8 Monitors, semaphores and rendezvous

The problem of providing ordered access to resources shared between processes has been solved traditionally by these three mechanisms. The monitor is still a useful paradigm for building objects in a distributed system. The rendezvous provides a mechanism for communication as well as synchronization. Semaphores are too low-level and inappropriate for distribution in that to distribute the semaphore mechanism requires provision of distributed mutual exclusion to the semaphore operations. However, they are widely used for controlling concurrency within an object or process inside a distributed system.

2.8.1 Semaphores

Semaphores were introduced by Dijkstra to give more elegant solutions to some of the concurrency problems in early operating systems work. A semaphore is a special type of integer variable that must be non-zero, and only has two operations available. These are shown in Figures 2.11 and 2.12. It is essential to note that these operations have to be implemented in an uninterruptible way, i.e. they are indivisible.

Semaphores may be used to protect critical regions of code simply since they make strong synchronization. Unfortunately, they are not useful for distributed applications, since they are implemented by local variables and special instructions which are not available between different address spaces. However, since semaphores are well understood, many programming solutions are known using them. It is possible to show exact equivalence of semaphores to other mutual exclusion techniques.

```
wait(s)
If (s > 0)
    s = s - 1;
else
    <we are suspended>;
```

Figure 2.11 Semaphores – wait.

37

Semaphores

```
signal(s)
if (someone else (P) is suspended due to a wait on s)
    wakeup (P);
else
    s = s + 1
```

Figure 2.12 Semaphores – signal.

2.8.2 Monitors

The monitor is an extension of early operating system designs. Early operating systems provided resource control by running users' programs uninterruptedly, by having complete control of I/O and by having exclusive use of some parts of memory. This monolithic monitor may be provided as a more decentralized tool for the applications programmer: a monitor is a collection of procedures with private data, plus an initialization routine. Entry to the procedures in a monitor is defined to be mutually exclusive (i.e. a strict monitor has only one client at a time). To provide synchronization between processes calling these routines, there is a pair of routines like semaphores. Since the monitor has private (safe) data to count events with, we only require the blocking and waking functionality. This is shown in Figure 2.13.

```
wait(c)
    This process is placed on a FIFO queue awaiting
    the condition to become true and suspended.

signal(c)
    The first (if any) process on the queue waiting for
    c to be true, is woken up.
```

Figure 2.13 Monitors.

2.8.3 The Ada Rendezvous

Ada (DoD 1980) is now the preferred language for software for US defence contractors. It is designed to provide good data abstraction, in an object-oriented way; what are relevant for this chapter are the tasking and inter-process communication paradigms available in Ada.

In Ada, the normal set of modularizing definitions are available, including the facility to "package" a number of procedures/functions together, with a separate public declaration, and private definition/implementation. As well as this, a module, like a package, can be declared as a *task*. A task is a unit of activity and tasks can be executed concurrently.

EXAMPLE 1i, Top level of a window task:

```
procedure Window is
task get_mouse;

task body get_mouse is
begin
  wait_for_mouse_events;
  deal_with_mouse_events;
end get_mouse;

task get_kbd;
task body get_kbd is;
begin
  wait_for_kbd_events;
  deal_with_kbd_events;
end get_kbd;

begin
  wait_for_messages_from_network;
  update_screen;
end Window
```

Figure 2.14   Use of tasks.

```
procedure Window is

task mouse is
  entry get_input(dev: in device);
  entry do_output(net: out network_cx);

task body get_mouse is
begin
  accept get_input(dev: in device) do
    event = input(dev);
  end get_input;

    action = decode(event);
  accept do_output(net: out network_ck) do
    output(net, action);
  end fo_output;

end mouse;

......similar for kbd......

begin
  mouse.get_input(mouse);
  kbd.get_input(kbd);
  mouse.do_output(net);
  mouse.do_output(net);
  ...
end Window
```

Figure 2.15   Use of rendezvous.   39

The activation of tasks is defined by scope. Nested task declarations are children of some main task, and are activated when the main parent task begins as in Figure 2.14. The Ada language includes a synchronisation facility called the rendezvous. The rendezvous allows arbitrary processes to synchronize with each other and exchange data at that point.

Somewhere in the **task** specification, there are one or more **entry** declarations. These are analogous to procedure (method) declarations in a package (class). There is a corresponding **accept** statement which contains the declaration of the executable statements that implement this entry. The **accept** and corresponding call to this rendezvous are *strongly* synchronized. This means that the called task is suspended at an **accept** until the caller calls this entry. The caller is then suspended until the called task completes execution of the end of the accept statement/block.

```
procedure Window is

task mouse is
  entry get_input(dev: in device);
  entry do_output(net: out network_cx);

task body get_mouse is
begin
  accept get_input(dev: in device) do
    event = input(dev);
  end get_input;

    action = decode(event);
  accept do_output(net: out network_ck) do
    output(net, action);
  end do_output;

end mouse;

......eimilar for kbd......

begin
  select
    when is.mouse
      mouse.get_input(mouse);
  or
    when is.kbd
      kbd.get_input(kbd);
  mouse.do_output(net);
  ...
end Window
```

Figure 2.16 Guards and priorities.

The `entry` and call can pass in, out and in-out parameters. In this sense the rendezvous is analogous to a remote procedure call (RPCs are discussed later in this chapter). Its use is illustrated in Figure 2.15.

Let us suppose two active processes are proceeding with their execution. In a symmetric way, whichever reaches the rendezvous first, waits. When both reach the rendezvous, a single transaction takes place. The transaction is exclusive so that consistency problems are avoided.

The second example is rather artificial. It would almost certainly deadlock unless events arrived strictly alternately from the mouse and keyboard – an extremely unlikely situation. It is possible to schedule the rendezvous with delays and priorities. By default, some notion of fair scheduling is expected. A `select` statement allows a task to choose from one of several possible rendezvous. The `select` may be "guarded" by a `when` clause.

We can solve the problem in the last example, and even improve it, by introducing priorities to make sure that mouse events are dealt with more promptly than keyboard ones (this is reasonable when a fast-tracked mouse might traverse several hundred pixels in the time it takes to type a character). This is illustrated in Figure 2.16.

2.9 Distributed systems and concurrency

2.9.1 Shared memory

Some early distributed systems provided inter-process communication by modelling shared memory. A global naming scheme is usually used for all shared objects in the distributed system. Read or write access to shared objects will appear identical whether the object is local or remote, and takes the form of assignment. Often special hardware is used to trap assignments to or from remote objects (usually by enhancing a memory management subsystem). The shared memory paradigm is difficult for the typical applications programmer. Message passing and remote procedure call are more familiar.

2.9.2 Message passing

Message passing is commonly used in real-time systems, and is also familiar to object-oriented programmers, although it is sometimes hidden behind the method invocation mechanism. Usually, message passing is provided by some built-in system primitives such as these:

```
send(port, data)
receive(port, source, data)
```

Message passing is often non-blocking. This means that one process may continue execution immediately after it has sent a message to another. It is also sometimes synchronous. Synchronous message passing involves no buffering, but it does require strong synchronization between sender and receiver.

Message passing may or may not be reliable. If it is reliable, it is a requirement that the underlying communications system make sure of this. Message passing is appropriate to applications that are highly sensitive to latency. One important example of this is in distributed graphics systems or window systems.

2.10 Worked example of networked windows

Windows are multiple views on what multiple tasks (processes) are doing on your workstation. A workstation here is anything with one or more bitmap displays and capable of some kind of multi-tasking. When you have a multi-tasking system (like Unix) it's nice to take advantage of being able to run a lot of things at once, for instance, compile a program, see the errors, edit it elsewhere whilst also having the program specification in front of you. It is pretty inconvenient having a lot of paper as well as a terminal, and not too nice having lots of terminals on the table or desk; hence windows. Because workstations from different manufacturers have completely incompatible hardware, lots of different window systems have evolved.

2.10.1 Portability and network window protocols

A networked window system is portable because of one thing: the display functionality is separated from the application functionality. This can be done by constructing a standard protocol that allows application programs to talk to the display process. The display process (of which there is one per physical display per machine) is called the "server", while the application programs are "clients". In other words, the roles of client and server are reversed from those of CPU or file serving.

There can be lots of application programs. Each application program can have 0, 1 or more windows, which may or may not be visible at once on the screen. One consequence of this design is that a client can talk to a display server on a different machine (or indeed several machines!). The most common client program is a terminal emulation window – an application that is usually running a command interpreter, but can run anything else that does terminal I/O.

2.10.2 Window managers

A window manager looks after all the windows on the display. It allows you to use a pointing device (a mouse) to ask for more or less windows of a particular kind (by use of menus). It allows you to move windows around, resize them, close and open them, turn them into icons, and so on. The display server is not a window manager. The window manager is actually another client of the display program (i.e. it is independent of the display hardware too). See Figure 2.17. The window manager intercepts bits of protocol between the display server and the other applications, and then informs applications of special things (such as the fact they should resize or be redrawn). Thus it implements the *policy*.

Networked window systems mainly use (reliable) messages to communicate between client window processes and the graphics display server. An important

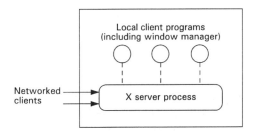

Figure 2.17 The X-Windows process and communications model.

reason is that the server must receive events (such as input from a mouse) and transmit them to the client program, without incurring too much delay. If application-level acknowledgement were required (such as is implied by a procedural type interface) the system would be a minimum of two times less responsive.

This messaging system is often bound up for the programmer in a library of standard procedures which often have no return values or out parameters, and thus can simply send the message and return. Thus the applications programmer sees the server directly as a library resembling a conventional device-independent graphics systems. Examples of such systems include the X-Windows system and the NeWS system. They are of increasing importance in distributed systems, since it is possible to distribute graphics processing more widely, and move a large part of what was once mainframe-type processing on to the user's desk. This is possible through the change in relative cost of graphics workstations and LAN technology.

Engineering tradeoffs can be made in the way in which the protocol operates between the application and the server, whether simply moving procedural data between the two, or moving graphical objects or actual programs (active objects). The key design decision in many networked window systems is the use of messages rather than RPC mechanisms, which are described in the next section.

2.11 Remote procedure call

Remote procedure call is exactly what it sounds like. A procedure with some piece of program on some processor (i.e. in another address space) is made available to other processes in some way, and may be called (invoked) exactly as if it were local to the caller's process. The pioneers of the RPC idea were Birrell and Nelson (1984).

Remote procedure call systems follow the client/server model very closely. A server implements the procedure. A client calls it. Usually, the distributed applications programmer starts by defining some procedure or set of procedures in an *Interface Definition Language* (IDL). The interface defines the procedures and their parameters together with associated type information.The procedure is written to conform to this interface. Then a number of clients can be written to call this interface. There are several levels of software necessary to support this system,

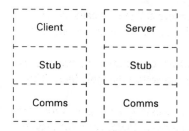

Figure 2.18 RPC layers.

above the normal communications systems. These are illustrated in Figure 2.18.

The appropriate communications semantics vary between different RPC systems, but are always request/response in pattern. Some systems demand different levels of reliability, such as exactly-once semantics, others are at-least-once. Exactly-once systems attempt to mimic the failure mode of local procedure call, while at-least-once systems may result in multiple executions of the remote procedure at the server. Some systems limit the size or number or types of procedure parameters; others have no practical limits. The "stubs" at each end have three functions:

- They mimic the missing code: the client stub mimics the procedure and the server stub mimics a caller.
- They *marshal* and *unmarshal* the arguments to a procedure. This means that the stub code must accumulate the arguments (typically from the stack) and wrap them in an appropriate format to send over the network.
- The server stub must dispatch incoming calls to the appropriate procedure when more than one is supported. In some systems, the server may queue incoming calls, while in others it may rely on the caller to retry.

Different RPC systems allow concurrent threads of procedures to be executing. The server stub is effectively executed in parallel to any of the procedures, dispatching calls and replies as they happen and not blocking. The sequence of events for a typical remote procedure call is as follows (see Fig. 2.19):

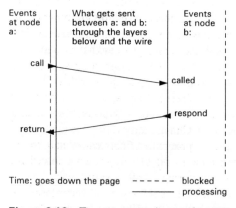

Figure 2.19 Time sequence diagram for a remote procedure call.

1. If this is the first call (to this instance of the server) the client program locates the server (perhaps by making a call to a well-known server which provides the instance-to-location mapping service). There are a number of other mechanisms possible here.

2. The client program reaches a remote procedure call (i.e. it calls its "stub").
3. The stub code marshals the arguments and uses the communications subsystem to send them to the appropriate server.
4. The client program is then blocked from further execution, awaiting a reply. Some systems permit the client to continue and collect the reply later. This is called "non-blocking RPC".
5. The server stub then performs the reverse processing, calling the procedure as if it were the client. If the procedure has out parameters or return values, these are then marshalled by the server stub, transmitted back to the client, and unmarshalled there.
6. The client program continues as if an ordinary procedure call had returned.

How does this relate to the object-oriented approach outlined in Chapter 1? The server is an instance of an object, implementing some class. The set of procedures are the implementation of the methods for that class. Some RPC systems are not restrictive about which processes are clients or servers. Many allow a client to be a server and vice versa at different points in their execution. Some allow RPC calls to a client that is awaiting a reply. This is sometimes restricted to calls back from the server that has been called. This is on the basis that this "callback" is essentially mutual recursion, and a fully transparent RPC system should allow all normal procedural patterns.

2.11.1 RPC and threads

Many systems now incorporate support for programmers to break their application processes into lightweight processes or "threads". These are typically implemented by providing multiple execution stacks within the same address space, thus saving on the context switch overheads of saving registers and process state.

These packages were developed first and foremost for the programmer creating a server. A server that deals with many RPC clients can be implemented in a number of ways. One approach is for a single server process to deal with each request in turn. Another approach is to create a new server process for each request (this is generally costly and used only for applications with long-lived effects). A third approach is to create a pool of servers, and schedule each request to the next free server (or least heavily loaded) in the pool. The way this is done is discussed further in Chapter 6, and a little in Chapter 12.

Once these packages became widespread, programmers also used them for an entirely different reason. A threads package allows the programmer to control concurrency. Instead of blocking the client during a call, a server can create a thread, and return immediately to the client, thus providing a reliable message at the level of application access. Or, alternatively, a client can create a thread, which makes a call, whilst the "main thread" of the client code continues with other useful work.

Combining threads with RPC provides a full general communications system, although this is at the expense of exposing the programmer to the problems of concurrency control. However, if the distributed application has this requirement, these may be unavoidable complexities anyhow. One example of how RPC, threads and messages are interrelated is discussed at some length in Chapter 8.

2.11.2 Interface compiling

An interface is a collection of one or more procedures and functions. It is effectively the implementation of the object. When a server runs, it provides these procedures and functions as a package to one or more clients. This "running" interface/server is called an *instance*.

Interfaces are often defined in a language which is either part of or an extension to the system language for the distributed system. In Chapter 3, we look at some of the ways interface languages have evolved. Typically, the interface language allows:

- naming of the interface
- naming of the procedures
- naming and typing of parameters

An interface compiler (often a preprocessor for the application programming language) produces the stub code, which together with an RPC run-time support system allows the functionality described above. Most RPC systems limit the types available to a remote procedure. This is often a consequence of the base language. For instance, in a non-type-safe language, it is difficult to pass arbitrary pointers safely, since they may reference local memory in the client (or returned pointers may reference memory in the server). This means that arbitrary graph structures and even trees are frequently not allowed as parameters to remote procedures.[3] The Ada rendezvous differs from RPC in this respect.

Global variables may be accessed by the called task. It is hard to see how this might be implemented on multiple processors without shared memory. Some RPC "stub compilers" generate a checksum (Wilbur & Bacarisse 1987) based on the procedures, types of arguments, and order of types in the specification. This checksum, or *signature,* is then inserted in the header of a request/call packet to act as a simple run-time check that the receiver (server) can use to see that the client has been compiled using the same interface definition. (Some systems go further and seed the checksum with the *version* of the stub compiler to ensure compatibility at RPC version level.)

Many systems do not allow procedures or functions as parameters. This is usually a consequence of the lack of support for functions as first-class variables in

---

3. CORBA stub compilers do allow you to pass pointers (this is how "out" and "inout" parameters are implemented and is addressed further in Chapter 7). What happens is when the pointer gets into the stub, the stub does a copy: once when making the invocation, and once after unmarshalling the results. Thus the illusion of a pointer is maintained. So in CORBA IDL "out" and "inout" might be regarded as being equivalent to C's "*" operator. However, you are restricted to passing structures that are definable in the IDL. In particular, you are not allowed to pass structures that contain pointers to other structures (instead they must contain the structure). Allowing structures to contain pointers to other structures would complicate (intolerably) the life of the stub compiler writer. There is more about this in Chapter 7.

the base language type. Systems have been developed in research laboratories based on functional languages that allow closures to be passed as parameters – in other words the set of required information for the server to call a function in the client and that function only to be determined at run time.

A common optimization employed in RPC systems is to check whether a call is local, and to avoid the message buffer copy in this case (use of a memory management unit or shared memory system is feasible to map the buffer between the separate process virtual address spaces on a single machine).

2.11.3 ROS and ASN.1

Reality Checkpoint   The ISO has developed a set of standards for invoking operations and an accompanying external data representation standard for parameter typing called Remote Operations Service (ROS) (CCITT 1986) and Abstract Syntax Notation 1 (ASN.1) (CCITT 1985). ROS is not strictly an RPC system, especially since it defines no order on requests and replies. ROS and ASN.1 are described in some detail in Chapter 7.

RPC systems started out with the marvellous work of Birrell and Nelson at Xerox PARC. Since then, they have got larger and slower almost exactly as fast as workstations have got faster, so that today we see typical ROS or RPC performance almost no different from that achieved at the beginning of the 1980s. There seems little explanation for this, but a remarkably similar thing has happened to operating systems and window systems at the same time.

2.11.4 Naming, location and binding

When a remote procedure or function is called, there must be some mechanism to bind the call to the appropriate instance of the procedure. There may be many servers that implement this particular procedure. There are three choices for when the binding is done:

1. It can be at compile time. The location of the procedure is compiled into the client.
2. It can be at load time. When the program is linked and loaded to run, the programmer or system indicates which set of remote instances are the ones this application will use.
3. It can be at call time. When the client reaches the call to the remote procedure, the decision is made which instance to bind to.

Sophisticated RPC systems define one of the base types of the interface language to be an "instance". This allows clients and servers to pass instances of clients and servers amongst themselves. It makes the definition of the interface to the binding service itself cleaner. It is the first step towards providing some notion of inheritance in an RPC system. The location service has itself to be located. There are several approaches:

- It is at a well-known location. ("Well-known" is a euphemism for "wired-in constant").

- Clients broadcast (multicast to a well-known multicast address) for the location service.
- All clients implement some aspect of the location service.

This last case is complex. The idea is that every host that implements a particular service advertises the fact, and this is made known since all services include the location mechanism for that service (by inheritance).

2.11.5 Scaling of naming/binding mechanisms

The scaling of different location services must be considered in terms of number of messages required to locate a given service as well as in the usual scaling of software. Clearly a single central naming/binding service scales well for messages, but rather poorly for performance since it would be inundated with messages. Multicasting for the service (i.e. the opposite extreme of full distribution) may be expensive in network traffic, but is ameliorated by caching results. As we shall see with directory service work, something in between is usually the correct engineering choice.

2.11.6 ANSA trader

The ANSA project developed a "trader" which provides the basic binding service mentioned above. One interesting aspect of the trader is that it is possible to express requests to resolve locations of services together with *constraints*. These constraints are a set of simple expressions on simple attributes of the service. Thus it is possible to ask such questions as: "Where is an instance of service X, not more than n hops away?" or "Where is a printer server that can handle ASCII and PostScript with a zero-length queue?"

Another interesting idea incorporated within the trader is the idea of linking multiple traders together. How you do this and what search policy you specify is a design decision which allows you to make some of the tradeoffs discussed in the preceding section.

2.11.7 Directory services

The CCITT and now ISO X.500 directory service provides something rather more complex than a simple name/location service. We shall see how the directory may be used for storing network management information in Chapter 9. For the moment, we describe the operation of the directory. X.500 assists in locating services and routeing by maintaining databases (often distributed) of name–name and name–address mappings. They may map user-friendly names onto network names. These are in use in wide area networks such as the Internet and thus contrast with many simpler nameservers in use on LANs. Standards for directory and name services include the Name Registration Scheme (NRS) and Domain Name Scheme (DNS), which allow the user to specify destination services by user-friendly names. Services located in this way are hosts, mailboxes and other services. These services are built as distributed databases on the network.

Usually the user does not interact directly with such services. A user supplies the name of a service, and some quality of service that is required (e.g. "Get me Jones, and 'quickly'" or "Send this to Boston, 'Second Class'"). The user program dealing with the request asks a "resolver" to find the service. The resolver may (but need not) try various places until a satisfactory answer is found, and carries out the original request directly. The CCITT X.500 series of standards came into effect in 1988, defining a standard for global naming. A directory contains entries that describe communication entities. A communication entity may be virtually anything about which there is information that can be stored (e.g. humans, computer processes, services). There is considered to be one global directory service. This is much in the style of the Xerox Grapevine Global model, but much has been learned from the scaling problems that Grapevine had.

A user accesses the directory service by the use of a Directory User Agent (DUA). A Directory Service Agent (DSA) accesses the directory, and communicates with other DSAs and DUAs. The Directory Service Functional Model is illustrated in Figure 2.20. A user interacts with the DUA to formulate a query. The DUA then interacts with the directory system, by communicating with one or more DSAs. The DSAs may then communicate with each other to resolve the query. An example of an entry in a directory service for an individual might be as illustrated in Table 2.2.

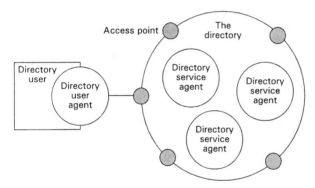

Figure 2.20   The distributed directory model.

The protocols being considered for DUA–DSA and DSA–DSA interactions are based on Remote Operations Service (ROS). They are known as the directory access protocol (DAP) and the directory service protocol (DSP). The data held in the directory is in the form of attribute/value pairs, and thus can be arbitrarily complex. The set of operations allowed on the directory includes searching on keys as well as the usual resolver-type interaction.

Table 2.2   Directory entry example.

Attribute	Description	Value
C	Country	GB
O	Organization	UCL
OU	Organizational unit	Mail service

49

Recursion versus iteration (chaining and referral)

Information in the directory is arranged to form a tree, as are the directory servers themselves. Each server holds some part of the directory tree, most of which is information relevant to the local operations of the system the directory server resides in. It is possible for servers to hold information on behalf of other parts of the directory information tree, and it is reasonable in some circumstances (e.g. a small site without the capacity to run a directory service – i.e. cost reasons; or to provide mutual backup between two sites – i.e. reliability).

When a directory user accesses a server and makes a query, it is possible that the query is for information held in other directories. There are two different approaches for how to proceed:

1. Recursive: the directory chooses another directory and calls it "on behalf" of the user. This next directory may choose to do the same if it cannot resolve the query. This is known as *chaining* (Fig. 2.21).

2. Iterative: the directory returns a "pointer" to another chosen directory. This is known as *referral* (Fig. 2.22).

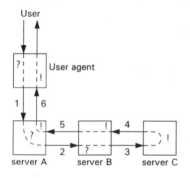

Figure 2.21 Chaining.   **Figure 2.22** Referral.

These two mechanisms permit location transparency, although the second requires more intelligence in the directory user agent.

In both cases, the results may be cached by the user or indeed all along a chain. This achieves some performance transparency as well as location transparency. The mechanism by which the directory servers choose other servers to chain or refer to is self-consistent. The mapping of the structure of the directory information tree onto the tree of directory servers must be held in the directory itself.

There are two important engineering design decisions here. One is the choice of cache timeouts. The other is when to chain and when to refer. A model implementation (Kille 1988) relies on the slow-changing nature of directory information and uses large cache timeouts. QUIPU uses chaining for the first interaction (e.g. DUA to DSA) and thereafter uses referrals. This is justified on the grounds that the DUA is simplified and that only the "first" DSA need "switch" connections – i.e. only the first DSA needs to hold in non-local parts of the tree.

(!) Reality Checkpoint   The directory has not had the success that it should have had so far. In practice, other less well-designed systems are in common use in the worldwide Internet. The existence of the Domain Name System (largely a read-only, non-searchable hierarchical database of networked object name/address pairs) has meant that there is less infrastructural requirement for X.500 systems. This has been a pity.

2.11.8 Recursion and callback

If an RPC system is to be truly location- and access-transparent, it should provide the same semantics as local procedure call. Most procedural languages provide recursion. To this end, a remote procedure call system should provide recursion remotely as well. In this sense, a client may also be a server if some of its procedures are available to other clients. Callback is illustrated in Figure 2.23.

A choice is usually made as to whether the client may be called by servers as a result of calls to those servers, or by arbitrary clients at any time. If the first choice is made, this is sometimes known as "callback". The clients/servers reverse roles as calls result in a tree of processes with a thread going from root to branch causing possible further trees of processes. To maintain the integrity of the group of processes in the tree, it may be necessary to carry a "conversation" marker in call and reply messages. The restriction of callback to the already involved processes can simplify exception handling ("orphan extermination", see Fig. 2.24).

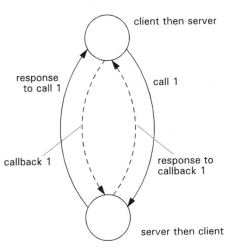

Figure 2.23   Recursion and callback.

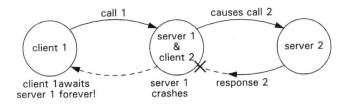

Figure 2.24   Partial failure leaving RPC orphan.

51

2.11.9 Concurrency control

When a server is called, there are a number of choices as to how the global state of the server program is maintained:

1. The server may be "static": persist through all the calls from all its different clients. Any global state changed by calls may affect other calls.
2. It may be "dynamic": created to service each call, and then evaporate after each and every call, usually losing any accumulated state. This approach was taken by the Xerox Courier system (Xerox 1981), for instance.
3. It may be "static", but only service calls from a single client. When a client first calls the server, a new instance is created. This persists until the client indicates its last call, or is destroyed.

The consequence of choosing the first mechanism rather than the last two is that concurrent access to the server may result in interleaved changes to the global state. This may require special mechanisms separate from the RPC system to allow the programmer control over this concurrency.

One solution is to wrap up all servers as a monitor. Another extreme is that taken by Sun RPC: it constrains the programmer to ensure that all calls are idempotent (Sun 1986). This means that if a call is repeated the server returns the same result. This can only be the case if all calls are cast in a form that identifies all the states they refer to, and that servers are stateless. This does have one advantage, which is that crashes of server are of no concern to the programmer (apart from availability/performance reasons). However, it can lead to unnatural interfaces.

The dynamic server approach can be made to perform well if some lightweight process mechanism is provided (e.g. threads, as in Chapter 11). In this type of system, it is possible to have concurrent server processes without creating/destroying the full context associated with normal users processes.

2.11.10 Multicast

Many applications have a requirement for multidestination delivery. This has implications for naming and access mechanisms:

- The targets for multidestination are groups of servers. They may be providing identical services, or replicated services, or they may be providing choices of differing but similar services.
- Some way of choosing which of the group (all or some or one) is needed at compile and at run time.
- The groups may be slowly changing (static) or rapidly changing (dynamic). A group management scheme is needed.

In any language-integrated RPC system, some mechanism is needed for collecting replies and either mapping them into an array of results or providing hooks for voting/selecting a reply. The different models are illustrated in Figure 2.25.

Group communications for applications are not well understood. It would appear that multicast protocols provide a simple packet/message optimization, but that they do not simplify real group communications problems except for the

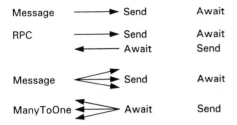

Figure 2.25 Message patterns and inter-process communication (IPC).

"which of" type of query. Many systems use one-to-one communication and model groups inside the application (Birmand 1991). Chapter 3 shows how replicated servers are built in this way. In the most general case, you have both client and server groups. If a server (group) is invoked by a client group then you also need to have mechanisms for collecting invocations and determining which invocations belong to which groups (naming activities).

2.11.11 Upcalls
A common and elegant way of structuring IPC is the use of the "upcall" concept. If a pair of processes can be viewed as a producer and consumer to each other, it is often the case that one of the processes is an initiator. It is possible to provide a way for the initiator to register procedures with the recipient. When the recipient has information for the initiator, rather than waiting to be called, it asynchronously invokes the appropriate procedure in the initiator. This is analogous to a software interrupt, but allows the same kind of language support that the conventional RPC mechanism does.

2.11.12 Buffering schemes
A number of implementation decisions must be made in IPC mechanisms. Although these have no effect on the semantics of the system, they can greatly alter the performance. In any multi-tasking system with inter-process communication, there must be some scheme for controlling allocation and ownership of memory. Dynamic use of memory is often required for IPC, whether message passing or RPC, since it may not be known until call or send time how large the call parameters will be. There are several choices for buffering schemes with respective tradeoffs between efficiency and safety. Some are appropriate to message passing, others to RPC:

- The caller/sender may allocate buffers.
- For RPC, this may include space for return parameters, or else this may be allocated by the receiver.
- The ownership may be transferred to the receiver or not.
- The buffers may be copied to space allocated by the receiver.
- The caller may then free the call buffers.

- The caller may rely on the receiver to free the buffers for return parameters.

These schemes may be combined in various different ways. Object-oriented approaches make buffer handling in RPC-type systems much simpler, since lexical scope often determines when buffers or messages can be garbage-collected by memory management. An optimization in RPC systems is to use shared memory when the call is to a server that happens to be in the same address space.

Another useful optimization is to provide scatter/gather memory in the RPC application-to-stub and stub-to-protocol interfaces. It is often the case that the data representation scheme in use means that this optimizes the marshalling and unmarshalling of arguments. It is also possible that this interface actually extends as far as the network–hardware interface and thus avoids any copying of arguments or buffers at any stage. This can only be made safe when the underlying operating system is sufficiently sophisticated in its memory protection, or the programming language sufficiently type-safe.

2.12 Summary

In this chapter we have introduced the ideas of distributing of conventional programming technologies such as procedure call, and link editors, in the form of remote procedure call and binding services.

2.13 Exercises

1. Why can pointers (references) not usually be passed as parameters to a remote procedure call?
2. How would a fileserver interface differ if the RPC semantics were: Exactly once? At most once? At least once?
3. What are the appropriate properties of a protocol for a networked window system in terms of synchronization and reliability?

CHAPTER 3

Real time and reliable systems

3.1 Introduction

Time is of the essence. We say that someone is reliable if he is punctual. We say that an enterprise is reliable if, in the face of a problem, they try again. On the other hand, most commercial contracts contain penalty clauses to deal with "late delivery". Thus we can see that timeliness and reliability are inherently bound together. This chapter is about the mechanisms that an open distributed system must provide to ensure some required level of reliability and timeliness. In practice this means providing fault and performance transparency for each user or application. This is in contrast to the timeliness required by multimedia communication.[1]

First, we overview some of the standard reliability techniques appropriate to a distributed system. Secondly, we look at the special problems of shared resources in such a system. Thirdly, we look at how to provide higher reliability using transparent replicated objects.

3.1.1 Some definitions

A *fault* is a defect in a system that may, but might not, lead to an error. It may be permanent, transient or intermittent. It may in fact never betray itself. An *error* is a piece of information in a system that results from a fault and may cause a failure when processed in good faith. A *failure* is a deviation in the observable behaviour of the system from its specification. This can include the failure to provide some service within some specified interval.

The quality of a reliable system is often measured in terms of its *mean time between failure* (MTBF), its *mean time to repair* (MTTR), and its *availability*. The first is a reflection of how often something fails, the second how long it takes to become available again, and the last is the percentage of time it offers the specified service. The ability to be fault-tolerant can be based on many approaches.

These failure modes all increase the overall availability of the distributed system despite internal faults. They all do so with some associated cost to some aspect of the performance of the system.[2] In addition to these modes, timeliness brings another list of requirements:

---

1. As we shall see in Chapter 8, video and audio streams are better dealt with by separate mechanisms than distributed system control since they have completely different realibility requirements, which are generally statistical in nature. Their timeliness is also periodic (although even this is also potentially only statistical), and hence requires more design for control loops and clock access.

- *Tightness of deadline*
  There must be enforcement of bounds on delivery time for real-time systems. If a non-deterministic communications medium is used (e.g. Ethernet), then it must be used within the statistical performance bounds that are an acceptable risk.
- *Hiding sins of omission*
  Any retry mechanisms must be bounded by a best estimate of the time to expect an answer (cf. round trip time estimation).
- *Bounds on outages*
  Outages (or network link downtime) should not persist to the point of overburdening recovery mechanisms – i.e. the MTTR should be specified.
- *Priorities*
  If different systems need different service rates, it may be that this must be implemented right down to the lowest level to give the right performance.

3.1.2 How things fail

A model of failures gives a handle for how to provide fault transparency. Suppose that at some level of a system, a fault occurs. If we provide a mechanism to mask it, we can make our system operate correctly. If we do not, the fault may result in a failure.

Failures are usually categorized as follows:

- A crash is where a system ceases to run the programs that are intended.
- A system that fails "silent" is one that crashes and does not report its fault, and may even return valid (but meaningless) responses to messages.
- A "fail stop" system is one that guarantees that it will give no response when it crashes.
- A commission fault is one where a system silently fails to update the state of some variable in stable storage (say disk), but appears to have done so.
- A value fault is said to have occurred after some sequence of updates where the state in stable storage is not what was intended.
- A timing fault is where a system fails to meet some deadline.

Each type of fault has an appropriate method for hiding it so that the corresponding failure does not occur. Of course, each method will have an associated cost.

3.2 The object model and fault transparency

The object-oriented approach is a good way of providing fault confinement. Faults are unlikely to propagate from a well-defined module, except in a very restricted way in the form of erroneous messages which may be checked by other objects in a number of ways.

---

2. It is worth noting that many existing distributed systems still have lower availability than equivalent central systems since more components have a higher number of independent failure modes than one. Analyzing the dependencies between processes in a distributed system is extremely important as it allows the system designer to avoid this pitfall.

Fault detection and diagnosis may be based on comparing the kind of output expected from an object with the actual output. The ADT approach will help with this. In an open distributed system, one of the base methods in the class hierarchy may be the "liveness" test (echo/loopback facility). This will also help isolate and diagnose faults, including those to do with timeliness. Faults are often masked by various means based on replication or error correction. For replication of a service to be transparent to the application/user, there must be some agent that collects replies and performs some majority voting on these replies. The service provided by this agent can be derived from the non-replicated form of the service object.

In some systems, it may be sufficient to retry any failed operation. This relies on the fault model presented by the operation. For example, it will only guarantee freedom from a value failure if the retried operation is either idempotent (meaning that repeated completion of operations has the same effect) or has "all or nothing semantics". This may get round transient faults (e.g. network noise), but will not provide any bounds on the time to complete the operation.

Reconfiguration may be required when the number or rate of appearance of faults exceeds what can be handled by the mechanisms outlined so far. Providing this functionality in a distributed system often involves migration of objects, but when these mechanisms are used, they should not be visible to the application. One extreme case of reconfiguration is to employ some recovery technique to re-establish an earlier system state known to be correct. This may involve rollback or undoing of some number of logged operations. Once recovery is complete, it may be feasible simply to restart all the outstanding operations. If they are idempotent this is straightforward. If not, it may require informing the original end-user so that they may resubmit the original command (e.g. retype their request to withdraw x from a cash point).

A distributed system may be partitioned by a temporary network failure. An important aspect of fault tolerance is the ability to repair the system transparently. In a distributed system, faults and errors are more common and complex than in a centralized system. This is usually because of the communications infrastructure (the larger the system in geographical scale, the more likely errors in communication). It is also due to the heterogeneous nature of an open distributed system. It is not guaranteed that all components (workstations, servers, etc.) are of the same quality.

It must be stressed that in a distributed system, faults and errors may consist only of the *lack* of information. The primary way in which these types of conditions can be detected is by use of timeout and retry facilities. It is frequently found that an application that relies on a "reliable transport" of messages fails in obscure ways. Alternative approaches use self-checking server processes. Of course, the detection of a value fault can be handled by consistency checks at any point in a system.

In distributed systems, most of the facilities available to the conventional communications programmer should be visible to the applications programmer, but only when wanted. The object model provides us with a convenient way of inheriting base methods. These can include base exceptions for handling timeouts and such events.

Any operating system or application has to provide services within time constraints. Some constraints are looser than others. The time to deal with the arrival of data from a monitoring device (e.g. radar signal from air traffic control system) may be very much less than the time to deal with running a process for a user (e.g. formatting a document).

A system must provide varying degrees of reliability. Some data may not be recoverable and some sequences of events may not be repeatable. The relative costs of fixing or preventing faults are different at different stages of system design and implementation. Appopriate cost/benefit tradeoffs need to be made by the engineer when thinking about faults and their consequent failure, depending on loss of service availability, integrity or performance.

Examples
When data was being gathered from the Voyager Fly-by of Triton, the signals took several minutes to travel from the ship back to computers on Earth. There was certainly no opportunity to send a message to the ship requesting it to turn round, go back a few hundred thousand miles and re-film some area!

3.3 Conventional hardware and software reliability

Hardware support to enhance reliability of single processors has centred round the support for confining errors to processes and providing error correction for memory. I/O errors are usually dealt with by retry or replication of I/O devices.

Hardware support for software includes the use of memory management units to isolate the address spaces accessible to different processes. The natural extension of this is to have capability-based hardware where all resources are protected and only those processes with the correct capabilities may access a given resource.

Processes are usually grouped into several levels in a hierarchy. Typically, there are user and superuser privileged processes. In some systems, interrupt service routines (really transient processes) are divided into some number of levels of prioritized processes within the superuser priority. Access from lower priority to higher priority may not be allowed. All different priority processes run with different stacks, often protected by guardwords. Single instructions are usually provided to switch context (including all process state and priority). Most hardware architectures allow certain operations to be uninterruptible (e.g. test and set).

Some network hardware may provide some level of reliability. For example, some financial-service information networks provide at least duplicate links and transmit all information over both routes. This is not simply for resilience to line failure, but also so that errors in transmission can be detected by comparing received messages.

One secure system went even further in protecting the data from interference: access was made only through approved "black box" network interfaces which implemented all the required communications, including generating constant random traffic to prevent traffic pattern analysis by intruders and to provide very rapid network failure detection. Software reliability is currently based on various stages of testing. In the future, it may be possible to use automated program-proving techniques, especially when more systems are formally specified using methods like abstract data types (see Chapter 5).

The notion of "reliability growth" is inherent in the idea that a set of staged tests through the software development cycle will improve the quality of the system. These staged tests are as follows.

Development

During software development, errors may be detected. Based on the number of detected errors and on experience, an estimate can be made of overall non-detected errors. Based on the complexity of the program (branching of the call graph etc.), an estimate of the number of likely errors can be made. It is certainly true that the more channels a distributed application uses, the more likely it is to be error-prone. But testing parts of a distributed application in isolation rarely detects more than simple problems.

Testing

When the software is integrated, a set of coherent tests may be carried out, including deliberate error seeding of the program. Parts of the program are corrupted, and the effect on the rest of the system is observed. The results give some indication of the robustness of the program. This technique is useful in a distributed system. It is often vital to have checked whether a server is safe from rogue clients generating bad requests, and that clients will not fail badly when servers return meaningless results.

Validation

When software is complete, it is usually validated by running in a non-operational environment with test data taken from the real environment or with a distribution based on that from a real-world model.

The more tests run, the more confidence there can be in the reliability of the software. Unfortunately, this leads to excessive cost in testing. An alternative is to restrict the test data by choosing it from "likely" data – chosen by looking at the nature of input the program expects.

What makes distributed systems a particular challenge is the fact that they often exhibit a higher degree of non-deterministic behaviour than centralized systems (due to the inevitable concurrency). Thus the number of traces of the system can be extremely large.

In a distributed system, it may be possible to monitor a network, and replay all the messages in a test harness, and so test the new system with real data in a highly effective way. However, it is worth giving an example of a failure of a system to illustrate how hard this can be to do effectively. In a campus system, it was observed that a number of networked PCs crashed occasionally, but only late on Friday afternoons. The only known change to their software was the introduction of a recently written Ethernet device driver. The eventual bug was found to be that a periodic broadcast packet on the network, advertising the number of users on another particular machine, exceeded the buffer size for received packets in the PC. Normally, PCs only talked to each other, and therefore never sent large packets, or saw/received large broadcast packets. Most of the week the large machine had fewer users. But on a Friday, coursework was due in, so many more students used the machine. In software terms, the problem was that the check on the packet length was after the check on who the packet was for (and subsequent copy of the packet into an insufficiently large buffer).

Operation

Operational testing is identical to validation, except of course for the cost of failures.

Maintenance

During maintenance (repairs, upgrades) it is always possible that reliability decreases. An example of the danger of maintenance in a distributed system is what happens when an upgrade to a system is then distributed to all the other machines in a system. If, for example, an error is introduced that means that machines are no longer able to contact one another, then it will be impossible to automatically rectify this fault. This has implications for the allowed rate of change of systems when they are distributed.

3.4 Software in distributed systems

A basic rule learnt in the Internet community in the USA is that in communicating systems, software should be "conservative" in what it transmits and "liberal" in what it receives. This means that if some large number of optional parameters are feasible when invoking a particular operation, avoid them unless they are required. However, on receiving an operation, be prepared to parse/check all possible options for sanity/correctness. A basic set of rules emerge for sanity checking:
- length
- counters
- source/destination
- checksums

3.5 Contracting for reliability

Meyer (1988) introduced the concept of contracting for software reliability. A class definition represents a statement of what an object of that class can and will do. Clients can expect a behaviour defined by the class specification together with a set of assertions that aid with the semantics of a module.

Assertions usually take the form of *preconditions* and *postconditions* that can be checked just before a method in the object is invoked and just after it returns. In a distributed system, these would be checked between receiving a request message and starting execution of the method procedure, and between completion of the procedure and returning a result message.

Failure of these assertions leads to exceptions. These can be helpful when constructing *transaction* systems (see below). As well as pre- and postconditions, an object-oriented system allows the programmer to identify class invariants. For instance, in the class defined in Chapter 1 for printer spooling, there is a queue which is a finite ordered set of items to be printed. A class invariant for this might be:

$$0 \leq lengthOf(Queue) \leq MaxQLength \qquad (3.1)$$

The use of class invariants and pre- and postconditions decreases the number of states/cases in the event of failure in an object. Pre- and postconditions are also tested at well-known points of synchronization, and we shall see that this aids in isolating faults in the distributed execution (and decreases the time spent uselessly blocked in a distributed environment under error conditions). Of course, many applications (e.g. interactive window systems like X-Windows) map exceptions into total failure. This gives us a strong hint as to the base method for exception handling in a distributed system!

We shall see later how careful use of exceptions can help isolate problems in a distributed system. Another important concept in Meyer's approach is that of side effects in functions, and whether they should be allowed. In a distributed system, we have no choice but to allow side effects, in that state must be stored somewhere, though it may simply be in the output to some static storage, or control of some device (autoteller outputting notes).

3.6 Analyzing timing constraints

As indicated above, timeliness can be just as important as correct results. The usual way that time constraints are worked out starts at the lowest level (closest to the hardware), and works upwards through lower-priority processes.

If we consider the source of interrupts (say a disk/asynchronous terminal line or network interface):

- At some level, data will be blocked into frames or octets.
- At some level of timing, there will be a maximum bit rate.
- There will be a maximum wait time by which we must start processing these blocks.

When analyzing the interrupt- or upcall-driven code, we simply count the lines of code (or profile the code). Interrupt service code usually dequeues data, processes it (inline – rarely branching or calling other procedures), then enqueues a processed block (or amalgamated blocks) for a higher-(lower-)priority process.

By scheduling the most *urgent* service routines highest, but also making them shortest, we can work out the percentage of the CPU time that is used by them. Then, from what is left, the next priority processes worst-case arrival rate of events can be calculated, and the corresponding time to handle these. This can go on until the only processes left to run are non-preemptive user processes, and the CPU "bandwidth" or spare cycles left is what the end-user gets. A robust system for detecting timing violations and avoiding faulty detections requires the use of synchronized clocks.

In a distributed system, this whole analysis is much more complex, as events may be transmitted over a shared network to remote processes. Since the network is shared between arbitrary machines/processes, the time for messages to traverse it may be effectively non-deterministic (i.e. has no obvious upper bound).

This is an undesirable situation, so usually bounds are imposed on message times, both by the network (time-to-live field in packets) and by the end-systems (end-system to end-system timeouts).

3.6.1 Watchdog timers

"Watchdog timers" are often used both in hardware and in software to detect errors. Software is required to periodically probe some timer. If the system fails to do this at some prearranged frequency, an alarm is raised. In a distributed system, this is a very useful technique. Many systems rely on probes, not simply to test the liveness of a service, but to make fault detection more timely so that use of an alternative can be chosen more quickly.

3.6.2 Synchronization mechanisms

We have described the synchronization mechanisms between end-systems when they communicate. We now discuss synchronization between instances of communication. In a distributed system, many concurrent applications may attempt to access the same object simultaneously. The classic example is that of access to a bank-account database as shown below. Two clerks start to update the same bank account as they clear two separate cheques:

```
A:
1. Read account P -> x
2. x = x + 42
3. Write account P <- x


B:
1. Read account P -> y
2. y = y + 23
3. Write account P <- y
```

Consider the different order in which these operations can occur. If B.1 happens between A.1 and A.3, or A.1 happens between B.1 and B.3, account P would be short 23 or 42 dollars respectively. Any other ordering has the desired effect. What is required is some synchronization mechanism. It is worth noting for now that if A and B had been accessing different accounts, or A and/or B only read the account, then no synchronization would be necessary. The solution is to provide a locking mechanism. Each application must acquire a lock before attempting its set of operations. Setting locks must be indivisible with respect to the normal operations.

Locks should apply to groups of operations at an appropriate level of granularity. There is a tradeoff between concurrency and blocking, which will need adjusting based on the number of commonly linked operations by a single client versus the number of clients concurrently carrying out operations.

A problem then arises as to when to release the locks. Next we see how transactions help structure these sets of operations.

3.7 Transactions

We have seen that concurrent access to a shared object by separate clients can lead to consistency problems. The mechanism that is employed to avoid these problems is *atomic* transactions. With knowledge that the service is shared, the client program may be written, specifying that some sequence of operations on the shared object is not to be interleaved with operations by other clients. Essentially, a group of operations is structured into a single *atomic* operation which is called a *transaction*. The four properties of an atomic operation are referred to conventionally by the useful acronym "ACID" – atomicity, consistency, independence and durability.

A major consequence of transactions is the requirement for mechanisms for failure recovery. If the client or the server fails *during* a transaction, the transaction must appear to have either:

* completed successfully
* failed completely

This means that the state of the system at each end must be *recoverable*.

The transaction is a mechanism that was devised for database systems. Its purpose it to maximize *consistency* of stored data. This consistency must be maintained in the face of failures, and without placing unnecessary restrictions on any concurrency between different applications accessing the data. Its properties include the following:

* A transaction consists of an arbitrary sequence of operations, bracketed by a StartTransaction and an EndTransaction.
* The transaction is said to be *atomic* if
  - either all the operations succeed, and the overall transaction succeeds.
  - none appear to succeed, and the transaction fails – *failure atomicity*.
* If more than one transaction is executed concurrently, then the effect must be the same as if the separate transactions had been executed one at a time (but in no specific order). This property of concurrent transactions is known

as *serial equivalence*. (The transactions are *serializable*). This is achieved through use of some concurrency control mechanism such as locking, timestamp or optimistic concurrency control (see below).

- If one of some concurrent transactions fails (does not complete), its results (intermediate or terminal) are not hidden from the other transactions.

Transaction services are sometimes offered on file systems as well as database systems. In an open distributed system, transactions are a way of offering this failure atomicity on any object in the system. To provide a transaction service, certain functions are required:

- The transaction must be *recoverable*. Either the transaction can be reversed (there is an inverse operation, and the current operation is reliably logged), or else some previous version of the data/object is available.
- When each operation is invoked after the transaction is started, it is logged or else the operation is made on a *tentative* version of the data.
- When the client ends the transaction, if all the operations have succeeded, the server will return to the client the fact that the transaction is *committed*.
- If the client finds some fault or error, it may abort the transaction. This causes the server to wind back the state of the data as if no operation had been invoked.
- If the server fails for some reason (lack of resources or error), it must wind back to the same previous state (this may be after a restart) and report to the client that the transaction has failed.

All of these functions require stable storage (e.g. disk-battery-backed RAM).

Transactions are another tool to make programming distributed applications easier. The atomicity property means that the programmer does not have to be concerned with consistency. They can group operations in a transaction arbitrarily, without concern for what failures may occur in the client, server or network. They are guaranteed that the stable storage holding the data will either contain successful results, or no change. The serializability of concurrent transactions means that each application programmer is sealed off from all others. They need not concern themselves with the order in which operations are invoked in different applications. Applications are shielded from handling errors caused by other applications by the way transactions hide tentative intermediate updates.

3.7.1 Example
Going back to the example of a printer spooler from Chapter 1, we can see that the operations in this service are in fact made up of several suboperations, and that some of these operations should be implemented as transactions.

Add "file" to printer queue - succeeds, returns q#, or fails
This must transfer a local file to a remote spool area and place a new entry in the queue. Several failures are possible (the file transfer fails due to network failure, the spool area is full, the queue itself is full, etc.).

Remove q# from queue – succeeds, returns ok, or q# not in queue
This must check that the q# is not currently printing and that the remover is the owner of the queue entry.

List queue
This should read the queue as it stands and not keep listing new entries if they are added halfway through the list queue operation.

We can see that the first two operations write things in the queue (and spool area), while the third merely reads it.

3.7.2 Concurrency control

In Chapter 2, we introduced the idea of concurrency and the requirement for concurrency control. In this section, we look at some concurrency control techniques in some detail.

Locks

If you want to stop two people using a single room at the same time, an obvious technique is to provide the room with a lock, and the people with a single key. Locks in concurrent systems are a logical extension of this. Locks are divided into two classes:

Shared ("read") locks

Shared locks are used to exclude updates but allow shared read-only access to an object from a transaction. (Recall, in our print spooler example there are no problems with concurrent "list" operations, but "add" should be exclusive of "list".)

Exclusive ("write") locks

Exclusive locks exclude all other accesses and are used for write/update access to an object from a transaction.

When a transaction starts, it then attempts to acquire appropriate locks on the items/objects it is going to access. When it is done with these items, it releases the locks. This mechanism is known as *two-phase locking*.

To maximize the concurrency in the system, the right locks must be used in the right way:

- Locks should apply to the smallest granularity of object that is sensible. For instance, two processes accessing different records in a file should not be excluded.
- Locks should be released as early as possible. For instance, a read lock can be released as soon as the appropriate value has been read, but a write lock cannot be released until the entire transaction involving the write operation is complete. However, it is safest to hold both read and write locks until the end (as I believe is the usual practice). Otherwise, other transactions could

be affected by an intermediate state of this transaction. Consider releasing read locks early:

```
T1:
x = y;
z = y;

T2:
y = y +1
```

If T1 releases and reclaims its read lock on y, there could be unfortunate effects.

- Locks should be acquired in the same order when accessing the same object. This last point is vital for avoiding deadlock.

As we saw in Chapter 2, deadlock is caused by two concurrent processes each acquiring resources that the other requires; in this case the resource is the lock (the right to access the object). Deadlock can be dealt with by either avoidance or detection.

Deadlock avoidance involves imposing some ordering on the transactions in the system. This is problematic, as transactions may be data-dependent; that is, it may not be known in advance what will be the set of transactions the system will undergo.

Transactions or locks may be timed out. This will lead to failure/aborts and retries, which may mean undue work, and may not stop the same situation arising again (possibly immediately), although suitably randomized timeouts may help.

Thirdly, one can allow deadlock to occur, and detect it, and then abort some suitably random selection of transactions. Detection is based on keeping a list of all the processes waiting for and holding each lock (or resource). By scanning this list (known as a "wait-for graph"), we can detect deadlock by the presence of loops. In a distributed transaction system, deadlock is very much harder to detect since the processes executing transactions/locks are distributed, and no single machine can reliably hold the wait-for graph for the whole system.

If it is possible to choose sensible values, we can use the timeout mechanism to abandon potentially deadlocked distributed transactions. However, as we have discussed, the communications system often has effectively unbounded delays in delivering a (correct) message, so we may abort successful transactions unnecessarily. There is an engineering tradeoff to be decided by measuring the values for an actual system. Some systems do not require absolute consistency – it may be acceptable for different users to perceive different levels of accuracy in the information they receive (e.g. weather forecasts at sea are more important to ships than to those ashore).

3.8 Timestamps

We have seen that a distributed transaction system requires concurrency control. One mechanism used is to add a timestamp to each transaction. The mechanism is quite simple. A "write" transaction updates an object and adds its timestamp to the object. If a further "read" or "write" transaction attempts to access the object and has an older timestamp than that of the object (i.e. that of the latest correct successful transaction), this transaction is aborted.

This mechanism avoids the need for locks altogether and therefore avoids any deadlock problems. It does so, effectively, by serializing all transactions by a notion of global time in the distributed system. Of course, we still need to provide failure atomicity (say by two-phase commit), but most importantly we need to provide global synchronization.

A global clock is useful for other things too, such as distributed deadlock detection (and see Chapter 4). Mills (1994) suggests that clocks can be synchronized to a high degree of accuracy even compared with the variation in message transit delay between distributed computers. In fact, we do not necessarily require global synchronization of clocks so much as global ordering of related events.

The rules for working out this ordering are simple (due to Lamport (1978)). The clock here need only be a counter at a location that is incremented with each event:

- If two events are co-located, then the local clock will determine their ordering.
- If an event e1 causes a message to arrive at a separate host, which "causes" another event e2, then e2 happens "after" e1.
- If e1 "causes" e2 and e2 "causes" e3, then e3 happens "after" e1.
- If e1 "causes" e2, and e1 "causes" e3, then e2 and e3 have no special relation and are effectively "simultaneous".

Each host keeps monotonically increasing the "logical" clock with each event, which it can use to "timestamp" messages so that other hosts can track the order of messages from this host.

3.8.1 Optimistic concurrency control

Optimistic concurrency control differs from the use of locks fundamentally, in that it is based on the assumption (observation) that in many systems the vast majority of operations are independent. To this end, it avoids the expensive synchronization and checkpointing necessary for transaction systems.

The distributed system is divided into a number of logical recovery units. Each of these periodically checkpoints its state, and continuously logs the stream of messages arriving at it, in such a way as to be able to roll back its state to the previous checkpoint. The state intervals of the system are partially ordered by a "causal relation". This is so that when there is a fault that leads to some partial failure in the system, the task of rolling back the whole system to a known state is a tractable one, since the system is modularized.

The idea of optimistic concurrency control is that by analyzing the dependencies, one can generate "commit guards". Commit guards are effectively the list of other recovery-unit states that this execution is dependent on. Rollback based on logged state is only necessary if at some later stage it turns out that one of the recovery units failed, perhaps with a lost message. Usually, systems built around this approach also engineer their networks to make message loss a rare event. Thus this is really an approach for partitioning up the recovery problem into smaller pieces so that the cost of keeping enough information to carry out rollback is not too high in any one part.

3.8.2 Recovery mechanisms
There are three classes of *failure* in a distributed transaction system:
- The client can fail.
- The transaction service (including communications channel) can fail.
- The stable storage can fail. (Stable storage refers to storage such as disk or tape that persists after power outage – of course, it still has failure modes, such as physical damage, but these are normally much rarer than power loss.)

If the client fails, it will happen either during the transaction or after commitment. In the first case, the service simply undoes the transaction. If the transaction service fails, the client and server can wait for recovery and retry, or independently assume failure, and wait to issue aborts/undoes. If the stable storage fails, the enterprise should acquire more reliable hardware by spending more money![3] Client and transaction-service failure involve recovery mechanisms. We describe these techniques next.

3.8.3 A commit log
A commit log is used to track the necessary state to make decisions during an n-phase commit process, or else to unroll back to any pre-committed state:
(a) It either contains inverse operations or records the state of the object prior to the start of the transaction. These can be used to revert in the case of abort or failure during the transaction.
(b) It also contains an effective duplicate of the operations and parameters of the transaction, since it must be feasible to replay the transaction if there is a system failure immediately after commitment.

This log must be in stable storage to maximize reliability.

In (b) above, failure of a distributed transaction service includes network failure. Network failure can be seen as temporary or long-term inability of the application and transaction service to contact each other (loss of messages or network partitioning).

---

3. It is absolutely impossible to achieve 100% reliability. The aim of the engineer should be to reduce the chances of failure to the point where the expected loss is acceptable and at an acceptable cost. This may involve moving the probable modes of failure to components for which the MTBF can be accurately assessed.

3.8.4 Two-phase commits

Although a distributed system could suffer a number of failures of a different kind simultaneously, the normal approach to increased reliability is to consider this unlikely, and deal with network failures and service failures separately. This has led to the two-phase commit protocol:

```
Phase 1
1. Log intention to run this transaction on S's in TA's stable
storage.
2. TA starts Timer
3. TA requests S's "can i commit?"
4. S's reply and log "ready", "abort", or TA times out.
5. TA proceeds with either "Commit" or "Abort" for Phase 2


Phase 2

1. TA records Commit or Abort
2. TA reports Commit or Abort to S's
3. S's now proceed as if normal Commit
4. S's acknowledge
5. TA records "complete"
```

A transaction agent (TA) acts on behalf of all the servers (S) involved in sub-transactions in this transaction.

Considering failures, either the TA or the S's can fail, or the messages 1.3, 2.2 and 2.4 can be lost. The resulting cases are:

```
The transaction succeeds.
Either the transaction blocks because S's or TA blocks.
The transaction fails.
```

3.9 More about multiple-readers/single-writer and the object model

Since we base our model on abstract data types, in the simple case of a single client/server thread, we may be able to analyze the types of parameters in a method/operation and identify which involve updating a server, and which do not.[4] From this we can find out which operations can be concurrent and which cannot. Those that require locking for read inherit this operation as a side effect, while those that lock out all readers and other writers inherit the appropriate operation.

Since read-type operations, or write operations on independent items, are not dependent, they cannot affect consistency, and can be eliminated from this analy-

---

4. In general, this is a very hard problem, since many programming languages make it hard to tell whether a piece of code necessarily alters the state of variables that it references.

REAL TIME AND RELIABLE SYSTEMS

sis syntactically. This approach is adopted in the ANSA Atomic Object Model by adding certain information to the interface definitions of object methods: a concurrency control manager decides which atomic operations to schedule, based on "concurrency predicates" that are added to the object definition by the programmer. These will state how operations that share arguments/objects can be interleaved and ordered. They are illustrated in Figures 3.1 and 3.2. There are two types of predicate:

- Ordering predicates control which operations can be interleaved within a tree of dependent atomic actions in a single tree. If, for example, updating some database requires several suboperations and these are all defined as part of a single superclass, then we would define some ordering predicates on the suboperations.
- Separation predicates allow the concurrency control system to determine which operations from different (independent) trees of operations may interleave, and which must be separated by use of locks or other mechanisms to hide partial states of the transaction from other operation trees.

A concurrency predicate is in the form shown in Figure 3.1. One then forms a concurrency evaluation matrix for all the operations. This is shown in Figure 3.2.

```
predicate = (opi(args) [| or -> or []} opj(args)
        ........
        ........
        (opm(args) [| or -> or []} opm(args)

1. |, ->, [] indicates that opj can be invoked either in parallel with
opi, or must always follow (sequence) or is a mutually exclusive
choice.

2. args is a list of arguments with associated modes
args = [arg, mode]*
where mode indicates "read only" or "read/write".
```

Figure 3.1 Concurrency predicates.

Each entry shows how the addition of a new operation, opx, relates to outstanding operations. It shows the synchronization operator (as in 1. in Fig. 3.1) and the set of argument lists associated with the current outstanding operations. From these and the modes, we can determine whether the new operation is allowed now, or must be scheduled as a pending operation. If we schedule it for later, it is queued until all the outstanding operations complete and commit or abort.

	opi	...	opn
opi			
:	?,m		
opn			

Figure 3.2 Concurrency evaluation matrix.

70

If operations are nested or related by callback, then the situation is a lot more complex. If a nested operation only ever appears in the same "place" in the nesting/hierarchy, then we can apply locking at the top (outer) level, but if two clients may access the same operation, one directly, the other indirectly, then there's a problem.

The current approach is to examine the dependencies that exist between transactions that perform operations on a common object. If the transitive closure of all dependencies (order in which the transactions operate) forms a partial order, then the transactions can be serialized. If there are cycles, then the order is ambiguous.

3.10 Commitment, concurrency and recovery (CCR)

This is the part of the ISO Common Applications Service Elements which provides some of the functionality outlined above.

In the ISO standardization work on Job Transfer and Manipulation protocols, a requirement for application support for synchronization, consistency and commitment was realized. Since the OSI model (see Chapter 6) is designed to avoid duplicate functionality, and the standards bodies decided that these features should be available to other applications too, they form a separate standard. CCR is now available for the ISO File Transfer, Access and Management (FTAM) protocol as well. CCR is designed to handle end-system crashes during critical operations and loss of network connectivity between one update and another. CCR allows the applications programmer to build a tree of processes/activities. The top of the tree is some master and lower down are subordinates. This is called the "atomic action tree".

Just as we have described above, the protocol CCR defines follows the normal rules:

1. A superior issues a C-Begin to start an atomic action.
2. Actual data starts to be exchanged, and (locally specific) concurrency control mechanisms are used.
3. The superior issues a C-Prepare primitive, indicating that it has finished the set of operations that make up this action.
4. The subordinate issues a C-Ready, indicating that it can now ensure either commitment to this action, or rollback. The superior issues a C-Commit or a C-Rollback
5. The subordinate acknowledges the C-Commit or C-Rollback, having released all concurrency controls.

Note that once a superior has issued a C-Begin, it must eventually complete or rollback. This ensures that the subordinate always (eventually) frees the concurrency controls (and therefore allows other clients/superiors to access the resource).

CCR contains the amusing concept of "heuristic commitment and rollback". This facility allows subordinates to decide to commit or rollback after losing contact with a superior (say after sending it a C-Ready), based on *guesswork*! CCR contains part of the ideas of timing out atomic actions (and locks/deadlock arising from them) by defining a "period of use" for any data item. CCR also includes the notion of nested atomic actions. One action can be "wrapped" around others (just as a single simple action is made out of some number of non-atomic operations).

3.11 Fault tolerance

So far in this chapter we have described techniques for isolating faults and helping the distributed applications programmer avoid some of the pitfalls of synchronization and consistency in a distributed system. We have not described how a distributed system can *improve* availability in any way.

The starting point is to recognize that although there are more possible independent failure modes in a distributed system than there are in a centralized one, applications may not need many of the hosts or storage systems to be capable of running.

Then we should take note that there is a high degree of replication of hardware, communications and operating system facilities in a distributed system. Some of these components (e.g. CSMA/CD and FDDI/DAS local-area network technology) are highly reliable, and have no dependent failure modes. Other components may not be very reliable but are inexpensive to replicate (e.g. microprocessors, small disks, memory).

The aim of reliable distributed system software is to take advantage of the hardware replication or reliability to place, replicate or migrate processes and data (methods/objects) to avoid/mask failures.

3.11.1 Replication/redundancy

Many distributed systems are (ironically) less reliable than centralized ones. A distributed file system without replication has more failure modes than a centralized one, since the network between client machines and the fileserver can fail as well as the fileserver itself. Replication mechanisms for objects in a distributed system can be subdivided into two main classes:

- hot or cold standby
- active replicas with voting

When the objects are changing rapidly, for instance in a rapidly updated file system, the second approach is essential.

Replicated services lead to the requirement for *distributed two-phase locking*. If several copies of an object are held replicated, the two-phase locking mechanism described in Section 3.7.2 must be extended to deal with this. If locks are granted independently on copies of the object, then it might be possible for two separate transactions to acquire locks on separate copies and create inconsistencies in the replicated file.

There are a range of solutions. One is to designate a primary object, and locks always apply there – this can reduce availability of the object if the primary fails. Another extreme is to propagate a lock for access to all copies of an object. This is costly. Cost is reduced by only insisting that a write lock must be applied at all sites, and a read lock at any one site.

3.11.2 Nested transactions

Replicated servers are wrapped up in "meta-servers", so that the replication is transparent. These are called "nested" transactions. The idea is generalized in most real distributed-system platforms to provide a way of creating hierarchically structured servers built out of other servers. The idea is to get the same gain for a distributed system that hierarchical modularization gains for single programs. There is a consequence of this: that the fault/failure models must reflect the nesting of services; and some care is needed in making sure that a system built out of nested servers does not have less fault tolerance than a monolithic one.

3.11.3 Version management

To achieve failure transparency in a system that allows nested atomic operations, a reliable system must maintain versions of objects in stable storage (i.e. storage that has a much lower failure rate than the operations system).

There is one version per outstanding transaction. The concurrency control system makes use of the interface to the version management system to provide independent versions of the object to independent operations. When an operation commits, the version manager ensures that changes are only reflected in the stable store after all ancestor operations commit.

3.11.4 Replication

Many systems in safety-critical areas use replication of vital components to improve reliability. It is important to note that such systems also provide high availability. These two characteristics are not the same thing.

A low-level technique for increasing integrity of information on a disk is to mirror the disk and use a simple comparator. If the data ever differs, we then force a failure. This means that the *integrity* of the data is twice as good, but even if the comparator has 0% failure, a failure of either disk means the whole system fails. Thus the system has half the availability, at best.

In a distributed system, this is even more critical to appreciate, since the network that connects components may be far less reliable even than the components themselves. Network partitioning will reduce the availability of distributed replicated objects.

A third characteristic of replicated services is that they may provide better performance for read access, but are generally slower for update access. To see why, we must consider how the replication is made transparent whilst providing exactly the same view of the data to all clients. Consistency must be maintained, and the mechanisms for maintaining consistency have a cost. This cost is simply because a replication system is usually implemented by making all the operations that applied to a unique object into *atomic* operations that have a set of sub-operations on each of the replicated object. Thus locks or optimistic concurrency control with rollback and recovery are required, with all the overheads described in the previous section.

In some systems (such as name and directory servers) updates are far less frequent than reads. In these services, the master/slave model of replication is simpler. A master service holds the state that is downloaded to slaves. Multiple slaves provide higher performance and availability for reading. Updates only happen on the master, which then restarts the slaves one by one with the new version. There are other systems in which it doesn't matter if the information is only slightly out of date, e.g. the latest weather. Then we can afford to propagate updates lazily (i.e. as a read request to a replicant server arrives). The design tradeoffs here are similar to those for cache designs.

Some systems allow write access to proceed even when network partitioning means that consistency cannot be maintained. This is so that availability is maintained. It is a reasonable engineering tradeoff. In this case, we need a scheme to deal with the rejoining of the distributed system after repair.

This will be based on voting about versions of objects. Various schemes exist for distributed voting between replicated but possibly inconsistent servers and clients:

Majority consensus

The normal majority consensus algorithm is used for clients updating replicated servers:

- A client has previously read some version of some item (timestamped).
- When the client updates, it submits the new version to some server together with the old ones.
- This server then either broadcasts to all the others or simply chains through them (rather like the directory service mentioned in Chapter 2).

To ensure that the servers converge on an update being accepted or rejected, there is now a voting phase, while the update is "pending":

- The servers recursively ask the next server if this is okay (and tell them all the servers that so far have okayed the update).
- If the update's timestamp is more recent than each server's stored value, they okay it.
- When the number of okays in the consensus message is a majority of the servers, the update starts to be applied.

Suitable use of timeouts ensures that we can operate this scheme even with a minority of servers unavailable.

Weighted voting

Weighted voting schemes allow for weights to be associated with the different replicated objects, both for read and update access. Then read operations need some quorum of votes before they proceed, while updates need some different quorum (Herlihy 1986). In this way, we can get higher read availability for older copies, whilst maintaining high integrity for writing. This is an important property in distributed systems, since there are often system objects that are rarely updated, but frequently read (e.g. executables on workstation disks).

3.12 Object migration

One of the properties of objects mentioned in Chapter 1 was that of activity. Objects can be passive or active, and this relates to their use.

Migration of passive objects is relatively straightforward. It is a generalization of file migration. An object store management system will keep statistics as to accesses and use of passive objects and can decide to relocate an object closer to clients if necessary.

Migration of active objects is a great deal harder. In an open distributed system, we have an underlying assumption about the heterogeneous nature of the systems, software and hardware. An active object is instantiated as executing code and associated state. The state is not only private variables, but also outstanding service to clients. Even if the system implements an interpreted pseudo-code for the instructions of the object, it would be extremely complex to "replug" all the clients to a relocated object.

We would argue for initial process placement as being a more appropriate and technically feasible way of load balancing in open systems. This can also be supported by the argument that an open system may require negotiation before placing a process. This overhead may often outweigh the benefit of moving an already active object.

Both ANSA and ODP have the concept of relocation, which avoids the problem of having to replug all clients. An interface reference contains a sequence of interfaces to relocation servers. The mechanisms moving an object update associated relocation servers. If a client tries to invoke a service that has moved, the infrastructure can consult the relocator (all this can be done transparently to the application). This is discussed in great detail in Chapters 7 and 11.

3.13 Exception handling

We define an exception to be the occurrence of an abnormal condition during execution of a program. Generally, an exception is caused by a failure which was caused by an error.[5]

Exception handling mechanisms have been added to some programming languages and many embedded systems. These mechanisms are based on the requirement for well-defined behaviour such as atomicity. A piece of software must succeed or fail. Thus an exception must provide only two possibilities:

---

5. In software terms, the error was in software that did not meet its specification. The fault/failure was the inability of the software to then meet its design. The exception is then caused by there being no further way this part of the software can proceed.

1. Tidy up and report failure to a higher authority
2. Retry (perhaps another way)

We can further refine our idea of exceptions (especially in distributed systems) by observing that there are four places an exception can occur:

1. An object is being asked incorrectly to do something it cannot
2. There is a fault in the object
3. The object invokes an operation in another which is faulty
4. There is a communications failure

Case 1 can be dealt with by preconditions on operations preventing this object being corrupted by faults elsewhere. Case 2 must be dealt with by raising a higher-level exception (and will require maintenance). Case 3 requires a retry mechanism where we may choose an alternative if possible. Case 4 may be dealt with by retry to an alternative.

Implementing exception handling is hard. It is only just being introduced to C++ at the time of writing.

Examples of exception handling include the following:

- Remote execution of some part of the program – failure must lead to total failure of the program.
- Remote use of floating-point hardware – failure might map to local emulation rather than total failure.
- Remote name service (e.g. Yellow Pages) – failure to get an answer (timeout) might map to retry (typical behaviour with multicast idempotent services).
- Load sharing systems (e.g. European Space Agency telemetry monitoring and analysis systems).
- Distributed authoring systems through e-mail.

3.14 Summary

In this chapter, we have introduced the notions of timeliness and reliability. We have seen that a simple RPC system can be enhanced to provide atomic operations, and that by annotating an interface specification we can provide enough information to implement objects that provide failure transparency. At the same time, concurrency transparency is provided through analyzing the concurrency predicates, so that independent atomic operations can execute in a timely way, while dependent ones are serialized correctly.

(!) Reality Checkpoint   Open real-time systems are a long way off in reality. The mission-critical nature of real-time systems has meant that the cost of a single supplier is balanced by the value of testing and the stability of the system they supply. Until distributed real-time systems are far better understood, it is unlikely that we will see many multivendor systems running air-traffic or health-system control.

3.15 Exercises

1. Why is a system with workstations and a fileserver less reliable than a central mainframe?

2. Explain the tradeoffs between availability and consistency in the implementation of a replicated object.

3. Two banks use an atomic operations system to implement their customer-account databases. Show how we can combine these to allow transactions to take place between the two banks.

CHAPTER 4

The nature of security

with Robert Cole, Hewlett-Packard Laboratories, Bristol

This chapter discusses the need for security in a distributed system and the basic principles of security in distributed systems. Security is not a component of a distributed system that can be added as an afterthought. Security is a quality that a system has with regard to the information in the system and the processing of that information. As such, security has to be designed into the system from the beginning. Unfortunately, there is no readily agreed definition for security, so it is impossible to say "this system has security" in the same way we may say "this car is red". This is because each system has different requirements for security which are set out by the users of the system.

The person responsible for the security of a distributed system is called the "security administrator". This person will translate the enterprise requirements for security into a security policy and ensure that the appropriate mechanisms are used in the distributed system to enforce that policy.

The security requirements for each system are set down in a security policy, which is a set of statements that the components of the system must adhere to. The statements will dictate the way the system will be run such that, if the policy is correctly maintained, then the system will be secure as defined by the policy. Examples of policy statements might be:

- Only a goods inwards clerk is able to add items to the inventory files.
- Only an accounts payable clerk can raise a cheque against an invoice.
- All documents that are classified as "company confidential" must be kept on computers that are not available to non-employees.
- All data transferred between company computers must be encrypted for confidentiality.
- Computers in secure computer rooms cannot be used with operator privileges from terminals outside the computer room.

To support the implementation of the security policy a number of security concepts have to be designed into the system, discussed in this chapter. The placement and use of security mechanisms to implement the concepts will be dictated by a model.

The problems of security in distributed systems (as opposed to stand-alone computers) are compounded by the need to protect information during communication and by the need for the individual components to work together. The problem of getting all of the individual components of the distributed system to work as a single unit requires some degree of trust.

 Reality Checkpoint   There is no such thing as an insecure network. Only end-systems need be secure. The network can do little to help with security (although users of it could do a lot to undermine it!). This is the key to understanding where security mechanisms are placed.

4.1 Threats and protection

To understand the need for security in a system it is necessary to understand what threats or attacks the system is subject to. A threat is a potential violation of security. The security policy of a system will identify the threats that are deemed to be important and will dictate the measures that are to be taken to protect the system against those threats. It is not possible to provide a detailed discussion on threats in such a general text; however, the primary threats against which most security is directed are:

Disclosure

Information kept within the system should be protected against disclosure to unauthorized persons. Note that this can include who is talking to whom and even the fact that someone is talking at all. (Imagine companies that normally compete discussing a merger by electronic mail – share dealers would be tempted if they even knew of such conversations. Imagine a list of people who subscribe to particular sets of bulletin boards. Junk mailers and advertisers would dearly like such information to target their output.) So there is explicit disclosure of information, but never forget the implicit information in the act of communication itself. Under some circumstances, it may be that someone wishes to prove that they originated *some* information but wish to repudiate the contents. Thus a separation of authentication and privacy can be seen to have requirements from both secrecy and revelation.

Corruption

Information in the system must be protected against unauthorized change. Obviously, we do not want the integrity of our work to be compromised.

Destruction or loss of information

Where this occurs information is effectively unavailable for use within the system. If information has value, then the cost of its loss is clear.

Denial of service

The resources of the system must be protected so that they are available for use by authorized persons. This means preventing unauthorized use of the resources. In some systems, it may be reasonable to share resources that are idle. In others, this may prevent timely reaction (e.g. safety-critical systems, or again, share-dealing systems, where time is of the essence).

Covert signalling

This is not generally a direct threat to an organization, but is indirect. The use of their communications channels to carry another organization's messages surreptitiously may deny them revenue. The usual urban myth cited here is the technique of telephoning football scores long-distance by ringing tones on a deliberately unanswered phone at an agreed time.

Denial of service is a threat that is covered to some extent by the security concepts used to protect against disclosure and corruption. For example, if access to a system is controlled by access-controlled quotas, then to deny service to other users may be prevented. Other measures fall into the area of physical security which is outside the scope of this text. Consequently the rest of this chapter will concentrate on the first three threats. In general, passive attacks are very difficult to detect – the general defence is to try and prevent them. Conversely, active attacks are easier to detect, but perhaps harder to prevent. A combination of passive attack and replay can lead to denial of service and is particularly pernicious.

An important threat that has to be tackled in any system that is being used by humans is that someone may subvert the system to their own gain. In other words, they may commit some form of fraud or damage by using the legitimate operations of the system. The most common technique that is used to overcome this is to ensure that no single individual (not even the security administrator) can carry out all of the actions necessary to commit a fraud. For instance, no one who is allowed to enter invoices into a system will be allowed to authorize payment of invoices. This would stop someone entering their own fictitious invoices to obtain payment. There are lots of examples in other areas: two keys are necessary to open a bank vault, and they will be held by different people, or two different keys will be necessary to launch a nuclear missile. The concept behind these examples is that of *separation of duty*. To ensure that this concept may be used in a distributed system it is necessary to provide the underlying mechanisms, particularly access control and authentication.

Threats can be further classified into intentional or accidental, which is self-explanatory; and active or passive. An active threat is one that will result in some unauthorized activity in the system which can cause corruption, loss, or destruction of information. An active threat can also cause a denial of service by monopolizing resources within the system. A passive threat is one that does not intrude on the system and utilizes no resources or activity within the system. However, a passive threat can lead to disclosure of information, for instance by passive wire-tapping, or monitoring the radiation from a VDU.

The security facility that is used to protect against disclosure is that of confidentiality. This means the information in the system is protected by appropriate confidentiality mechanisms (see Section 4.7 below). The security facility that is used to protect against corruption, or partial loss of information, is integrity. Unfortunately, although integrity will tell you that your information has been corrupted it would be better if some form of prevention were available. Similarly for confidentiality: this will provide some protection to data once it has been obtained by a third party, but it would be better if the data were only made available to those authorized to see it. The main mechanism used to prevent unauthorized access is that of access control.

The disclosure of information is usually achieved by copying the information from some part of the system, when it is on some storage device, when it is moving through the system (especially over communications links), or when it is being manipulated by processes within the system. It is impossible to tell if information has been copied, since there is no evidence left with the original information. The strategy for preventing disclosure relies on making the data representing the information indecipherable if it is copied!

We are using the concept of information to represent what is stored in the system and data to represent the idea that information is stored in some set of symbols (usually a bit pattern) for manipulation. Information represents the semantics, data represents the syntax. Confidentiality is provided by translating the data in such a way that it can only be turned back into its original format by entities authorized to have access to the information.

Any other entities would only be able to access the gibberish version. The corruption of information is difficult to prevent, hence the need for access control, but this can be detected since there is evidence left with the information that a change has taken place. It is not necessary to transform data to detect corruption, usually a checksum is carried with the data. The checksum is calculated in such a way that only entities authorized to change the data can compute a valid checksum.

Eventually, an authorized entity will want to access or change the information in the system. Distinguishing authorized access from unauthorized access is the concept behind access control.

4.2 Access control and authentication

The objects used in this description of security are those units of the distributed system that are subject to security: they are a modelling concept. The reader should not confuse these objects with those used in a programming environment, or objects used in other parts of the book. There is a relationship between security objects and programming objects, but it is usually not one-to-one.

In an object-oriented distributed system *access control* means controlling the interaction between the objects and providing the objects with facilities to control access to information within themselves. It is important to realize that just controlling object interaction is insufficient in many systems since it is not feasible to make the security objects small enough to represent individual items of information. For instance, in many current systems a database is treated as a single object supporting the methods of the database management system. The security of the object system cannot be used within the database; however, there is a need to apply access control within a database. This situation may be avoided by using an object-oriented database.

Before an object can be allowed access to another object the identity of both objects must be established so that the appropriate access-control rule can be applied. The identity of the accessed object is often taken for granted, since it represents the information or resources of the system. It is the identity of the accessing object that is usually in question. The process of establishing the identity of an object in the system is called *authentication*. There are two types of entity in a distributed system that are the subject of security: the objects (which model all activity within the system) and human beings. A distributed system is built by humans to be used by humans for humans. Thus all activity within a system is carried out on behalf of some human or other. We can consider the objects in a distributed system as working on behalf of (as a proxy for) a human.

The most easily understood aspect of authentication is that of identifying humans. The user identity-password technique is a well-known mechanism. The essence of human authentication consists of two or more steps. First, they must identify themselves to the system (the purpose of the user identity). Then, the human and the computer may exchange one or more secrets. The idea is that only the individual human and the computer know the secrets – therefore if the correct secrets are exchanged then the human can only be the claimed human. It is sometimes necessary for the computer to authenticate itself to the human by providing some secrets; this may be particularly important where communications links are used by the human to access the computer.

One of the main purposes of authentication is to distinguish the users of the system for the purpose of accountability. All security activity in a distributed system will be audited by the system and a log of the events held in some archival form. This log, sometimes known as an "audit trail", is analyzed to see if the security policy of the system is being properly implemented. Every action in the system will be attributed to some user who will then be held responsible for that action. Only by correctly identifying users can they be held accountable for their actions. When humans know that they are accountable they are usually less inclined to do things they shouldn't.

Within the distributed system each object will have two identities that will be used for security purposes: the identity of the object itself (i.e. the object-identifier, some unique system-wide object-identifier), and the identity of the human on whose behalf the object is currently working. Some objects will have been designed to interface to humans: these would handle the man–machine interface and perform the authentication of individual human users. If an object invokes another object then the invoked object will be working on behalf of the same human as the invoking object. In most systems it is the human identity that an object is currently using that will determine the access privileges of the object.

The concept of one object invoking another on behalf of a third object is called *proxy*. Every activity of invocation in a system must begin somewhere, let us call that object the *principal*. The identity and privileges of the principal will be the main ones for determining what the invoked objects may do. For the purposes of an example let us call the principal object "A". A calls object B to carry out some function for it. To complete this function, B calls object C. When B calls C, B is acting as a proxy for A. If it is necessary for object C to invoke a further object, then C will be acting both as a proxy for A, and as a proxy for B.

Objects in the system will be authenticated when they are created by the object infrastructure. The allocation of a unique object-identifier and the placing of the object within the infrastructure is effectively all the authentication an object needs. The question of how the infrastructure is authenticated, and who authenticates the entity that authenticates the infrastructure are important problems in the design of actual systems.

An identity, in a security sense, is usually thought of as a token of privilege. That is, the holder uses the identity to obtain privileges (access rights) which allow a human user to obtain real work from the distributed system. From the other side, an identity should also be seen as a token of responsibility that is used by the system to track operations on objects and consequently the activity of a human within the system. Identities are used for three major purposes in a distributed system:

- *Access control*
  This is the use of the identity to obtain privileges within the system.
- *Audit*
  This identity is used by the system to record the activity of the owner and establish responsibility.
- *Charging*
  This identity will be used to accumulate charges for resources used within the distributed system.

These three identities do not have to be the same – a different identity may be required for each use. Each identity will require a level of granularity, the level to be set by the security and charging policy of the actual system. For instance, the charging policy may determine that all charges are accumulated on a department basis. This would mean that everyone in the same department would have the same charging identity. The same policy may require that each individual needs to have their actions recorded in the audit; so every person has a different audit identity. Perhaps the department is responsible for three different tasks in the distributed system; then only three different sets of privileges are required to complete these functions and only three access-control identities are needed. A combination of access-control privileges required for a specific set of related operations is often called a "role". A person using the system would have to indicate to the login object their name and their secret, which would establish their identity. They would then need to indicate which role they wanted to take so they could be allocated the access-control privileges for the required function. Obviously, if the granularity of two types of identity coincides then they can be served by the same identity value. It is possible for a system to allow anonymous users whose identity cannot be determined by any of the objects in the system. In this case a special audit identity is issued which cannot be traced within the system to any individual. However, the device that authenticates the anonymous user produces an audit record containing the actual identity of the user and the special audit identity. Then the user can be tracked only by examining the audit records of the system.

4.3 Authorization

Access control is actually made up of two components: authentication and authorization. Authentication has been briefly discussed above. Authorization is the function of looking up the identities of the client and server objects in a table of access-control rules. These rules may require a number of additional pieces of information to be taken into account: time of day, current objects already accessed, etc. The actual rules will be carefully derived from the security policy of the system. In fact, the access-control rules will be the most obvious manifestation of the system security policy. The result of the authorization function will be a decision, yes or no, on whether the access may proceed. In practice, the authorization function usually coincides with the part of the system that will enforce the decision. However, it is worth remembering that these two operations: making the decision and enforcing the decision, are separate and can be carried out in different parts of the system if required.

There are two sets of rules in the distributed system: those for authentication and those for access control. The authentication rules determine who can use the system and what privileges they will have according to the way they have authenticated themselves. These rules have a long-term effect, in that once someone has been authenticated and is using the system then they are not invoked again. The authentication rules also have a large-grain effect in that the privileges given out as a result of a successful authentication can be used to carry out a number of operations affecting a number of objects. The rules for access control provide fine grained control of a system since they determine which privileges are required to access individual objects. These rules are invoked every time that access to an object is required so they also provide fine control in time. A good design of a system will ensure that the two sets of rules complement each other in their scope of control.

4.4 Access control schemes

Discussions on access control usually concentrate on one of two basic schemes: access-control lists and capabilities. A third scheme, used in military system access control, is often governed by a label-based scheme where every object has a label and an identity. Each of these can be considered as a single technique on a spectrum. The spectrum is concerned with where the authorization information is kept: with the accessing object, with the accessed object, or split between both of them. Each of the schemes recognizes that the access-control rules need to be kept somewhere and that the set of possible rules for every possible object interaction is very large. We look at this spectrum next under the headings of access-control lists, military security classifications, and capabilities.

In the access-control list scheme nearly all of the information is kept with the accessed object. The information takes the form of a list of all the objects that are allowed to access a particular object. The only information that is needed from the accessing object is its identity, which is used to look up the access-control list and make a decision. Where the set of object identities allowed to access another object is quite small, or can be kept in an abbreviated form, then this scheme has the advantage that the access-control information is kept with the objects that are to be protected. Lists can be kept small by having groups of objects with the same access rights share a single role identity; then the role identity of an accessing object is used to check for entries in the list. A negative access-control list contains a list of identities that are *not* allowed to access an object – a sort of blacklist. Negative lists are useful when all the members of a group or role except a few individuals are to be allowed access to an object. They are also used when an individual is to be taken out of a role or group but not all the group lists have been changed, or that individual may still be using the system when their rights are to be revoked and they have already obtained the role privileges.

In a capability scheme the information is kept with the accessing object. A capability is a right to use some object, just like a prepaid ticket on a train. Every object would have a set of capabilities for all of the objects it might need to use. The only information required of the accessed object is its identity so that it can be compared with the capability that is being used in the attempt to obtain access. Just as there are techniques for limiting the size of an access-control list there are techniques for reducing the number of capabilities that an accessing object must keep. Because all of the access-control information is with the accessing object it can be seen that this is the opposite, or complementary, scheme to access-control lists. A problem with capabilities is making sure that an object has all the capabilities it needs and that objects do not acquire capabilities they are not entitled to (that is, capabilities have to be protected against copying).

A scheme that is used with military systems is one based on the use of labels and classification. Information in the system is given a classification, say `secret` or `classified`, and users of the system are rated to some level, `secret` or `classified`. There is a strict relationship between the classifications such that (for example) all `classified` information is available to a user with a rating of `secret`, as well as all `secret` information. In addition to these classifications, information is placed into categories, or compartments, such as `naval`, `nuclear`, or `HQ`. Users are given access to certain compartments. To decide if a user has access to a piece of information (or even should be told that it exists) the user's level must be greater than or equal to the classification of the information, and the user must have access to the compartment which the information has been assigned to. A problem with this scheme is that it does not help to discriminate different users of the same level – other access-control mechanisms have to be used. The classification and compartment idea can be readily translated to the commercial world, using `company confidential`, `restricted` for classification and `accounts`, `personnel` for compartments.

4.5 Trust in a secure system

If the point of security in a distributed system is to protect resources against both wilful and accidental misuse then there will need to be some enforcement. If there is any possibility of some entity obtaining resources it is not entitled to then there needs to be protection within the system. This protection can be provided by a number of different techniques, a few of which are described later in this chapter. However, underpinning all of the protection techniques is a matrix of trust. Various components supporting the security system have to be trusted to carry out a particular function. Which components are trusted and what they are trusted for will depend on what the security requirements are and the design of the actual system. In a very secure system the number of trusted components is kept very small and they are built very carefully. Unfortunately, such systems are expensive and involve a considerable overhead. Many commercial systems compromise by having more trusted components; this is potentially less secure, but requires a lower overhead. In the discussion above on authorization we assumed that there was a trusted component that would enforce the access control decision made by the authorization function. The system is also trusting the authorization function to make a proper decision in line with the prevailing security policy. In discussing security for distributed systems it is not possible to say much more about trust without describing a specific system.

When designing a distributed system the designer must make a conscious decision about which parts will be trusted, and with what functionality. There needs to be a clear distinction between the trusted parts and the untrusted parts so that the proper mechanisms can be used to keep them apart. For instance, the boundary between a user process and the operating system on a conventional computer is protected by hardware mechanisms that prevent the user's process from accessing the operating system through any other path than that allowed for by the designer. The designer must install a boundary and decide which parts of the system are within the boundary and need to be trusted, and consequently which parts are not to be trusted and must lie outside the boundary. The boundary will need to be protected by mechanisms, the strength of which will determine the strength of a lot of the system security.

Where components cannot, or should not, be trusted with some function they may still need to use or invoke some security facility. In these cases special techniques can be applied, usually based on cryptography, to support the use of security. For instance, in the above description of capabilities in access control the problem of an object acquiring a capability it is not entitled to was described. This can be overcome by having the function that issues capabilities include the identity of the object to which it is issued in the capability. Of course, the object trying to use the capability needs to be authenticated to make sure it is not faking its object identity (assuming the identity of somebody else who is entitled to that capability). The capability is then sealed, in some way, so that the receiving object cannot change it. Then the access-control function can check that the capability is being used along with the correct object identifier; it can also check the capability to see if it has been modified. The objects in the system are not being trusted to look after the capabilities, but they can still hold them and use them. However, using a cryptographic seal means that some cryptographic keys have to be distributed, and that requires some further trusted components. The problem of key distribution is discussed in Section 4.7 on cryptography.

Trust is in fact a rather subtle idea. When you receive a piece of information, there is a great deal of context which causes you to trust it. Whether it is from a trustworthy source, via a trustworthy channel, is not all that is needed. At least you need to know that the source is not joking.

4.6 General models of computer security

A number of general models for computer security have been developed in the past for use in stand-alone situations. A designer of a distributed system will find that customers will want to talk about the new system in terms of these models. These models are applicable to a distributed system, though the boundary and mechanisms to support the trust barrier are necessarily different. This section describes two such models: the military model of multi-level security, and a more recent model of commercial security which is still being developed. The multi-level security model is very important as it is the basis for a well-known set of criteria that the US government is using to procure computer systems for most of its requirements. The criteria are set out in DoD (1985), which is known as "the orange book", and in NCSC (1987), which is known as "the red book". These criteria have become very important for all types of computer security as they are the only available criteria that are widely available and being used. The new commercial model is an attempt to begin work towards a similar set of criteria for purchasing systems for commercial applications.

4.6.1 Multi-level security

This is a concept that arose in the early 1960s when the military started considering the use of computers to hold information having different levels of classification. In a military (or government) environment information is graded according to its sensitivity, the grade, or classification, ranging from unclassified, through secret, top secret, etc. The purpose of the classification is to restrict access to people having the same or higher clearance. A clearance is an ability, or trustworthiness, to see information graded at that or a lower level. Additionally, information is compartmentalized into groups, such as `nuclear`, `NATO`, or `naval`. A person wishing to have access to a piece of information would also have to be cleared to see information in all of the compartments to which the information has been assigned. For instance, if we had some information classified as [`secret`; `naval`, `nuclear`] and a person cleared to [`top secret`; `NATO`, `nuclear`] they would not be allowed to see the information, even though they have a higher classification than the information, because they do not have access to the `naval` compartment.

A multi-level system is one in which information of different security levels is stored. The problem of multi-level security is two-fold:

1. To provide adequate access control to meet the classification and compartment labels (such access-control schemes are called "label-based" schemes)
2. To prevent the leakage of information from a high classification to a lower classification

The first problem is entirely one of access control and is discussed above. The second problem is one of information flow. The problem is described in the following scenario. Suppose an object with top-secret clearance accesses another object with a classification of top secret, as allowed by the access-control rules. The client object may then access another object that is unclassified; this is also allowed by the rules. The client object may then read information from the top-secret object and write it to the unclassified object. The top-secret information has then been *written down* to an unclassified level. To prevent this the system must monitor which objects a client has accessed and prevent such a sequence from occurring. In an object-oriented system this would mean that an object that has accessed another object at some classification level would not be allowed to access another object at a lower classification for writing, but could read from it. Thus the access-control system must have a memory for the lowest possible classification available to an object.

Note that this scheme is oriented at preventing disclosure; a similar problem also exists for corruption. To maintain the integrity of information, integrity levels can be applied to objects. A high-integrity object will be allowed to access a low-integrity object, but a low-integrity object will not be allowed to access a high-integrity object. The write-down problem of disclosure is reversed for corruption to prevent low-integrity information contaminating high-integrity information.

Multi-level security, especially concerning protection against disclosure, is a fairly well-understood problem. This understanding is the result of considerable research, funded by the needs of military security. Commercial security has the same concerns as military security, but the emphasis is different.

4.6.2 Commercial security

In a landmark paper, Clark & Wilson (1987) put forward some basic ideas on commercial security that were intended to be the basis of commercial security evaluation criteria, similar to the orange book used by the military to evaluate systems for military applications.

The basis of the Clark–Wilson model is the idea that the information in a commercial system represents a model of some aspect of the enterprise that owns the information. If the data is a stock list for an inventory system, or if the data is a set of ledgers in an accounting system, then both of these have a physical representation that they can be checked against. The actual stock can be counted and the money held by the company can be checked to see if they match against the data in the computer system. A commercial enterprise is likely to be more concerned that the information represents a true picture of reality than that some of the information is disclosed in some way. Of course, every enterprise needs to keep some information secret, but, Clark and Wilson argue, the integrity of the information is more important than its confidentiality in most commercial systems. They note that an important mechanism used in commercial security is that of *separation of function*. This means no single person is allowed to carry out a function, or sequence of functions, that will result in an undetected fraud. For instance, no one person would be allowed to enter new stock into the system as well as check out stock. This person might be tempted to adjust both entries. Similarly, the accounts receivable clerk and the accounts payable clerk are two separate functions. In this way, at least two people must get together to commit a fraud. Any one person committing a fraud would be found out as soon as the stock or account information is balanced. On a computer system, the information can be reconciled very quickly and frequently.

To provide the *separation of function* Clark and Wilson propose two components in a commercial system. First, there are a number of data sets which contain high-integrity information. This information has been reconciled and is, as far as possible, a true representation of the actual physical system it is modelling. Processing of this information is carried out by high-integrity processes which always leave the data in a similar state of high integrity. There will be a number of functions that can operate on a single data set. Various people will be allowed to invoke particular functions on particular data sets. Careful examination of which functions and which data sets a single person has access to will ensure that the separation of function principle is maintained. A special function is required to turn a non-integrity data set into a high-integrity data set. Once a data set has integrity, the condition that executing a function with a high-integrity data set results in a high-integrity data set ensures that the information cannot be corrupted. Once the system is started with high-integrity data then the system will continue to run with high-integrity data. The careful reader will have realized that this assumption depends on being able to build processing functions with integrity guarantees. Of course, it is currently very difficult and very expensive to produce such software, and no existing commercial system carries such guarantees.

A final component of the system is a function that doesn't modify the data, but merely checks its integrity. This function is used by the security officer to ensure that the system is running correctly. Of course, the security officer will not have access to any of the usual functions that will modify the data sets.

It can be seen that the Clark–Wilson model requires a three-dimensional access control model: people, functions and data. This will require a two-stage access-control function in which a person's right to invoke a function object is checked first. Then the right of that function object, used by that person, to access a particular data object has to be checked. This can still be handled either by a capability system, in which a person is issued with function–data-set capabilities, or by access-control lists, with both functions and data having access lists.

4.7 Cryptography

The use of cryptography underlies many of the mechanisms used to enforce security. The principle of cryptography is to use a special piece of information, called a "key", in some carefully designed mathematical function such that it is impossible to reproduce the effect or reverse the effect of applying the function to the data, without the key. Keeping the key secret ensures that only those who are intended to reverse, or reproduce, the effect can actually do so. In some cases the algorithm for the mathematical function is well known so that it can be widely implemented and used for general communication; in other cases the algorithm is also kept secret, which is more secure but is not useful in a wide heterogeneous user environment. This is a compromise that has to be made in having widely available security that can be used by lots of people. Since the key is kept secret it can also be used as part of an authentication scheme, as explained below. A lot of effort by very clever mathematicians has been employed in devising the mathematical functions, and also in finding ways of breaking them. A lot more effort is currently being put into this area as distributed systems become more widespread. This section will describe two basic cryptographic procedures without invoking any of the mathematics that underlie them. The point this section makes is that for any cryptographic mechanism, the difficult aspect of using cryptography is the appropriate distribution of the keys. To provide confidentiality, using cryptography, on a piece of data the data is translated by the cryptographic algorithm using the key as a special starting condition. All of the data is transformed in one go, using the key. The data in its original form is called the *plaintext*; when it has been enciphered (that is, processed by the cryptographic algorithm) it is called *ciphertext* and is meant to be unintelligible. This simple translation can be described as:

$$E_k(P) = C \qquad (4.1)$$

where E_k represents the encipherment function using key k, P is the plaintext and C is the ciphertext. Obviously, to recover the plaintext from the ciphertext a reverse transformation is required which is called "decipherment":

$$D_k(C) = P \qquad (4.2)$$

To provide integrity it is not necessary to translate the plaintext into another form; instead some fixed-size checksum is provided as a result of putting the data through the algorithm. The checksum can be thought of as the remainder from the function when all of the data has been processed. The checksum is then a function of the value of the data and the key. If the data is changed then a different checksum would be calculated – consequently any change to the data can be detected by recalculating the checksum. The integrity checksum is usually kept with the data in the storage system or when the data is sent over a communications link. The checksum is also known as a *seal*; a *certificate* is a combination of some data and the associated seal. Often the seal may include details of the algorithm used to calculate the checksum and an identifier of any key used. Data that is protected for confidentiality is automatically protected for integrity; if the encrypted data is changed then the original data will not be recovered after decryption by the receiver. To allow for this a known value is placed with the data so that the receiver can tell if decryption has been successful. If the ciphertext is changed in any way then the original plaintext cannot be obtained, and the change will be detected. Most of the algorithms used for confidentiality protection would result in some completely unintelligible output if corrupted ciphertext were used. However, it is common to add in some well-known information that can be easily checked when the decipherment has been completed.

There are two classes of functions, or algorithms, used in cryptography: secret-key (or symmetric) algorithms, and public-key (or asymmetric) algorithms. These two classes have different uses because of the different characteristics of the algorithms.

4.7.1 Secret key (or symmetric) technique

The symmetric algorithm is the classical technique that has been known about since Roman times when Julius Caesar used a very simple technique to protect his messages as they travelled by courier. The basis of the symmetric algorithm is that a single key and the same algorithm are used for both encipherment and decipherment. Thus

$$D_k(E_k(P)) = P \tag{4.3}$$

This complete mapping places some constraints on the algorithms that can be used since the mapping of the E function from the plaintext onto the ciphertext must be symmetrical with the mapping of the same function from the ciphertext to the plaintext. When a symmetric key algorithm is used for sending information the recipient will know that the data came from the authentic sender if the correct secret key can be used to decipher the message and it makes sense. This provides authentication of origin, that is, the technique allows the recipient to be confident that the identity of the sender is known, as long as the key really is a secret known only to the authorized sender and recipient. To ensure that the deciphered data is not gibberish the plaintext usually contains some easily identifiable pattern so that it can be checked by a computer.

The protection provided by the symmetric algorithm relies on keeping the key a secret, confined to those who need to carry out the encipherment or decipherment of the data. For instance, if this technique were to be used to provide confidentiality on a piece of data (to protect it from a disclosure threat), then every object that needed to access the data would have a copy of the key. If these objects were distributed around the system then that key would have to be sent to each of the objects. When symmetric keys need to be distributed this must be done with confidentiality.

The most widely used symmetric algorithm is known as DES (Data Encryption Standard) and was originally approved by the US government for commercial use though this approval has now lapsed. Since no other algorithms have been approved (nor are likely to be) and since a number of hardware implementations of this algorithm have been produced it is widely used in banking and some allied commercial applications. Symmetric algorithms can be made to work quite fast and are considered to be quite satisfactory for use on processing quite large amounts of data for confidentiality and integrity. They are used to protect information on storage systems as well as during transfer between computer systems.

4.7.2 Public key (or asymmetric) technique

A number of problems in using symmetric algorithms in distributed systems, mostly to do with key distribution, led to the development of public-key or asymmetric algorithms. The principal idea is that a pair of keys are used with a single algorithm. Of this pair, only one needs to be kept secret while the other is made public knowledge. Currently only one algorithm is widely known to be suitable for general use: it is called RSA after the inventors, Rivest, Shamir and Adleman (Rivest et al. 1978). This algorithm relies on the fact that factorizing very large numbers into two primes is a very hard problem and should take a computer a long time. The keys used are the two factors. Unfortunately, there is only empirical evidence that this is true, which means that no one has found an easy way, although no one has proved that an easy way does not exist either. Improvements in theory and technology continue to make the problem a little easier all the time.

The basis of the public-key system is the two keys, one kept secret by the owner (K_s) and the other made publicly available (K_p). Information that is enciphered by one key can only be deciphered by the other. So, to make information confidential to the owner it is encrypted by the public key, then only the owner (or authorized holders of the secret key) may decipher the data to use it; similarly, to protect information for integrity it is checksummed using the secret key. Anyone having access to the public key can check the integrity of the data, but only holders of the secret key can change the data. Obviously, this mechanism reduces the number of entities in a distributed system that need to know the secret key. The primary use for public-key systems is in an environment involving a large population; in this sense they are very important for distributed systems. To send data with confidentiality it is enciphered with the public key of the recipient:

$$E_{rp}(P) = C \qquad (4.4)$$

(E_{rp} means enciphered using the recipient's public key), and on receipt it is deciphered with the recipient's secret key:

$$D_{rs}(C) = P \qquad (4.5)$$

Since the public key is common knowledge anyone can send a confidential message to a known recipient. Integrity is achieved in the same way. To obtain authentication of origin a second transformation needs to be applied. Since the recipient's public key can be used by anyone it does not prove who the sender is; to do this we need a secret from the sender. To provide this component the sender's secret key is used in a separate transformation of the data:

$$E_{ss}(P) = C \qquad (4.6)$$

which is then transmitted and deciphered by

$$D_{sp}(C) = C \qquad (4.7)$$

at the recipient end. Note that the actual secret used by the sender is not sent, only the effect of the secret which can be checked. This is an important advantage in using public keys for authentication (the distribution of the public keys apart). If authentication and confidentiality are required then the two transformations are carried out on the data: the sender would do

$$E_{rp}(E_{ss}(P)) = C \qquad (4.8)$$

and the recipient would reverse both of these as

$$D_{rs}(D_{sp}(C)) = P \qquad (4.9)$$

For this to work the mathematical function must be chosen so that

$$P = D_p(E_s(P)) \quad \text{and} \quad P = D_s(E_p(P)) \qquad (4.10)$$

which is currently only true of the RSA algorithms, as stated above. Public-key algorithms appear to have the advantage over secret-key algorithms in that the secret key does not have to be known by every party in a communication. It also means the computer system can apply protection using the public key. In the above examples the secret key only needs to be known by one entity – all the others use the public key. In practice, the algorithms for public keys take a lot longer to transform the same amount of data than a symmetric algorithm, consequently they are not used on large items of data. This limits their use in general communications support.

4.7.3 Key distribution

The major problem in using cryptography lies in distributing the keys to the entities that need them and not to any other entities. The keys used in symmetric algorithms need to be distributed with confidentiality. Of course, the best way to provide confidentiality is to use cryptography. Keys that are used to encipher and decipher data are called *data-encrypting keys*. Other keys are used to encipher data-encrypting keys so that they can be distributed and held in computer systems – these keys are called *key-encrypting keys*. If a data-encrypting key is compromised then all of the data protected by that key may be compromised. If a key-encrypting key is compromised then all the data-encrypting keys protected by that key and consequently all the data protected by all of the data keys is compromised. It is important to protect the key-encrypting keys and often more expensive and secure algorithms are used.

Just as key-encrypting keys can be used to protect data-encrypting keys when they are distributed it is possible to use further key-encrypting keys to distribute key-encrypting keys. A hierarchy of keys is used to make up a whole scheme so that keys can be changed and distributed as required. The requirements for the key distribution system will be set out in the security policy and are therefore different for each system. Since the keys may be distributed through the same communication channels that are used for the data, and consequently need protecting in the same way as the data, it is not possible to distribute all of the keys in this way. One or two keys at the top of the key-encrypting key pyramid have to be distributed by some other means, often a courier or a special letter. The invention of public keys was meant to alleviate the problem of key distribution by allowing one of the keys to be public. The public key does not need to be protected, so no key-encrypting keys are needed to keep it confidential. Unfortunately, a key also needs to be distributed with authentication. If someone wanted to carry out a fraud they would only have to intercept the distribution of the public key and substitute their own. When using a public key, for instance in the authentication mode above, it is essential that the recipient uses the real public key of the sender, otherwise someone else could pretend to be the sender simply by supplying their own public key at the appropriate time. The need to distribute public keys with authentication also requires the use of cryptography. Schemes have been worked out to store and distribute public keys, one such scheme having been made into a standard as part of the ISO directory service (Kille 1988).

Public-key mechanisms do have some advantages in their distribution (for instance, they can be placed on letter headings and widely published to overcome the authentication problem), but their implementation results in very slow processing rates. Currently it can take half a minute to process 512 bits using a software version of the RSA algorithm. The secret-key mechanism has distribution problems but implementations are quite efficient now and a software version can easily do 100,000 bits/second. For these reasons, public-key mechanisms are usually limited to use in key distribution systems and secret-key mechanisms are used to protect the actual data in a system.

4.7.4 Blocking

Most cryptographic algorithms are implemented to encipher fixed-sized blocks of data, often a power of 2 such as 64 or 512 bits. This means each block will stand on its own and not be related to any other. Thus it might be possible to break the protection on a single block and replace it without being detected. It also means that the individual blocks could be rearranged, thus breaking the integrity of the data, without being detected. This independence also gives more information to someone using crypto-analysis to break the algorithm and find the key. To make crypto-analysis of the ciphertext more difficult and to ensure that data that is enciphered together cannot be rearranged, a method known as "cipher block chaining" is used on larger pieces of data. This method requires the cryptographic algorithm to produce some remainder value from its calculation of the ciphertext. This remainder is then used, with the key, as input to the encipherment of the next block, and the remainder from the second block is used to encipher the third block, and so on. Thus the order of the data in the plaintext is used in the encipherment process, and any reordering will detected as the result from the decipherment would be gibberish. A seed value has to be used in place of a remainder for the first block; this is known as an "initialization vector". The initialization vector can be as secret as the key, or it could be made known, depending on the application.

4.8 Key distribution

A classic problem in security in distributed systems is that of how to distribute the keys. In the traditional world without computers and networks, it is done *out-of-band*, by meeting, letter, phone call, etc. In networks, now, we usually have a two-level system of trusted servers (e.g. the X.500 directory server or even a secure subset of World Wide Web servers has been suggested). These can hold public keys publicly, and private keys for individuals with access control appropriately set.

More recently, as networks have merged into the Internet spanning all countries and walks of life, a fully distributed trust model has also emerged, and is displayed in PGP (pretty good privacy). Here, instead of a hierarchy of agency-approved trusted key managers, certified with the authority of governments, individuals form a web of trust, by listing those they trust to introduce them to others, and vouch for the authenticity of a public key. This has social advantages, but suffers from one potential disadvantage, which is that the revocation of a key can be difficult to archive globally.

The interesting thing about the PGP model of distributed trust is that it is more open, and at the same time can be made more inherently secure, than a system where an arbitrary central authority delegates trust.

4.9 Practical security approaches?

The Internet represents a perfect social environment to promote the development of secure systems, since it is so open.

Unfortunately (because of the false sense of security they provide), the prime technique used commercially to prevent attacks is the use of "firewalls".

A firewall is simply a filter that is placed at the edge of an enterprise's network that permits a restricted subset of packets or types of communication through. Typically, this is done in one of two simple ways:

- *Packet filters*

  Basically, most modern packet switches and routers can be programmed to exclude packets by arbitrary bit-patterns, in either direction. This has a performance impact, and also requires intimate knowledge of the protocols, but can be made quite effective. For example, it can restrict which hosts can initiate which types of sessions in each direction.

- *Application-layer relays*

  This is the simplest firewall technique. Basically, most, if not all, applications can be staged via a special-purpose system, placed on the boundary of an enterprise's network. This requires a second stage of authentication, and means that direct attacks on internal systems may be rendered impossible. It may also render external access very inconvenient.

(!) Reality Checkpoint   Firewalls encourage system managers to be lax about the security behind them. If a firewall is breached, this means your systems are wide open. It is better to consider the costs of either not being networked or else securing all your systems properly.

4.10 Summary

In this chapter, we have examined the nature of security in distributed systems. We have covered authentication and encryption techniques and looked at the idea of trust.

4.11 Exercises

1. Design a distributed system for a political election. Note that not only should such a system provide guarantees of authenticity, non-repudiation and non-replay, but it must also protect the identity of voters!

2. What are the salient features for a distributed online publishing system to provide guarantees that people can identify the authentic manuscript they might retrieve?

3. Consider the design of a data compression technique for video or audio – how might cryptography be applied inline to provide secrecy?

CHAPTER 5

Languages and formal methods

with Mark d'Inverno, Westminster University

This chapter of the book presents and outlines some of the techniques used and being developed for distributed system description or specification. We look in particular at process algebras such as LOTOS and CSP, and languages such as Z, based on predicate calculus. Process algebras are good at analyzing protocols to study liveness properties such as the absence of deadlock. They are less good at analyzing and modelling internal state. In contrast, Z and similar formalisms are excellent at modelling state and state changes that will be important in a system. There are less good for studying liveness properties. There have been attempts to combine the strengths of both, but this is still the subject of active research.

5.1 Why protocol description?

The ISO term is formal description technique (FDT). A Formal Description is a guide for implementors and also allows dissemination of a protocol through manufacturers. It allows humans to reason about protocol.

It simplifies the job of designing new protocols by providing a common framework for the common parts of any protocol (this is analogous to using Algol type language to specify sequential algorithms).

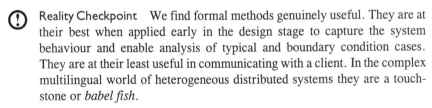 Reality Checkpoint   We find formal methods genuinely useful. They are at their best when applied early in the design stage to capture the system behaviour and enable analysis of typical and boundary condition cases. They are at their least useful in communicating with a client. In the complex multilingual world of heterogeneous distributed systems they are a touchstone or *babel fish*.

5.2 Why protocol specification?

In the short term, we can manually and semi-automatically check protocols. In the long term, we will be able to generate protocols from specifications in specialist languages. We can *validate* a protocol – check that a protocol is free from syntactic errors, and is simply self-consistent. We can *verify* protocol – can check that the protocol does actually provide the required functionality:
- free from deadlocks (states that it can't leave)

- free from livelocks (states that conspire to lock out others)
- free from (useless) unreachable states
- free from busy idle behaviour
- may be able to analyze the performance of the protocol
- can study event scheduling within the protocol
- can match event scheduling in network (other layers) to those in the protocol
- can exploit the genuine parallel nature of network components

5.2.1 Some common specification systems

The first protocols were specified in a sort of structured English – text. This is very difficult to check for anything. Flowcharting has been used, but is an unnatural framework for specifying concurrency and leads to very large charts. It does, however, allow for some automatic checking and generating of parts of a protocol.

More powerful techniques are:

- *State diagrams* – like Markov diagrams
  These are very useful to humans, but get large and are not machine-readable.
- *Petri nets*
  These are a variety of state-transition graphs. They can help check protocols, but are not intuitive for the human implementor.
- Grammars such as Backus–Naur form
  These can be bent to describe formats and sequences of actions in a protocol. They are well known to programmers, but are not so useful for checking for concurrency problems.
- *Format and protocol languages*
  These are most promising for the future.

5.3 Format and protocol languages

Historically, these start with the IBM system, FAPL, which was used to specify large parts of the Systems Network Architecture (IBM 1988). It is an extension of PL/1 to include finite state machines (FSM) and state transition. RSPL was developed at the technical university in Berlin to specify protocol sequences and alternative actions.

ISO formed two committees to work in this area, and the two draft proposals for systems are:

- ESTL or Extended State Transition Language ("Estelle"), which is an extended FSM approach, based on ISO standard Pascal
- LOTOS or the Language of Temporal Ordering Specification, derived from the Calculus of Communicating Systems and related to Communicating Sequential Processes

LOTOS is based on some firm mathematics in temporal logic, which allows the proof of behaviour of the processes described.

5.4 Protocol validation

This section of the chapter outlines two commonly used methods for protocol validation based on FSM descriptions of a protocol.

Looking at a protocol specification, we can identify all the events that occur and all the states that a protocol entity can be in. Consider a protocol that operates between two end points, or processes:

1. First, uniquely number the events, positively for input (rx/arrival) and negatively for output (tx/transmission).
2. Second, uniquely number all the states of the protocol, 0, 1, 2, etc.

We can identify sequences of states, simply by starting in each state, listing all sequences of possible events, and seeing what the resulting state for an end point is. A *unilogue* is a sequence of states which starts and ends in the same state, but not going through that state in between, e.g. 0–1–0, 0–1–2–1–0, etc. A *duologue* is a pair of these unilogues for two end points of a communication. The *duologue matrix* is the set of all possible duologues (unilogue pairs).

Protocol validation is done by designing a function that operates on the duologue matrix, which for each member produces the values:

```
+1, if the member is well behaved.
0, if the sequence pair cannot happen.
-1, if the sequence pair is an error
```

This function can be determined by considering the cases:

- post-transmission condition (every case where one end transmits, the other should be in a receiving state)
- deadlock or pre-reception condition (every case where one end is waiting to receive, but the other does not transmit)

A duologue is "occurable" if it satisfies these two conditions, and "well behaved" if all states are reached as well.

Limitations of this method are:

- All sequences of states must be finite.
- There can only be two end points of the protocol.

This last point is a very severe drawback in realistic distributed systems, where there are typically hundreds of end points.[1]

5.4.1 State perturbation

This method of validation is based on the idea of generating all derivative states from a starting state (e.g. an idle state), and exhaustively checking the legality of the sequences generated. The word *perturbation* is used to mean all state changes that are visible externally from the protocol end point, like transmission of packets, reception of a packet on a channel, etc. The validation method involves generating all legal trees of state sequences, and therefore can result in infinite-sized

---

1. Forming transitive closure of a state-transition matrix is usually achieved using Warshall's algorithm.

output. There exist methods for limiting the expansion of the tree to include only interesting cases. Loop detection is essential for finding a stable sequence.

5.5 Language of temporal ordering specification (LOTOS)

LOTOS is fully described in ISO (1989a) (See also Bolognesi & Brinksmma 1987). It is based on Milner's (1989) Communicating Concurrent Systems. Here we give some examples of its use in specifying some commonly found functions of protocols.

5.5.1 Processes

Just about everything in LOTOS is a process. Processes are black boxes, with carefully defined interactions with the outside world, which are the only ways of influencing their behaviour. The general form of a process definition is

```
process <process-id><parameter-part> :=
        <behavior expression>
endproc
```

Process parameters are lists of gates and values that the process may be instantiated with. For example, a recursive definition:

```
process Buffer [in, out] :=
        in?x:t;
    ; out!x
    ; Buffer [in, out]
endproc
```

Note that a process definition may be recursive, indicating that the process continues, rather than implicitly running the *stop* process at the end. A process is defined as *event gates* at which *events* cause process interaction.

```
a?x:t - a process is prepared to accept a value of type t at
        gate a; When this happens, the value is in x.

a!e    - a process is prepared to output a value e at gate a.
```

Processes may be built up together to form more complex processes. The composition of basic components of complex processes is done with various operators.
- Where you want to override operator precedence, or for clarity, "()" brackets may be used.
- The ";" operator builds sequences of processes as we saw in the first example of a process.

- The "[]" operator denotes a choice of alternative paths of execution for the process. For example, a user interface to a connection protocol might be specified as follows:

```
Process User [port] :=

        port?x:int
     ; connect [port]
  [] port?b:buff
     ; write[port]
        User[port]
endproc
```

- The "||" operator allows us to specify parallel processes.

When two parallel processes offer to synchronize with events at the same gates, the conflict is resolved by some mechanism internal to the system: in other words, some internal event that is not a choice of the environment of the processes (e.g. a user typing something or a cosmic ray!), causes a choice. Internal events may be written i.

The "[>" operator allows us to specify the disruption of one process by another:
given

```
Process Activity [a, b]  :=
        a
     ; b
     ; Activity [a,b]
endproc
```

and

```
Activity [a,b]  [> Disrupt
```

at any point in `Activity`, `Disrupt` can come along and do whatever it does, and then `Activity` is finished with completely.

The "\\" or "hiding" operator is used to hide gates from the environment, so that a process may selectively filter which gates it is prepared to receive events on, as it wishes.

The "≫" or "enabling" operator is equivalent to the sequencing operator, except that execution stops, so long as the previous process terminated via the *exit* process.

An example of a complex process to make breakfast might be that shown in Figure 5.1.

```
Specification (* Making_Breakfast *)

(* Normal Sequence *)
process breakfast[cup, plate] :=
        normal_breakfast[cup, plate]
    ; go_to_work
    ; stop
endproc

(* Example of Input and guarded action *)
process normal_breakfast[cup, plate] :=
        cook_breakfast[cup, plate]
    >> (
            ; eat_breakfast[cup, plate]
            ; wash-up
        )
        hunger ? ask_ourselves : bool
        (ask_ourselves) -> normal_breakfast[cup, plate]
endproc

process cook_breakfast[cup, plate] :=
        put_kettle_on
    ; make_tea
    ; cup!tea
    || (
            put_water_on
        ; put_eggs_in
        ; plate!eggs
        )
    || (
            put_toast_in
        ; toaster_on
        ; plate!toast
        )
endproc

(* Note must be able to accept eggs and toast and tea in any *)
(* sequence, or we get deadlock                              *)
process eat_breakfast[cup, plate] :=
    ( cup?tea:imbibable
    || plate?boiled_eggs:edible
    || plate?toast:edible
    )
    ; eat_up_now_its_getting_cold
endproc

(* news is usually an internal event *)
process 9_am_news :=
        i
    ; turn_everything_off
    ; throw_everything_in_sink[cup, plate]
    ; stop
endproc
process smell_burnt_toast :=
        i
    ; toast_to_sink
    ; stop endproc
(* Disruptions *)
normal_breakfast[cup, plate]
        9_am_news normal_breakfast[cup, plate]
    || smell_burnt_toast
endspec
```

Figure 5.1 Example LOTOS specification (over).

104

5.6 Variables, values and expressions and LOTOS

LOTOS uses ACT.1 to define a language for types and algebras, so that variables and expressions may be included in a protocol specification. ACT is an abstract data type language, akin to object-oriented language. This means that one specifies not only types for variables, but also the set of operations allowed on these types.

Typical specifications include:

- sorts (the sorts of things we are defining)
- opns (the operations on these sort of things)
- sort (a sort identifier for use when defining variables of this sort)
- eqns (defining legal equations on these sorts of things)

5.7 Estelle

Estelle is fully described elsewhere (ISO 1989b) (See also Budkowski & Dembinski 1988). Here we just give some examples of its use for specifying some commonly found functions of protocols.

5.7.1 Overview

Estelle is an extension of ISO standard Pascal. The extension is mainly concerned with expressing finite-state machines and their associated states, transitions and events:

- State identifiers are chosen by the user, according to some understanding of a particular system. They form an enumerated set of constants, and each is associated with some module or modules.
- Transitions are specified between states, and have associated transition blocks which contain almost standard Pascal definitions of the actions to be performed on a transition.
- A specification is made up from modules, which interact via channels and interaction points.
- A module is essentially either a process (which may be a system – top-level – process), or else an activity. The intention behind this is to enable the specification of active chunks of a system, and passive (i.e. event-handling) pieces of a system. In implementation, this might be reflected in the difference between modules that are scheduled and run continuously until they explictly complete, and modules that are fired up on a one-off basis.
- A module definition contains a list of interaction points at which events will occur. These are essentially a list of the channels that the module will accept events on, or will generate events on.
- A channel is essentially a queue on which a process or activity can generate events. The channel definition says what the relationship of any modules using the channel should be (i.e. which module will generate what events on a channel, and which will accept events on a channel).
- The association of modules via channels, with interaction at the end points is controlled by connecting and disconnecting the modules to and from a channel.

```
Specification PanicStations systemprocess;
{
    Some const and type declarations
    in normal Pascal
}
    Channel recall(user,provider)
    by user
        TryToRemember(Fact);
    by provider
        Inspiration(Fact);

    module Student process
        brain brainstorm: recall(user);
    end; {of Student Header}

    module Conscience process
        brain OverActive: Inspiration(provider);
    end; {of Conscience Header}

    body StudentBody for Student;

    {some local types/variables etc}

        state bone_idle, frantic; { State Declaration }

        trans { From bone_idle to frantic on remembering Coursework }

        priority high
        from bone_idle
        to frantic
        provided    ( Deadline - TodaysDate < OneDay
                        and
        NumberCourseworksToDo > 1 )

        when
            brain.recall;
        begin
            StartSomeKindOfWork;
            {The Complete spec will involve another interaction with
            the environment which causes the student to become idle
            again - via some event like}
        end;

    body ConscienceBody for Conscience;

    {some local types/variables etc}

        begin
            while(alive)
            begin
                delay;
                output brain.Inspiration;
                end;
            end
            begin
                init conscience with ConscienceBody;
                init student with StudentBody;
            end; {of module initialisation}
        end. {of spec}
```

Figure 5.2 Example Estelle specification.

Modules may be parameterized. Process-type modules are dynamic, and are initialized (created/instantiated) or destroyed as a system runs.

A module may have a separate body and header, so that we can define a consistent service supported by a module without going into detail of how the service is provided. (For example, a train or a plane will get you from London to Edinburgh, but they work in a totally different way. They might be parameterized by cost – e.g. the plane is usually cheaper, but not during the Festival. And they certainly have internal interactions that are different, e.g. with the railway tracks provider or runway provider).

5.7.2 Example of a specification
An example of a specification of a frivolous system in Estelle is shown in Figure 5.2. This example illustrates that the system behaviour is directly captured by a set of modules in a conventional programming language, together with the state transitions and associated guards.

5.8 Communicating sequential processes (CSP)
CSP is a programming language and is the basis of Occam, a lower-level programming language for parallel architecture computers. CSP forms the mathematically strict background (originally for design of Occam) and is partly a programming language, partly a notation.

It also allows us to make statements about programs like:
- This program is the same as that (behavioural equivalence)
- This program will not deadlock.
The basic idea is that of a process:
- A process is defined as the set of events that are relevant – this set is an alphabet.
- The behaviour of a process is defined by a set of process names and operators.
We describe behaviour in terms of the operators shown in Table 5.1.

Table 5.1 CSP operators.

Operator	Symbol
Prefix (then)	$\rightarrow$
Choice	▯
Parallel	‖
Non-deterministic or	⊓
Interleave	⦀

5.8.1 Process descriptions
By convention, we use upper case for processes and lower case or mixed cases for events. A process is some expression involving events and operators. For exam-

ple, a process (say *GAME*) describing a computer game might have an alphabet: *InCoin*, *OutCome*. Its (top-level) behaviour might then be expressed as:

$$GAME = (InCoin \rightarrow OutCome \rightarrow GAME)$$

Note that a process can be recursive – this is how we describe repetitive behaviour in CSP.

To describe behaviour that can vary (a bit more interesting) we use the choice operator:

CLEVERGAME = (*InCoinLarge* → *OutCome* → *OutCome* ⫿ *InCoin* →
  OutCome) → *CLEVERGAME*

(assuming *InCoinLarge* is part of the alphabet of *CLEVERGAME*).

Other features are as follows:
- Mutual recursion is also allowed.
- There is a special process called *STOP*. It stops.
- There is another special set of processes called *CHAOS*. It is indistinguishable from any other process with the same alphabet, but doesn't stop (i.e. its traces satisfy no specification). *CHAOS* can generate all possible traces for a given alphabet (it takes an alphabet as its argument).

5.8.2 Pictures

Just as in other parts of software engineering, we draw pictures of processes:

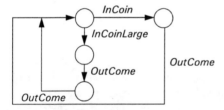

Of course, this is equivalent to:

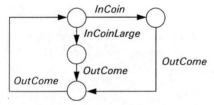

So a CSP picture is a bit like a Markov diagram or state-transition picture.

5.8.3 Traces

A trace of a process is a log/record of the events/actions it has undertaken (like a tape recording). A specification is a predicate (some expression in terms of variables in the trace) that we would like to be true about a process. A trace can go on for ever (e.g. a trace of the *GAME* process). Traces are written as $<a, b, c, \ldots>$. The empty trace is denoted by $<>$. A trace of *CLEVER-GAME* might be:

$<InCoin, OutCome, InCoinLarge, OutCome, OutCome>$

Operations on traces include:

- Catenation: $s\hat{\ }t$.
  This simply appends trace t to trace s. Note that $f(s\hat{\ }t)$ is $f(s)\hat{\ }f(t)$ (for classes of functions that map sequences of events to sequences of events).
- Restriction: $s \lceil A$
  All the symbols not in alphabet A are removed from the trace s.
- Most important is ordering
  If s is a copy of an initial subsequence of t, it is possible to find an extension u of s, such that $s\hat{\ }u = t$. Thus we can define an ordering: in some sense $s \leq t$.
- Other useful operations include s_0, the head of a trace; s', the tail of a trace; and $\#s$, the length of a trace.

Also note the following:

- $traces(STOP) = <>$
- The traces of both our *GAME*s includes infinite sequences:

$traces(GAME) = \{<>, <InCoin>, <InCoin, OutCome>,$
$<InCoin, OutCome, InCoin>, \ldots\}$

- $traces(c \to P \square d \to Q) = \{<>, (t_0 = c) \text{ and } traces(P), (t_0 = d) \text{ and }$
  $traces(Q)\}$

i.e. the trace will include $t_0 = c$ or d, then the initial subsequence of P or Q. An example of a specification is:

$$\#(traces(GAME) \lceil OutCome) \leq (\#(traces(GAME) \lceil InCoin)) \qquad (5.1)$$

and

$$\#(traces(GAME) \lceil InCoin) \leq \#(traces(GAME) \lceil OutCome) + 1 \qquad (5.2)$$

must both be true. Informally, a coin doesn't buy you more or less than one game and the *GAME*s machine cannot be better than that one coin ahead. (In some sense, we have "contracted" in the software engineering sense, not to rip off the customer or the games manufacturer.) [2]

5.8.4 Program transformation
We would like to be able to write an obviously correct implementation of an algorithm in any concurrent programming languages, in general, and then mechanically transform the program into one with identical behaviour but more efficient

2. See Meyer (1989).

performance. By "mechanical transformation" is meant a transformation, selected from some bag of tricks by the programmer or a clever program, that can then be applied mechanically, and that is known to produce a precisely equivalent program. The problem lies, of course, in selecting and proving the bag of tricks, and in deciding how to use them on a particular program.

We now wish to show that a given process satisfies a specification. This is done by proofs!

Combining the two parts of the specification for *GAME*, and subtracting *OutCome* from both sides of (5.1) and (5.2):

$$0 \leq \#(traces(GAME)\lceil InCoin) - \#(traces(GAME)\lceil OutCome) \leq 1 \quad (5.3)$$

or writing $length(trace(PROC))\lceil event$ as $tr\lceil event$:

$$0 \leq tr\lceil InCoin - tr\lceil OutCome \leq 1 \quad (5.4)$$

Now if *P* sat *S* and $S \Rightarrow T$, *P* sat *T*. i.e. if a specification *S* implies a specification *T*, then everything satisfying *S* must satisfy the (weaker) *T*.

Now (induction!): *STOP* satisfies $tr = <>$ (obviously), and this implies

$$0 \leq tr\lceil InCoin - tr\lceil OutCome \leq 1 \quad (5.5)$$

since

$$<>\lceil InCoin = <>\lceil OutCome = 0 \quad (5.6)$$

Assuming some process *X* satisfies

$$0 \leq tr\lceil InCoin - tr\lceil OutCome \leq 1$$

then $(InCoin \rightarrow OutCome \lceil X)$ satisfies

$$tr \geq <InCoin, OutCome> \quad (5.7)$$

or

$$(tr \geq <InCoin, OutCome> \text{ and } 0 \leq tr\lceil InCoin - tr\lceil OutCome \leq 1) \quad (5.8)$$

This implies *GAME* does satisfy spec since:

$$<>\lceil InCoin = <>\lceil OutCome = <InCoin>\lceil OutCome = 0 \quad (5.9)$$

and

$$<InCoin>\lceil InCoin = <InCoin,OutCome>\lceil InCoin =$$
$$<InCoing,OutCome>\lceil OutCome = 1 \quad (5.10)$$

and

$$tr \geq <InCoin, OutCome> \quad (5.11)$$

imply

$$tr\lceil InCoin = tr+1 \text{ and } tr\lceil OutCome = tr\lceil OutCome + 1 \quad (5.12)$$

Note: *STOP* satisfies every spec that can be satisfied by any process. Also, any process defined only using prefix, choice and guarded recursion never stops.

5.8.5 Laws of Then and Choice

- $(x \rightarrow P \,\square\, y \rightarrow Q) = (y \rightarrow Q \,\square\, x \rightarrow P)$ (5.13)

  In other words, "Leave the room and shut the door behind you, or sit down and listen" is much the same as "Sit down and listen or leave the room and shut the door behind you".
- $(x \rightarrow P) \neq STOP$ (5.14)

  That is, "some event, then do whatever" is a process that can do something!
- Two processes are the same if the initial events are the same, and subsequent events are too!

5.8.6 Concurrency

We are usually only interested in concurrent processes that eventually interact. If two processes have the same alphabet (of events) and run in "lockstep", we have simultaneous engaging by each process, i.e. each is concurrently behaving as if it was on its own. In other words, in our example where the games player and *GAME* are processes, if we consider the events in their alphabet, *InCoin* and *OutCome*, they (in some sense) engage simultaneously in each. This is written:

$$PLAYER \,\|\, GAME \qquad (5.15)$$

At the top level of a concurrent system, only the interactions are interesting.

5.8.7 Laws of concurrency

- $P \,\|\, Q = Q \,\|\, P$; i.e. parallelism is symmetric.
- $P \,\|\, (Q \,\|\, R) = (P \,\|\, Q) \,\|\, R$; i.e. we do not care what order you said things were parallel in.
- $P \,\|\, STOP = STOP$; i.e. deadlock is infectious.
- $(c \rightarrow P) \,\|\, (c \rightarrow Q) = (c \rightarrow (P \,\|\, Q))$, e.g. if the alarm rings then we run out, and the alarm rings then we start shouting, is the same as: the alarm rings and we run out shouting.
- $(c \rightarrow P) \,\|\, (d \rightarrow Q) = STOP \ (c \neq d)$

  In general, if both of two processes offer a choice of initial event the combined processes will only engage in events they both offer. This lets us rewrite concurrent systems in terms of choice and prefix: e.g. if

$$P = (a \rightarrow b \rightarrow P \mid b \rightarrow P) \qquad (5.16)$$

and

$$Q = (a \rightarrow (b \rightarrow Q \mid c \rightarrow Q)) \qquad (5.17)$$

then

$$(P \,\|\, Q) = (a \rightarrow b \rightarrow P) \,\|\, (b \rightarrow Q \mid c \rightarrow Q) = a \rightarrow (b \rightarrow (P \,\|\, Q)) \ (5.18)$$

So we now have a processes that could be defined:

$$X = a \rightarrow b \rightarrow X \qquad (5.19)$$

5.8.8 Non-determinism and general choice

Non-determinism may or may not actually occur in the known computing universe. It is, however, a convenient fiction, a useful abstraction, when the internal mechanisms that determine the choice are hidden from us. If we prefer to say that the choice of what happens next is beyond the scope of our program then we use non-determinism. If our simple computer game program now includes whether the player wins or loses:

$$Alphabet(GAME) = (InCoin, Win, Lose)i \qquad (5.20)$$

then
$$GAME = (InCoin \rightarrow Win \sqcap Lose \rightarrow GAME) \qquad (5.21)$$

Now the traces of this include

$$< InCoin, Win, InCoin, Lose, \ldots >$$

as well as $\quad < InCoin, Lose, InCoin, Lose, InCoin, Lose, \ldots > \qquad (5.22)$

5.8.9 Laws of non-determinism

- $P \sqcap P = P$
- $P \sqcap Q = Q \sqcap P$
- $P \sqcap (Q \sqcap R) = (P \sqcap Q) \sqcap R$
- $x \rightarrow (P \sqcap Q) = (x \rightarrow P) \sqcap (x \rightarrow Q)$
  i.e. choice distributes over non-determinism. So does $\parallel$ and so does any $f(P)$, where f is a CSP operation.

5.8.10 Refusals

A refusal is a subset of the events/actions that a process can partake of, that at some particular time we wish to exclude. For instance, if a process specification says that it must have at most five more things input than output, then while there are five things "buffered", we refuse input events.

5.8.11 Communication – input, output and pipes

Input and output in CSP are semantically identical with those of Occam (a programming language for transputer processor – a building block for parallel computers!). Communications is a special event: c.v., where c is a channel, and v is a value that appears on the channel. Using this, a copy process might be written:

$$COPY = (left?x \rightarrow right!x \rightarrow COPY)$$

As a convenient shorthand for processes that have a single input channel and a single output channel, finally, we have a pipe operator for connecting them via this channel, while at the same time hiding it (this is another example of the hiding abstraction, where the level of specification is raised to conceal details about ordering that are not relevant): If

$$P = (\text{something} \rightarrow \text{right!x} \rightarrow P)$$

and
$$Q = (\text{left?x} \rightarrow \text{somethingelse} \rightarrow Q)$$

then $(P \parallel Q)$ is such a common thing that we write:

$$P \gg Q$$

(subject to alphabetic constraints!).

5.9 Introduction to the specification language Z

Mathematical set theory has the notion of type – for example, integers, booleans. Z allows another type, the schema type. A schema consists of two parts separated by a horizontal line. In the upper half we have what is commonly referred to as the *declarative* part of the schema. Here we define our variables by stating their type. In the second half, or bottom half, commonly referred to as the *predicate* part, we show how the variables are constrained.

```
__ SCHEMA – NAME _____
  declarations
 _____
  predicates
|_____
```

Modularity and abstraction are important assets of Z, and are coped with by allowing schemas to be written in the declarative part of other schemas:

```
__ SCHEMA2 _____
  SCHEMA1
  more declarations
 _____
  more predicates
|_____
```

This should be read by imagining the schema *Schema1* expanded, with all of its declarations joining the *more declarations* of *Schema2* and all its predicates being moved under the dividing line to join the *more predicates* of *Schema2*

The way operations are described in Z, for a given schema, is to relate the variables of the state after the operation (primed) to the variables of the state before the operation (unprimed). So for an operation *OP* on a schema *Schema1* we would have

```
__ OP _____
  SCHEMA1
  SCHEMA1'
 _____
  Show how the variables of the before and after state are related
|_____
```

The notion of change is made explicit by the delta schema, which expresses the

113

fact that some state has changed in a schema, without the need to repeat the entire definition:

$$
\begin{array}{|l}
\hline
\Delta SCHEMA1 \\
\hline
SCHEMA1 \\
SCHEMA1' \\
\hline
\end{array}
$$

So a delta schema says we have some previous state, and some next state, and that the state has changed. The converse of this is where an operation produces no change:

$$
\begin{array}{|l}
\hline
OP \\
\hline
SCHEMA\ 1 \\
SCHEMA\ 1' \\
\hline
\textit{All the variables of the before and after state are unchanged} \\
\hline
\end{array}
$$

This is written: $\equiv Schema1$

Other notation is best described by example. Consider the following schema:

$$
\begin{array}{|l}
\hline
EXAMPLE \\
\hline
a, b\ :\text{N} \\
x, y\ :\text{N} \times \text{N} \\
p, q\ :\text{P}(\text{N} \times \text{N}) \\
f, g\ :\text{N} \rightarrow \text{P N} \\
seq1, seq2 : \text{seq } [Names] \\
name : \text{P } Names \\
\hline
a > b \\
\exists z : \text{N} \mid z > a \bullet z < fst\ x \\
\forall n : (\text{N} \times \text{N})\ n \in p \bullet fst\ n = snd\ n \\
q = \{s, t : \text{N} \mid s > t \wedge t < s \bullet (s, t)\} \\
\forall n : \text{N} \bullet fn = \{\text{m} : \text{N} \mid m < n \bullet m\} \\
g = \{1,\ 2,\ 3\} \lhd f \\
seq1 = [mary,\ sally,\ john] \\
seq2 = \{1\} \lhd seq1 \\
name = \text{ran } seq2 \\
\hline
\end{array}
$$

In the declarative part of the schema we declare our variables:
1. a and b are natural numbers.
2. x and y are pairs of natural numbers.
3. p and q are drawn from a subset of the natural numbers.
4. f and g are functions that take a number and return some subset of numbers.
5. $seq1$ and $seq2$ are sequences of names. In Z, each sequence is thought of as a function from the natural numbers to the set of names.

6. The variable *name* is a subset of names.

We consider the predicate part of the schema, one line at a time:

1. *a* is bigger than *b*.
2. There exists a number that is bigger than *a* but smaller than the first element of the pair *x*.
3. Any pair of numbers contained in the subset of pairs of numbers *p*, must have equal values, e.g (3,3).
4. The set *q* is constructed of pairs of numbers that satisfy the condition of neither being greater than the other (i.e. they are the same), so *p* and *q* have a similar structure.
5. *f* is the function that takes a number and returns the set of numbers that has all the numbers up to but not including that number.
6. *g* is the function that is like *f*, but only defined for the values 1, 2 and 3. This is known as *domain restriction*.
7. This line gives an explicit value for *seq1*, which, in Z, is equivalent to the function { 1 → *mary*, 2 → *sally*, 3 → *john*}
8. This line tells us that *seq2* is like *seq1* but restricted to the first element, i.e. *seq2* = *mary*, or equivalently *seq2* = { 1 → mary}.
9. This line says that the variable *name* has the value that is given by the range of *seq2*, or specifically *name* = { *mary* }.

Finally, writing *EXAMPLE.f*, for example, refers to the variable *f* as defined in the schema *EXAMPLE*.

5.10 A multimedia conference specification in Z

This section presents the specification, design and implementation of a text-based multi-way interactive conferencing program. The motivation was frustration with the limitations of the Unix[3] talk program.[4] The system will be described in three parts: the user interface, the distribution mechanism for users' contributions and the floor-control scheme.

There are certain limitations to the ability of humans to assimilate textual information. We look at how these are reflected in the design of the windowing interface to the conference, and how they affect the floor-control system. People have evolved many complex ways of interacting face to face.

Underlying mechanisms are emerging for multidestination delivery of data. We shall see how these can be used by the conferencing system.[5]

5.10.1 Requirements

The central purpose of our description is to present as complete a model of floor control as possible, so that implementors of conferencing systems have a general framework from which to derive any specific policies they require.

---

3. Unix is a trademark of AT&T Bell Laboratories.

4. The talk program was originally written by Kipp Hickman.

5. "A floor so cunningly laid that no matter where you stood, it was beneath your feet" – Spike Milligan.

Higher-level tools are now available to help specify the set of distributed operations in a system. We have used these to decompose the various control messages and the flow of users' data around the conference.

5.10.2 Motivation

The conferencing facility available on most modern telephone exchanges is extremely useful. Many commercial analogue video/audio conferencing systems offer a similar service. What characterizes these services is the lack of structure to the conference; a common complaint is that it is hard to work out which person on a screen is the new speaker. We shall outline the design of a conferencing system for windowing workstations and look at some of the possibilities for powerful *floor-control mechanisms* beyond the simple-minded (and probably unmanageable) multi-way version of talk.

Talk is a simple-minded program that divides the screen on a dumb terminal into two areas. What the user types appears in "their" half on their screen and in the "other" half on the other terminal. The users may type simultaneously, and the sequence of output will be interleaved almost arbitrarily on the other user's screen. The program is extended over the network so that users with terminals attached to different hosts may use the facility in a network-transparent way (excepting delays). This is done using a reliable byte stream protocol appropriate for one-to-one communication. The system is limited to two parties.

5.10.3 User interfaces

We look at how the conference appears to the user on the screen. How much text output can a human easily assimilate, and in what way can the current speaker (typist) be best identified? Can the ease of use of the conference be aided by semantic hints in the display? We consider the use of Searle's illocutionary acts as a way of classifying the users' input (Searle 1975, Winograd & Graves 1988).

We do not examine in detail how a conference is started, how people are invited to join or ask to join, how they find out about a conference in the first place, or how the conference is closed down. These concerns are briefly discussed in the section on related work.

5.10.4 Distribution

End-system communication in a conference is characterized by requiring *one-to-many* or *many-to-many* communications channels. Some commercial conferencing systems make use of the underlying broadcast nature of the communications medium (e.g. analogue video conferencing systems over satellite channels).

Our (high-level) model of the conference is that there is a unidirectional channel from each user to every other user. We picture a user as a possible speaker or a possible listener. If a user is speaking to more than one listener, then the conference *may* make use of underlying multicast or broadcast mechanisms as an optimization. That is outside the scope of this design.

5.10.5 Floor control

How is the conference managed? We propose a general floor-control system, where the users may specify the style of floor control that they wish for the conference in as abstract a way as possible. This entails choosing whether the conference is "chaired" in the most general sense. If the conference is not chaired, is there a queuing system to gain the floor, and, if so, what is the queuing discipline? Are users time-sliced in a manner similar to operating-system process scheduling? Can a user pass on their place in a queue to another, and, if so, can they regain part of their time? How may subgroups be split off from the main thread of a conference; how may they rejoin; how might conferences be merged; are there mechanisms for mumbled and muttered asides? What are the possibilities for displaying these floor-control policies on the screen?

5.10.6 Related work

Although this work is concerned with conferencing, we have tried to avoid duplicating work by other researchers in the area of shared workspaces and multidestination delivery protocols. A brief survey found that most of the work falls into these two areas, and little into the areas either of structuring exchanges of text between humans, or of distributed floor-control algorithms (although mechanisms are often discussed).

- Sarin & Grief (1985) discuss computer-mediated analogue voice conferencing. Windows/panels are used to indicate speakers and chair and to control access. The communications model is message-passing/distributed.
- Ahuja et al. (1988) studied the networking requirements for the Rapport multimedia conferencing system. Unix sockets are the communication mechanism. Voice is carried separately (i.e. not on the same LAN).
- Bonfoglio et al. (private comm.) describe a framework for real-time conferencing. A prototype was implemented under a Unix environment.
- Egido (1988) describes video conferencing support for group working . This paper reviews the teleconferencing literature and reasons for the comparative failure of video conferencing compared with other networking services.
- Suzuki et al. (1986) discuss Unix kernel support for conferencing between users of window-based workstations. Their model incorporates existing (single-user) applications for multiple users without modification of the application. They discuss a four-phase structure of a conference: planning (invitations to join), setting-up (chair selection), progress (changing rights/windows), and completion (minutes circulation).
- Forsdick & Crowley (1989) describe the Bolt, Beranek & Newman real-time multimedia conferencing system. The mmconf facility based on Diamond/Slate, and its integration with the wideband network conferencing system is described in a collection of BBN technical reports. It includes some floor control, but with a fixed policy.
- Other work includes Chess & Cowlishaw (1987), Palme (1987) and Olivetti (1990).

5.10.7 The user interface

The user interface consists of:

- a user window, which accepts input when focus is on the window (usually when the mouse or pointer device is in (or clicked in) this window)
- a number of other-participant windows, which show the text the other participants are typing[6]
- a control window to show join/leave and participant information such as bids to gain the floor and the current floor sequence
- a set of buttons/display panels for expressing out-of-band human communication such as warnings/threats and so forth

The part of a conferencing system that has been most interesting to researchers in the past has been the user interface. A great deal of work has been done on multimedia user interface design which we have not attempted to cover here. However, in a simple text-based conferencing system, a number of interesting problems and possibilities arise. This is discussed in the section that follows.

5.10.8 Readability and usefulness

A great deal of the research into legibility has been done in the printing world (NFER 1989). The functions of colour, typeface, font size and so on are reasonably well understood, although there are some ergonomic differences between screens and the printed page.[7]

On readability, the basic rules of thumb for the following parameters have been established:

- accuracy
- comprehension
- speed

There is some understanding of how complexity and style of grammar affect comprehension. However, we have found that there has been little work so far on the structure of real-time conversations. Nor is there a great deal of work on conversations with more than two participants. As our starting point we considered a classification of *speech acts* from Searle so that we could start to identify multiparty protocols. Searle classifies speech into five illocutionary acts:

- assertive (suggesting that someone should do something)
  e.g. "assert", "claim", "argue"
- commissive (stating that we will do something)
  e.g. "commit", "promise", "threaten"
- directive (ordering someone to do something)
  e.g. "request", "order", "solicit"

---

6. The n-way distribution of input to the other-participant windows was achieved by modification to the X-Windows server to field events to multiple clients.

7. For "back of the envelope" calculations, we should note that reading speeds as high as 900 words per minute have been recorded, although speech comprehension can go even higher. Interestingly, although the bandwidth of the eye is around 1 Gbps, neurologists claim the bandwidth of the nervous system into the brain is closer to 300 bps! Of course, a lot of preprocessing is occurring!

- declarative (naming/reassigning that such and such is the case)
  e.g. "declare", "name", "abbreviate"
- expressive (stating feelings about something)
  e.g. "thank", "apologise", "greet"

We can use these acts to help structure the exchanges in a conference. A directive, for example, should always require an answer, agreement or acknowledgement, and the conferencing system will make provisions so that the person to whom the directive is made will be forced to make a reply before they can continue with the conference. An assertive will normally beg a question (directive), an argument (an assertive not logically consistent with the last-made assertive), or evidence or opinion backing up the previous statement (an assertive or expressive). Breaking down communications into these categories enables us to semi-structure (precompile into the conferencing system) conversations in advance, enabling the users to be guided and understood more efficiently in their communications (Campbell & d'Inverno 1989).

Even more importantly, though, placing statements under particular speech-act headings will remove a significant number of ambiguities as well as giving the hearer a quicker route to understanding the speaker's intentions. The proposition "Close the door", for example, could be a promise or threat, but equally could be a request or order. Placing all propositions under their speech-act heading will enable the hearer to remove many of the ambiguities that arise through the loss of information that happens when a speaker's tone and expression are unavailable.

Not only can we use these acts to give more structure to the exchanges of text between users, but we can use them to give weight to their *bids* for the floor. This has been used by other workers in the area, although only for offline systems rather than real-time ones.

Mechanical protocols generally come from a very limited range of the set possible, e.g. ARP "who-has", RPC "request-response", or the TELNET IAC (interpret as command), "do, don't, will, won't". We believe that the use of speech acts allows a much wider expression for exchanges without losing structure altogether (Xerox 1981, Plummer 1982, Postel & Reynolds 1983). The Coordinator is a system that, by exchanging messages restricted to some types chosen to express some of the same ideas as speech acts (though not in real time), allows better time management of actions (Winograd & Graves 1988).

5.10.9 How to show who spoke last, and who will be next

Floor control is not necessary for "off the cuff" conferences – the talk model suffices. This is a "free for all", where all users may type simultaneously, and their input updates all the appropriate output windows on all other users' conference screens (many per screen).

When floor control is operating, we need to show the order of speakers. One possibility is that the current speaker has the large central window. The windows for past speakers form a spiral of decreasing sized areas on one side (for less recent speakers). The people waiting to speak form a similar spiral on the other side.

5.10.10 Starting and continuing the conference – attention

In the first place, a user must request or be asked to enter the conference. We assume that some single user starts the conference, and has either previously invited other users, or else uses some tool to locate and ask them. A third possibility is that they can detect a new conference and request to enter. This part of the distributed operations is out of band from the exchange of text and out of band from the floor-control mechanisms.

5.10.11 Queues and shows of hands

One possibility for showing who wishes to speak, and with what urgency, is to place an icon for each user (either a small photograph or a name tag) on the screen some distance from the "floor" window. As the time approaches for them to speak, the icon moves closer to the floor. One possible implementation of this (due to John Taylor at UCL) was a step-functioned "fish-eye" lens model of the area around the floor, with icons nearer the centre naturally being larger.

5.10.12 Why is X appropriate?

The X-Windows system is essentially divided in two parts: client programs and the display server. These communicate by a well-defined protocol, which allows the client program and display server to be on separate machines. There is an access-control mechanism to prevent a client program arbitrarily accessing the display server on another machine without first being given permission.

The server allows a program to create and manage a number of windows on a display/machine. A client program can be a window manager, which keeps track of a set of other applications. Any X application can notify other applications of events that it has asked the X Server to notify it with.

5.10.13 The talk model

The original talk program had two parts:

- the daemon
- the user interface

The daemon is used to find users and invite them to join a talk. The user interface allows someone to request to talk to someone. This causes the daemon to invite the other user to join and then to plug together the inviter's and invitee's talks (all within the appropriate window on the appropriate machine). To extend this to multiple end points, we attempted two alternative approaches:

- *Centralized*

  We maintain the talk daemon approach roughly as it is. This is the means by which active or passive joins are propagated to a machine. We create a single daemon which creates the conference clients (see below), for each conference, and tracks them by name (which maps to machine/port), and also create a corresponding list of users. This is implemented simply by letting the conference clients be windows on the corresponding users' workstation consoles. In other words, the conference is a single program which is an X-Windows client of many display servers.

- *Replicated or distributed*
  We allow the control of the conference to be distributed in the same way as the conference itself. This approach entails a number of autonomous conference programs, with some other means of communication than the X Protocol. We used multiple TCP Socket connections from each conference program to all the others.

We now present an open systems approach to defining the service interface to the conferencing system. The notation is that of the Remote Operations Service (CCITT 1986), using the Abstract Syntax Notation 1 (ASN.1) (CCITT 1985) to define the operations and parameters available between the conferencing programs. An outline of the objects and ports available in the various servers, available to clients, is given at the end of Chapter 6. For the centralized approach, we can decompose the system into three services, and analyze some design decisions for the services:

- *The conference server*
  This maintains the conferences for the users. It handles requests to create or destroy a conference, to join or leave a conference, and to send messages to the members of the conference. There may be one instance of the conference server per site, handling all conferences on all machines, or one per machine, or one per conference.

- *The location server*
  This is used by a user program to find where another user is logged in. There must be one of these per machine. However, does the client ask a location server, and the local location server ask all the others for the location? It may tell the user where the other location servers are, and then they have to repeat asking until they find the user. Another design decision might be for the location servers to continually (say every couple of minutes) inform each other of the users on their machine. In our case, we made use of the *rusers* RPC service.[8]

- *The ping server*
  The user uses this service to ask another user if they wish to join the conference. In our implementation, we made use of the *write* facility.

The user program is then a client of these three servers, typically the conference server (to create and join the conference), then the location server (to find another user), then the ping server (to ask the other user if they want to join), then the conference again to send messages to the set of users in the conference.

5.10.14 Star/mesh duality and rings

The most important property for the *n*-way conference to maintain is that of global sequencing. There are essentially two classes of distribution mechanism for this kind of application:

---

8. The location service is of general utility, and so is separate from the ping service.

- *Mesh*

  Each conferee runs a program that maintains a set of windows on their screen/display server (all in a box, one input window, one output window per other conferee, and some control panels/button boxes), and uses one (TCP) connection per other conferee to exchange conference proceedings (broadcast for data, more complex for floor control protocol). This is styled like the BSD talk facility.

- *Star*

  A central conference server per conference maintains an (X) connection to each conferee's display server, with the same appearance as above.

The main problem with the first mechanism is that extra protocol is required to maintain global sequencing of the input and output to the conference, otherwise the appearance of separate interleaved conversations may become reordered on some (or even all) of the conference displays. A common optimization is to organize the conferees in a logical ring and pass a token round for sequence control.

The second mechanism does not have the same problem, since the central conference server can act as a global sequencer. Simply by blocking input from all subsequent users until the input from the last user has been successfully output on all the displays, we ensure ordering. However, this mechanism does have two related problems: first, there is a large load on the central server, and second, the central server is a single point of failure.[9]

Either scheme would benefit from a reliable multicast protocol such as that described in Nirman & Joseph (1987) and Crowcroft & Paliwoda (1988). In contrast to either of these, a distributed shared-memory model for distributed programs could be used (albeit, in a distributed system, this must be on top of some message-passing mechanism which would then require all the global sequence that the mesh approach needs). We have then just exchanged the sequence problem for that of controlling concurrent access to shared memory. Our pilot implementation used the central server model for reasons of simplicity.

5.10.15 A general floor-control conference model

The floor control of a conference is the mechanism for managing which user(s) are allowed to speak to which listeners. In our model, we make no assumptions about the distribution mechanisms. We require a communications channel from each user to all the others. (This might be optimized through the use of multicast mechanisms.)

The floor-control mechanism assumes some out-of-band channel to *make bids* to be placed in a queue of speakers, and requires some out-of-band channel to turn on and off some *valve* on the connection from any speaker/user to some others. Of course, we do not say that the user at the end of an open channel is necessarily listening. This model is not restricted to text conferencing.

---

9. On a practical note, both mechanisms run out of Unix file descriptors at about 16, 32 or 64 conferees (depending on the version of Unix), but that should be adequate for most purposes.

In specifying a conference, we have made a number of design decisions that could be changed. We assert that, given this general model, it is not difficult to define most other desired models of conference.

5.10.16 Modularity of this conferencing system

A conference is made up of four different facets:

1. The *FLOOR* schema which is the set of channels open at a given time and previously requested by one of the current people in the conference.
2. The *ASIDES* schema which looks after individual asides between the users of the system.
3. The *QUEUE* schema which maintains an ordered list of bids, which are made up of the identity of the user, the current users, a desired floor (by default, a floor where the requester has a communication channel with all the people of the conference), the type of speech act (by default an assertion), and the time of the request. It also has a weighting function which ranks the bids.
4. An *ALLOWED* schema, which restricts the type of floors allowed in a given schema.

So then our total schema for the conference is:

$$
\begin{array}{|l}
\_\_CONFERENCE _____ \\
\ FLOOR \\
\ ASIDES \\
\ QUEUE \\
\ ALLOWED \\
\hline
\ somepredicates \\
\end{array}
$$

5.10.17 The *FLOOR* schema

Given the set of all people P, a floor is a set of ordered pairs of people, where each ordered pair suggests a directional communication channel from the first of the pair to the second. Of course, the floor should only be made up of the users currently in the conference, and we must keep track of the users of the system. Then all this information is captured by:

$$
\begin{array}{|l}
\_\_FLOOR _____ \\
\ floor : P(P \times P) \\
\ users : P\,P \\
\hline
\ floor \subseteq users \times users \\
\end{array}
$$

By way of example we define some types of floor. The first is the floor where everybody has a communication channel with everyone else – except themselves:[10]

```
  OPENFLOOR _____
  FLOOR _____
  floor = {x, y : P | x, y ∈ users • (x, y)} – {x : P | x ∈ users •(x, x)}
```

Another is the (we imagine) very common floor where one speaker talks to all the other people in the conference:

```
  SPEAKERFLOOR _____
  FLOOR _____
  ∀p, q : P | p, q ∈ floor • fst p = fst q
  #floor = #users – 1
```

5.10.18 Useful functions

First let us define the set of functions which take the set of users and a floor and return the number of users to whom that user is talking, that is, the number of open channels from that user, to other users:

```
  SPEAKER? _____
  speaker : P(P × P) → P → N
  ∀f : P(P × P), u : P
  speaker f u = n
  ⇔
  #{p : P | (u, p) ∈ f • p} = n
```

There are two cases. For a floor f, and a user u, either

1. $speaker\, f\, u = 0$

   in which case p is only a listener of the current floor.

2. $speaker\, f\, u > 0$

   in which case p is talking to someone in that floor. In this case we say, unsurprisingly, that p is a speaker of the floor f.

Next let us define the notion of the maximal speaker of a floor f. This is/are the user/s that is/are speaking to more conference users than anyone else:

```
  MAXIMAL _____
  maximal : P ↔ P (P × P)
  u maximal f
  ⇔
  ∀p : P | speaker f p ≤ speaker f u
```

10. It is an internal matter that a speaker can hear themselves in a human conference. Similarly, we feel that in a computer-mediated conference, a channel between the keyboard and screen (or camera and monitor) of a given user is out of the scope of the actual conference (at least for the reason that it cannot be floor-controlled).

5.10.19 Operations on the *FLOOR* schema

The first operation we define is that of a new user joining the conference system. And by default we join them to the listeners of any maximal speaker, so:

$$
\begin{array}{|l}
\_\_ \textit{ADDUSER} _____ \\
\hline
\textit{u?} : \mathrm{P} \\
\Delta \textit{FLOOR} \\
\hline
\textit{u?} \notin \textit{users} \\
\textit{users}' = \textit{users} \cup \{\textit{u?}\} \\
\textit{floor}' = \textit{floor} \cup \{q : \mathrm{P} \mid (q \text{ maximal floor}) \bullet (q, \textit{u?})\} \\
\end{array}
$$

(Note that in all examples "*u?*" represents the person initiating the operation.)

Of course, the user may not be very happy about this, and so we define operations where they can stop having to listen to a speaker. So if a user *u?* wishes to stop hearing the speaker *p?*, we have:

$$
\begin{array}{|l}
\_\_ \textit{REMOVE} - \textit{LISTEN} - \textit{SPEAKER} _____ \\
\hline
\textit{u?}, \textit{p?} : \mathrm{P} \\
\Delta \textit{FLOOR} \\
\hline
\textit{u?}, \textit{p?} \in \textit{users} \\
(\textit{p?}, \textit{u?}) \in \textit{floor} \\
\textit{floor}' = \textit{floor} - \{(\textit{p?}, \textit{u?})\} \\
\textit{users}' = \textit{users} \\
\end{array}
$$

And, correspondingly, any user should be able to get to hear any speaker of a floor (this operation is optional and may not be allowed).

$$
\begin{array}{|l}
\_\_ \textit{REQUEST} - \textit{LISTEN} - \textit{SPEAKER} _____ \\
\hline
\textit{u?}, \textit{p?} : \mathrm{P} \\
\Delta \textit{FLOOR} \\
\hline
\textit{u?}, \textit{p?} \in \textit{users} \\
\textit{speaker floor p?} > 0 \\
\textit{floor}' = \textit{floor} \cup \{(\textit{p?}, \textit{u?})\} \\
\textit{users}' = \textit{users} \\
\end{array}
$$

The first predicate in the above schema states that *p?* is already speaking – there is not much point listening to them if they are not. If the speaker wasn't specified, then the default would be for a channel to be set up from the maximal speaker of the current floor to the user *u?*.

Next, we give the converse of the operation of a user joining a conferencing system, namely leaving it. We suggest at this point that in order for a user to leave a conference they must *not* be a speaker of the current floor. If that is true, then we close any open channels involving the user and remove the user from the variable *users*:

```
┌─ LEAVE – F ─────────────────────────────────────────
│ u? : P
│ ΔFLOOR
├──────────────────────────────────────────────────────
│ speaker u? floor = 0
│ floor' = floor – {p : P | (p, u?) ∈ floor • (p, u?)}
│ users' = users – {u?}
└──────────────────────────────────────────────────────
```

Then, finally, we specify an "I've finished" operation: that is, when a speaker has finished what they wanted to say. If there are other speakers as well as the person finishing, we just close all the open channels for which P is the speaker:

```
┌─ FINISHED1 ─────────────────────────────────────────
│ u? : P
│ ΔFLOOR
├──────────────────────────────────────────────────────
│ speaker floor u? > 0
│ ∃p : P | p ≠ u? • speaker floor u? > 0
│ floor' = floor – {p : P | (u?, p) ∈ floor • (u?, p)}
│ users' = users
└──────────────────────────────────────────────────────
```

However, if the "I've finished" operation is engaged where the initiator is the only current speaker, then the floor becomes empty (i.e. there is a special case of finishing). In fact, the floor becomes what the highest ranked bid requests (we shall see this later); so we write, for the time being:

```
┌─ FINISHED2 ─────────────────────────────────────────
│ u? : P
│ ΔFLOOR
├──────────────────────────────────────────────────────
│ speaker floor u? > 0
│ ~∃p : P | p ≠ u? • speaker floor u? > 0
│ floor = ∅
│ users' = users
└──────────────────────────────────────────────────────
```

5.10.20 The ASIDE schema

An aside is where a user sets up a private one-way link with some other user. The analogy is sitting next to someone at a conference and whispering in their ear. We stipulate that any user may only have one aside where they are the speaker, and one where they are the listener. That is, for a given $u?$, the most asides allowed would be a $(u?, p)$ and a $(q, u?)$. Of course, if $p = q$, then we would have a conversation in progress, since both the channels $(u?, p)$ and $(p, u?)$ would be open. This is, of course, merely a design decision and is used for the purposes of exposition. Here is the ASIDE schema:

```
┌─ ASIDE ─────────────────────────────────────────────────────
│ users : P P
│ asides : P(P × P)
├─────────────────────────────────────────────────────────────
│ asides ⊆ users × users
│ ∀ p, q : P × P | p, q ∈ asides ∧ p ≠ q • (fst p ≠ fst q ∧ snd p ≠ snd q)
└─────────────────────────────────────────────────────────────
```

Now some of the operations we wish to perform on our *ASIDE* schema are as follows: a user may, at any time, set up an aside with another user, if the initiating user does not have an aside with someone else or the recipient of the requested aside is not the "hearer" in another aside. That is:

```
┌─ ASIDE1 ────────────────────────────────────────────────────
│ u?, p? : P
│ ΔASIDE
├─────────────────────────────────────────────────────────────
│ u? ∈ users
│ p? ∈ users
│ u? ∉ (fst * asides)
│ p? ∉ (snd * asides)
│ asides' = asides ∪ {(u?, p?)}
└─────────────────────────────────────────────────────────────
```

Or there may be a request for a two-way aside. The preconditions for this are even stronger (that neither user is involved in any asides):

```
┌─ ASIDE2 ────────────────────────────────────────────────────
│ u?, p? : P
│ ΔASIDE
├─────────────────────────────────────────────────────────────
│ u? ∈ users
│ p? ∈ users
│ u? ∉ (fst * asides)
│ p? ∉ (fst * asides)
│ u? ∉ (snd * asides)
│ p? ∉ (snd * asides)
│ asides' = asides ∪ {(u?, p?)} ∪ {(p?, u?)}
└─────────────────────────────────────────────────────────────
```

Similarly the operations of removing an aside are straightforward. Here is the operation of removing a unidirectional aside (which was originally set up by the same user):

```
┌─ REMOVE – ASIDE1 ───────────────────────────────────────────
│ u?, p? : P
│ ΔASIDE
├─────────────────────────────────────────────────────────────
│ u? ∈ users
│ p? ∈ users
│ {(u?, p?)} ∈ asides
│ asides' = asides – {(u?, p?)}
└─────────────────────────────────────────────────────────────
```

And, of course, we could similarly get rid of a two-way aside.

If we extend the analogy of the aside in a conference, then a user may wish to remove an aside channel that they didn't initiate, by moving somewhere else or by telling the person initiating the aside to shut up, as in a real conference. So we define a *REMOVE – UNWANTED – ASIDE* operator. The only difference here is that the aside (*p?, u?*) is removed rather than (*u?, p?*):

```
┌─ REMOVE – UNWANTED – ASIDE1 ─────────────────────
│ u?, p? : P
│ ΔASIDE
├──────────────────────────────────────────────────
│ u? ∈ users
│ p? ∈ users
│ {(p?, u?)} ∈ asides
│ asides' = asides – {(p?, u?)}
└──────────────────────────────────────────────────
```

When someone leaves the conferencing system then any asides they are involved in must be removed:

```
┌─ LEAVE – A ───────────────────────────────────────
│ u? : P
│ ΔASIDE
├──────────────────────────────────────────────────
│ u? ∈ users
│ asides' = asides – {p : P | (u?, p) ∈ asides • (u?, p)} – {p : P | (p?, u)
│     ∈ asides • (p?, u)}
│ users' = users – { u?}
└──────────────────────────────────────────────────
```

5.10.21 The *QUEUE* schema

This consists of an ordered sequence of ranked "bids" for desired floors. The bids are ordered, or ranked, by a weighting function *W*, which scores each bid. First, let us describe a bid:

```
┌─ BID ─────────────────────────────────────────────
│ FLOOR
│ requester : P
│ id : N
│ time – of – request : Time
│ s : SPEECH – ACT
├──────────────────────────────────────────────────
│ request ∈ FLOOR users
└──────────────────────────────────────────────────
```

A bid can only be made if the *users* part of the *FLOOR* schema contains the requester.

So now, we can give our schema for *QUEUE – BIDS*:

```
┌─ QUEUE - BIDS ─────────────────────────────────
│ W : Bid → N
│ queue : seq[Bid]
│ users : P
├─────────────────────────────────────────────
│ ∀ p, q : Bid | ⟨|p, q|⟩ in queue • W p ≥ W q
└─────────────────────────────────────────────
```

Then we say that change of state of the *QUEUE - BIDS* schema does not affect the weighting function:

```
┌─ ΔQUEUE - BIDS ────────────────────────────────
│ QUEUE - BIDS
│ QUEUE - BIDS'
├─────────────────────────────────────────────
│ W' = W
└─────────────────────────────────────────────
```

Default values of the bid would be that the *FLOOR.users* became equal to the current variable *users*, and that *FLOOR* is given the value *SPEAKERFLOOR* with the requester as the sole speaker and the type of speech act as assertion.

Now there are two operations that affect this schema independently of the other schemas mentioned. First, requesting a bid:

```
┌─ NEW - BID ────────────────────────────────────
│ b? : Bid
│ ΔQUEUE - BIDS
├─────────────────────────────────────────────
│ ran queue' = ran queue ∪ { b?}
└─────────────────────────────────────────────
```

Secondly, removing a bid; of course, a precondition for this will be that the bid was actually made by the person removing the bid:

```
┌─ REMOVE - BID──────────────────────────────────
│ u? : P
│ id : N
│ ΔQUEUE - BIDS
├─────────────────────────────────────────────
│ ran queue' = ran queue - {b}
└─────────────────────────────────────────────
```

Then for completion (we shall use this operation later), the operation of removing all one's own bids from the current queue of bids:

```
┌─ REMOVE - ALL - BIDS ──────────────────────────
│ u? : P
│ ΔQUEUE - BIDS
├─────────────────────────────────────────────
│ ran queue' = ran queue - {b : Bid | b ∈ ran queue ∧ b.requestor = u? • b}
└─────────────────────────────────────────────
```

5.10.22 The ALLOWED schema

This just gives the set of allowed floors:

```
__ ALLOWED _____
  allowed : P P (P × P)

```

Alternatively we might want to define "allowed" as being a function from the current users to the set of allowed floors:

```
__ ALLOWED _____
  allowed : P P → P P(P ´ P)
  _____
  ∀u : P P , p : P(P × P)
  p ∈ (allowed u) → p ⊆ (u × u)

```

It is not important at this stage, but we assume that it is defined as in the former case.

5.10.23 Promoting (or applying) all the operations to act on the CONFERENCE schema

Let us complete our conference schema, by adding all the operations to the schema (this is really just an example of modularization and locality):

```
__ CONFERENCE _____
  FLOOR
  ASIDES
  QUEUE – BIDS
  ALLOWED
  _____
  asides ∩ floor = ∅
  floor ∈ allowed
  ∀ f : Bid | f ∈ ran queue • f floor ∈ allowed

```

(Note that asides are independent of floors. The predicate *asides ∩ floor* = ∅ states that no channel can be an aside as well as part of the current floor. This also says that we need only one two-way channel between each pair of users. It allows us as well to know easily which channels of the system are open at any time by considering the value of *asides ∪ floor*.)

So we now we write down our operations, and because of our modularity, a lot of this promotion is trivial. For example, the operation of asking to be able to hear another speaker in the current floor is just written:

```
┌─ CONF – REQUEST – LISTEN – SPEAKER ─────────────────────
│ Request – Listen – Speaker
│ ≡ ASIDES
│ ≡ QUEUE – BIDS
│ ≡ ALLOWED
├──────────────────────────────────────────────────────────
│ floor ∪ {(p?, u?)} ∈ allowed
└──────────────────────────────────────────────────────────
```

We can do this precisely because this operation doesn't affect any other part of the conference system.

Here is another example. Consider what happens when a new aside is requested – does this affect any of the other schemas? No, of course not. All we must do is make sure that the requested aside is not an existing channel in the current floor (since we must have that the intersection of *asides* and *floor* is empty). Thus:

```
┌─ CONF – ASIDE1 ──────────────────────────────────────────
│ ≡ FLOOR
│ ASIDE1
│ ≡ QUEUE – BIDS
│ ≡ ALLOWED
├──────────────────────────────────────────────────────────
│ (u?, p?) ∉ floor
└──────────────────────────────────────────────────────────
```

Here is just one more example; making a bid merely changes the state of the *QUEUE – BIDS* schema, so promoting the operator to act on the whole conference is again trivial:

```
┌─ CONF – NEW – BID ───────────────────────────────────────
│ ≡ FLOOR
│ ≡ ASIDE
│ NEW – BID
│ ≡ ALLOWED
└──────────────────────────────────────────────────────────
```

Many operators will promote just as easily.

Now, though, we must describe the operations that affect more than just one part of the conferencing system. For example, let us start with what happens when the lifetime of a floor comes to an end. Remember how this happens? Well, a speaker stops talking and if they are the last speaker of that floor then the current floor will be replaced by the floor requested by the highest-ranked bid. We do not in any way, though, wish this change of floor to interrupt existing asides – why should it? Here goes: we use the *FINISHED2* schema defined before. Note that an aside is overwritten when the channel is part of the new floor. (This is to maintain the truth of the predicate *asides* ∩ *floor* = ∅.)

___ *CONF – NEWFLOOR* _____

FINISHED2
$\Delta ASIDES$
$\Delta QUEUE – BIDS$
$\equiv ALLOWED$

—————————————————————————————

#queue > 0
queue' = (tl queue)
floor' = (hd queue) • floor
asides' = asides – (hd queue).floor
users' = (hd queue).users

_____

This only really leaves us to clear up what happens when a user joins or leaves the conferencing system. First, let us describe what happens when they join. We suggest at this time that a new user not only becomes an audience for all the maximal speakers of the present floor, but also for all the maximal speakers in all the floors of the requested bids:

___ *CONF – ADD – USER* _____

ADDUSER
$\Delta ASIDES$
$\Delta QUEUE – BIDS$
$\equiv ALLOWED$

—————————————————————————————

$\forall\, n : 1..\#\, queue \bullet (\{n\} \lhd queue').users \cup \{u?\}$

$\forall\, n : 1..\#\, queue \bullet (\{n\} \lhd queue').floor$
$\qquad\qquad \cup \{q : P. \mid q\; maximal\, (\{n\} \lhd queue).\, floor \bullet (q, u?)\}$
asides' = asides

_____

If a user wishes to leave a conference then they should first remove all the bids they have made that are currently in the queue of requested bids. This operation was described earlier (*REMOVE – ALL – BIDS*), and is easily promoted:

___ *CONF – REMOVE – ALL – BIDS* _____

$\equiv FLOOR$
$\equiv ASIDE$
REMOVE – ALL – BIDS
$\equiv ALLOWED$

_____

Once this has succeeded and the user has no bids in the queue, they may leave the system. In other words a precondition of leaving the conference is that no bids are currently in the queue that have been made by the person wishing to leave the conference:

$$
\begin{array}{|l}
\hline \underline{\text{CONF} - \text{LEAVE}} \\
\textit{LEAVE} - F \\
\textit{LEAVE} - A \\
\Delta \textit{QUEUE} - \textit{BIDS} \\
\equiv \textit{ALLOWED} \\
\hline
\sim \exists\, b : \textit{Bid} \mid b \in \text{ran } \textit{queue} \bullet b.\textit{requestor} = u? \\
\forall n : 1..\# \textit{queue} \bullet (\{n\} < \textit{queue}').\textit{users} = (\{n\} \lhd \textit{queue}).\textit{users} - \{u?\} \\
\forall n : 1..\# \textit{queue} \bullet (\{n\} < \textit{queue}').\textit{floor} = (\{n\} \lhd \textit{queue}).\textit{floor} \\
\qquad\qquad\qquad -\{x, y : P \mid (x = u? \lor y = u? \bullet (x, y)\} \\
\hline
\end{array}
$$

5.10.24 More useful operations

Someone may want to join a conference and simultaneously make a bid, but not require to hear any of the conference, until the floor of that bid manifests itself:

$$
\begin{array}{|l}
\hline \underline{\text{WAIT} - \text{TILL} - \text{TURN}} \\
u? : P \\
b? : \textit{Bid} \\
\Delta \textit{FLOOR} \\
\Delta \textit{ASIDES} \\
\Delta \textit{QUEUE} - \textit{BIDS} \\
\equiv \textit{ALLOWED} \\
\hline
u? \notin \textit{users} \\
\textit{asides}' = \textit{asides} \\
\textit{floor}' = \textit{floor} \\
\textit{users}' = \textit{users} \\
\text{ran } \textit{queue}' = \text{ran } \textit{queue} \cup \{b?\} \\
\hline
\end{array}
$$

It should be noted that unsuccessful operations have not been specified (i.e. we have not considered error handling) for reasons of brevity.

5.10.25 Pictures of floors

We can picture each floor in one of two ways:

- Two columns of users, with lines joining each on the left to each on the right of that for which the channel has the *valve* open (Fig. 5.3). An open floor has all lines (except horizontal ones) filled in.[11]
- A 2D matrix, with all users listed along the top, and down the left. An entry is then coloured differently for an open or closed valve.

As shown in Figure 5.4, an open floor has all entries except the diagonal filled in.

---

11. In our model of a conference, horizontal lines don't exist.

	P_1	P_2	P_3	$\cdots$	P_n
P_1	–	–	–	$\cdots$	x
P_2	–	–	–	$\cdots$	–
P_3	–	–	–	$\cdots$	–
$\cdots$	–	–	–	$\cdots$	–
P_n	x	–	–	$\cdots$	–

This example has only p_1 talking to p_n

Figure 5.3 Floor control.

	P_1	P_2	P_3	P_4
P_1	–	x	x	x
P_2	x	–	x	x
P_3	x	x	–	x
P_4	x	x	x	–

This example is an open floor

Figure 5.4 Floor control.

5.10.26 Negotiations

We have not discussed the ordering function that is used to decide how bids to change the floor are queued. To do this, we need to introduce the idea of *negotiation*.

A negotiation would make use of an open-floor conference to decide what the ordering function should be. A negotiation is a sequence of bids exchanged between the users concerning the ordering function. These bids are made using particular speech acts. All negotiations converge by increasing the strength of statements about the desired algorithm, by increasing priority of speech acts made by *ps* in requesting it – i.e. bound the time to reach agreement (or else leave the conference in disgust), by only negotiating in one direction (e.g. for a more restricted ordering function). Other mechanisms might be feasible, but harder for the user to comprehend. We argue that our model is reasonably "natural".

5.10.27 Offline components of a conference

Many references to conferencing facilities refer to bulletin boards or centralized mail systems, where the conversations are *asynchronous* or offline.

Even though our system is intended to be real-time (*synchronous*), we do not want to exclude the possibility of interworking with offline facilities. One possibility is that of providing proceedings automatically for the conference. Since our implementation is text-only, we can consider logging all input, and tagging it with the user, the current floor, and any speech act used. This log can be made available to new conference members. Simple heuristics might be used to replay part or all of the past to a new user, showing the structure of the conference so far. This can be based on the observation that people who speak often and loudly generally end up controlling the floor (or being evicted). Thus we can identify the threads of control through the conference by looking at the priorities of speech acts used by frequent speakers.

In general, the system should allow for the introduction of old documents at the beginning or during the conference, and the production of new documents during or after. We have not implemented any more than the bland input of text by a given speaker to all of the current floor. Obviously, multiple read/write access to offline documents would be desirable, but that is a large research area in itself. However, interaction with the simple structure of messages should be reasonably simple to add on. Much more experience is required in this area before we can commit ourselves to a particular design.

5.10.28 The implementation

A pilot implementation of a text-only system was undertaken using X-Windows version 11 release 3, and MIT's Athena project's Widgets, on a set of Unix workstations (from various different vendors: one advantage of the choice of X is its machine-independence). The star (shared-memory) model was used; a single process runs the conference with X protocol connections to each display. An example of the actual user interface is shown in Figure 5.5.

Some simplifications were found to be necessary after experience with several users:

- *rate* – changing the layout as the speaker changes is unsatisfactory
- *complexity* – there is too much clutter for expressing illocutionary acts
- *quality* – a 19 inch monitor isn't big enough!

The current implementation includes the *valve* to allow floor control, but none of the rich floor-control mechanisms have yet been implemented. These will be added. Reports from users are that floor control is definitely required when more than two users are present. The main reason given is simply to limit the amount of text appearing at once.[12]

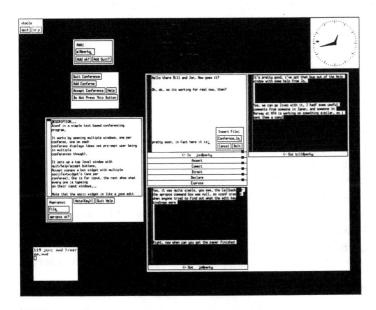

Figure 5.5   A text-based X conferencing system.

---

12. The program was posted on the bulletin board "comp.sources.x" and users as far afield as Finland, Crete and Japan have commented.

5.10.29 Conclusions

The separation of the distributed operation of the exchange of "speech" in the conference from the floor-control mechanism has led to the possibility of implementing an "open-floor" conferencing system, and then adding floor control.

The only operations necessary to add floor control are those required to allow or prevent use of a channel from each user to any other. The extra state incurred in the conference server processes is the 2D matrix of user-by-user channels, with each entry showing allowed/disallowed.

```
const BUFFSIZE 4096

type struct xwin {
  Widget   w;
  Arg      warg[8];
  int      nwarg;
  char     buff[BUFFSIZE];
  XtTextSource  source;
  int      x_nlines;
  int      x_ncols;
  int      x_line;
  int      x_col;
  char     cerase;
  char     werase;
           enum ValveState{Open, Closed} -- can we speak or not
} xwin_t;

const MAXCONF 8
type struct xconf {
  Display  *dpy;
  Widget   toplevel, tbox, ab, qb, pop, box;
  Widget   hb, hpop, hbox, htxt, hq;
  Widget   lab[MAXCONF];
  int      live;
  char     user[128]
  char     display[128]
  char     *disparg[3];
  xwin_t   me;
xwin_t       them[MAXCONF];
} xconf_t;

xconf_t Conference[MAXCONF];
int numberofthem;
}
```

Figure 5.6 State of the floor.

In the future, we hope to implement the floor control mechanisms described and integrate them with the open-floor conferencing system we have. We will then be able to experiment with floor control.

5.10.30 Conference state
The state required in each conference program is predominantly maintained by the X Server process. The structures in Figure 5.6 show what other information is required for each conference.

5.11 Summary
In this chapter, we have looked at several different formal specification techniques, and tried to see how they might be applied to distributed systems. It is early days for the large-scale use of such systems, but methodologies and languages such as Z hold out a strong promise, especially when coupled with object-oriented program design methodologies.

5.12 Exercises
1. Specify a set of printers using Z, showing some properties that are safe.
2. Specify a print spooler in LOTOS, CSP or CCS and show that it doesn't deadlock, and is always printing one job.

CHAPTER 6

Communications support

with Graham Knight, University College London

6.1 Introduction

We have dealt, so far, with distributed systems in terms of the semantics of the operations they support, the problems of synchronization, consistency and so forth. All interactions within a distributed system involve the transfer of messages. Such transfers require there to be some underlying communications system. In this chapter we look at this communications system and the way in which it can be designed in order to support "open" distributed systems. "Open" distributed systems require "open" communications which, in turn, implies an agreement on the part of the participants on a set of communication "standards" to which all will adhere. It is desirable that such standards have some degree of consistency and coherence and fit into a reasonable, concise abstract model. Standards defined in this way are often dignified with the name communications "architecture".

There are many more-or-less "open" communications architectures: for example, IBM's Systems Network Architecture, DEC's Digital Network Architecture, and the set of standards associated with the US ARPA (Advanced Research Project Agency) network. However, the key architecture for a book on open distributed systems is that developed by the ISO for Open Systems Interconnection (OSI). OSI standards are important not only because they were developed specifically to support open communications involving equipment from different manufacturers, but also because they introduce a vocabulary and an abstract "reference model" of a communications system which is widely applicable. It is not the purpose of this book to give a complete development of the OSI standards: there are many other books that do this well. Our purpose here is twofold: first, to establish the modelling concepts inherent in the OSI architecture, and, secondly, to consider the suitability of the OSI work for the support of distributed systems. In practice, most distributed systems use the Internet protocols. However, our model is similar enough, and, dare one say, less well expressed, if better coded.

As mentioned before, the distributed systems programmer inevitably sees more of the underlying system than the traditional applications programmer on a centralized system. We believe that a firm grasp of the underlying communications technology is essential.

6.2 Technological point of view

6.2.1 The wire

The wire is in reality a wide range of services, ranging from a modem with an acoustic coupler, attached to a conventional telephone, right through to a high speed digital packet-switched network (e.g. SuperJANET). The range of wide area (national and international) networks extends a long way, as we can see in Table 6.1.

Table 6.1 Network ranges.

Phone	Trunks	Packet-switched
600 million	10,000s	100s
Modems/PCs	Modem/muxes	DTEs/gateways
French home use	Banks, etc.	Research

6.2.2 Switching methodologies

In switched digital networks the switching nodes can operate in three different ways:

- *Circuit switching*
  The switches on a route establish a physical circuit between two hosts for the duration of the communication session. This is how the telephone system operates.
- *Message switching*
  The sending host parcels up data into long messages which are transferred step by step over each link between the switches and delivered to the recipient.
- *Packet switching*
  This is like message switching, but the parcels are short, so that the switching nodes can store numbers of them in memory.

Packet switching is favoured for computer communication for the following reasons:

- It makes good use of the links. Between bursts of data between one pair of hosts, other hosts may use the same links and switches.
- Delays through storing short packets in switches are short compared with storing long messages.
- Switches need less memory/buffer space to hold packets for forwarding than for messages.
- Hardware to implement packet switches is now relatively cheap.
- Switches and links may break during a communication session, but alternative routes be found.
- Packet-switched networks have been in use for over 15 years. Early examples are the now decommissioned US ARPANET and the UK National Physical Laboratory Network.

- The PTTs provide international packet-switched networks.
- National networks now exist with millions of attached computers.

For a packet to get from one host to another through a series of switches, each switch on the route needs to know where the packet is going. The range of network characteristics is wide. For WAN (wide-area networks) characteristics are:

- Data rates are from 300 bps up to hundreds of Mbps.
- Error rates are of the order 1 in 10^5.
- Delays range from 100 ms to seconds.
- Bit serial interfaces are used.

For LAN (local-area networks):

- Data rates are from 10 kbps to 140 Mbps.
- Error rates are of the order 1 in 10^9.
- Delays are of the order of milliseconds.
- Frame or byte-level interfaces are used.

6.2.3 Transmission shortcomings

Packets are placed on the network. What is their fate next? Even if the network is essentially a reliable bit pipe, it is possible for it to break, independent of the end-hosts communicating. Practice shows that it is in fact far more likely to break than, for instance, the terminal interface device on a mainframe, or a disk controller. If the network is packet-switched, then things can go wrong in more subtle ways. Depending on the type of network, a variety of disasters can befall a packet:

- The network may not know how to get this packet to its correct destination.
- Most importantly, the packet can just get lost because of lack of memory or a temporary fault in some component.
- Next, a packet can be corrupted by electrical (or other) noise on a wire, or by faulty software.
- Packets can be delivered to the remote end in a different order than they were sent in.
- The same packet could be delivered many times to a destination.
- Packets could be delivered by the network to a destination host faster than the host can deal with them.

The consequences are that there must be mechanisms for hosts to indicate where they wish to communicate with – just as file systems allow us to indicate which file we want to read or write. There may be a single wire leading out of a host, which then splits in some way to go to multiple destinations. This means we need to have some kind of addressing mechanism, so that we can multiplex communication between many hosts on a network.

The user needs some level of reliability. This can vary between some statistical level – digital voice or video may only require some percentage of data per second to be delivered so that a reasonable result can be constructed by the receiver (e.g. humans only need 30% of the sound of someone's voice to be able to understand 90% of what is being said). The user may need to restrict the rate at which data arrives. Real-time applications like voice and video require fairly exact rates of arrival. Print servers may support much lower data rates than typical modern networks.

6.2.4 Intermediate devices in a network

In a packet-switched network and in store and forward networks we have special-purposes boxes, variously called:

- Bridges – these connect LANs, of possibly different media access and/or physical technology.
- Switches – these connect multiple communications links, and have a virtual or logical circuit model of what is connected to what.
- Gateways – these are devices that translate one protocol stack or layer to another.
- Router – this is an intelligent device like a switch, but maintains no state between one packet and the next except that needed to carry out the forwarding function.
- Relays – this is the ISO term for all of the devices above.

These will normally run real-time operating systems, and perform many of the same functions as general-purpose end-hosts, except for the upper levels which are not required in intermediate nodes, except in so far as they may be needed by network management applications, for example. There is often special hardware support to facilitate communications, such as:

- clever interfaces
- clever buses (e.g. binary tree buses)
- specialized use of memory management units (MMUs)

Depending on the architecture of the network, and the choice of end-host protocols, these intermediate nodes support different complexities of protocols, usually ranging from connectionless to connection-oriented.

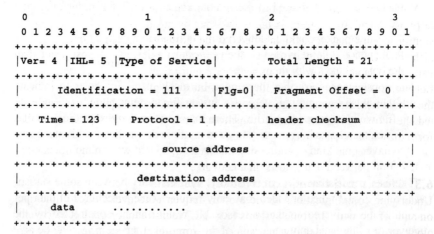

Figure 6.1 Example of an Internet Datagram.

By way of example, the DoD Internet Datagram protocol is a commonly used format for a packet, used on LANs (Ethernets) and WANs (the Internet). It is shown in Figure 6.1.

There are many common Internet protocols, of which IP, in Figure 6.1, and Novell IPX are most widely used. The key fields in the packet header are the source and destination addresses which allow the packet to be forwarded along the way (just as addresses on envelopes permit postal sorting offices to forward letters), and the protocol field which indicates what upper-layer service is being carried by the packet (i.e. what is in the data part of the packet!). The other fields are largely concerned with internal book-keeping. The order of bits and bytes must be unambiguously specified too.

The order of transmission of the header and data described in this book is resolved to the octet level. Whenever a diagram shows a group of octets, the order of transmission of those octets is the normal order in which they are read in English. For example, in Figure 6.2 the octets are transmitted in the order they are numbered.

```
 0                   1                   2                   3
 0 1 2 3 4 5 6 7 8 9 0 1 2 3 4 5 6 7 8 9 0 1 2 3 4 5 6 7 8 9 0 1
+-+-+-+-+-+-+-+-+-+-+-+-+-+-+-+-+-+-+-+-+-+-+-+-+-+-+-+-+-+-+-+-+
|       1       |       2       |       3       |       4       |
+-+-+-+-+-+-+-+-+-+-+-+-+-+-+-+-+-+-+-+-+-+-+-+-+-+-+-+-+-+-+-+-+
|       5       |       6       |       7       |       8       |
+-+-+-+-+-+-+-+-+-+-+-+-+-+-+-+-+-+-+-+-+-+-+-+-+-+-+-+-+-+-+-+-+
|       9       |      10       |      11       |      12       |
+-+-+-+-+-+-+-+-+-+-+-+-+-+-+-+-+-+-+-+-+-+-+-+-+-+-+-+-+-+-+-+-+
```

Figure 6.2 Transmission order of octets.

Whenever an octet represents a numeric quantity the leftmost bit in the diagram is the high-order or most significant bit. That is, the bit labelled 0 is the most significant bit. For example, Figure 6.3 represents the value 170 (decimal). Similarly, whenever a multi-octet field represents a numeric quantity the leftmost bit of the whole field is the most significant bit. When a multi-octet quantity is transmitted the most significant octet is transmitted first. This is the simplest possible form of presentation syntax.

```
 0 1 2 3 4 5 6 7
+-+-+-+-+-+-+-+-+
|1 0 1 0 1 0 1 0|
+-+-+-+-+-+-+-+-+
```

Figure 6.3 Significance of bits.

6.3 Clocks and time in distributed systems

Underlying communications services often deliver a bit-level clock to time data on and off the wire. In some systems (e.g. E1/Megastream or the UK electricity clock cycle) this is globally guaranteed to some level of accuracy. However, higher-level protocols usually rely on networks built out of LANs connected via routers and long-haul links. In such systems, applications may be attached to different networks. Hence although each network may have its own bit-level clock, there is no common bit-level clock available to both applications. Hence a clock is needed at a higher level available to both end points. A high-level clock synchronization mechanism is then often useful to provide coordinated time. Examples of such systems are the Network Time Protocol and the Digital Time Service, which use periodic exchanges of timestamped messages to estimate network transit delays and thus derive clock differences. A hierarchy of time servers is formed based on the measured accuracy and reliability of reports. Nowadays, enterprises will even site atomic clocks or satellite-fed Global Positioning System receiver-based clocks at a number of key places on the network to support such a service. Few distributed systems make use of this, but it could be very powerful in optimizing performance. However, having global application-level agreement on time can save application-level handshake phases in many situations.

6.4 Communications system modelling

Communications systems are extremely complex and standards can only be defined for them if the problem is decomposed into manageable portions. The starting point for this decomposition has to be a model of what a communications service does.

We can view a simple communications service as a "black box", as in Figure 6.4. In OSI terminology, outside the black box there are "service users" (usually two) and inside there is a "service provider". In this case, the service offered is very simple: user A may "request" that data be transferred and the provider may "indicate" to user B that data has arrived. This is about the simplest service that can be offered – it is roughly that offered by the letter post. As we shall see, opinions vary widely as to what is the most appropriate service for a black box to offer.

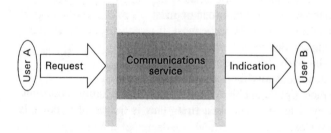

Figure 6.4   Unconfirmed service of communicating entities.

In Chapter 2 the RPC model was discussed. In that model, messages are paired so as to carry parameter values into and out of the remote procedure. Such a service could be built by adding some information to the data transferred (probably a sequence number) to allow replies to be matched correctly to the corresponding requests. We would then have built a new black box outside the original one.

The black box analysis can be taken in the other direction. Our original black box may be able to transfer messages of arbitrary length. However, real systems often impose limits on message length. If we look inside our black box, we will see another black box corresponding to such a "real" system. Our black box builds on the inner black box service (by fragmenting messages into suitably sized chunks and reassembling them on the other side) in order to provide the service we require.

This gives us the basic decomposition of a communications system. It consists of a series of nested black boxes each of which adds something to enhance the service offered by the black box it contains. The first task for the designers of communications system standards is to decompose the problem into a set of black boxes and make a broad allocation of functions to each. Next, they can make the definitions of the services offered by the black boxes precise. Essentially an object-oriented approach is followed. The designers are specifying what the objects (the black boxes) do, rather than how they do it. Languages do exist for formally specifying the interface to and the behaviour of communications services; however, most often, reliance is placed upon a sort of formalized English. We looked at more formal languages in the previous chapter.

6.5 Protocols

The object-oriented approach to system design is applicable to most large computer systems. One of its strengths is that the implementor of an object has complete freedom to choose appropriate algorithms to achieve their purpose so long as the end result is an object that conforms to specification. For communications services the situation is a little different since the objects themselves are distributed. A service A is implemented by enhancing service B. This enhancement is performed by a pair of processes, X and Y, one in each of the communicating systems. It is quite likely that X and Y will have been implemented by different people. If this is to work, then the distributed algorithm which defines the interactions between X and Y must itself be standardized. These distributed algorithms are called "protocols", and the processes that implement them at each end of a communications service are called "protocol entities", or "entities" for short.

Communications protocols may be extremely complex, specifying complicated message sequences to recover from loss or mis-sequencing of messages. Alternatively, they may be very simple, specifying little more than the format of the messages that will be exchanged. Naturally, the degree of complexity depends mainly on the amount by which the underlying service needs to be enhanced.

Drawing nested boxes to any depth strains both typography and the reader's eyesight. Instead, it is conventional to represent the boxes as in Figure 6.6 and to stack these vertically to illustrate the complete architectural model (Fig. 6.7). Figure 6.5 shows a pair of similar protocol entities (peer entities) exchanging messages with each other in order to implement the distributed algorithm. The net effect of all this is to provide the service represented by the outermost box. The

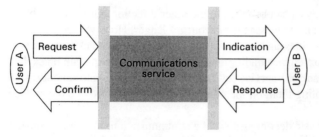

Figure 6.5 Confirmed service model of communicating entities.

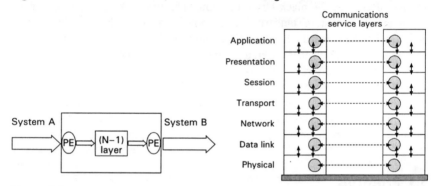

Figure 6.6

Figure 6.7 ISO OSI service and protocol layers.

messages exchanged between service users and provider are shown by the vertical arrows. The messages exchanged by the peer entities are, of course, transported through the use of some subordinate service, and thus each service provider is also a user of the service below (except for the bottom one, of course!).

It is worth introducing some OSI jargon here. The vertical arrows in Figure 6.7 represent "service primitives" – the requests and indications that the service reports. In most cases there will be some data associated with these primitives which is being passed across the service interface. An individual lump of this data is called a "service data unit" (SDU).

The horizontal arrows in Figure 6.7 represent the protocol messages that are formed by the protocol entities and exchanged with each other. These messages consist of two types of information: "protocol control information" (PCI), consisting of the sequence numbers, checksums, etc. required by the operation of the protocol; and "user data", which is the data (submitted in SDUs) that the service is supposed to be transporting. Together, the PCI and the user data constitute a "protocol data unit" (PDU).

There is obviously a relationship between SDUs and PDUs. This is not necessarily simple as there may be good reasons to split one SDU into several PDUs or to lump several PDUs into one SDU when requesting the service on the layer below.

6.6 Service types

The services described in the examples above have appealingly simple behaviours. Unfortunately, practical communications services often have rather more complex behaviours and a number of irritating questions must be asked about them. For example:

- What guarantee does the service give that the data will be delivered at all?
- What guarantee does the service give that the data will not be corrupted on the way?
- What guarantee does the service give that the data will not be delivered to the wrong address?
- Is data submitted in one lump guaranteed to be delivered in one lump?
- Is there any chance that a message will be duplicated and delivered twice?
- Does the service offer confirmation of receipt (like certificate of postage)?
- Does the service offer confirmation of delivery (as in recorded delivery)?
- Will successive data requests be delivered in the order they are submitted?
- How long will delivery take?
- Are there constraints on the size of messages?

All these (and other) questions must be answered before the service definition can be considered complete. The answers define the quality of service (QoS) being offered. Often, the purpose of enhancing a primitive service is to remove some of this complexity so that the top-level service provides a nice clean, simple and easily understood service that the distributed system designer can use to transport their messages. This is related to the approach of "selective transparency" discussed in Chapter 1, used in distributed applications design. There are two main views about what this nice, clean, simple and easily understood service should look like.

In Europe, public data communications services have been developed by the PTTs (post, telephone and telegraph authorities). It has been natural for them to think of data communications as being analogous to the telephone system and so the communications service they offer has a strong resemblance to the telephone service. Their service changes state in the course of the communication. Initially it is in an idle state in which only "connection requests" are allowed (the telephone is on the hook and all you can do is lift it up and dial). Once a connection has been established we enter the connected state. Here you can request "data transfers" (speak) or "disconnects" (put the phone down). Quite reasonably, this type of service is called "connection-oriented" (CO).

The key feature of a CO service is the existence of shared state information between the two ends of the communication when they are in the connected state. At the minimum this information tells us that two identified users (A and B say) are bound to a particular connection (C say). A then knows that any data it sends on C will be delivered at B (ignoring errors and other difficulties for the moment), and vice versa. In practice, the CO service offered by the PTTs involves the two users in rather more shared knowledge and offers amongst other things:

- guarantees that data will be delivered in sequence and un-corrupted
- the ability of either end to control the rate at which data is sent by the other ("flow-control")

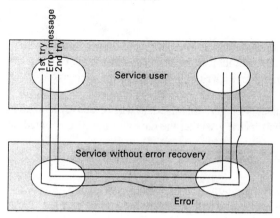

Figure 6.8 Error recovery provided by the service user.

- confirmation of delivery

This sort of service is supposed to resemble that which would be provided by a highly reliable dedicated physical circuit. Consequently, it is called a "virtual circuit" (VC) service (see Fig. 6.9).

In contrast, the simpler service of Figure 6.8 is called "connectionless" (CL). Here there is a single state and only one type of request – "data transfer". CL services have been supported by two main groups: the purveyors of local-area networks and disciples of the Internet community. We shall return to the CL vs CO argument later.

6.7 Relationships between services

The stack of services depicted in Figure 6.7 gives rise to the term "layered architecture". The positions of the various services in the stack define the possible relationships between them. For example, a protocol entity in layer 4 is a user of the layer 3 service and a provider of a service to layer 5. It would be illegal for a layer 4 protocol entity to try to use the service of layer 5. The OSI model imposes this layering principle in a very rigid way:

- All the layers must be present; a layer (N) entity must use the layer (N–1) service and cannot miss it out and go straight to layer (N–2)
- The model prescribes exactly what an (N) layer service should do. (Originally there was just one service in each layer, now there are two, one CO and one CL.) It is not possible to define a new variant of an OSI (N) layer service without stepping outside the OSI model

Many experts consider that this rigidity unnecessarily constrains distributed system design. The DARPA architecture is much more flexible. In this, although the basic hierarchical relationships between layers or modules remain, the additional constraints identified above for the OSI model are not applied. Thus it is possible to have several alternative services at the same level in the hierarchy. As long as the ordering is preserved, it is permissible to omit an intermediate service

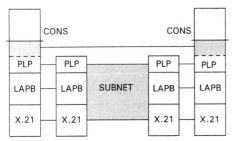

Figure 6.9 Interworking using a connection-oriented service model at the network layer.

Figure 6.10 Network service access points (internal addresses) and routeing.

and map directly into one below. This flexibility makes it especially easy to introduce new types of service and new technologies.

This flexibility provides justification for calling the DARPA architecture a "hierarchical", one rather than a "layered" one. One of the problems facing the designers of distributed systems based on the OSI model is the fact that they are stuck with a set of services and protocols that cannot be altered in any way. Since these were originally designed with the needs of particular applications in mind they are unlikely to be ideal for new application types.

6.8 The ISO reference model

It is appropriate now to look at the ISO OSI Reference Model (OSI RM), both because it is important in itself and because it establishes a vocabulary that we will use in the rest of the chapter.

The ISO OSI Reference Model and the standards that are associated with it were drawn up in order to define a series of conventions by which computers of different types and from different manufacturers could communicate with each other. Manufacturers – especially small ones – are generally favourably disposed to such standards as they enable the creation of an "open" market for their products, which would otherwise be dominated by proprietary standards over which they have no control.

As noted before, the concept of "layering" is used to decompose the problem.

6.8.1 Terminology and conventions

The ISO has developed its own set of jargon to describe the concepts in the model and in the related standards. We have already surreptitiously introduced some of this "OSI-speak" and it is used extensively in what follows. Some of the important terms are summarized below.

Table 6.2 Transport service primitives.

Service	Request	Indication	Response	Confirm
T.CONNECT	*	*	*	*
T.DATA	*	*		
T.EXPEDITED_DATA	*	*		
T.DISCONNECT	*	*		

A service definition is a document defining a particular layer service. Usually it defines a set of several services provided by a layer. Each service is described in terms of four service primitives:

- request – the user of a service asks it to carry out an action
- indication – a service informs a user of some event
- response – a service indicates to a user that an answer has been forthcoming
- confirm – a service indicates to a user that a request has been carried out

An operation is begun when the local service user generates a request primitive across the local service interface. This should result in the generation of a corresponding indication primitive across the remote service interface. In some cases a reply will be required from the remote service user. This is triggered by the generation of a response primitive across the remote service interface which should eventually result in the generation of a confirm primitive across the local service interface. By way of example, Table 6.2 shows the set of primitives that are defined for the OSI Connection Oriented Transport Service (layer 4).

In general, the primitives mentioned above have parameters associated with them. For example, a TCONNECT request will include the address of the remote host while a TDATA request will include data for transfer across the network. Primitive requests cannot be issued in a completely arbitrary way and there are usually rules governing which primitives may follow which and which are legal when the system is in some particular state. In the transport service example above, a TDATA req cannot be issued in advance of a TCONNECTconf. OSI service definitions include a state table specifying these temporal orderings.

6.8.2 The seven layers

The seven layers of the OSI model may be divided into two groups (Fig. 6.7). The upper three layers are concerned with applications – the synchronization of activity within a set of distributed applications, the representation of data, the management of associations, concurrency, etc. These are called the "upper" or "application-oriented" layers.

The lower four layers are concerned with the technology in use – error and flow control, routeing, etc. These are the "transport-oriented" layers. Note that the transport service interface forms the boundary between these two groups. The idea is that the application-oriented layers should not have to worry about the vagaries of the technological differences in the lower layers – the transport layer should mask all these. Thus the functionality provided by the transport layer has a great significance in determining the nature of the communications service available to the applications.

Generally speaking, the boundaries between the lower three layers reflect boundaries that already existed when the OSI effort began. The upper layers are more interesting as they attempt to separate out common functionality required by applications which had not previously been the subject of standardization. This should be a "good thing" as it should prevent new applications from re-inventing the wheel. It is these upper layers that are of most interest from the point of view of distributed system designers. Notice that you can separate out two aspects of a protocol layer:

- Signalling
- data

In the telecom world, this separation is made obvious, since almost all signalling is done at the beginning and end of a communications session. In the data communications world, it is less obvious, since signalling-type activities may be required almost every time some data is sent or received.

In summary, the functions of the layers are:

- 7) *Application Layer*
  This defines services for specific applications, file transfer and electronic mail, for example. Both the syntax of the service elements to be exchanged between application entities, and the actions they should perform are defined. Often, service elements from different applications will have broadly similar semantics: for example, all OSI applications have initialization and termination phases.

- 6) *Presentation layer*
  Before communication can take place between application entities, there must be agreement both on the "abstract" syntax of the messages that may be exchanged and the way in which this abstract syntax should be represented as a sequence of bits. This latter form is called a "concrete" or "transfer" syntax. The presentation layer handles the negotiation of abstract and transfer syntaxes and translates between native data representations and the transfer syntax.

- 5) *Session layer*
  The session layer manages the duplex communication channel provided by the layers below. It provides service elements for initializing the channel, for synchronizing the two ends, for determining which end has the right to transmit next, and for resynchronizing in the event of errors.

- 4) *Transport layer*
  The transport layer provides an "end-to-end" network-independent communication service with known reliability and performance characteristics. It is up to the transport layer to provide this service irrespective of the service provided by the layer below. A range of transport protocols of increasing complexity has been defined in order to cope with the different qualities of service (QoS) that might be provided by the layers below.

- 3) *Network layer*
  The network layer takes account of the fact that communication takes place across real networks such as Ethernets and public X.25 networks. Each of

these (called "real subnetworks" by ISO) is likely to provide a slightly different "subnetwork service". The network layer builds on these to provide a common OSI Network Service, though great differences in the QoS may remain.

Computers are attached to subnetworks and are identified by their points of attachment to subnetworks. An important function of the network layer is the provision of addresses for computers that are global throughout the OSI world. Communication often takes place across a series of interconnected subnetworks. The routeing of traffic between subnetworks is also a network layer responsibility.

- 2) *Datalink layer*
  This provides framing, error and flow control on a single physical link – for example, a piece of wire. This definition is appropriate mainly to mesh-style WANs which consist of a collection of packet switches connected together by links.
- 1) *Physical layer*
  This provides mechanical and electrical interface definitions.

6.8.3 The LAN lower layers
In the LAN model, the lowest two ISO layers are replaced by three layers:
1. The logical link control (LLC) layer
   This allows several "logical" links to exist on the shared medium and indeed several to exist between a pair of attached systems. Three classes of LLC are provided:
(a) unacknowledged connectionless service
(b) connection-oriented service
(c) acknowledged connectionless service
   The service provided by a CO logical links is the same as that provided by the OSI datalink layer which assures compatibility between the LAN and WAN worlds at the datalink service interface.
2. The medium access control (MAC) layer
   This defines the procedure to be used for sharing the medium: for example, CSMA-CD as used in the Ethernet.
3. The physical layer

6.8.4 Historical perspective
When ISO came to define the services to be offered by their layers, they were heavily influenced by the existing "X.25" service developed by the PTTs and consequently defined virtual circuit-type services. (Unfortunately ISO treat "connection oriented" as synonymous with "virtual circuit-oriented" ignoring the additional reliability and flow control features that the latter implies.) Thus the original OSI model was CO from top to bottom.

The first addendum to the OSI Reference Model introduced CL working. Gradually CL layer standards have been developed and these now exist for the datalink and network layers. CL transport layer standards are under development. These developments are important for open distributed systems since a large part of the non-OSI work that has been carried out on distributed systems has assumed an underlying CL service. The Internet is the largest network in the world, and is CL, and was built in some senses independently of OSI.

6.9 Naming, addressing and routeing

The OSI addressing scheme is intended to support global communications. In principle, every process in the world can be identified by an address that is guaranteed unique. Unfortunately, possessing the address of the process you want to contact is not much use unless it is possible to discover a route to it, and here OSI is somewhat less helpful.

Consider a print spooler and a client resident on two systems. These are both "application processes" and contain within themselves the "application entities" (AEs), which are the parts that are involved in OSI communication. As far as OSI is concerned, the objective is to put AEs in touch with each other. AEs have names; the OSI word for these is "titles". Hence "application entity titles" or AETs. Usually AETs are chosen to be meaningful to people, so we will call ours "printspooler" and "printclient". Note that there could be several instances of the print spooler active simultaneously; all of these would have the same AET. Thus an AET identifies a process type rather than a process instance.

The first step for the client is to map the AET to an "address" which will identify where the AE can be found. In the OSI model, addresses are attached to Service Access Points (SAPs). One way of thinking about the distinction between SAPs and addresses is to think of the difference between a telephone socket and the phone number associated with that socket. An (N)-SAP is the place where an (N + 1)-Entity accesses an (N)-Service. The N refers to the layer we are considering, so that a P-SAP refers to the presentation-layer service access point. This is analogous to the addressing scheme used in the telephone system where the address (telephone number) is associated with the point at which one accesses the service (the plug on the wall) rather than with the entity doing the accessing (the telephone hand-set). This means that an AE will be identified by the address of the P-SAP to which it is attached. So the mapping we require is:

```
Application Entity Title -> P-SAP Address
```

As far as OSI is concerned this mapping implies a look-up operation in some table known as a "directory". No particular way of implementing a directory is implied, in particular, the use of the ISO/CCITT standard directory service is not assumed. In the case of RPC-type systems, servers may move between systems fairly frequently and the provision of some form of readily available service to locate application services is of paramount importance. This is one of the functions of an RPC binder.

Starting from the P-SAP address, we need two pieces of information:
- something that will identify the host on which the print spooler can be found
- something that will identify the print spooler process on that system

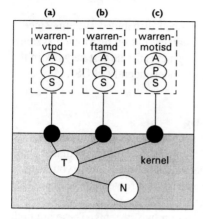

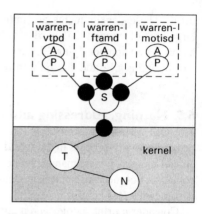

Figure 6.10 Multiple process and multiple SAPs.

Figure 6.11 Multiplexing at the SAP.

The first of these is a Network Service Access Point (N-SAP) address which identifies the point at which the host accesses the network. Fortunately, it is easy to extract the N-SAP address from the P-SAP address since the latter is defined as:

```
P-SAP Address := P-SEL + S-SEL + T-SEL + N-SAP Address
```

Here, the "selectors" (SEL) are locally meaningful values that identify entities (and ultimately the application process) on the remote host.

Let us suppose we are using the OSI CO stack. The first step then is to try to establish a presentation connection so we issue a P-Connect-Request with the P-SAP address as a parameter. The presentation entity needs first to establish a session connection, so it strips the P-SEL (thus generating an S-SAP address) and issues an S-Connect-Request to the session layer. This process continues down through the layers. Now, let us return to the example. Suppose the P-SAP address is as in Table 6.3.

The fact that two of the selectors are NULL reflects the fact that only one level of demultiplexing is required. Here is what happens:

1. An N-Connection is established between the client and server transport entities. How this is done may be very complex, involving finding routes across several interconnected subnetworks. We will ignore the details for now.
2. The client transport entity uses the network connection to carry a T-Connect PDU which includes the T-SEL "prspl".
3. At this point, we must consider the process structure of the server system. Let us assume that the network entity is in the operating system kernel and that the transport entity is represented by a user process that fields all incoming T-Connect PDUs. T-ent-proc examines the T-SEL and maps this (probably via a local table) to a file containing the executable binary for the print spooler. The print spooler is now invoked and handles all subsequent packets.

We can now see why only a T-SEL was needed. This is a result of the particular

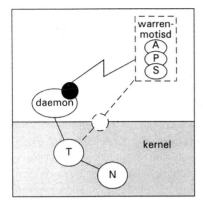

Table 6.3 Presentation service access point.

P-SEL	S-SEL	T-SEL	N-SAP address
NULL	NULL	"prspl"	abcd123456

Figure 6.12   Dynamic process/server model.

process structure on the service system. Other structures would use different selectors, possible all three.

T-ent-proc is an example of a "generic server". This sits on a system and fields all incoming calls and then invokes the specific server required. An alternative model – and one probably more appropriate in our case – would have the print spooler invoked at boot time "listening" for incoming requests directed at its T-SAP. To an extent, the generic server model is the one favoured by OSI because there are no explicit "listen" primitives. However, it is quite possible to employ either model in an OSI system.

6.10 Connection-oriented or connectionless?

The arguments about the superiority or otherwise of connectionless and connection-oriented services have raged loud and long. The whole issue is confused by the fact that the adoption of a CL service in one layer does not preclude the adoption of a CO service in the layer above – all that is needed is a protocol sophisticated enough to provide the enhancement. The best example of this is transmission control protocol (TCP), which is CO and enhances the CL internet protocol (IP) layer. Equally, it is possible for a protocol to mask the presence of connections in the layers below and to present a CL service to the layers above. Given that this flexibility exists, the CO vs CL argument is really concerned with what is most efficient and convenient for a particular application.

Let us look first at the main characteristic of a CO service – the long-term association it maintains between its two users. Figures 6.11–6.13 show a server with multiple clients. It is often desirable that the server should operate as a "stateless" server.[1] This means that there should be no long-term associations between the

---

1. We need to distinguish between application-level and protocol-level state. It is usually desirable to minimize the statefulness of the protocol. It is often desirable to be able to change the state of the server in response to interaction with clients.

server and the clients. Any such associations would be difficult to manage as the server has no idea how many there will be in advance, and the amount of state information required in each case might eat up precious memory. Interactions between the server and its clients, then, are inherently CL and require a CL communications service. If all that is available is a CO service, then something will have to be done to make it appear to be CL as far as the server is concerned.

One way would be to set up a different connection every time the server communicates with a client, but this would be very inefficient if the data transfers are small, as the messages sent to establish and remove the connections are essentially wasted. A way to reduce this overhead would be to leave the connections in place once they had been established and to disconnect only when activity on them seemed to have ceased. However, this just reintroduces the association management problem, but in a lower layer. This can cause serious problems in some operating systems. For example, in Berkeley Unix systems each association would correspond to a so-called *socket* and the number of sockets that an individual process may use is strictly limited. It is not hard for quite modest servers to run out of sockets when operating above CO communications services.

CO communications services are not all bad news for clients and servers though. Often it is convenient if clients and servers receive speedy notification of each other's demise or of a communications failure. A CO communications service will usually inform its users if the association has been broken for either of these reasons. With only a CL communications service available, clients and servers would have to institute their own polling regime and maintain the relevant state information themselves.

So far, we have looked at the impact of long-term associations on the applications themselves. The other layer in which they are important is the network layer. It is here that routeing takes place, and in a complex network many routeing decisions have to be taken in order to establish a path to the final destination. If the network layer service is CO then it is common to make use of the long-term associations in the way the networks operate. For example, a path across the networks is established when the connection is set up and remembered for its duration. All packets belonging to the connection then follow the same path. This means that the routeing decisions have only to be made once and all the resources the connection needs at the intervening nodes can be reserved in advance. With CL operation routing decisions have to be made for each packet and there is a danger that too many packets will be routed via a particular node, thus causing "congestion". However, in some circumstances the fact that every packet is routed individually is considered a virtue as this enables packets to be routed round failed nodes. This robustness in the face of failed nodes was one of the main reasons a CL network was chosen by DARPA. DARPA anticipated failure of some nodes in the event of nuclear attack!

As noted previously, most CO services offer reliability guarantees as well as long-term associations, that is, they offer virtual circuits (VCs). Proponents of the VC approach argue that the reliable, sequenced, flow-controlled service provided by a VC relieves the end-systems and the applications from concerns about errors. This is undoubtedly true and the sort of applications that currently run above the VC service provided by X.25 networks exploit the inherent reliability of the service. However, there are two major flaws in this argument:

- The applications may not want that much reliability. They may be willing to sacrifice reliability for increased throughput. The case often cited is that of packetized voice; here, the loss of the odd packet will go unnoticed, but a long delay caused by the retransmission of a lost packet is unacceptable.
- There are other players involved in the chain linking two applications apart from the network service. There are the transport and higher layers implemented in the hosts, together with infrastructure provided by the operating system in which they are embedded. Whilst these are usually highly reliable, they are unlikely to be completely error free. More important are the issues raised by inter-networking. If two highly reliable networks are linked by a relay system that is unreliable, then the complete concatenated network is itself unreliable. An application that is serious about reliability will have to provide its own error-control procedures to cope with this possibility. Once these are in place, the error-control procedures in the VC-oriented networks are being duplicated, so they might as well be abandoned (Saltzer et al. 1984).

So which is best? The balance seems to lie with CL services and these seem to be the choice when the choice can be freely made. However, WANs seem likely to offer mainly CO services for some time to come. Truly "open" distributed systems must be able to operate above either service type.

6.11 Programming interfaces

So far in this chapter we have taken a rather abstract view of communication services, specifying their behaviour in terms of a set of primitive operations that may be performed upon them. If these services are to be realized on systems, then the primitive operations will need to be mapped to constructs in a programming language. In a conventional language such as "C", it is natural to make a correspondence between the abstract primitive operations and function calls; the parameters of the primitive operations become the parameters of the function calls. For the transport service considered earlier we might have:

```
T_CONNECT_req(t_address, ...);

T_DATA_req(connid, user_data, ...);
```

There are many decisions still to be made about how these functions should behave. Some of the key ones are:

- How is the interaction with the service to be synchronized? For example, when a function returns does it mean:
  - The request has been accepted by the service and will be carried out at some time in the future.
  - The request has been accepted and a request has been transmitted.

- The request has been received by the remote entity.
- The operation is complete, which would mean that a `T_CONNECT_conf` had been received.
- How are "asynchronous events" like the unexpected receipt of data to be handled?
- How are the parameters to be represented as types from the language?
- How are the buffers that carry the user data to be handled? (Usually buffers are obtained from a pool to which they must subsequently be returned.) Which layer should request the allocation and which should request the freeing?

There are no "best answers" to these questions and different implementors will make their own choices. They are free to do so since, as yet, there are no standards for programming interfaces. This is a little unfortunate since it might have been hoped that one benefit of standardization would have been the easy portability of service implementations. We can now see that two implementations can conform to an OSI service in an exemplary way but be completely incompatible with respect to programming interfaces. Mapping one such interface to another is by no means a trivial task.

6.12 OSI application-layer support for distributed systems

It is in the upper layers that OSI has been most innovative – specifying common services that had previously been performed on an ad hoc basis within applications.

In the lower layers the services offer only a few "service elements". Usually you can connect, send data and disconnect, and not do much else. In the application layer things are much more complex. There are service elements relating to specific applications such as file transfer, electronic mail, and so on. There are also more general service elements which are used by several different sorts of application. These are of interest to the distributed system designer as they are the basic building blocks from which new applications can be made. We consider these below.

6.12.1 Association control

In the discussion of CO and CL communications services above we noted that it was sometimes desirable that two (or maybe more) application entities should form a long-term association. Most of the OSI applications defined to date assume that this is desirable. The Association Control Service Elements (ACSE) are designed to manage these associations. There are four elements:

```
A.ASSOCIATE
A.RELEASE
A.ABORT
A.P_ABORT
```

The last three are concerned with breaking associations by agreement, by fiat from one end, and as a result of some inadequacy of the service provider respectively. The most important parameters of an **A.ASSOCIATE.req** are:

- The P-SAP address to which the remote application entity is attached.
- The application context name, which specifies the activity in which we are about to engage (file transfer, electronic mail, etc.).
- Presentation context information, which is concerned with how information is to be represented in transit. This is considered in the next section.
- User data. Since **A.ASSOCIATE** is used to set up an association on behalf of some application, there will usually be some application-specific initialization data to be transferred.

In practice, **A.ASSOCIATE** does little more than collect together the parameters to be placed in a **P.CONNECT.req**. In future it may do more; it would be an excellent place to implement application-entity mutual authentication, for example.

6.12.2 Remote operations

In Chapter 2 we examined the remote procedure call paradigm in the construction of distributed systems. OSI contains a similar concept in the form of the Remote Operation Service Elements (ROSE). The objectives are much the same – the provision of the invocation–response semantics that are familiar from local function calls. However, there are two main differences from the classic RPC model:

- First, ROSE assumes a CO environment; you have first to establish an association before a ROS.req can be issued.
- Second, there are none of the language binding mechanisms normally associated with RPC. Rather than ape the syntax of any particular programming language for the operation's parameters and responses, ROSE specifies these using OSI specification language ASN.1 (Abstract Syntax Notation 1) which is described below.

In addition to providing a disciplined way of handling the parameters and responses associated with the normal execution of a remote operation, ROSE deals with abnormal terminations. There are two ways in which abnormal termination can occur: the remote application entity can reject the operation on the grounds that the parameters are illegitimate, or it may find that, although the parameters are okay, the operation cannot be performed for some external reason.

6.12.3 Atomic actions

The commitment, concurrency and recovery service elements (CCR) are OSI's means of providing atomic transactions. As discussed in Chapter 3, CCR implements atomic transactions by means of a two-phase commit protocol. It contains the elements shown in Table 6.4.

6.12.4 OSI Presentation-layer support

Earlier in this chapter we noted that in OSI, the parameters of a remote operation were specified in a language called ASN.1, which is ISO's (initially CCITT's)

Table 6.4 CCR service primitives.

Element	Action
C.BEGIN	Begin transaction
C.PREPARE	Prepare to commit
C.READY	Slave is able to do the work
C.REFUSE	Slave is unable to do the work
C.COMMIT	Commit the transaction
C.ROLLBACK	Abort the transaction
C.RESTART	Notify failed transaction

response to the perceived need for a language in which to express the syntax of information independent of any particular programming language. In many respects, ASN.1 resembles the data type definition facilities of a programming language. It specifies a range of primitive types (integer, boolean, etc.) and constructors (sequence, set, etc.) via which more complex types can be built. Many standard OSI applications use ASN.1 to express the syntax of the operations they support.

6.12.5 ASN.1 principles

ASN.1 (or Abstract Syntax Notation number 1) is a presentation transfer syntax used by application-layer protocols for representation of the information exchanged between application entities. It specifies both high- and (in practice) low-level structure of actual data on the network.

High-level information means application-specific data-structuring and value constraints. In a "tuned" context-specific way, applications can define complex structures, pass data or carry out transactions regardless of underlying differences such as byte-order or language constraints.

Low-level information means a machine-independent encoding scheme. Although there is the possibility of divergent encoding schemes, such as encryption, in practice CCITT-aligned standards are using a common octet-level encoding method.

The syntax of ASN.1 displays several properties:

- The notation is BNF (Backus–Naur form) defined. It forms a self-consistent and testable grammar that allows specification to be provable and testable.
- By sticking to the production rules defined within the ASN.1 BNF, all valid instances can be produced.
- Unlike BNF, which is typically used to present language grammars or systems without considering actual transfer of data, ASN.1 actually defines the encodings of its objects. When reduced to its lowest form, all legal ASN.1 structure is an octet stream, a sequence of octets of data.
- The encoding is defined to be language-, host- and network-independent.
- This encoding is not always optimal and is often highly context-specific.

It is important to note that ASN.1 is BNF-defined but is not BNF itself. When reading the ASN.1 specification be sure to differentiate between them. For exam-

```
struct  passwd  \{ /* see getpwent(3) */
        char    *pw_name;
        char    *pw_passwd;
        int     pw_uid;
        int     pw_gid;
        int     pw_quota;
        char    *pw_comment;
        char    *pw_gecos;
        char    *pw_dir;
        char    *pw_shell;
\};
```

Figure 6.14   Example of a data stucture.

ple, consider a fragment of "C" code showing the definition of a simple data structure that could be used to represent the contents of a line in /etc/passwd. This data structure consists of a series of pointers to strings, and embedded integers. At run time a given instance of this structute is as in Figure 6.14.

If the content of file /etc/passwd is

```
george:0vMadwH/QR13s:1111:902:G.Michaelson:/usr/staff/
george:/bin/csh
```

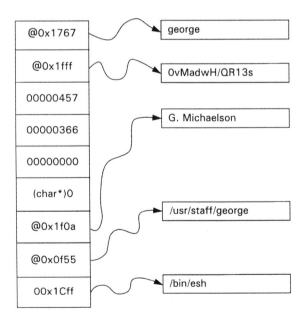

Figure 6.15   Data structure at run time.

then an instance of struct passwd at run time would appear as in Figure 6.15. Assuming that the separate field sizes were as on a typical 32-bit RISC-architecture machine.

- char * pointer is 4 bytes
- int is 4 bytes
- structure is not "contiguous" memory

Note:
- Size of structure is machine-dependent.
- What is the size of a (char *) pointer?
- What is the size of an int?
- Encoding of values is machine-dependent.
- Strings are null-terminated.

A typical ASN.1 representation of this structure is shown in Figure 6.16. A more complex example is illustrated in Figure 6.17.

```
    passwd   ::= SEQUENCE \{
        pwname      IA5String,
-- must not exceed 8 chars in length
        passwd      Printable String,
-- any character EXCEPT ':' which delimits entries in /etc/
passwd
        uid         INTEGER,
        gid         INTEGER,
        quota       INTEGER OPTIONAL,
-- only present if quota checking enabled
        comment     IA5String,
        gecos       IA5String,
        dir         IA5String,
        shell       IA5String
        \}
```

Figure 6.16 ASN.1 version of C data structure.

Note that Figure 6.16 assumes the following about memory templates for objects:
- All objects occupy minimum space.
- Octet order is defined for the integer-valued defined objects.

The above example shows three of the predefined objects in ASN.1.
- A simple structure is introduced by the keyword SEQUENCE.
- This simple structure consists of INTEGER and IA5String named sub objects.
- There is one Printable String object.

```
      -- definitions for a hypothetical ROS for cash dispensers
      CashDispenserDefinitions ::=

BEGIN
      PinType ::= [APPLICATION 1] Numeric String

      -- a PIN is a 4-digit secret code issued per cashcard
      SortingCodeType ::= [APPLICATION 2] SEQUENCE \{
         BankNo      NumericString,
         BankSubNo   NumericString,
         BranchNo    NumericString,
         -- all are 2 digit sequences such as 80-02-83
      \}

      ACNameType ::= [APPLICATION 3] IMPLICIT SEQUENCE \{
         given Name   IA5String,
         familyName   IA5String
            \}
      ACNumber ::= [APPLICATION 4] Numeric String

      Card Status ::= INTEGER \{ stolen(0), overdrawn(1), valid(2) \}
      CurrencyType ::= INTEGER \{
            Sterling(0), Scots(1), Punt(2), ECU(3)
      \}
      -- we handle all sensible currencies

      AmountType ::= [APPLICATION 5] SEQUENCE \{
         Currency CurrencyType,
         Value  INTEGER,
      \}
      CardStrip ::= [APPLICATION 6] SET \{
         [0]  pin PinType,
         [1]  sortingcode SortingCodeType,
         [2]  acountholder ACNameType,
         [3]  acountnumber ACNumber,
         [4]  status CardStatus OPTIONAL,
         [5]  balence AmountType OPTIONAL
         [6]  ptherinfo ANY
      \}

END
```

Figure 6.17 Example of an ASN specification: cash dispenser.

- There is an OPTIONAL component.
- Comments are embedded into the definition and layout is used just like in normal programming languages to delimit and aid "parsing" of the structure.
- Unlike most languages ASN.1 has a rich set of primitive types and few con-

struction types. This is because the constraints of open-systems-oriented networking require that the notation be able to control use of network- or technology-specific objects as tightly as possible.

- Most construction types in programming languages are simply "user-friendly" variations or abstractions of simple types like arrays or sets. These can be built up quite easily in ASN.1, but the definition of primitive objects that conform to interworking standards requires central control.
- The notation provides as many defined types as possible, and facilities for new definitions and extensions have been made.
- IA5String is a type that defines objects of any length, but consisting only of characters in the IA5 alphabet. The "C" definition didn't actually constrain the values in this way, but a hard-typed language such as Pascal could easily have done so.

The list in Table 6.5 has only two construction types: the SET and the SEQUENCE. Using these along with a MACRO notation and a CHOICE selector, arbitrarily complex structures can be built up. In the table we note the following:

Table 6.5 ASN base data types.

ID code	Data type
0	End-of-contents
1	Boolean
2	Integer
3	Bit string
4	Octet string
5	Null
6–15	Unassigned
16	Sequence
17	Set
18	Numeric string
19	Printable string
20	T.61 string
21	Videotex string
22	IA5 string
23	UTC time

- Subtypes and ranges can also be defined from the primitive types, allowing finer control of the value of the primitive elements.
- The use of named types provides some clarity for readers since names like T.61 string and Videotex String don't really tell you much about the context.
- By its nature ASN.1 can be ambiguous. Although definitions can carry a lot of tagging and identification this increases the volume of transmitted octets hugely.
- Typically reduced definitions are used where the context can define the encoding of following objects. This is not without its dangers, and you should be very careful to determine whether a piece of ASN.1 defines something of global or localized significance.
- Annexe A to CCITT X.409 is a guide for the use of ASN.1, which can help avoid creating such ambiguities. Example: an ASN.1 definition for autotellers.

Here is a small set of ASN.1 definitions for objects that might plausibly be exchanged during the use of high-street cash dispensers, assuming anyone was rash enough to attach them to an OSI network:

- New types are defined using an "overloading" facility that redefines the predefined types for this application, thus defining application-wide types that have global significance, e.g. PinType.
- New UNIVERSAL types are defined by international agreement and cannot

be preempted, but private and application-specific types can be created at will.

- Where context permits, the use of IMPLICIT types helps to reduce the coding overheads; the context will implicitly define the object, so a distinct marker is not required.
- Sets, unordered lists of items, typically require the use of set-specific tags, to ensure each item can be discriminated.
- Wildcard types can be included into constructs using ANY; thus definitions can be made open-ended to encompass later extensions.

6.12.6 Remote operations service (ROS)

In the general sense, any application carried out across a network can be considered a remote operation or set of operations. The ISO network standards (CCITT 1986) define a notation and methodology for specifying these operations which has several advantages over ad hoc methods previously used:

- The application is decoupled from underlying network "environments" since the operation is defined at a network-independent level. This makes it highly portable.
- The specification is rigorous and can be made unambiguous, reducing errors of interpretation and implementation. Operations become "provable" and "testable". See Figure 6.16 again for an example.
- The notation is simple to learn and very powerful.
- Online checking and automatic generation of code is possible.
- Existing specifications provide re-use and extension or tailoring. Productivity is increased.

The intention of ROS is to make remote operations look as similar as possible to a localized procedure call. To allow a "generic" implementation a single point of call and set of returns are provided, and the user-specified requests are "fed" through this invocation. This invoke-point allows for arbitrarily complex arguments to be passed, using the ASN.1 encoding mechanism.

Typical uses of ROS are for the implementation of "interactive" protocols, applications-level exchanges between two or more processes where there may be bidirectional exchanges of requests or data. Examples include mail systems, directory services and file transfer systems.

ROS and abstract data types

To achieve portability, network independence and self-consistency, ROS represents applications, objects and operations using the concept of abstract data types. The most familiar application of abstract data types is in computer languages, where a set of built-in types such as "integer" or "character string" can be used to specify other context-specific complex types.

The use of abstract data types displays several useful properties:

- Data structures are classified by their behaviour into a set of types.
- The set of behaviours for a given type are specified as a set of "atomic"

operations for that type.

- The operations specify what happens, and not how it happens. Furthermore this specification is programming-language-independent.

The last point can be seen as a disadvantage, since you still have to find out how to implement a given operation. That remains a general problem in computing!

As long as the set of type-operations is the only point of contact for each type, (i.e. it is a strongly typed syntax as in Pascal or Algol) this can be seen as an object-oriented architecture.

This method for specifying the states and changes of abstract data is naturally extensible to complete systems.

ASN.1 and ROS

The basis of the representation and implementation of remote operations in ISO specifications is the ASN.1 syntax as defined in ISO/CCITT X.409:

1. All data types and their encoding are defined in ASN.1.

```
    OPERATION MACRO ::=
BEGIN
    TYPE NOTATION ::= "ARGUMENT" NamedType Result Errors | empty
    VALUE NOTATION ::= value (VALUE INTEGER)

    Result ::= empty | "RESULT" NamedType
    Errors ::= empty | "ERRORS" "{" ErrorNames "}"
    NamedType ::= identifier type | type
    ErrorNames ::= empty | IdentifierList
    IdentifierList ::= identifier| IdentifierList "," identifier

END
```

Figure 6.18 The remote operations macro.

```
    ValidatePIN OPERATION
    ARGUMENT SEQUENCE {
        accountnumber ACNumber,
        submittedPIN PinType,
        bankid SortingCodeType
        }
    RESULT accountStatus

    ERRORS { badpin, wrongbank, unspecified }
    ::= 1

-- ValidatePIN takes the user submitted PIN and checks it against
-- accounts at the specified branch. error returns cover for
-- non-connected banking firms and mistyped PIN.
```

Figure 6.19 Example of a remote operation.

2. The remote operation, its parameters, returns and error conditions are defined using the ASN.1 "MACRO" facility (see Figs 6.17, 6.18).
3. Actual Remote Operations invocation is implemented using a set of operational protocol data units (OPDUs). These are also defined in ASN.1, and may be mapped on to any suitable underlying network layer, typically the session layer or a reliable transfer service (RTS).

Note the following points about remote operations:

1. The representation of an operation is an integer.
2. The arguments of the operation may be any ASN.1 construct.
3. The result of the operation may be any ASN.1 construct.
4. The error list of the operation is a list of integers identifying the possible error returns.

Thus a minimal Remote Operation with no arguments, errors or result is represented as an integer returning nothing. The ERROR macro is

```
ERROR MACRO ::=
BEGIN
  TYPE NOTATION ::= "PARAMETER" NamedType empty
  VALUE NOTATION ::= value (VALUE INTEGER)
  NamedType ::= identifier type type
END
```

For example,

```
badPIN ERROR ::= 1
```

defines the error return **badPIN** to be a simple value with no arguments, and

```
  balanceExceeded ERROR
PARAMETER cashlimit INTEGER
::= 2
```

defines the error return **balanceExceeded** to take one integer argument, the allowed cash limit.

Mapping the ROS macros into OPDUs

The ROS operations, the results and errors have a set of four protocol data units called Operational Protocol Data Units that sequence the exchange of ROS events. Client and server processes use these OPDUs to implement the ROS exchange:

```
OPDU ::=
  CHOICE { [1]Invoke, [2]ReturnResult, [3]ReturnError, [4]Reject }
```

Not defined in ROS

- No mention is made in the ASN.1 of how to ensure synchronous or asynchronous operation.
- Similarly, localized dependencies such as how many outstanding requests may be supported or timing constraints are not specified.

- An ROS exchange would typically consist of a connection phase, a series of ROS invocations and responses and a disconnection. Certain applications might demand a level of "atomicity" not provided within the specification. This must be managed by higher-level decisions of how ROS is used.

6.12.7 Event cycle in a ROS exchange

Figure 6.19 shows the sequence of events that form an ROS exchange between two hosts A and B:

- ROS exchanges must go through a connection phase, but this is not defined in terms of OPDU. Instead, appropriate mappings are made into the underlying services connection events to pass the application-specific information that identifies the communicating processes. Each application must define this itself but X.400 shows two such mappings into session and RTS services.
- During the execution phase remote requests are made in the `Invoke` OPDU, each being marked by a unique Invoke-ID which identifies that specific invocation from all others outstanding. Although many processes are

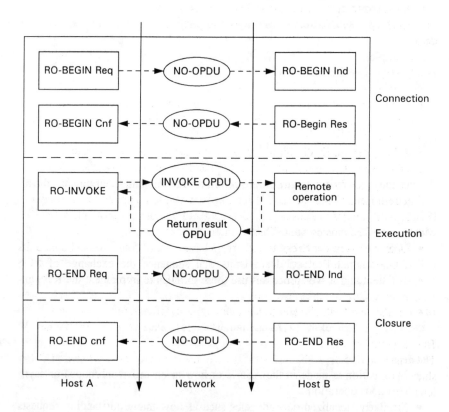

Figure 6.19 Remote operations exchange.

fully synchronous and cannot support multiple outstanding requests, ROS allows for asynchronous operation.

- Valid returns are replied in the `ReturnResult` OPDU, whereas recognized errors detected in the remote process return in `ReturnError` OPDU.
- ROS-level problems are flagged by the `Reject` OPDU which encodes the ROS level failure. Recovery is not defined in the ROS protocol.
- There is no need for ROS requests to be one-directional. Suitable token management can be used in the underlying layer to control direction in synchronous mode. Asynchronous processes can in theory be written to handle requests in either direction: in other words, the initiator of the connection does not have to be the only process issuing invoke requests.
- ROS requests do not have to generate responses. It is possible to make valid invocations and ignore the result of the request if your ROS definition permits.
- At the end of the exchange a disconnection phase is used, which again does not map into OPDU, but uses underlying facilities.

6.12.8 Octet-level encoding of ASN.1

In ASN.1 all objects actually transmitted are encoded as octets or sequences of octets:

```
read BITS from right to left
read OCTETS from left to right
```

There is a standard encoding schema which allows for extensions, and permits length-delimited and typecast objects to be constructed:

- All objects are finally represented as an ordered sequence of octets.
- Objects are length-delimited as a "counted" sequence of octets.
- New types of object can be defined out of the "raw" defined objects.

The representation of octets and octet-sequences should always conform to the ISO/CCITT standard to ensure that ordering and identification of octets and bits within octets remains correct. This is simply defined as:

- Octet $i-1$ is to the left of octet i.
- Bit $j+1$ is to the left of bit j.
- "First" and "last" refer to leftmost or rightmost depending on whether bits or octets are being referred to.
- "LSB" and "MSB" refer to least and most significant bit respectively

The data element

The basic unit of an ASN.1 specification is the data element or "element" for short. This is a variable-length object but always has three fields (each of variable length):

- Identifier distinguishes one type of entity from another.
- Length specifies the length of the contents.

- Contents is the actual "body" of the element.

The identifier determines the interpretation of the contents. The contents may itself be a data element or combination of elements defined by context or specification. The size and encoding of each of these "fields" depends on circumstances as laid out below:

- The identifier field is one or more octets in length, and identifies the "type" of element. This in turn governs the interpretation of the contents field.
- A field consists of a number of subfields, bit sequences that encode various attributes of the identifier and by extension its contents part.
- Class (two bits) defines the "scope" of the identifier within this and other specifications.
- Form (one bit) defines the "nature" of the contents, simple or complex.
- Code (upwards of five bits) encodes the "identity" of the identifier, the (possibly context-dependent) mark that allows its recognition. The context of the code is determined by the class.

6.12.9 Identifier

Four classes of types are distinguished. The class is encoded in bits 8 and 7 of the first octet of the identifier (see Table 6.6).

Table 6.6 Identifier classes.

Class	Value
Universal	00
Application-wide	01
Context-specific	10

- *universal*

  These apply across all applications – basic types defined in ASN.1.
- *application-wide*

  These are local to a specific application but global within that application.
- *context-specific*

  These apply within a restricted context of the application, e.g. tags within a set or sequence.
- *private-use*

  These are arbitrary identifiers chosen by the "user".

Two forms of identifier are distinguished by bit 6 of the first identifier octet (see Table 6.7):

Table 6.7 Two forms of identifier.

Form	Value
Primitive	0
Constructor	1

- *Primitive*

  The element is atomic.
- *Constructor*

  The element has contents – one or more primitive or constructor elements.
- *Identifier codes*

  The last five bits (bits 5 to 1) of the first identifier octet and any extension octets are used to construct the ID (identifier) code of the element.

  – Within one octet up to thirty identifiers may be defined.

  – Further identifiers are formed with extension octets.

The construction of extension octets is by the following rules:

1. Bits 5–1 of octet 1 are all set to 1.
2. Each extension octet encodes the remaining binary value, the last octet having bit 8 clear.
3. Thus bits 7–1 of all extension octets plus bits 7–1 of the last octet are concatenated to form one bitfield encoding the unsigned binary integer ID code.
4. The ID code is formed from the shortest number of octets possible: no leading extension octets can have bit 8 clear.

Valid ID Code octets will take the form:

```
\centering
C       denotes class-bits
F       denotes form bits
I       denotes ID code
0/1     show binary digits
```

In Table 6.8 the length specified is the length in octets of the contents of the element. It is itself variable in length, taking two forms shown in the table.

Table 6.8 Length encodings.

Form	Size	Constraints
Short	1 octet	Lengths up to 127 octets (preferred form)
Long	2–127 octets	Lengths over 127 octets (to 2^{1008})

The interpretation of the contents field depends upon the ID code and any context dependency implied by the ASN.1 specification. Octets are sequenced exactly as the ASN.1 order implies: items in linear order in a specification occupy successive octets of the contents.

- Read the ASN.1 spec from top to bottom!
- Read each item from left to right!

6.12.10 ASN.1 Predefined types

The 16 universal types are defined in ISO/CCITT X.409. These types, shown in Table 6.5, form the basic elements from which all other ASN.1 constructions can be defined. ID codes 0, 16 and 17 are "special":

- Code 0 denotes end of contents when indefinite-length objects are used. This requires that the input stream be scanned continuously, object by object, until this "token" is recognized, so indefinite-length objects are frequently encoded as sequences of known length "fragments" to improve processing overheads.
- Code 16 introduces an ordered list of items of any type.
- Code 17 introduces a set of unordered items of any type.

Since the last two items allow for recursive use, and a notation for choice also exists, any set- or sequence-derived structure can be built.

ASN.1 construction rules

These are the Backus–Naur form (BNF) representations of the basic rules for constructing and reading ASN.1 specifications.

You must be careful to distinguish between:

- BNF notation for specifying the ASN.1
- actual ASN.1 syntax itself

In the BNF, not all terminal objects are quoted, following the practice of quoting symbols which may conflict with BNF but allowing plaintext to be entered unquoted where it is unambiguous.

General BNF rules used (from X.400):

- Symbols rendered in bold are non-terminals.
- All other symbols are terminals.
- The terminals "::=", "string", "identifier", "number" and "empty" are quoted to distinguish them from the BNF operators, and any built-in non-terminals listed immediately below them.
- Non-terminals whose first letter is capital are defined in the grammar.
- Other non-terminals, of which there are four are defined here:
- Non-terminal string is a sequence of zero or more characters.
- Non-terminal identifier is a sequence of one or more characters chosen from the capital letters, the small letters, the decimal digits and the hyphen; the first character must be a letter. Case is significant and distinguishes one identifier from another.
- Non-terminal number denotes a non-negative integer and has two forms. The first specifies the integer's value in decimal (radix 10) notation; it is a sequence of one or more decimal digits. The second specifies the integer's value in hexadecimal (radix 16) notation; it is a sequence of one or more hexadecimal digits followed by the letter "H". (To aid clarity, binary values may be subscripted with "2", hexadecimal values with "16", and decimal values left unsubscripted.)
- Non-terminal empty denotes the null or empty string of symbols.

Comments are embedded in the notation, preceded by two hyphens "--" and ended by two hyphens or the end of a line.

6.12.11 Definitions

Type definition is

```
TypeDefinition ::= identifier "::=" Type
```

An example is

```
PrimaryColour ::= INTEGER { red(0), yellow(1), blue(2) }
```

The type **PrimaryColour** is defined as an **INTEGER** of value 0, 1 or 2 which are named as **red**, **yellow** and **blue** respectively. These value specifications may then be freely used within legal contexts to represent their respective values. An object of type **PrimaryColour** would be constrained to one of these values.

Value definition is

```
ValueDefinition ::= identifier Type "::=" Value
```

An example is

```
DefaultPrimaryColour INTEGER ::= yellow
```

Along with the type definition, this allows constant values to be assigned to meaningful names, and then used (in context) to set values:

```
MacroDefinition ::= identifier MACRO "::=" BEGIN MacroBody END
MacroBody ::= TypeProduction ValueProduction Supporting Productions

TypeProduction ::= TYPE NOTATION "::=" AlternativeList
ValueProduction ::= VALUE NOTATION "::=" AlternativeList
SupportingProduction ::= ProductionList | empty
ProductionList ::= Production ProductionList Production
Production ::= identifier "::=" AlternativeList

AlternativeList ::= Alternative AlternativeList " " Alternative
Alternative ::= SymbolList
SymbolList ::= Symbol | SymbolList Symbol
Symbol ::= Terminal | NonTerminal | EmbeddedDefinitions

Terminal ::= "string"
NonTerminal ::= ProductionName | RegularBuiltinNonTerminal
  | SpecialBuiltinNonTerminal
ProductionName ::= identifier -- of a supporting production
RegularBuiltinNonTerminal ::=
  "string" | "identifier" | "number" | "empty"
SpecialBuiltinNonTerminal ::= type --any type
type (identifier) --a type to which a name is assigned
value (type) --a value of the specified type
value (identifier type) | --a value to which a name is assigned

EmbeddedDefinitions ::= < EmbeddedDefinitionList >
EmbeddedDefinitionList ::= EmbeddedDefinition |
EmbeddedDefinitionList EmbeddedDefinition
EmbeddedDefinition ::= TypeDefinition ValueDefinition
```

The `MacroBody` definition follows the normal rules of BNF, specifying the production sequences defining the result of macro expansion:

- To ensure unambiguous expansion ALL terminals must be quoted within macros.
- The reference name VALUE must occur once only in the macro.
- Embedded definitions may be included, which are expanded during parsing of the macro. This is an alternative to specifying choices that are made during actual use of the specification and can be considered analogous to compiled-in rather than run-time decisions.

Module definition is

```
ModuleDefinition ::= identifier DEFINITIONS "::=" BEGIN   ModuleBody
END
ModuleBody ::= DefinitionList empty

DefinitionList ::= TypeDefinition |
ValueDefinition | MacroDefinition
```

An example is

```
  ColourDefinitions ::= BEGIN PrimaryColour ::= INTEGER { red(0),
yellow(1), blue(2) }
  defaultColour PrimaryColour ::= yellow
END
```

The module name can be used to discriminate between named objects of grouped definitions by the concatenation: ModuleName"."identifier as, for example,

```
ColourDefinitions.PrimaryColour
```

Built-in types are defined:

```
  Type ::= BooleanType | IntegerType | BitStringType |
OctetStringType | NullType | SequenceType |
SetType | TaggedType | ChoiceType | AnyType
  Value ::= BooleanValue | IntegerValue | BitStringValue |
OctetStringValue | NullValue | SequenceValue
SetValue | TaggedValue | ChoiceValue | AnyValue
```

The built-in types are used in the recursive definition of other types and construction of complex types. Each type is matched by a value or set of values.

Boolean type is defined:

```
BooleanType ::= BOOLEAN
BooleanValue ::= TRUE FALSE

-- FALSE is all bits zero, TRUE is any other combination of bits.
```

Integer type is defined:

```
IntegerType ::= INTEGER |
  INTEGER { NamedNumberList }
IntegerValue ::= number | - number | identifier
NamedNumberList ::= NamedNumber |
NamedNumberList , NamedNumber
NamedNumber ::= identifier (number)
```

The contents are encoded as a two's complement binary number, of the shortest possible number of octets. MSB = bit 8 of octet 1; LSB = bit 1 of last octet. No more than the first nine bits may be all 0 or all 1.

Bitstring is defined:

```
BitstringType ::= BIT STRING |
  BIT STRING { NamedNumberList }
BitstringValue ::= "string" B | "string" H |
  { IdentifierList }
IdentifierList ::= identifier |
  IdentifierList, identifier
```

When `Bitstring type` is defined as type constructor it is as if it was defined

`universal 3 IMPLICIT SEQUENCE OF BIT STRING`

This is typically used with indefinite-length encoding when the length is unknown or very long, so that each substring can be encoded with known lengths.

OctetString is defined:

```
OctetstringType ::= OCTET STRING
OctetstringValue ::= "string" B | "string" H | "string"
```

When `Octetstring type` is defined as type constructor it is as if it was defined

`universal 3 IMPLICIT SEQUENCE OF OCTET STRING`

This is typically used with indefinite-length encoding when the length is unknown or very long, so that each substring can be encoded with known lengths.

Null type is defined:

```
NullType ::= NULL NullValue ::= NULL
```

Sequence type is defined:

```
SequenceType ::= SEQUENCE | SEQUENCE OF Type |
  SEQUENCE {ElementTypes}
SequenceValue ::= { ElementValues }

ElementTypes ::= OptionalTypeList | empty
OptionalTypeList ::= OptionalType |
  OptionalTypeList , OptionalType
OptionalType ::= NamedType | NamedType OPTIONAL |
  NamedType DEFAULT Value |
  COMPONENTS OF SequenceType
NamedType ::= identifier Type | Type
```

```
ElementValues ::= NamedValueList | empty
NamedValueList ::= NamedValue |
  NamedValueList , NamedValue
NamedValue ::= identifier Value | Value
```

The SEQUENCE is the ordered list constructor. Items must occur in the order of the specification. The OPTIONAL construct allows for variant structures, but also introduces an element of ambiguity that can only be resolved by careful use of TAGGING and reference-naming options.

The COMPONENTS OF structure allows other sequences to be referenced by their type, the effect being to insert the members of its argument as members of the sequence within those of the sequence being defined.

Set type is defined:

```
SetType ::= SET | SET OF Type | SET {MemberTypes}
SetValue ::= { MemberValues }
MemberTypes ::= OptionalTypeList | empty
OptionalTypeList ::= OptionalType |
  OptionalTypeList , OptionalType
OptionalType ::= NamedType | NamedType OPTIONAL |
  NamedType DEFAULT Value |
  COMPONENTS OF SetType

NamedType ::= identifier Type | Type

MemberValues ::= NamedValueList | empty
NamedValueList ::= NamedValue |
  NamedValueList , NamedValue
NamedValue ::= identifier Value | Value
```

The Set type is the unordered list constructor. As for SEQUENCE constructs care must be taken to disambiguate any construction that uses OPTIONAL or COMPONENTS OF forms.

Tagged type is defined:

```
TaggedType ::= Tag IMPLICIT Type | Tag Type
TaggedValue ::= Value

Tag ::= [ Class Number ]
Class ::= UNIVERSAL | APPLICATION |
  PRIVATE | empty
-- the normal context for a context- specifically tagged data
-- element is a Sequence, Set or Choice
```

Tags allow already allocated identifiers to be re-used, the attached type being either explicit or implicit. CHOICE and ANY may not be tagged. Tagging is provided to allow already typed objects to be further distinguished. The IMPLICIT

176

facility allows complex type information to be "taken as read" so that the context and tag becomes sufficient to identify the remaining data.

Choice is defined:

```
ChoiceType ::= CHOICE { AlternativeTypeList }
ChoiceValue ::= identifier Value | Value
AlternativeTypeList ::= NamedType |
  AlternativeTypeList , NamedType
NamedType ::= identifier Type Type
```

The Choice Constructor allows for variant structure in specifications. As with Set and Sequence care must be taken to disambiguate components. A variant form is the BOUND CHOICE:

```
BoundChoiceType ::= identifier < ChoiceType
BoundChoiceValue ::= Value
```

The representation is that of the chosen alternative. The alternatives must have distinct identifiers, typically achieved by use of the tagged type.

Any is defined:

```
AnyType ::= ANY
AnyValue ::= Type Value
```

The built-in type ANY allows any other defined type to be substituted. Defined types have been built up using the above rules and definitions, and are included as "predefined" by agreement amongst the standards bodies.

IA5String is defined:

```
IA5String ::= [UNIVERSAL 22] IMPLICIT OCTET STRING
-- values as defined in Reference Version of International
-- Alphabet No. 5

Bit Eight of each octet is zero since IA5 is a 7- bit code.
```

NumericString is defined:

```
NumericString ::= [UNIVERSAL 18] IMPLICIT IA5String
-- Digits 0 - 9 and Space only allowed characters
```

This represents the ordered set of zero or more characters encoding numeric information in textual form.

PrintableString is defined:

```
PrintableString ::= [UNIVERSAL 19] IMPLICIT IA5String
-- Allowed Characters: A-Z a-z 0-9 space ' ( ) + , - . / : = ?
```

This defined type allows compatibility with Telex-like devices, i.e. restricted character-set machines.

T.61String is defined:

```
T.61String ::= [UNIVERSAL 20] IMPLICIT OCTET STRING
-- values as defined in Recommendation T.61
```

T.61 is an 8-bit code that allows diacritically marked characters to be passed as a pair of codes.

VideoTexString is defined:

```
VideoTexString ::= [UNIVERSAL 21] IMPLICIT OCTET STRING
-- Values as defined in Recommendation T.100 and T.101
```

Bit 8 is set to zero, and control-codes apply to output devices as specified by the VideoTex standards.

Generalized Time is defined:

```
Generalized Time ::= [UNIVERSAL 24] IMPLICIT IA5String
-- value as in ISO 2014, ISO 3307, ISO 4031
```

The interpretation of the character sequence is as follows:
- Where local time only is present, the generalized time is a string consisting of the date (as in ISO 2014) followed by local time of day, using one of the forms specified in ISO 3307.
- Where the UTC time only is present, the representation is as above, followed by the letter "Z" to denote UTC-time source.

UTC Time is defined:

```
UTC Time ::= [UNIVERSAL 23] IMPLICIT IA5String
```

The construction of UTC time is as follows: either ten (YYMMDDhhmm) or twelve (YYMMDDhhmmss) digits denoting the time, followed by either the letter "Z" or an offset of the form "+hhmm" or "-hhmm".

6.13 A distributed system example

Using the Remote Operations facility for reliable applications support, we will design and build (and hopefully document) a simple text-based conferencing system, akin to the Berkeley Unix talk program, but capable of supporting multiple users in the conference. An outline of the objects and ports available in the various servers, available to clients, is given below. Compare this with the Z specification of the conference floor-control system in Chapter 5.

We can decompose the system into three services, and analyze some design decisions for the services:

- *The conference server*
  This maintains the conferences for the users. It handles requests to create or destroy a conference, to join and leave a conference, and to send messages to the members of the conference. There may be one instance of the conference server per site, handling all conferences on all machines, or one per machine, or one per conference.
- *The location server*
  This is used by a user program to find where another user is logged in. There must be one of these per machine. The client may ask a location server, and the local location server ask all the others for the location, or it may tell the user where the other location servers are, and they have to repeat asking until they find the user. Another design decision might be for the location servers to continually (say every couple of minutes) inform each other of the users on their machine.
- *The ping server*
  The user uses this service to ask another user if they wish to join the conference.

The user program is then a client of these three servers, typically the conference server (to create and join the conference), then the location server (to find another user), then the ping server (to ask the other user if they want to join), then the conference server again to send messages to the set of users in the conference. The conference program is a client of the user program to transmit messages that other users have sent to the conference to these users. The system is illustrated in Figure 6.21.

```
InteractiveCommunicationModel
DEFINITIONS ::=
BEGIN

OBJECT ConferenceServer
  PORTS {
    Conference[S]
  }
  ::= ??

OBJECT PingServer
  PORTS {
    Write[S]
  }
  ::= ??

OBJECT LocateServer
  PORTS {
    Locate[S]
  }
```

Figure 6.21 Interactive communications system in ASN.1 (continued overleaf).

```
       ::= ??
         -- need 3 versions
         -- a) local users
         -- b) rwho based
         -- c) rusers based

OBJECT LocateClient
  PORTS {
    Locate[C]
  }
  ::= ??
    -- Find where users are logged on

OBJECT PingClient
  PORTS {
    Locate[C],
    Write[C]
  }
  ::= ??
    -- Ping specified users (locate first)

OBJECT ConferenceClient
  PORTS {
    Locate[C],
    Write[C],
    Conference[C]
  }
  ::= ??
    -- Do conference stuff. Remainder is
    -- needed to tell others how to join!

Locate PORT
  CONSUMER INVOKES {
    FindUser
  }
  ::= ??

Write PORT
  CONSUMER INVOKES {
    WriteToUser
  }
  ::= ??

Conference PORT
  CONSUMER INVOKES {
    Join, Leave, SendMessage
  }
  SUPPLIER INVOKES {
    NewMember, MemberLeaving, ReceiveMessage
  }
  ::= ??

END
```

Figure 6.20 Interactive communications system in ASN.1 (continued from previous page).

6.14 OSI – a critique

The OSI model is often criticized as being overly complex, offering too many choices. It is usually contrasted with the Internet or TCP/IP protocol suite by such critics.

It is hard to separate the implementation from the specification when analyzing these criticisms. For example, the idea that there are too many layers simply does not hold water. A TP4/CONP (the ISO Connection Oriented Transport Protocol in its appropriate class for running over the ISO datagram network protocol) implementation could be almost exactly as efficient as a TCP/IP one. Indeed there exist implementations that are that efficient.

The model has its use as a reference to compare different protocol systems, and should be considered a major success as that model. The ISO protocols that instantiate the model in ISO stacks are a completely separate matter.

The concept of layers introduced in the OSI model has two motivations:
1. Primarily technically, but secondarily politically, it is a modularization technique, taken from software engineering, and reapplied to the systems engineering of communications architectures (a term used instead of "model").
2. Secondarily technically, but primarily politically, each layer (module) can be implemented by a different supplier, to a service specification, and must only rely on the service specifications of other layers (modules).

Reality checkpoint   Why has this approach gone astray? There are two reasons (at least), one technical, and the other political:

1. The layering, imposed politically, essentially reflects a protectionist approach to providers, such as PTTs and software and hardware vendors. But the world has moved on, and now we have much more mix and match, and the walls between types of provider have been broken down. Now, you might get your host from an entertainment company, your operating system from a PTT (e.g. Unix from AT&T), the communications software from a university (TCP/IP on a PC from UCL), and so forth.
2. Software (and other) engineering has moved on a bit, and now software re-use (through object-oriented and other techniques) means that we can take pieces of code in other people's products and efficiently and safely adapt them to our requirements.

    A trivial concrete example might be use of bcopy (memcopy) by anyone in any layer of Unix applications, despite its being designed for the operating system originally, with overloaded assignment in C++ perhaps being a better way to present it to the programmer – but what we don't have is millions of different copy functions, one for each layer of software.

    Basically, the layer/service model is like an extreme version of Pascal where you can only declare functions local to their use, and they can therefore only be used there! Of course, the opposite extreme of C (all functions are global) may be too anarchic as well, although that argument is really to do with managing type complexity rather than the function namespace size.

6.15 Networked windowing systems

We introduce networked windowing systems here; from the point of view of distributed systems they are really a communications mechanism. They have interesting requirements from the lower layers that distinguish them from other conventional communicating applications. We shall see in Chapter 8 how they can be distributed to multiple users.

Because all these machines have completely incompatible hardware, lots of different window systems have evolved. A consortium of computer manufacturers, software vendors and researchers decided to rectify this, by designing and implementing a free, portable windowing system. They called it X.[2]

6.15.1 Portability and the X protocol

The X-Windows system is portable for one reason: the designers separated the display functionality from the application functionality. They did this by constructing a standard protocol (a set of rules, and format for records exchanged according to those rules), allowing application programs to talk to the display process.

The display process (of which there is one for each physical display attached to a machine) is called the "server", while the application programs are "clients".

You can have lots of application programs. Each application program can have 0, 1 or more windows, which may or may not be visible at once on the screen. One handy consequence of this design is that a client can talk to a display server on a different machine (or indeed several machines!).

The most common client program is a terminal emulation window – usually the xterm (terminal emulation) application, which is normally running a shell (Unix command interpreter) for you, but can run anything else that does terminal I/O.

NB: the model of client and server is the reverse of that you may be used to in distributed systems. In a distributed file system, your workstation is a client, and the server-under-the-stairs with lots of disks is the server. In a networked windowing system, the large machine in the basement with lots of CPU cycles is the client, and your workstation (display) is the server.

6.15.2 Window managers

A window manager process looks after all the windows on the display. It allows you to use a pointing device (mouse) to ask for more or less windows of a particu-

---

2. Most windowing systems derive from the Xerox PARC systems developed for Xerox workstations a long time ago. These spawned the MAC, MS-Windows and Suntools/Sunview systems, amongst others.

lar kind (by use of menus). It allows you to move windows around, resize them, close and open them (turn them into icons), and so on.

The display server is not a window manager. The window manager is actually another client of the display program (i.e. it is independent of the display hardware too).

The window manager (there are lots: uwm, awm, iwm, twm, vtwm, aixwm, mwm, olwm, and so on) intercepts bits of protocol between the display server and the other applications, and then informs applications of special events (like the fact that they should resize or be redrawn or what have you).

There is an "inter-client" protocol to allow the sideways communication that is now going on. One problem with X is that this is "policy-free". In other words, either the designers could not make up their minds how it should work, or they preferred not to force any particular choice on the users. This leads to problems. For instance, some window managers default to intercepting mouse and key events in contexts where a client application would want the event.

6.15.3 Running X, a window manager and so on

When you login to a workstation, usually you just have a shell running. On DECstations and Vaxstations, X is run for you. On X Terminals, a display manager program on some client machine will run some kind of login session on the terminal (which is running the display server – one performance disadvantage for an X terminal is that the window manager may be running in the client machine, so events may have to make an extra round trip time if the window manager is interested in them).

Otherwise, to run X-Windows, you have to set up quite a lot of parameters, but it is worth the effort, as your productivity goes up pretty fast after that. You need to initialize X in some way – this means you need to start a display server for your display.

You then need at least one application – e.g. an xterm running a shell. The process model of X is roughly as shown in Figure 6.22.

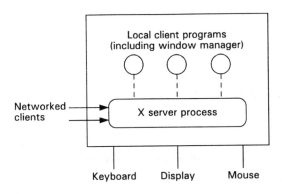

Figure 6.22 Process model of X.

6.15.4 Programming with X

There are several different ways of programming with X. Note that (like all Unix programs/commands) the X applications like xterm, xclock, xcalc and so on, are all just programs written using some of these techniques, just like you may write programs.

You do not have to know a thing about the display server, the window manager, or the X Protocol. Instead, what you need is one or other of the various X libraries.

6.15.5 The libraries

The lowest-level library is called Xlib. This provides a simple way for a client program to create a window, show it (map) onto the screen, and put various graphical things (including text) in the window. This is illustrated in Figure 6.23. (Inside the Xlib is all the stuff to implement these simple functions, and to turn the parameters into messages that are sent, using the X Protocol, to the right display server.) The next library is called the X Toolkit (it is made of two parts: the intrinsics and the Athena widgets libraries). There are several other toolkit libraries – the main contender for standards (i.e. what you will find on lots of makes of machine) is MOTIF. A C++ library that is very easy to use and very elegant is called "interviews".

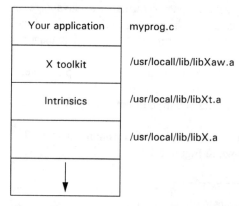

Your application	myprog.c
X toolkit	/usr/locall/lib/libXaw.a
Intrinsics	/usr/local/lib/libXt.a
	/usr/local/lib/libX.a

Figure 6.23   Library and protocol layers model of X.

Nowadays, toolkits are emerging at ever higher levels. The latest fad is for the one associated with the tool language, Tcl, called Tk.

6.16 Summary

In this chapter, we have looked at underlying communications services and protocols. We have seen how packet-switched networks come in a variety of structures, and introduced a number of interesting failure modes for systems to have to correct.

6.17 Exercises

1. The Byzantine Generals problem is as follows. Two generals are on hills on either side of a valley. They each have an army of 1000 soldiers. In the woods in the valley is an enemy army of 1500 men. If each general attacks alone, his army will lose. If they attack together, they will win. They wish to send messengers out through the wood to agree when to attack. However, the messengers may get lost or caught in the woods (or brainwashed into delivering different messages). How can the generals devise a scheme by which they attack either with high probability or not at all?

2. A network runs a dynamic distributed routeing algorithm. This is a scheme to permit automatic avoidance of broken links and routers. In what way does this differ from a distributed application such as an electronic mail system?

CHAPTER 7

CORBA – An industrial approach to open distributed computing

Nigel Edwards, HP/APM

This chapter looks at an industry standard for open distributed processing being developed by the Object Management Group (OMG). The OMG is a consortium operated as a not-for-profit company based in the USA. The objective of the OMG is to create a standard for interoperability between independently developed applications across networks of computers. The OMG's member organizations include most of the major information technology vendor companies and many end-user companies. It works by adopting interface and protocol specifications within the context of a jointly agreed Object Management Architecture or OMA. These specifications are usually developed by a number of members working in collaboration.

The OMG focuses on distributed objects as a vehicle for systems integration. The key benefit of building distributed systems with objects is encapsulation: data and state are accessible only through invocation of a set of defined operations rather than allowing direct access. It is much easier to cope with heterogeneity (different implementations of the same service), because differences in data representations are hidden. In turn, this makes application and system integration easier.

Objects also make system evolution easy: new services and implementations can be introduced that support the same operations as the services they replace. It does not matter that the implementation and internal state of the new services is different. Old or legacy information systems can be wrapped or encapsulated inside an object, so that in time they too may be replaced as the system evolves.

The Common Object Request Broker Architecture or CORBA is the central component of the OMA and there are already several commercial implementations available. To position CORBA properly, we first need to understand the framework within which it fits: the Object Management Architecture.

7.1 The Object Management Architecture (OMA)

Figure 7.1 shows the main components of the Object Management Architecture (Soley 1992). The Object Request Broker or ORB is the central component: it provides all the other components with the ability to communicate (make and receive requests and responses). It encapsulates the underlying platform (i.e. the operating system and network) and provides many of the transparencies discussed

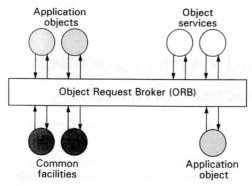

Figure 7.1 Main components of OMA.

in Chapter 1. Ideally, an ORB should make the following aspects of distribution transparent to an object that is communicating with other, potentially remote, objects:

- location: whether or not the other objects are on the same machine
- access path: the route taken by messages exchanged with the other objects
- relocation: movement of the other objects from one machine to another
- representation: the format of data associated with the other objects
- communication mechanism: what inter-process communication mechanism or protocol is used
- invocation mechanism: how the other objects' methods are executed (e.g. details of processes, threads, dynamically linked libraries)
- storage mechanisms: the details of any storage that may or may not be used by the other objects
- machine type: any differences in machine type
- operating system: any differences in operating system
- programming language: in what programming language the other objects are implemented
- security mechanisms: the specific mechanisms used to control access to the other objects[1]

Any changes in the above for a particular object should not force the recompilation (or relinking, reloading, etc.) of other objects. This allows changes to be made dynamically to the implementation of an object without affecting other objects, either its clients or its servers. Thus it is easy to introduce new implementations and replace existing services.

There are many possible different interfaces that could be provided by an ORB satisfying the above requirements. The standard interface for the ORB component of the OMA is called Common Object Request Broker Architecture or CORBA. This is described in Section 7.2 of this chapter.

---

1. It is possible to enforce simple policies transparently such as the partitioning of users into secure and insecure groups. However, certain application domains such as electronic commerce will require security to be handled explicitly by the application.

The most important feature of CORBA is its Interface Definition Language or IDL. This language is used by the other components of the OMA to specify the services they offer to each other using the ORB.

Object services are basic services that other objects might find useful. Examples include:

- naming services which, if given the name of a service, will supply a reference that can be used to invoke that service
- lifecycle services which can be used to control objects, including creating, deleting, moving or modifying them
- persistence or storage services which can be used to store state

Object services are specified using CORBA's IDL. More details and some specific examples of object services are given in Section 7.4 of this chapter.

Common facilities also provide services that other objects might find useful. Common facilities can be thought of as an "application toolkit", whereas Common services are an "infrastructure toolkit". Object services will be available for all ORBs.[2] In contrast, common facilities are optional, but if they are provided they must conform to OMG specifications. Examples of common facilities include:

- user interface facilities
- compound document facilities
- services specialized for a particular application domain (e.g. financial)

Common facilities are specified in IDL; more details about these services are given in Section 7.5 of this chapter.

The services provided by *application objects* are specified using IDL; however, these services are not standardized by the OMG. Examples of application objects include: email, spreadsheets, CASE tools, data-querying tools, CAD tools. In OMA an application consists of a collection of interworking objects. Usually the collection will consist of one or more application objects and a number of object services and common facilities. Although object services and common facilities may provide the functionality required by an object, it is not mandatory for that object to use this functionality: it may choose to implement the functionality itself or use a non-standard service provided by an application object.

7.2 The Common Object Request Broker Architecture (CORBA)

This section summarizes the CORBA 1.2 specification as defined in OMG (1993), which is the most up-to-date specification available at the time of writing. This document is 178 pages long, so our text necessarily omits certain details. Shortly, a new specification will be published on CORBA 2.0 (OMG 1995e). The text indicates those additions and amendments which, to the best of the author's

---

2. Soley (1992) actually says that object services will be available on all platforms whereas common facilities are optional. Unfortunately this does not define what a platform is; we assume it means ORB.

knowledge, are likely to be made in CORBA 2.0.

The code examples included in this section were developed using a CORBA-compliant platform called Orbix.[3]

7.2.1 The object model

An object is an entity that encapsulates state and provides one or more operations acting on that state. These operations can be requested by clients. An operation is defined by a signature written in IDL (see Section 7.2.2) which includes:

- a specification of the parameters required
- a specification of the results
- a specification of the exceptions that may be raised when the operation is invoked
- an execution specification of the semantics of the operation (not to be confused with a full semantic description).

The execution specification specifies one of two different execution semantics: at-most-once and best-effort. The former requires the operation to be performed exactly once if it returns successfully; the operation is performed at most once if it returns an exception. Best-effort operations are request-only: they do not return any results, so the requesting client receives no reply and does not synchronize with completion of the operation.

To invoke an operation, clients must identify the receiving object. Object references are used for this. An object reference always identifies the same object. However, the same object may be identified by more than one object reference (for example, each client may have a different object reference).

When an object receives an invocation from a client, it may invoke operations on other objects before returning a result to the client. The client has no way of telling if other objects were invoked.

When a client invokes an operation on an object, the object may not be immediately accessible to the ORB supporting the receiving object. For example, code for the operations (methods) and persistent state may have been stored in a file system. If this is the case the object is said to be "deactivated". Before the operation can be executed the object must be activated. This might require the ORB to instantiate a process containing the object's state and methods.

An interface is a set of possible operations that a client can request of an object. Interfaces are specified in IDL. In OMG (1993) an object may support multiple interfaces. Given an object reference, a client may invoke any operation within any interface supported by the object.

It is probable that the intention of the original CORBA specification was for objects to have only a single interface. However, as the specification stands, it neither explicitly allows multiple interfaces per object nor explicitly prohibits them. Hence interpreting the specification as allowing multiple interfaces per

---

3. Orbix is a registered trademark of Iona Technologies Ltd. The version of the platform used predates the CORBA C++ mapping, so there are some minor deviations from the current standard (OMG 1994).

object is consistent with that specification. This may change in the future (see Section 7.6.4 which also explores some of the advantages of having multiple interfaces per object and distinguishing interfaces explicitly).

Objects can be created and destroyed as a result of operations; the mechanisms for this are transparent to the client. The result is perceived by the client as an object reference that identifies the new object.

7.2.2 The Interface Definition Language

The Interface Definition Language or IDL is used to specify the components of the ORB as well as services that (application-level) objects make available to clients. IDL uses a C++-like syntax for defining the operations supported in an interface. It completely specifies the parameters, results and exceptions for each operation, but does not specify the semantics of that operation (apart from whether it is best-effort or at-most-once). This means that two implementations may satisfy the same IDL specification, but have completely different behaviours. A simple example of an IDL specification is given in Figure 7.2. It defines two interfaces: one is a bank account, the other is the interface to a bank responsible for giving customers access to their accounts by giving them an interface to an "account" object.[4]

The specification begins with a couple of type definitions and then defines three user exceptions. Exceptions are named errors that can be returned by an operation instead of its normal return value. These help the programmer to deal with run-time failures efficiently, which is important in building robust systems. The CORBA specification defines a number of standard exceptions that any operation can return (e.g. "INV_OBJREF" for invalid object reference). An operation can return a user-defined exception such as "NoSuchAccount" only if it is named in the operation's signature. We will see several examples of how application programmers can use exceptions in later sections.

Next in the IDL specification is the definition of the interface "Account". This begins by defining the structure "AccountRecord". The main difference between IDL structures and structures in C is that a definition of a structure also implicitly defines a type of the same name; hence, the type "AccountRecord" can be used in the rest of the specification. The interface has three operations: "Credit", "Debit" and "List". "Credit" takes a single "in" parameter (the amount to be credited to the account) and returns no results: neither "out" parameters nor a return value. "Debit" is similar, but can return (or raise) the exception "InsufficientFunds" (as well as the standard system exceptions). Presumably this exception would be raised if the customer were to exceed their overdraft limit by debiting the requested amount. The operation "List" takes no "in" parameters, but returns a single result of type "AccountRecord" as an "out" parameter. This result would be used to show the customer their current balance and provide some information (in the form of a string) about the last access to the account.

---

4. The specification from which this example is taken also includes a management interface for creating and deleting customer accounts in the bank.

```
typedef unsigned long AccountNumber;
typedef unsigned long PersonalIdentificationNumber;

 exception NoSuchAccount {};
 exception InvalidPin {};
 exception InsufficientFunds {};

 interface Account
 {
 struct AccountRecord {
 string owner;
 float balance;
 string lastaccess;
 };
 void Credit(in float Amount);
 void Debit(in float Amount) raises (InsufficientFunds);
 void List(out AccountRecord List_R1);
 };

 Interface SBank
 {
 Account Access(in AccountNumber acct,
     in PersonalIdentificationNumber pin)
     raises(NoSuchAccount, InvalidPin);
 };
```

Figure 7.2 IDL for SBank and Account.

The interface "SBank" provides a way for customers to gain access to their accounts. Each bank account has associated with it both an account number and a personal identification number or PIN. The single operation provided by the interface "SBank" takes a PIN and an account number, returning a value of type "Account". In other words, it returns to the customer an object reference which can then be used to access the account.

There are two ways to implement the "Access" operation that returns a reference to an "Account" object. One assumes that "Account" objects already exist, so an implementation of "SBank" would store object references and hand them out in response to invocations of the "Access" operation. An alternative implementation would be to store the state associated with an account, creating "Account" objects on the fly when the "Access" operation is invoked. Which of these alternatives is used will be invisible to the client program.

Since none of them are preceded by the tag "oneway" (indicating best-effort), all the operations are at-most-once if an exception is returned, or exactly-once if they return successfully.

The "SBank" interface illustrates two important points about CORBA. The first is that object references can be treated as first-class entities: passed as operation parameters and returned as results. Thus clients can obtain references to and communicate with objects that were not known to them at compile time. The second point is that CORBA objects should not necessarily be thought of as large, expensive entities in terms of the storage and processing resources they require. An efficient implementation on an operating system such as Unix would need to allow many CORBA objects to share the same process. Given such efficient support, the CORBA programmer can use distributed objects as an abstraction and encapsulation mechanism in exactly the same way as objects are used by C + + or Smalltalk programmers.

A language mapping defines how the CORBA IDL types map onto the type system of the target language. In addition, the mapping also specifies how certain ORB interfaces must appear to programmers using the language. OMG (1993) specifies a mapping for C. At the time of writing, several language mappings have been defined or are being defined including those for C + +, Smalltalk, Ada and Cobol.

The full definition of IDL is given in OMG (1993, 1995e).

7.2.3 The Object Request Broker

In this section we use the terms "object" and "client" to distinguish between the entity receiving a request to execute an operation (the object) and the entity sending the request (the client). These are just roles. A client may itself support a number of operations; when these operations are invoked it will be acting in the role of an object.[5]

The most important function of an ORB is to enable a client to invoke an operation on a potentially remote object. Although this is a simple requirement, satisfying it is not so simple! In Section 7.1 we described the aspects of distribution that an ORB must make transparent to the programmer making a remote invocation. To achieve this, the ORB must hide the underlying protocols and networks used to send the invocation and receive the results.

A client identifies the target object by means of an object reference. The ORB is responsible for locating the object, preparing it to receive the request (it may need to be activated), and passing the data needed for the request to the object. Once the object has executed the operation identified by the request, if there is a reply needed, the ORB is responsible for communicating the reply back to the client. An ORB consists of several logically distinct components (see Figure 7.3). Everything (including the IDL stubs and skeletons) apart from the client and object is regarded as part of the ORB.

The CORBA specification OMG (1993) defines the interfaces explicitly labelled in the diagram. There are several interfaces that are not defined by the specification: the interface between the ORB core and the IDL stubs, the interface

---

5. Another name for the object role is "server". OMG (1993) uses the term "object" and we have followed this convention.

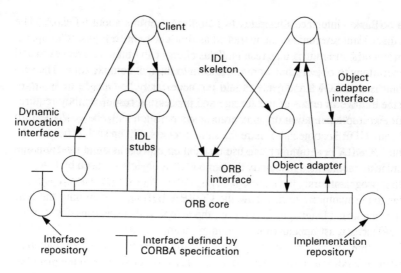

Figure 7.3 Basic structure of an ORB.

between the object adapter and the IDL skeletons; the interface between the object adapter and ORB core. By not defining these interfaces, the CORBA specification allows many different implementations. For example, one implementation may choose to provide more functionality in the IDL stubs and object adapter and less in the ORB core. Another implementation may make the converse choice. The important point is that clients and objects should not observe a difference (modulo performance differences). This is because CORBA has specified the interfaces through which they interact with the ORB. Also, CORBA specifies the rules by which objects interact with each other through interfaces defined in IDL. Hence porting object implementations from one CORBA implementation to another should be trivial.

There are some things that may make porting object implementations non-trivial:

- CORBA does not define fully the interface used by the object adapter to activate objects (giving a full definition is difficult because exactly what constitutes activation will vary between different operating systems).
- CORBA allows there to be several alternative object adapters, but only defines the interface provided by one.
- The ORB interfaces are specified in IDL with an English language description of the semantics of each operation defined in an interface; different implementations may interpret the English specification differently.

Nevertheless porting between CORBA implementations will be significantly easier than if nothing were defined at all! Some of the ambiguities that may cause porting difficulties will be removed by conformance tests (see Section 7.6.6).

The ORB interface provides a number of operations that can be applied to any object. Although they are provided by the ORB, the language binding (the defini-

194

tion of how the language is supported in CORBA) makes it look as though the operation is implemented by the object to which it is being applied. The operations provided by the ORB interface include:

- operations to convert object references to strings and vice versa
- the "`release()`" and "`duplicate()`" operations for managing memory used by objects and object references (discussed in Section 7.2.5)
- the "`get_interface()`" operation needed for the Interface Repository discussed in Section 7.2.7
- the "`create_request()`" operation used in conjunction with the Dynamic Invocation Interface discussed in Section 7.2.6

A given environment may have more than one ORB. Thus OMG (1995e) includes facilities to allow objects to select an ORB at initialization.

7.2.4 IDL stubs and skeletons

Both IDL stubs and skeletons are generated by a program called a "*stub compiler*" from the IDL definition of an interface. The OMG has defined the mapping of IDL to a number of languages (including C, C++ and Smalltalk). Thus, for a given language and for a given interface definition, the client–stub and skeleton-object interfaces are fixed (see Figure 7.3).

The job of the stub and skeleton is to hide the details of the underlying ORB from the application programmer, making remote invocation look similar to local invocation. For example, the C++ code the client programmer has to write to invoke the "List" operation of "Account" is shown below (the CORBA environment variable "`IT_X`" is used to carry exception information, as discussed in Section 7.2.5):

```
Acc->List(lresult, IT_X);
```

When the client invokes the "List" operation it is invoking the operation of that name provided by the IDL stub that typically resides in the same process as the client. The IDL stub drives the underlying ORB to invoke the remote object. There are many different ways in which to achieve this. In the following we consider one possible implementation. We assume the ORB is implemented using the TCP/IP protocol suite and specifically is using UDP (User Datagram Protocol) to communicate. However, the reader should note that ORBs can be built using a variety of different protocols to communicate and the TCP/IP protocols may not always be the most appropriate ones to use.

When the client invokes the IDL stub "List" operation, the stub obtains a buffer and writes into the buffer an encoding of the operation name and each of the parameters of the operation. This is known as "marshalling"; the inverse process of reading and decoding the contents of a buffer is known as "unmarshalling". The operation name and possibly the object reference will be marshalled into the buffer also.

The stub will then hand the underlying ORB core the buffer, together with the object reference. The routines invoked by the client stub in the ORB core are probably in the same process as the IDL stub and client (perhaps linked in as a run-time library). The ORB core's job is to locate the remote object, prepare it to receive the request, and finally hand it the request (in the form of a buffer) so that it can execute the appropriate operation.

There are two cases to consider:

- the case when the remote object is already active
- the case when the remote object is passive

In the former case the task of the ORB core in the client process is to locate the IP address of the remote object's host machine and the port number on which the remote object's ORB core is listening. Once it has done this, the client-side ORB core will send the remote ORB core the buffer, fragmenting it if the buffer is too large. The client-side and remote-object ORB cores need to deal with any failures that may occur, such as lost or duplicated packets, giving the illusion of reliable communication.

The task of locating the remote object's ORB core may be quite complicated if the remote object is mobile: a sophisticated infrastructure is required to locate it. ANSAware (APM 1993), demonstrates how such an infrastructure can be provided, although it is not CORBA-compliant.

The arrangement of libraries and processes at the remote object will be similar to that at the client. Typically the remote object will be contained in a process linked with the IDL skeleton, the basic object adapter, and some routines provided by the ORB core. A process may contain many objects and IDL skeletons (in ODP terminology it is a "capsule" (ISO 1995)). This arrangement is shown in Figure 7.4.

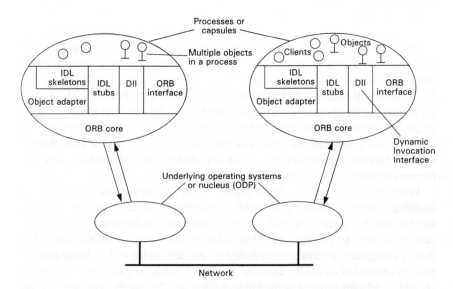

Figure 7.4   Multiple objects contained in a process or capsule.

Once the remote object's ORB core has received the buffer and correctly re-assembled it (if it was fragmented), the object reference is unmarshalled to determine which object should receive it. If the object is not resident in the capsule, an error is returned to the client-side ORB core. The remainder of the buffer is then passed to the IDL skeleton for the object. The IDL skeleton unmarshals the operation name, "List", and the parameters for the operation. It then invokes the object's "List" operation, passing it these parameters. A C++ implementation of the "List" operation is shown below. (Note that the implementation class "Account_i" inherits from its interface class "Account" which is generated by the stub compiler from the IDL definition of the interface.)

```
void Account_i::List(Account_AccountRecord& List_R1,
  Environment& env)
{
List_R1.owner = strdup(owner);
List_R1.balance = balance;
List_R1.lastaccess = lastaccess;
}
```

Once the "List" operation has executed, control returns to the IDL skeleton. The events that occur to send the results back to the client are symmetrical with those that occur to send a request to an object. The IDL skeleton obtains a buffer and marshals any results that are needed into that buffer. The results needed include any "out" or "inout" parameters (in this case "List_R1"), the CORBA environment variable, and the value returned by the operation. The CORBA environment variable is used to carry exception information; it should not be confused with Unix environment variables. The buffer is then passed to the ORB core to be sent to the client. The ORB core needs to determine the IP address and UDP port to which the buffer must be sent. These may have been contained as a field in the object reference received as part of the original request, or may have been sent as a separate parameter.

Eventually the client's ORB core will receive the reply buffer. It checks that the client is indeed present in the capsule and passes the reply buffer to the appropriate IDL stub. The IDL stub unmarshals the results and returns control to the client. Client programmers see this as execution of "List" terminating. What is actually happening is termination of the IDL stub's "List" operation rather than the remote object's "List" operation, but this distinction is invisible to them.

Invocation of a remote object that is passive is similar to the above, but includes a number of extra steps in which the remote object is activated so that it can receive the request. In CORBA object activation is the responsibility of the object adapter. In practice the object adapter may well be implemented as a library component (linked in with the object and IDL stubs) and a second part that is a component of an ORB "daemon" process running on each host. The part of the object adapter running in the ORB daemon will be shared by all objects running on a host. See Figure 7.5.

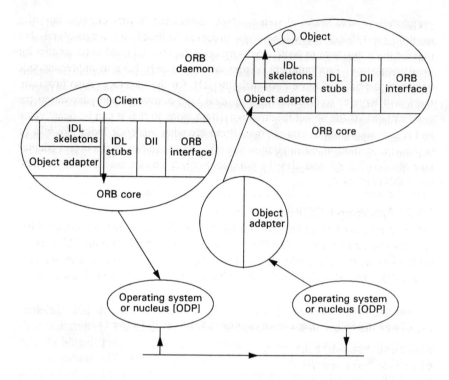

Figure 7.5 Use of ORB daemon to invoke an object (ODP is open distributed processing).

To activate an object the daemon might instantiate a process, running an implementation of the object with any persistent state for the object retrieved from a persistent store.

Once the client-side ORB core has determined the IP address and UDP port of the remote object, it would contact the ORB daemon on the remote host which is listening on a well-known UDP port. The ORB daemon would tell the client ORB if the object was already active and listening on its old UDP port. Alternatively it would return a new UDP port if the object was passive and had to be reactivated (the old UDP port might not be available). Once the client's ORB core is sure of the UDP port on which it can contact the remote object, it will send the request as described above.

It is unlikely that a client would contact the ORB daemon for a remote object for each invocation. Rather it might contact the service the first time it uses an object reference, if a communication error occurs (e.g. no reply), or if it had not used the object reference for a long time. This means that if a client sends requests frequently to an object the ORB daemon will be involved infrequently.

In concluding this section we note that the IDL stub and skeleton hide many of the unpleasant details of distributed programming from the programmer, satisfying many of the transparency requirements discussed in Section 7.1. For client programmers, the syntax of remote-object invocation is very close to that of a local (C++) object. They have to be prepared to handle extra exceptions, but otherwise do not have to write any more code than would need to be written for local invocation. Programmers of remote objects only have to implement one operation for each of those defined in the IDL for the interface. Also programmers will have to write some code to deal with activation and passivation (or deactivation), if the object requires persistent store so that it can be deactivated and reactivated without loss of state. Precisely what this code looks like will be dependent on the implementation of the ORB and specifically the object adapter (see Section 7.2.8), and also the persistent-object service (see Section 7.4 and also OMG (1995c)).

7.2.5 An example CORBA application

This section gives further details of the bank example to demonstrate how CORBA applications can be built. The C++ source code for the "SBank_i" class is shown below; this class inherits from the "SBank" class (generated by the stub compiler). The IDL definition for the "SBank" interface is given in Figure 7.2.

```
// SBank_i.cc
// Class SBank_i implements the SBank IDL interface

#include "SBank_i.h"
#include <stream.h>
#include <string.h>
#include <memory.h>

// constructor
SBank_i::SBank_i(char* name, AccountList* new_list) :
SBankBOAImpl(name)
{
 my_list = new_list;
}

// destructor
SBank_i::~SBank_i() {
}

// implementation of Access
Account* SBank_i::Access(AccountNumber acct,
 PersonalIdentificationNumber pin, Environment& env)
{
 Account_i* the_account = my_list->Find(acct);
 if (the_account == (Account_i*) NULL)
 {
 NoSuchAccount* e = new NoSuchAccount;
 env = e;
```

```
}
else if (the_account->pin != pin)
{
InvalidPin* e = new InvalidPin;
env = e;
}
else
{
the_account->_duplicate();
}
return the_account;
}
```

The constructor for the class takes an AccountList object (containing the accounts) and a name. The name parameter allows clients to bind to a named object. This is explained further in Section 7.2.8.

The "Access" operation takes an account number and a PIN, returning an object reference that can be used to access the account. The CORBA environment variable is used to raise an exception if an error occurs. First, the operation looks up the account in its list of accounts, returning the exception "NoSuchAccount" in the CORBA environment variable if it cannot find an account with a matching number. Next, it checks the PIN is correct, returning the exception "InvalidPin" in the CORBA environment variable if the PIN is incorrect. If no errors have occurred, the "`_duplicate()`" operation is invoked on "`the_account`", and finally the object referenced is returned.

The use of the "`duplicate()`" operation needs further explanation. An ORB provides two operations for allocating and releasing resources associated with object references: respectively "`duplicate()`" and "`release()`". Orbix (IONA 1994a) keeps track of how many references there are for an object, which is called the "reference count". When an object is created, its reference count is 1; should its reference count ever drop to 0 it is deleted. This helps to avoid orphan objects that nobody will ever use (i.e. the build-up of garbage). The "`duplicate()`" operation increments the reference count for an object while the "`release()`" operation decrements the reference count. This illustrates one way in which an ORB can solve the distributed garbage collection problem; other ORBs may use different methods.

Orbix calls the "`release()`" operation on all object references returned from operations. So, if the "`duplicate()`" operation is not called on an object before returning a reference to it, the reference count could drop to zero and the object would be deleted. In the above example, although the operation always returns "`the_account`", "`duplicate()`" is called only if there is no exception raised.

The other interface defined in Figure 7.2 was "Account". The implementation of the corresponding "`Account_i`" would have the same structure as the implementation shown for "`SBank_i`".

The simple bank teller program
The code below is for a simple bank teller that uses both the "Account" and
"SBank" interfaces. It also illustrates how CORBA programmers can use exceptions to deal with errors, in this case using the "TRY, CATCHANY, RETRY"
macro facilities provided by Orbix.

```
// SBankTeller.cc
#include "SimpleBank.hh"
#include <stream.h>

#include <stdio.h>
#include <stdlib.h>

// Commands that teller program can execute on an account
char *cmd_list[] = {"credit", "debit", "list", (char*)
NULL};

// Min & max number of arguments for each command
int minargs[] = {6, 6, 5};
int maxargs[] = {6, 6, 5};

const int INVALID_CMD = -1;

void PrintUsageAndDie(char* prog)
{
 cerr << "usage: " << prog << " bank acct pin credit value"
<< endl;
 cerr << " " << prog << " bank acct pin debit value" << endl;
 cerr << " " << prog << " bank acct pin list" << endl;
 exit(1);
}

main (int argc, char **argv) {
 // Check program has been given enough parameters. If not,
 // give error & quit.
 if (argc < 4)
 {
     PrintUsageAndDie(argv[0]);
 }

 // Check whether the "command" parameter is a valid command.
 int cmd_no = INVALID_CMD;
 for (int i = 0; cmd_list[i] != (char*) NULL; i++)
 {
     if (strcmp(argv[4], cmd_list[i]) == 0)
     {
         cmd_no = i;
         break;
```

```
      }
   }

   // If the command was not a valid one, print error message &
   quit.
   if (cmd_no == INVALID_CMD)
   {
      PrintUsageAndDie(argv[0]);
   }

   // If the wrong number of arguments have been given for this
   command,
   // give error & quit.
   if (argc < minargs[cmd_no] || argc > maxargs[cmd_no])
   {
      PrintUsageAndDie(argv[0]);
   }

   // Read in the account & PIN */
   AccountNumber accno;
   (void)sscanf(argv[2], "%ld", &accno);
   PersonalIdentificationNumber pin;
   (void)sscanf(argv[3], "%ld", &pin);

   // Try to access the given account using the given PIN

   // First, need to import the SimpleBank interface,
   // which provides the Access operation.

   SBank* Bank;

   TRY {
      // bind to SBank object
      char name[20];
      sprintf(name, "%s:SBank", argv[1]);
      Bank = SBank::_bind(name, nil, IT_X);
   } CATCHANY {
      cerr << "Bind to object failed" << endl;
      cerr << "Unexpected exception " << IT_X << endl;
      exit(1);
   } ENDTRY

   // Access the account.
   Account* Acc;
   TRY {
      Acc = Bank->Access(accno, pin, IT_X);
   } CATCHANY {
      // If the access fails, print the reason & quit
```

```
      cerr << "Access(" << argv[2] << ", " << argv[3]
         << ") failed, reason: " << IT_X << endl;
      exit(1);
  } ENDTRY

  // Otherwise, take the appropriate action, depending on
what command
  // has been given.

  float value;
  switch(cmd_no)
  {
  // Credit
  case 0:
      (void) sscanf(argv[5], "%f", &value);
      TRY {
        Acc->Credit(value, IT_X);
      } CATCHANY {
        cerr << "Credit(" << form("%.2f", value)
           << ") failed, reason: " << IT_X << endl;
      } ENDTRY
      break;

  // Debit
  case 1:
      (void) sscanf(argv[5], "%f", &value);
      TRY {
        Acc->Debit(value, IT_X);
      } CATCHANY {
        cerr << "Debit(" << form("%.2f", value)
           << ") failed, reason: " << IT_X << endl;
      } ENDTRY
      break;

  // List
  case 2:
  {
      Account_AccountRecord lresult;
      TRY {
        Acc->List(lresult, IT_X);
      } CATCHANY {
        cerr << "List() failed, reason: " << IT_X << endl;
        break;
      } ENDTRY
      // If operation succeeds, display account details
```

```
    cout << "Details for account" << endl;
    cout << "\towner: " << lresult.owner << endl;
    cout << "\tbalance: " << form("%.2f", lresult.balance)
<< endl;
    cout << "\tlastaccess: " << lresult.lastaccess << endl;
  }
  break;
  }
  Acc->_release();
}
```

The first ORB operation that the program invokes is `SBank::_bind()` (details of this operation are discussed in Section 7.2.8). If this is successful it takes the name provided and returns an object reference that can later be used to invoke the named object. The ORB may set various internal data structures to deal with the invocation when the reference is used. The `SBank::_bind()` operation can raise a number of exceptions, including standard CORBA exceptions such as **NO_RESOURCES** and **INITIALIZE** (ORB initialization failure). Any exception will be contained in the CORBA environment variable **IT_X** and is handled by the block of code between the **CATCHANY** and **ENDTRY** statements which prints the exception and terminates the program.

Next the "Access" operation is invoked on the SBank object; recall that this returns a reference to an account object. In addition to the standard CORBA exceptions, this operation can also raise the exceptions "NoSuchAccount" and "InvalidPin". These are handled by the block of code between **CATCHANY** and **ENDTRY**.

The rest of the program uses the same principles to invoke one of the "Account" object's operations. At the end of the program the "`release()`" operation is invoked on the "Account" object which will decrement the object's reference count (maintained by the ORB). This may cause the "Account" object to be deleted.

7.2.6 The dynamic invocation interface

The dynamic invocation interface (or DII) provides clients with an alternative to using IDL stubs when invoking an object. The DII is useful for certain specialized kinds of applications such as bridges (see Section 7.3) and class browsers. It is anticipated that most CORBA clients will use IDL stubs. An object receiving a request cannot tell which of the two mechanisms is being used by the client.

In Section 7.2.4 we saw how the IDL stubs enable a client to use the same syntax for remote invocations as they use for local invocations. Using the DII involves the client in a number of extra steps.

First, the client needs to build up an argument list. Each element in the argument list consists of the following IDL structure:

```
struct NamedValue{
 identifier name; //argument name
 any argument; // the argument
 long len; // size of the argument (in bytes)
 Flags arg_modes; // in, out or inout
}
```

The CORBA IDL type "any" can express any IDL type. In C it is implemented as a structure consisting of two fields:

```
typedef struct CORBA_any {
    CORBA_TypeCode _type;
    void *_value;
} CORBA_any;
```

The type code indicates the type encoded as an "any" (e.g. a string representing the type name). The "_value" field is a pointer to a memory location containing the value of the argument.

The next step in using the DII is to invoke the "create_request()" operation on the remote object. This operation is implemented by the ORB, but the language binding makes it looks as though it is implemented by the remote object itself. The inputs to the "create_request()" operation include:

- the operation name
- the argument list
- a variable to contain the result returned by the operation

The result of the "create_request()" operation is an object reference to a "request" object which can be used to control the invocation. The request object supports a number of operations:

- invoke()
- send()
- get_response()
- delete()

The "invoke()" operation uses the mechanisms provided by the underlying ORB to deliver the request to a remote object. The remote object, together with its ORB core and IDL skeleton will deal with the request, as described in Section 7.2.4 (just as if it had come from an IDL stub). If the "invoke()" operation terminates successfully the variable containing the result will have been updated and any "out" or "inout" arguments contained in the argument list will have been changed.

The "delete()" operation destroys the request object and reclaims any memory associated with it.

The "send()" and "get_response()" operations can be used to make asynchronous invocations. When the "send()" operation is invoked on a request object, the call returns to the caller without waiting for a response to be delivered. The caller can then continue execution and retrieve the response at some later stage. The "`get_response()`" operation is used to discover if a reply has been received from the invocation. If "`get_response()`" indicates that the operation is done, the return value and "out" or "inout" parameters will be set in exactly the same way as if "`invoke()`" had been used to make the invocation.

The DII provides two operations for making multiple invocations simultaneously: "`send_multiple_requests()`" and "`get_next_response()`". The "`send_multiple_requests()`" operation takes an array of request objects and invokes the "`send()`" operation on each one. Once "`send_multiple_requests()`" has terminated there will be multiple request executions taking place; the degree of parallelism and ordering of executions is system-dependent.

The response can be retrieved by invoking the "`get_next_response()`" operation. This will return a pointer to a completed request object. If multiple request objects have completed there is no guarantee which one will be returned.

In some senses the dynamic invocation mechanism is less abstract that the IDL stubs. It hides fewer aspects of distribution than the IDL stubs, requiring programmers to do more work than if they had used IDL stubs. For example, programmers using the DII must explicitly build up requests, possibly invoking other (remote) objects to discover what parameters are required. However, the dynamic invocation interface is sometimes a very useful tool for building certain classes of applications.

One class of applications that can be built easily using the DII are class browsers. If the IDL stub approach to invocation were used, the class browser might have to be rebuilt to incorporate an IDL stub for the new class each time a new class were added to the library. By using the DII it can browse any class without having to incorporate the IDL stub. In Section 7.5 we will see how the DII is vital for building bridges or gateways between different ORBs. Indeed, the next revision of CORBA (CORBA 2.0; OMG 1995e) will include corresponding facilities for servers, the dynamic skeleton interface, specifically so that bridges can be supported.

The DII's support for asynchronous and multiple asynchronous invocations might also be useful if a thread package is not available. In many cases a threads package is available, so the programmer can make multiple invocations in parallel using IDL stubs. Client-side execution can be continued by creating a thread to handle each request (which will block until the reply is received) and one extra to run in the client. The latter approach to asynchrony will generally require the programmer to do less work as fewer calls to the underlying system will be required.

In summary, there are certain classes of application that might be best implemented by using the DII; the DII's support for asynchrony would be useful in the absence of proper support for threads. However, the IDL stub approach to invocation requires much less work on the part of programmers: they only have to make one call to invoke an object, rather than several calls to an API. Hence there is less opportunity for programmer error using IDL stubs. So the approach to CORBA programming should be to use IDL stubs wherever possible, using the DII only when absolutely necessary.

7.2.7 The interface repository
The interface repository is a service that provides access to interface definitions. It can be used both by the internal components of the ORB and also by ORB applications. The best way to understand the service provided by the interface repository is to regard each IDL definition as an abstract syntax tree (AST).

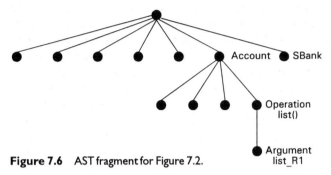

Figure 7.6   AST fragment for Figure 7.2.

Part of the AST for the IDL specification in Figure 7.2 is given in Figure 7.6. Attached to the root node is everything declared in the global scope – in this case the "typedefs", exceptions and two interfaces: "Account" and "SBank". Everything declared in the scope of the interface "Account" is attached to the node representing the "Account" interface: the typedef for the struct and the three operations. Attached to the nodes representing an operation will be one node for every argument declared in the scope of the operation. These are the leaves of the AST. Each node in the AST will also have a number of attributes associated with it. Every node will have an attribute that is its name. In addition, a node like the operation "Debit" will also have attributes such as its return type (void) and list of exceptions it can raise ("InsufficientFunds").

The interface repository treats every node in the AST as an object and provides a set of operations to discover the relationship an object has with other objects. For example, given a reference to the operation object "Debit", you could invoke the "`within()`" operation to discover in which interface this operation was declared. The result would provide an object reference to the interface object, "Account". Operation objects support operations that return references to parameter objects, references to exception objects (if the operation can raise any), and much other useful information about the operation.

Conversely, given a reference to the interface object "Account", the "`contents()`" operation could be invoked to return a list of interfaces to everything declared within the scope of the interface "Account". Included in this list would be a reference to the operation object, "Debit".

The definition of the interface repository in OMG (1993) includes a primitive object type for each IDL primitive, including: interface, operation, parameter, typedef and exception. It also defines the type codes for all the basic IDL types and how the type codes are constructed for complex types like structures. Thus, suppose an operation, called "foo", returns a value that is a structure type. If you ask the operation object, foo, (contained in the interface repository) for the type of the result value it returns, it will return a type code for the structure. The type code is parseable so that the fields in the structure can be determined.

An interface repository can be responsible for managing a great many IDL definitions written by different programmers. To provide a way of managing this it uses a notion of a module. For example, suppose two programmers, Dick and Dora, are working together on the simple bank project. Dick is responsible for the interfaces "Account" and "SBank", while Dora is responsible for the management interface, "SBankMgt". Both Dick and Dora could be assigned separate modules. The interface would then be contained in their respective modules. This is shown in Figure 7.7.

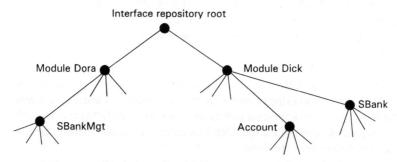

Figure 7.7 Use of modules in the interface repository.

Thus each interface repository appears as a container object, providing a number of operations to manage objects that it contains. If its "`contents()`" operation is invoked it will return a list of object references to the module object it contains. Similarly if the "`contents()`" operation is invoked on a module object, it will return a list of object references including references to other module objects and interface objects that it contains. Thus, starting from the root object (the interface repository object), it is possible to navigate through a structured space to any specific interface object that can provide all the information contained in the IDL specification of the given interface. Operations such as "`contents()`" retrieve information about objects one level down from the current object.

Each object in an interface repository has a unique (within the repository) identifier, as well as a name. For example, the unique identifier of the operation object named "Debit" might be `Dick::Account::Debit` (the actual structure of the unique identifier is opaque). The interface repository supports operations that will return a reference to an object associated with a given unique identifier. Another operation is supported that will return a list of objects that have the same given name (e.g. all objects called "Debit"). The reader is referred to OMG (1993) for details of these and other operations provided by the interface repository.

The interface repository may be implemented as an application object, like the "SBank" object. Alternatively, it may not exist as an object at all, rather the ORB may manage all the relevant information and make it appear to the application programmer that one or more interface repository objects exist.

An ORB is required to support a "`get_interface()`" operation that can be applied to any object reference. Given an object reference of type X, the result of applying the "`get_interface()`" operation to it is a reference to an interface object X, which is contained in the interface repository and defines the interface type X.

It may seem as though the interface repository is adding extra complexity for the CORBA programmer to deal with. However, most CORBA applications can be written without the application programmer ever having to use the interface repository. Indeed, at the time of writing, most ORBs work without using the interface repository at all. It is there if it is needed and may be useful for certain classes of application such as CASE tools, class browsers, gateways and applications determining type equivalence.

The interface repository can also be used by the dynamic invocation interface for type checking. IDL stubs can have type-checking information encoded into them by the stub compiler, since they are specific to a particular interface. In contrast, the DII can never know what interfaces it will be required to invoke, so it needs to have access to interface specifications (contained in the interface repository) if it is to do any type checking.

The early CORBA specifications (e.g. OMG (1993)) did not define any operations for installing new objects in the interface repository. However, at the time of writing, a new specification is under development (OMG 1995e) which is likely to include operations for installing objects in the interface repository.

7.2.8 The basic object adapter

OMG (1993) specifies the details of a single object adapter called the "basic object adapter" or BOA. An ORB may provide additional object adapters. In Section 7.2.4 we looked at how an object adapter is used to activate an object; recall that in practice it may well be implemented in two parts: part as a library linked in with an object along with the IDL skeleton, part as a component of an ORB daemon process running on each host. This section looks at other functions provided by the BOA as well as specific options for object activation.

The main functions of the BOA are:

- generation and destruction of objects
- activation and deactivation of objects
- invocation of objects through the IDL skeleton

In addition the BOA provides very minimal support for security. An object can invoke the `get_principal()` operation. This will return a reference to an authentication service responsible for the current invocation. The authentication interface itself and the details of any access controls are not specified in OMG (1993).

Just as interface definitions are stored in the interface repository, the BOA expects implementations to be stored in an implementation repository. A typical implementation repository might store compiled programs or shell scripts to start and initialize objects. The signature for the BOA's create operation is:

```
Object create(in ReferenceData id, in InterfaceDef IntDef,
  in ImplementationDef ImpDef);
```

The parameters `IntDef` and `ImpDef` are respectively references to objects in the interface and implementation repositories. The BOA implementation is free to use the `id` parameter in any way it chooses.[6] The choice will be affected by the environment provided by the host computer. For example, it might be the name of the file that is used to store the persistent state of the object; it is up to the object how it stores its state in this file – the BOA operation "`get_id()`" can be used to obtain the name of the file.

The "`create()`" operation returns an object reference to the new object. The "`dispose()`" operation, is used to destroy the object. Once the "`dispose()`" operation is invoked on an object reference the ORB will behave as if the object never existed. The implementation of the object itself is responsible for deallocating any persistent storage.

In Section 7.2.4 we described how the BOA must activate a passive object before it can receive an invocation. Object activation takes place in two stages. In stage one the BOA activates the implementation. This typically corresponds to starting the program that contains the object. A program may contain many objects, so in stage two of activation the BOA activates the particular object that is needed.

The BOA's activation policy describes how an object may be mapped to a process (or in ODP terminology a "capsule"). OMG (1993) requires the BOA to support four policies:

- activate only a single object per process
- activate multiple objects per process – this policy is shown in Figure 7.8
- run a new process to execute each operation
- allow an entity outside the BOA to activate the object

The last policy allows much flexibility, as it requires only that the activated object register itself with the BOA. (This would correspond to registering with the ORB daemon described in Section 7.2.4.)

Objects are responsible for deactivating themselves, by invoking the BOA's "`deactivate_obj()`" operation.

Figure 7.8 shows how the simple bank example might be started using the facilities provided by Orbix (IONA 1994a). A shell script to start the program is placed in the implementation repository using the Orbix "putit" utility: arguments to putit include the full pathname of the executable file and the name of the server program, in this case "SBank". This script will be run by Orbix when any client tries to access the "SBank" service.

---

6. Different implementations may make different choices, so this may lead to some portability problems.

```
// SBankServer.cc
// The executable file generated from this code should be
  // registered(under the name 'SBank') using
  // the 'putit' command.

#include <unistd.h>

  #include <stream.h>
  #include <CORBA.h>
  #include <exception.h>
  #include "Account_i.h"
  #include "SBankMgmt_i.h"
  #include "SBank_i.h"
  #include "SBankServer.h"

  int main()
  {

    // create an Account List object, to be shared
    // by the SBankMgmt and SBank objects
    AccountList* odpBankList = new AccountList;

    // create SBankMgmt and SBank objects
    SBankMgmt_i* odp BankMgmt = new SBankMgmt_i("odpBank",
                    odpBankList);
    SBank_i* odpBank = new SBank_i("odpBank", odpBankList);

    // Creation of other named banks here (code deleted)

    Orbix.impl_is_ready();

    cout << "server exiting" << endl;
  }
```

Figure 7.8   Creating objects in Orbix.

When the program is run it uses the C++ operator "new" to create objects of type AccountList, "SBankMgmt" and "SBank_i". The code for the "SBank_i" class is shown in Section 7.2.5. The server uses the name "odpBank" for the first "SBankMgt" and "SBank" objects it creates, and would use different names for other banks.

In Section 7.2.5 we saw how a client uses the "_bind()" operation to obtain an object reference to a named server. To obtain a object reference to the above "SBank" server, a client would have to invoke the "_bind()" operation with the parameter "odpBank:SBank". This would cause Orbix to run the server program registered as "SBank" (using "putit") and return an object reference to the object named "odpBank" created by that server. Further discrimination is possible: "_bind()" can also take the name of the machine on which the object is resident (e.g. outlaw.ansa.co.uk). This will cause Orbix to run the server

211

program on the named host.

Once the server has finished creating the bank objects it calls the "`impl_is_ready()`" operation; the objects created by the program are now available to clients.

The "`impl_is_ready()`" operation returns only after no clients have used the objects for some time – Orbix times out. In this case the program exits and the objects are destroyed. As explained earlier in this section, other options are possible in CORBA, including arranging for the objects to store state in a persistent store, so they can be activated when required. For an explanation of how Orbix supports this the reader is referred to the *Advanced programmer's guide* (IONA 1994b).

Although CORBA specifies the details of only a single object adapter (the BOA), some environments may contain many object adapters. Thus, OMG (1995a) includes details of how an object may select its object adapter during initialization.

7.3 Interoperability

An important goal of CORBA is to promote interoperation between different ORBs, so that clients in one ORB can invoke objects in a different ORB. This will allow programmers to build applications that use objects running on different ORBs provided by different vendors. The early CORBA specifications (e.g. OMG 1993) said very little about interoperability. This is being addressed in the CORBA 2.0 specification (OMG 1995e) which will follow the approach described in OMG (1995d).

Before considering the approach taken to interoperability it is important to realize that there will never be a platform, protocol or service that will be suitable for all applications; thus heterogeneity is inevitable. For example, some ORBs may be intended for computationally intensive applications and may use a communication protocol based on shared memory to achieve invocation times of the order of microseconds. Other ORBs may be targeted at long-lived applications that are needed to maintain data that has a life of many years. Given this constraint it is not practical to specify the internal communication protocol that should be used within an ORB. Rather the approach taken in CORBA 2.0 is based on a common communication protocol that can be used to communicate with objects running on different ORBs.

The protocol specified by CORBA 2.0 is called GIOP (General Inter-ORB Protocol) and its mapping to the Internet's TCP (Postel 1981) is called IIOP (Internet Inter-ORB Protocol). GIOP specifies a common data representation (or "on the wire" format) and also the messages and the format of those messages that can be sent between the client and server (object receiving the request) ORB. Included in the specification is a standard representation of object references. GIOP also specifies a number of requirements for its transport protocol. These include reliable at-most-once delivery of data, no reordering of data and support for fragmentation (to allow GIOP to send messages that otherwise might exceed the maximum packet size).

Some ORBs will be able to support IIOP as a native protocol, either as the only protocol they use for communication between objects, or by supporting multiple protocol stacks simultaneously. The latter approach requires the ORB to recognize which protocol a message is using – communication with objects in other ORBs will use IIOP. Unfortunately it is unlikely that all ORBs will be able to support IIOP as a native protocol. For such ORBs OMG (1995d) specifies a different approach to interoperability – bridges.

A bridge is an application that allows objects using one ORB to communicate with objects using another ORB even though the two ORBs do not use a common protocol. If an ORB cannot support IIOP as a native protocol, it can still interoperate by providing a so-called "half-bridge" between its internal protocol and IIOP. In this way two ORBs can interoperate even though neither can support IIOP as a native protocol. Figure 7.9 shows two ORBs interoperating using half-bridges to IIOP (the two half-bridges work together to form a full bridge). The two objects using the two different ORBs are said to be in different "domains".

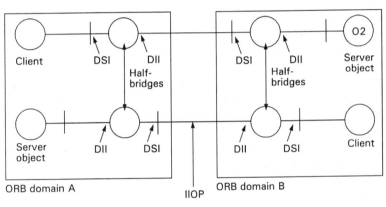

Figure 7.9 Two ORBs interoperating using half-bridges.

Notice that the bridges in Figure 7.9 use the dynamic invocation interface (DII) (see Section 7.2.6) and its corresponding server-side equivalent, the dynamic skeleton interface (DSI). This is because the bridges are generic: they can be used to invoke any object regardless of what interfaces that object has. The bridges could be built by using IDL stubs and skeletons, but in that case the bridges could not be used for any object except those whose stubs were incorporated into the bridges. Thus, adding a new object to either of the domains in Figure 7.9 would entail adding a new pair of bridges to make it accessible in the other domain. Using the DSI and DII avoids this problem.

One of the main difficulties with bridges is how to map between different representations of object references that are passed as parameters or returned as results. For example, how is a reference to an object O2 in domain B represented

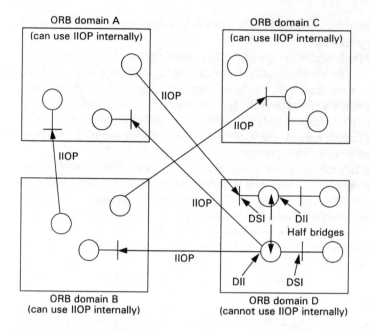

Figure 7.10 ORBs interoperating using IIOP and half-bridges.

in domain A? A simple answer is to say that it is actually a reference to the bridge that knows how to translate the reference to O2 in domain A to a reference in domain B. The problem is further complicated if the reference to O2 is handed out from domain A across another bridge to a third domain. OMG (1995d) lists several solutions to this problem and various tradeoffs that can be made.

All CORBA 2.0 (OMG 1995e) conformant ORBs are required to support IIOP either as a native protocol or by providing a half-bridge to IIOP. Figure 7.10 shows ORBs interoperating using a mixture of native IIOP and half-bridging to IIOP.

ORBs can also interoperate with other object platforms. Indeed it is important that they can, if they are to be used as a vehicle for systems integration. At the time of writing, a group within the OMG is investigating CORBA/COM interoperability (OMG 1994).

7.4 Common Object Services Specification

There are certain kinds of services that are generally useful, regardless of the application domain; examples include persistent storage and naming services. Rather than programmers having to reimplement such services each time they are needed, it would be better to re-use existing implementations. To promote this the OMG is working on the specification of standard interfaces for "Common Object Services" or COS. At the time of writing, the OMG has COS specifications in existence or under development for several services including: naming, event notification, lifecycle services, persistence, security, transactions, relationships and concurrency control. This section gives an overview of some of the services which are defined in OMG (1995c).

7.4.1 The naming service

In Section 7.2.8 we saw how Orbix clients use the "_bind()" operation to obtain a reference to a named object using facilities that are provided by the ORB. A different approach is to use the naming object service to keep track of the binding of names to objects. The naming service makes use of context. Contexts are rather like directories in a file system. A context contains a set of name-to-object bindings; in addition, other contexts can be bound to a given context to form a naming graph. Consider the naming graph in Figure 7.11, it shows a context "usr" to which the context "users" is bound; within the context users are two further contexts named "dick" and "dora". Both contexts and objects can be named and can be referred to by either their simple or their compound names. Thus "mbox" is the simple name of an object (ambiguous unless the context is known); "usr/users/dora" is the compound name of a context.

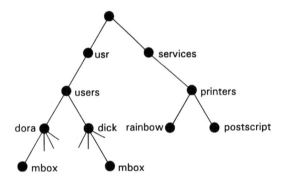

Figure 7.11   A naming graph.

The contexts "dick" and "dora" each contain a number of name-to-object bindings. Both have a binding for a name mbox. Unlike in a file system there is no general way of telling if the object bound to the name "usr/users/dora/mbox" is the same as the object bound to "usr/users/dick/mbox". The reasons for this are discussed in Section 7.6.3.

Within the COS naming service, names are treated as "pseudo-objects". This means that the language binding enables programmers to manipulate names exactly as if they were ordinary CORBA objects. However, there is no requirement to implement them as ordinary CORBA objects: implementations may make different choices for efficiency. This also has the benefit that the internal representations of names are hidden (object-oriented principle of encapsulation). Contexts are ordinary CORBA objects and can be bound to names in some context just like any other object.

The naming service defines the context interface containing operations that:
- bind an object to a name in the context
- delete the binding between an object and a name in the context
- bind a new context to a name in the current context
- delete a given context from the current context
- resolve a name to a given object (reference)

The resolve operation may return a reference to a naming context. For example, consider Figure 7.11 and suppose "`root`" is an object reference to the root naming context and "`foo`" is a reference to the name object "`/services/printers/rainbow`", then "`root->resolve(foo)`" will return a reference to the printer service rainbow.

On the other hand, if "`foo`" was a reference to the name object "`/services/printers`", "`bar = root->resolve(foo)`" would set "`bar`" to an object reference to the context service bound to the name "`service/printers`". If "`ref`" is reference to the name object "`rainbow`", "`bar->resolve(ref)`" would return a reference to the printer service rainbow.

As well as defining the naming context interface which is used to resolve name-to-object bindings, OMG (1995c) also defines the interface for name objects.

When an object is being initialized it will not have access to a naming service. Thus OMG (1995b) includes facilities for an ORB to provide an object with a way of listing a small number of object names and resolving these object names to an object reference. This facility allows the new object to discover about the rest of the world. For example, one object reference that could be provided like this is an object reference for the naming service.

In the future the OMG may well standardize a trading interface as part of Common Object Services. A trader allows clients to specify constraints on the values of arbitrary properties for a service to which it wishes to bind (e.g. location, cost and ownership). The trader will return to a client one or more object references that have associated with them the specified properties satisfying the specified constraints on values. Servers export their object references to the trader telling the trader what properties they have and the values of those properties. Thus the trader acts as a "match-making" or "brokering" service.

7.4.2 The event service

The standard CORBA interaction model is one in which a client sends a request to an object and waits for a reply. Threads can be used to allow other activity to continue in the client before the reply has arrived. However, sometimes a more asynchronous interaction model is convenient. For example, a source program might be changed. The program might just report that it has been modified and be completely unaware of a CASE tool that is notified of the event and then rebuilds parts of the system that used the program.

To support this type of interaction OMG (1995c) defines an event service. Conceptually an event service provides an event channel between one or more

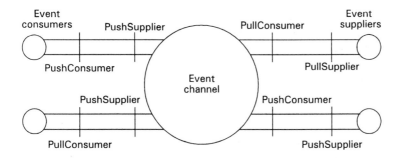

Figure 7.12 An event channel.

consumers and one or more producers. As shown in Figure 7.12, to use an event channel consumers and suppliers provide the event channel with a callback interface. The event channel is shown as a single object which is how it would appear to programmers of consumer and supplier objects. However, in practice it would probably be implemented by multiple collaborating objects.

For both consumers and suppliers of events there are two basic modes of interaction: "push" and "pull". In the push model of interaction an event channel pushes the event into the consumer by calling an operation in its callback interface, informing it that the event has occurred. In the pull model a consumer has to invoke an operation on the event channel asking for the event (if no event has occurred it can either return immediately or block until one does occur). In the push model of interaction for a supplier, the supplier invokes the "push()" operation on the event channel to inform it of an event. This operation takes a single parameter: the value of the event (no results are returned). Conversely, in the pull model, the event channel invokes an operation on the callback interface to see if an event has occurred or blocks until one occurs.

OMG (1995c) defines the interfaces that must be supported by event channels, consumers and suppliers to support both pull and push interaction. In addition it defines the (management) interfaces needed to connect producers and consumers to event channels.

It is envisaged that different event channels will have different semantics and support different qualities of service. For example, some event channels may store an event until it is consumed. Others may discard the event if there are no consumers interested in it, or store it only for a short period of time. The latter might be appropriate if the event is only valid for a short time (e.g. the latest temperature).

7.4.3 The lifecycle services
The lifecycle services defined in OMG (1995c) are designed to support creating, moving, copying and deleting an object. Three lifecycle interfaces are defined:
- the lifecycle object supporting copy, move and remove operations
- the factory interface used for creating objects

- the factory finder interface used for finding factories

An object that supports the lifecycle interface must provide operations for moving, copying and removing itself. To support the first two the object needs to understand the concept of location. The semantics of all three operations will be application-specific. For example, if an object is in some way linked to (or contains other) objects (perhaps it is part of a compound document), the "copy" operation may or may not copy all objects to which the object is linked (deep versus shallow copy). It is implementation-dependent whether or not these operations are atomic.

A generic factory interface is defined to create objects. A generic factory will usually invoke application-specific code to create an object of a particular type. A given factory represents an implementation at a particular location and is responsible for creating objects at that location. Factories are not special objects: their interfaces are defined in IDL, and to access a factory a client needs an object reference to it.

When a factory creates an object it is responsible for allocating resources to that object, including persistent store. The protocol between a factory and the object it creates is application-specific. For example, it may or may not include transfer of state.

To find a factory, the "FactoryFinder" interface is used. This enables a client to find a factory at a particular location. It is intended that there will be different FactoryFinder interfaces defined. The only one defined at the time of writing is the naming service (see Section 7.4.1). Using the naming service as a FactoryFinder is somewhat problematic since there is not explicit support for location in the naming service. It could be supported implicitly by associating particular contexts with a location (e.g. each network host could have its own context). (A trading service could support the concept of location more easily, as it allows arbitrary properties to be associated with object references.)

The result of invoking a "`create_object()`" operation on a factory will be a reference to the new object. The factory interface is one way of creating new objects. There are other ways: for example, in Section 7.2.8 we saw how the BOA can be used to create objects and how Orbix will run a program to create objects "on demand".

7.4.4 The relationship service

The Common Object Services Specification (OMG 1995c) defines a relationship service for managing relationships between objects. Examples of relationships include:

- "is employed by" which could relate an object representing a person and an object representing a company
- "is contained in" which could relate a chapter object to a book object

Relationships can be many-to-many: a company can employ many people and a person could work for more than one company. In addition, a relationship can relate multiple objects. For example, OMG (1995c) describes a ternary relationship between a library, a book and a person.

One other important concept defined by the relationship specification is that of "role". Thus a person object can act in the role of "employee" and a book object can act in the role of "container".

Both relationships and roles are first-class objects: OMG (1995c) defines the interfaces "RelationshipFactory", "Relationship", "RoleFactory" and "Role". The use of these services is best illustrated by example.

Suppose a programmer wanted to set up an "is employed by" relationship between a person and a company. First the employee role would have to be created by invoking the `create_role()` operation of an employee role factory, passing an object reference to the person object as an argument. The result would be a reference to an role object of type employee. Typically (although not necessarily) the role object would be co-located with the person object. Assuming the company's "employer" role object already existed, the next thing to do would be to create the relationship object. This is done by invoking the `create()` operation of an "is employed by" relationship factory with references to the employer and employee role objects as arguments.

The "Role" interface is the most complex defined by the relationship specification. It contains various operations for managing roles:

- It can enumerate the relationships in which it participates by returning a reference to each of the corresponding relationship objects (for example, an employer role object will typically be involved in many "is employed by" relationships).
- It provides an operation to return the other role object, if it is given an interface to a relationship object (for example, return the interface to the employee if given a reference to the "is employed by" object).
- It provides an operation for destroying the role object.
- It provides an operation for linking to another role in a newly created relationship (intended for use by the relationship factory).

Relationships and role objects do not require any state to be stored by the objects with which they are associated. So, no state change needs to be made to a person object as the various roles and relationships in which it is involved are changed. This allows immutable objects to be related and those relationships to be manipulated without activating the objects themselves that might be useful, for example, in a compound document system.

It is thought that one common use of the relationship service will be to manage graphs of objects (e.g. folder objects in distributed desktops and compound document architectures). Accordingly, a special set of services are defined by OMG (1995c) to manage these graphs. OMG (1995c) also defines two specific relationships: containment (a one-to-many relationship) and reference (a many-to-many relationship). The interfaces defined for these services inherit the general "Relationship" and "Role" interfaces described above.

7.4.5 The transaction service

As explained in Section 7.3, transactions provide guarantees which are useful for building dependable distributed applications. The common object services specification (OMG 1995c) defines a transaction service that is designed to be compatible with the X/Open DTP standard. Indeed it is intended that applications that use the transaction service should be able to interoperate with applications that conform to the X/Open DTP model.

To create a transaction, a programmer invokes the create() operation of a "transaction factory". This returns a reference to a "control" object which in turn contains operations that return references to a "terminator" object and "coordinator" objects which are used to manage the transaction.

The "terminator" object is used to commit or abort the transaction. The "coordinator" object manages the state of the transaction; this includes registering any objects that are participating in the transaction and any sub (or nested) transactions that are created within the scope of the current transaction. The "coordinator" includes an equivalence test which takes an object reference to a coordinator object and returns true or false depending on whether the reference is for the same object. This allows objects to compare the identities of two transactions (for further discussion of object equivalence see Section 7.6.3).

The terminator and coordinator objects are separate to allow an object to pass a reference to the coordinator, so that other objects can join a transaction while keeping private the reference of the terminator (and hence the ability to commit or abort the transaction).

Two other important interfaces defined by the transaction service are the "Resource" interface and the "TransactionalObject" interface. The "Resource" interface contains the operations that the transaction management system will invoke on a resource during the transaction, including **prepare()**, **rollback()** (or abort) and **commit()**. For example, the **prepare()** operation may cause the resource object to write into stable storage all state changes made during the transaction.

The "TransactionalObject" interface contains no operations; it is used to declare to the underlying ORB that the object is transactional. A transactional object is responsible for implementing all the object's operations. When the object is invoked it is responsible for registering a resource object with the transaction "coordinator". For example, a bank "Account" interface could be declared to inherit from both "TransactionalObject" and "Resource". The interface itself would declare operations like "**credit()**" and "**debit()**".

When "**credit()**" is invoked on the "Account" object it would register itself as a "resource" object with the "coordinator". When the transaction commits or rolls back, the transaction management system will invoke the operations provided by the resource interface to make permanent (or discard) any state changes made by the credit operation.

Many objects may be invoked within the scope of a single transaction. This means that the transaction context needs to be propagated to all these objects. This can be done either implicitly or explicitly. If propagation is explicit, a reference to the managing object (e.g. the "coordinator" or "control" object) is included as one of the parameters in the operation. In this case the argument would appear in the IDL definition of the operation. The alternative is implicit propagation. In this case the ORB recognizes that the operation is on a "TransactionalObject" and automatically includes the transaction context as a parameter, even though it is not mentioned in the operation's IDL definition.

The transaction service defines the interface between the ORB and a "transaction manager". The transaction manager is used by the transaction service to implement the transaction management objects such as the "coordinator" and "terminator". Essentially the transaction manager registers itself with an ORB and then the ORB uses it to ensure that the transaction context is propagated and that the transaction is properly managed. OMG (1995e) defines the mapping between the X/Open DTP "TX" interface and the transaction service operations. It is intended that an application can use either the "TX" interface to drive the transaction manager directly or the interfaces defined in the transaction service to drive it indirectly.

The transaction service is an unusual object service in that the specification requires the participation of the underlying ORB and specifies interfaces that the ORB must support. In particular, the ORB is responsible for propagating the transaction context (for implicit propagation) and also informing the transaction manager each time a request or reply is sent or received within a transaction. The transaction manager will examine the transaction context associated with each message to see if the transaction should be committed or aborted.

It is more normal for the services defined in the Common Object Service Specification (OMG 1995c) to be "application objects" which do not require special facilities in the underlying ORB.

A "transactional ORB" could be built by using a different object adapter, modified IDL stubs and skeletons, and re-using an existing ORB core (Fig. 7.4). Most of the ORB components would not require changing. Non-transactional objects would continue to use the existing object adapter and IDL stubs and skeletons.

7.5 Common facilities

So far this is the least well developed of all the components of the OMA. This is not surprising, since the scope of the problem is much greater than those faced by the groups working on CORBA and Common Object Services. The idea is that common facilities will provide application-level or user facilities that are interconnected by the underlying plumbing (the ORB and Common Object Services). Such services will have standard interfaces defined in IDL. OMG (1995a) defines the following categories for common facilities:

- User interface: this includes support for the general display and printing of objects, mechanisms for storing and presenting application help information, and facilities for user desktops.

- Information management: this includes support for information storage and retrieval (e.g. SQL and the World Wide Web), and mechanisms enabling objects to interoperate by exchanging data (e.g. EDI (electronic data interchange), ASN.1 (Abstract Syntax Notation), and various file formats for data interchange).
- Systems management: services in this class will deal with the control and management of networks and objects (including physical entities such as routers and nodes, and logical entities such as users and applications). Such services may include the sort of functionality currently provided by SNMP and CMIP (Stallings 1993).
- Task management: services in this category would support such concepts as workflow. Such facilities could provide support for objects migrating around the system from one user to another as a unit of work (e.g. an expense claim being processed). Other services in this category may provide support for agents – programs that migrate around the network acting on different objects. This kind of functionality is supported currently by languages such as Tcl (Ousterhout 1994) and Java (Sun 1995).
- Vertical market: services in this class support a specific market such as accounting, computer-integrated manufacturing and distributed simulation.

At the time of writing, no common facilities have been defined. However, the OMG working group has produced a document that describes the problem (OMG 1995a), and is working actively on compound document facilities.

7.6 Some practical issues
This section discusses some issues that arise when we use CORBA to build systems.

7.6.1 What applications are suited to CORBA?
A common misconception is that RPC systems have poor performance and are blocking. This is not so: modern ORBs are able to make RPCs at or near network speeds (Ethernet) with latencies of 1 millisecond or less. Blocking is easily avoided by using a thread to make an invocation, allowing the client to continue activity while the receiving object deals with the request.

CORBA is applicable to a wide variety of application domains, particularly those that fit the client/server or request/reply paradigm. One of the objectives of CORBA is to make it easier to build management and system integration applications. The idea is that distributed objects can act as gateways to existing heterogeneous information systems, integrating them into a uniform information space. The approach followed is similar to that used to build bridges for interoperability described in Section 7.3. Although CORBA technology is still relatively new, the early evidence of its suitability for this type of application is very positive (Drahota & Hutcheson 1994).

Certain classes of application are less well suited to CORBA. Security services are very necessary for certain application domains, and these are not developed fully at the time of writing. The major omission is that there is no support for timeliness and continuous media. Many applications (e.g. in telecommunications) need to deal with notions of time and control the scheduling of computations.

CORBA's lack of support for continuous media means that it would be extremely difficult to build the kind of multimedia applications discussed elsewhere in this book (see Chapter 8). Supporting such applications in CORBA requires enhancing IDL to describe streams and providing support in the underlying ORB to control quality of service (QoS), so that applications can control attributes such as jitter and latency. It is likely that support for streams and QoS will be added to CORBA eventually (OMG 1995b).

7.6.2 The need for a framework-based approach

In Section 7.3 we argued that there will never be a protocol, platform or service that is optimal for all problems. Section 7.6.1 argued that distributed objects (particularly CORBA) allow you to wrap, encapsulate and integrate this heterogeneity. This requires an ORB that can support multiple protocols and make it easy to plug in new protocols. Unfortunately CORBA does not specify the interface between the ORB and the underlying protocol stack.

CORBA blurs the ODP (ISO 1995) computational and engineering viewpoints. A more framework-based approach (as advocated by ODP), in which the internal structure and interfaces of an ORB were exposed, would make it easier to replace components of the ORB, especially the protocol stacks. This would help greatly with system integration: the legacy system's native protocol could be plugged into the ORB.

The disadvantage of the OMG specifying more of the internal structure of an ORB is that it restricts implementation freedom for ORB vendors. However, doubtless some ORB vendors who are targeting system-integration application domains will expose some internal interfaces to make it easier to plug in new protocols.

7.6.3 Object equivalence

There is no equivalence test on object references defined in CORBA. This is often surprising to people when they first study CORBA. The reason is that only the application can decide what is meant by "equivalence". Therefore equivalence operations need to be supported by the application object itself by providing an operation that takes an object reference and tests whether it is equivalent.

For example, consider a service that is replicated. For normal clients, we would want to consider the instances of the service as being equivalent. However, a management application would need to distinguish between the various instances. So in some senses the object instances are equivalent, but in others they are different.

Another example occurs when an object is handed two object references that happen to be to the same object in another ORB domain. In what senses are these references equivalent and in what senses are they different (e.g. an invocation might be routed through different gateways)? There is no general way of telling whether these references are equivalent: each may have been passed through different gateways and subjected to different processing.

The important principle is that ORBs should not be responsible for tracking equivalence relations – it is the responsibility of applications and application services. Indeed, COS (OMG 1995c) defines at least two services that have notions of object equivalence: the transaction service and the relationship service.

For a detailed discussion of object equivalence tests and the problems that can arise the reader is referred to Powell (1993).

7.6.4 Distinguishing between interfaces and objects

Perhaps the most obvious difference between CORBA and ODP (ISO 1995) is the way that ODP treats interfaces as first-class entities. In both ODP and CORBA an object can support multiple interfaces of different types. However, ODP treats interfaces as first-class entities: clients have references to interfaces that enable them to invoke the operations in that interface. A client needs a separate reference for each interface supported by an object to be able to invoke the operations in that interface. In ODP there is no notion of an object reference.

In contrast, CORBA has no notion of interface references. If a client has a reference to an object it can invoke any operation in any interface supported by the object.

Making interface references first-class entities has some important advantages:

- Different interfaces can support different functionality, for example there could be a separate management interface (this is more consistent with IDL in which interfaces are distinguished as separate entities).
- Different interfaces may have different access controls applied, for example not all clients may have access to the management interface.

Some may argue that this is introducing more complexity, but the benefits would seem to outweigh the costs. It is possible that the next revision of the object model will include a notion of interface references (OMG 1995b). One issue that needs to be resolved if such a model were adopted is whether or not there is a need for both object references and interface references.

7.6.5 Memory management and garbage collection

Distributed memory and resource management is a hard problem; it is very easy to end up with wasted memory and orphan objects (objects to which nothing has a reference and are hence never going to be invoked). In Section 7.2.5 we saw how Orbix uses the notion of a reference count to try and avoid orphan objects. This relies on programmers calling "`duplicate()`" and "`release()`" operations at the right time. Other approaches are possible – this is an area of active research.

A related problem is local memory management. For example, when an invocation arrives at an object the IDL skeleton is responsible for making the parameters available to the objects and may have to allocate memory to do so (e.g. a string). The problem is when to free this memory. If the stubs free the memory when the operation has completed, disaster will result if the object tries to access it later (e.g. it has stored a pointer to it). On the other hand, the object may never want to access the string again. In this case the right thing to do is to free the memory when the object completes the operation.

A safe, but aggressive solution to the above problem is for the stubs to free all memory that they allocate when the invocation has completed. This requires application programmers explicitly to copy any data for which memory is dynamically allocated (e.g. a string). A better solution is to use a language and implementation that can detect when memory has gone out of scope and garbage-collect it.

The CORBA IDL language mappings explicitly prescribe who is responsible for allocating and freeing memory for invocations in a target language. These rules are language-dependent; they are not implementation-dependent.

7.6.6 Conformance testing

At the time of writing, "CORBA conformance" is by vendor assertion. While it is possible to show that an implementation is not conformant (for example, the IDL compiler might not accept a known legal CORBA IDL specification), there are no official standard conformance tests to demonstrate whether an implementation conforms to CORBA.

Having no set criterion against which to measure conformance makes it impossible to evaluate whether or not an ORB is compliant. This will reduce application portability since it is likely that some ORBs that are asserted to be compliant are not compliant and will not be able to run an application that expects a CORBA-compliant ORB.

It is also worth noting that there are no conformance checks for an application, so it is impossible to test whether or not an application is expecting features that are not in the standard.

Conformance testing for CORBA is now the focus of active research. In particular, X/Open has developed a prototype CORBA 1.2 validation suite as part of a research and development project into automated test-suite generation from formal API specifications (the "ADL" project funded by the Information Technology Promotion Agency, an agency of Japan's MITI). The test suite is available by anonymous ftp from X/Open, but has no status as a conformance measurement tool either in X/Open or OMG.

Subject to being able raise the necessary sponsorship, X/Open expects by mid-1996 to have extended this work to cover the CORBA 2.0 C and C++ bindings, and subsequently to require the use of the resulting test suite for X/Open branding of CORBA implementations.

7.7 Summary

The Common Object Request Broker Architecture (CORBA) is the central component of the Object Management Group's (OMG) Object Management Architecture (OMA).

Perhaps the most important benefit of CORBA is the way it improves productivity by moving the programmer up several layers of abstraction. CORBA programmers do not require a deep understanding of protocols, application programming interfaces (APIs) or platform internals to build distributed applications.

The key to this is the idea of using an Interface Definition Language (IDL) to define the service being provided by an object. From this IDL definition a stub compiler can generate IDL stubs and skeletons. The IDL stub is placed between the client and the underlying platform. For the client programmer it makes invocation of a remote object look very much like invocation of an object in the same address space. The IDL skeleton is placed between the object or server and the underlying platform. For the server programmer it makes invocations from remote clients look very much like an invocation from the same address space.

Different Object Request Brokers (ORBs) from different vendors can interoperate using the Internet Inter-ORB Protocol (IIOP). If an ORB cannot support IIOP as an internal protocol, then the dynamic invocation interface (DII) and dynamic skeleton interface (DSI) make it easy to build a generic bridge application so that the ORB can interoperate using IIOP.

In addition to CORBA, the OMA also defines a number of common services such as naming and event channels which are useful for many applications. Common services will be available for all ORBs. The final component of the OMA is services called "common facilities". These services are optional, for example, they may be specialized support for a particular application domain such as finance.

CORBA is suitable for a wide variety of application domains and is particularly suited to the task of systems integration and building management applications. Currently CORBA does not provide support for timeliness or continuous media (e.g. video streams) and so could not be used to build some of the applications described elsewhere in this book.

Many of the OMG documents referenced in this chapter are available via anonymous ftp from `ftp.omg.org`. Other documents can be obtained from:

Object Management Group Inc.,
Framingham Corporation Center,
492 Old Connecticut Path, Framingham,
MA 01701-4568, USA

Telephone +1 (508) 820 4300
Fax. +1 (508) 820 4303
Email: `request@omg.org`

CHAPTER 8

Modelling and implementing distributed multimedia conferencing

with Mark Handley, UCL, and Ian Wakeman, University of Sussex

8.1 Introduction

In this chapter, we explore various aspects of multimedia conferencing. We look at shared windowing systems that permit multiple simultaneous users of an application that runs under a window system. We then look at shared applications that have been written with multiple users in mind, and look at managing shared data. We then look at conference management, and the problem of looking after all the different systems the users may have running. Finally, we examine how we can make use of multicast to improve the overall efficacy of such a system.

There is a lot of hype about multimedia conferencing. The main thing to grasp is that its usefulness increases with the distance you use it over. However, so does its cost (usually exponentially!), and so do cultural and social problems when you try to interact with people that you may never have met, over a limited-bandwidth link.

The systems described in this chapter were built as part of two European projects between 1989 and 1994. The first was the CAR project (Communications for the Automotive industry under RACE) which looked at computer-supported collaborative work for car designers. The second was the MICE Project (Multimedia Integrated Conferencing for Europe).

8.2 Multicast requirements for distributed applications

A Multicast Datagram Network Service in wide-area networks is a relatively new technique based on forming host groups and enhancing routers to form special-purpose forwarding information bases to these groups. This is mainly so that the number of copies of packets sent to replicated services may be reduced to near optimum in the same manner as on networks with a physical broadcast technology (e.g. satellite and Ethernets).

Multimedia conferencing is an application that often involves more than two end-systems, and could take advantage of a multicast network service. However, multimedia systems often employ application-level distribution. For instance, the voice portion of a conference is often sent by each participant to a central mixing service, which then sends the mixed portion to each member. To be best placed for each client, the mixing server may well be worst placed to use multicast to redistribute the mixed voice, compared with a forest of multicast trees rooted at each sender or rooted at each destination group.

With the video portion of a conference, it is often quad multiplexed by codecs (video coder–decoders), in a similar manner to audio mixing, or else bandwidth requirements preclude anyone but the floor holder of a conference being visible.

Clients of replicated databases distribute the same updates and retrieve the same records from more than one copy of the service and could also make use of a multicast network service. However, many transaction systems involve 2- or 3-phase commit protocols with each server in the replicated system for writing (although for reading, a majority read may suffice – however, we need to know what the majority is).

In this section we examine the snares and delusions that must be avoided when a multicast application uses a multicast network service. In particular, we distinguish between the savings of using a multicast system for data-packet replication and the overheads in establishing and maintaining group membership and group reachability.[1] In this case, there are two modes that could make use of multicast:

1. A periodic multicast "rwho", with the conference service cache the result of the multicast. We can also use this to find out the people we can conference with.
2. We can do a multicast to find out about the user when needed. Stations that have multimedia conference capabilities can then join the multicast group. Alternatively, only users that want to be found will join the multicast group.

In the CAR experimental platform, shared applications can be either collaboration-transparent or aware. Conference discovery can either use multicast to construct a conference finding service or can use that as an optimization between a real directory system and the application. All conference instances will be stored in the directory and local ones cached at the conference-finding daemon. Conference-finding requests will always be sent out on a local multicast address. A local conference will then return using the cached result at the conference-finding daemon. A non-local conference will then look up the real directory using DAP (directory access protocol).

In the next section, we briefly examine a centralized architecture for multimedia collaboration. Then we study in turn the use of multicast support for shared windows, audio, video and shared applications.

8.2.1 Conference servers, managers and replication/notification

Imagine we have a digitally switched video network connecting several offices and laboratories. The video is controlled by software running on a workstation and is transparently integrated into a multimedia conference. The conference video channel is controlled by the floor holder through the conferencing software and switches automatically when there is a change of floor. This degree of integration ensures that users view the video and applications as being one conference, rather than separate.

---

13. Multicast can also be used for user/conference location. User location involves identifying the current physical location of a given user and providing an invitation service as needed (or, as Cosmos Nikolaou called it, "User Locator").

The floor holder can also select quad mixing; this allows four conference sites to be visible to everybody, which is especially useful for small interactive conferences. The audio channel for a conference is open-channel, and so anyone can speak at any time. To prevent feedback, we employ an n-1 audio mixer, which returns mixed audio to a site from all the other sites, but not to the originator.

Many user trials show that in a collaborative conference much of the user's attention is taken up by the design applications. There tend to be quite long periods when a designer is concentrating on a design task, and often they do not explain verbally what they are trying to do. At these times, a video link is invaluable to find out what the other participant(s) are doing and whether they expect you to be doing something. For this purpose high-quality video is really not necessary. However, for larger lecture-style conferences, if video is required, greater bandwidth would be desirable.

These findings indicate that many users (especially designers) do not wish to sacrifice screen space for a video window, however small. For the purposes of interactive design conferences we also find that a frontal head-and-shoulders view does not include enough contextual information. Much better appears to be a view from one side, which allows the remote site to see the user from the waist upwards. Ideally it should include the workstation keyboard, so the remote site can clearly see when the user is busy. To create an illusion of co-presence, the camera and video display must be situated close together. This enables a user to talk to the image of the remote site and feel they are being talked to. The implication of this is that many users will not require the video to be displayed on the workstation screen, but rather on a separate monitor situated away to one side of the desk.

Using analogue video for local distribution provides us with maximum flexibility, and very high quality at relatively low cost. However, it is clearly not cost-effective to use analogue video for wide-area distribution, and the problems of scaling switch control are certainly not trivial. For wide-area distribution we employ both proprietary Picturetel and H261 video codecs, as well as lower-quality devices in workstations for capturing video and compressing to a usable data rate. As video codecs are currently expensive it makes sense to use them as a shared resource, and hence connecting them to our analogue video switch rather than to an individual workstation is a cost-effective solution.

Although car designers value the real estate of the workstation screen, it may prove much more cost-effective to display video there. We estimate that on workstations with greater than 100 MIPS processing power, H261 video compression will be possible in software without expensive hardware assistance. This is supported by findings at INRIA (Turletti & Huitema 1992) on current top-end workstations. As a result, digital multimedia will become much more widely available, which will have far-reaching effects for tomorrow's networks.

In a multimedia conference, events will occur that users should be informed about. If a new conferee joins the conference, all the existing conferees should be notified immediately that this has occurred, for it may affect the way they behave.

This is a high-priority event, and so the user should be distracted sufficiently from whatever they are doing to take notice of the event. The CAR system does this by sounding an audible warning and popping-up a new window containing the information.[2] Generally, though, this sort of warning proves too distracting for users if it is used for lower-priority notifications such as change of floor holder (though this would be a fairly high-priority warning if you were the old floor holder). The CAR system has an area set aside for these notifications however, trials show that users sometimes cover this with applications and then get confused.

Sometimes implicit notification can be used. An example of this is the video communication channel in the CAR system which switches to show the floor holder when the floor changes. However, this default can be overridden, and thus confusion can easily be created.

An example of a low-priority event is the resizing of a shared window by the floor holder. Here the notification received needs to be ignored until it becomes relevant – i.e. when the floor holder starts drawing in an area that can't be seen. Clearly there is a need to provide communication between conference sites of this information, but, irrespective of whether this is done using a shared window manager or using aware applications, the presentation of this information to the user presents some problems. In order to lessen the uncertainty of a user and thus their confusion, more information needs to be given, which may result in increasing confusion. The question is how to present this information in a way that will reduce the complexity, not increase it.

Which notification method is used for which event should depend on the user. High-priority events should always be intrusive, but lower-priority events should depend on the user's level of expertise.

8.3 Shared networked objects and windows

Computer-supported collaborative working is becoming a commonplace facility. The combination of shared applications with audio and video conferencing makes a very powerful tool. There is a great deal of work currently going on in the areas of network and workstation support for video and audio. In the past there has been some work on shared applications. This fell into two camps:

1. Replicating the application, typically through rebuilding the application so that it shares its persistent data through a shared file system. Of course, the main problem with this is it assumes that
    - you have source for the application

---

2. This is a good example of the inadequacy of a simple-minded implementation of the "client–server" model. Each conferee is running a conference management process and is a client of the multicast delivery system for each set of media. However, the conference service itself must multicast a request to each of these processes, reversing the roles. However, in many client–server programming systems (e.g. in the version of ANSA RPC used by the authors for the examples here), such a reversal is not permitted; thus we are forced to construct a CAR Library Notification Service which is a companion process for each client to serve these requests, and use local IPC mechanisms to report to the conference manager process.

- the users wish to use this particular application
2. Replicating the view of the application, typically through a shared window system.

These two approaches both require a coordination facility that determines which of the many concurrent users has control of change or input, whilst all the others see the same output. This is more easily achieved for the latter with the shared window approach. This has one major advantage over the other approach in that users may use any application they are familiar with that can run under the particular window system.

However, there is one serious drawback to sharing a view of a modern graphic user interface application. The cost of replicating the output can scale poorly. It has been achieved either through an intermediate agent (e.g. an X bridge) or by having the application treat n displays as 1 by replicating all output. In the former case, the load through the X bridge is excessive as soon as there are more than a very small number of participants. In the latter, the network traffic load is excessive. Modern network services include multicast where a packet destined for more than one destination can be optimally delivered by the network to only those segments/links that contain members of a multicast group. It is clear that we could combine this with a shared window system to minimize the traffic, thus countering the problems mentioned above.

8.3.1 Shared X

The standard client–server distributed window system model of computing implemented in the X-Windows system consists of a server process, which controls a workstation screen, and client (application) processes, which require their output to be displayed. The application sends requests to the server such as "Draw me a line", and the server sends back a reply to the application to confirm what happened. To make the model interactive, the server can send events to the application such as "The user just clicked the mouse button at position . . .". Applications can choose which types of events they are interested in, and so don't get informed about irrelevant events. These requests, replies and events are all performed or controlled by calls to functions in Xlib, the X library. The application process and the X server can be on the same machine, but they don't have to be – the Xlib functions just need to be told which display to use on which machine.

Shared X was intended to aid remote teaching by allowing the replication of the display and control of an X application on more than one display. To this end, a version of Xlib was developed that keeps a copy of all the state information pertaining to an application that is normally stored inaccessibly in the X server, and permits its duplication to other X servers. Programs can be recompiled using the Shared X library instead of the standard Xlib, but more typically the duplication is performed using a Shared X bridge, which converts standard Xlib requests into Xlib requests for each server. This bridge process sits between the client application and the server(s). It looks like a server to the client, and like a client to all the servers.

When the Shared X bridge receives a request from the client, it keeps track of any resources that would be created in the server, and then passes the request on to the servers. Replies and events coming from the servers to the client are filtered, as the application only expects to hear from one server, and hence a floor-control regime is imposed that only allows user input events from one server through to the application at any time.

One problem with Shared X is that it does not provide any form of distributed window management. Thus it is possible to have different-sized windows on different displays, and for one person to be working in a part of a window that is not visible to other users. A form of distributed window manager would be a desirable extension.

However the major drawback is the centralized design of Shared X. The problem with this model is that as the mapping is performed at the client, this results in a different request stream being sent to each X server, even though these request streams are supposed to perform the same task (albeit on different resources such as the colourmap).

The X protocol makes the complete distribution of this resource mapping difficult, as clearly only one consistent reply and event stream must reach the client. However, if the request and resource mapping were performed in a pseudo-server associated with each real X server, then the requests from the client could be multicast to the pseudo-servers. To do this, the pseudo-servers must implement a virtual X space, similar in concept to virtual memory. For instance, such a pseudo-server would map a virtual colourmap (which is the same for the client and all pseudo servers) onto the logical colourmap at its X server.

8.3.2 Shared NeWS/display PostScript

NeWS (network-extensible window system) is based on a very different paradigm than X. Rather than a specific protocol, NeWS is based on extensions to the PostScript page-layout language to handle displays and events. How to extend this to provide shared windows would be very different from natural extensions to X.

Shared X keeps external copy of the state information and resources that are normally inaccessible inside the X server. The PostScript language that NeWS uses allows the client application to build up new function definitions inside the NeWS server. The client can then call these new functions as required. To provide a Shared NeWS server we must duplicate these function definitions in any new NeWS servers joining a conference. This is relatively easy to do, and purely for the duplication of function definitions a centralized architecture may suffice. This will then allow the same PostScript function calls to be multicast to the NeWS servers. However, NeWS servers still contain state information that is not directly generated by the client, such as colour-map allocations. In order to allow multicast some mapping will still be required at each server. However, as NeWS servers are, by definition, extensible by the client, it should be possible for a bridge to download the mapping code directly into the NeWS server itself. In any case a bridge will still be required to arbitrate return values from the servers in order to present a consistent image to the client.

8.3.3 Multicast

Multicast is a facility that has been used to some benefit on local-area and bridged local-area networks to reduce the amount of traffic for protocols that are used for information dissemination. Multicast services are starting to appear in wide-area networks.

The Internet Protocol multicast routeing system distributes traffic across a minimum spanning tree of all the networks and routers where these are members of a multicast group. To join a multicast group, a process issues a group join, which is propagated globally. A similar scheme has been proposed for the ISO CLNS. Broadband ISDN networks based on the ATM (asynchronous transfer mode) service will necessarily support efficient multicast since they are aimed at cable TV as well as normal telephony and data services.

This scheme is scalable, and works well for such traffic as audio conferences. It makes an assumption that the group is symmetric in that no member of the group is more important than the others, and thus any member of the group can multicast to the group. For audio this is a reasonable assumption, as silence suppression decides which group member sends. If more than one member sends, mixing or filtering can always be performed at the receiver.

However, for shared windows we do not want more than one site sending simultaneously to a multicast group and, when there are many potential sources, it is the receiver that decides which one to receive from. What is required is for members of a conference to join a group at the start of the conference, but to be able to select from time to time whether they wish to be forwarded traffic from that group. We do not wish to use group join for this purpose as it is propagated globally, which is not necessary as we already know the group members.

What is needed is some traffic filter in the multicast routers and mechanism to send an activation message to them. This can be done in two ways:

1. It can multicast an "activate group" control message to the group. As this is multicast it will only propagate to the existing group routers.
2. It can send a message to the source, requesting activation of the group. The source then propagates the "activate group" message along with the existing stream of window packets to the routers downstream.

For video windows, this is even more critical, and the service must be extended. As the source must also end a synchronization point in the video for the new receiver, the second method ensures that this arrives after the filtering of the multicast stream has been removed. This filtering scheme could also be part of a more general scheme for hierarchically encoded video.

8.3.4 Audio

Audio services can make very good use of a real-time multicast facility. On a LAN or WAN (e.g. ATM) where multidestination packet delivery is efficient (e.g. order 1 for n destinations), each conferee simply joins the multicast group for a particular conference.

- *Conference service*
  The service required is to register and lookup a conference identifier to multicast group mapping.
- *Floor control*
  Floor control is achieved through normal vocal human interaction. Humans are used to this, and interaction with the workstation seems unnatural. However, a "microphone off" button and status display are useful for long-term information.
- *Traffic suppression*
  Silence suppression suffices to get efficient traffic limitation.

Even in a WAN without optimal multicast, the normal audio interactions involve only a single speaker, and therefore only a single multicast distribution tree of traffic at any one time (mostly). There is no need for floor control and traffic distribution to interact.[3]

8.3.5 Video

- *Conference service*
  The same service is required to register and look up a conference identifier to multicast group mapping as for audio. But we must also register a "callback" for floor-control interactions, and we may need to register subgroups of the video conference to allow conferees on lower-bandwidth lines to receive different samples of the video. Callback handlers are needed wherever another thread of control in a distributed system may wish to communicate asynchronously with this one.
- *Floor control*
  Workstations do not have sufficient display real estate to view more than a small number of video scenes. In fact, it would be distracting (and not particularly useful) since we can display more technical information such as a document or design under discussion. Therefore we want to have floor control interact with the video delivery system. There are two possible approaches:
  - Each conferee's video could be sent to a different IP group. We could use receiver selection by simply joining the right group(s).
  - Only a single or a small number of conferees could send at one time (selected by floor control). We could multiplex multiple video signals on screen (or select) based on source address.
- *Traffic suppression*
  Since a WAN can deliver more than a very small number of end-systems' video, we need intelligent multicast routers that interact with the floor con-

---

3. What about synchronization? There is some requirement for everyone to hear things at roughly the same time, so that no site has the advantage of getting everything first and always being able to assume the floor. If we don't enforce strict synchronization, then there must be some form of floor control where disadvantaged sites are compensated for their delay. Currently, we use an adaptive playout buffer to match everyone's delay. However, this is suboptimal for a conference with many local users and few remote. Further research is needed here.

trol scheme (Zhang 1993). It is not easy to see how we could employ any obvious form of "video silence suppression" any more than the common video compression algorithms already do.[4]

8.3.6 Replicated applications, data and multicast transactions

An alternative to replicating the interface to the application is to replicate the application itself (assuming we have access to the source). Processes are grouped so that messages concerned with changing the state of each replicant can be propagated by a multicast system to the group. These groups can be taken as host groups, or use a transport-level multiplexer (e.g. UDP or TCP ports) to have multiple process groups per host group.

The simplest model for replicating the application is to separate the access to any state in the application into read-only and modify operations. Then if the floor-control system is such an application, the modify operations are only permitted from one copy of the application to all the others (using multicast) and read operations from the other copies. Of course, since there is only one writer and many readers, the only consistency requirement is to synchronize the views all the applications have.

However, many users and applications require less strict floor control, and in these cases there will be multiple concurrent sources of read operations as well as write. This will entail concurrency control.

Since messages are not "idempotent" in the sense of a video or audio update, it is necessary to ensure uniqueness and reliability of delivery of group-addressed messages. It may be further necessary to ensure overall atomicity of messages and even global ordering. Each of these requirements entails further group and unicast messages, which reduce the gain from the basic multicast facility.

Factors contributing to the extra cost of carrying out atomic replicated communication using multicast:

1. How long do we wait before we can be sure that all messages have arrived before we sort them?
2. Arguments similar to those above can be made for storage.
3. Although unlikely, there will be cases when the timestamps on two messages are the same. We would need some arbitrary mechanism to sort the order. One way is to append the timestamp with host identifier/address.

A simple calculation shows the reduction in traffic for a 2-phase commit protocol, when using multicast, as in Figure 8.1.

The cost of using unicast for a complete 2-phase commit for the master is shown in Figure 8.2. The cost of using multicast for a complete 2-phase commit (assuming the master and all slaves are on the same multicast net) is shown in Figure 8.3.

---

4. But with a human level silence suppression, a privacy button becomes a "don't send anything at the moment", including video.

```
  MASTER            SLAVE (i=1..N)
  C-begin; {atomic action}
send(request_1);
send(request_2);
  ....
send(request_i);  receive(request_i);
  ....
send(request_N);
C_prepare;{Prepare to commit}
     C_prepare;
     if action can be performed
       then begin
         lock object;
         store an initial state;
         store the request;
         C-ready {the i-th slave
       end
       else
         C-refuse;


if all slaves sent C-ready
   then C-commit; {commit the action}
   else C-roolback; {abort the action}
wait for response
     if C-commit
     then begin
       do work;
       unlock object
     end
     send reponse;
```

Figure 8.1   2-phase commit protocol.


```
  N messages for "prepare to commit"
  N messages for "commit the action"

each slave:
  1 message for C-ready
  1 message for response

Total: 4N
```

Figure 8.2   Costs for 2-phase commit unicast protocol.

236

```
master:
  1 message for "prepare to commit"
In the worst case that all slaves carried out different
action, then the send requests before C_prepare will be
all different:
  N message for "prepare to commit"
  1 message for "commit the action"

each slave:
  1 message each for C-ready
  1 message for response

Total: 2N+2
Worst Case Total: 3N+1

As N -> large, we get about 50% saving for complete
transactions, or 25% in worst case
```

Figure 8.3   Costs for 2-phase commit multicast protocol.

8.3.7 Replicated transaction ordering: clock synchronization and timestamps

The most stringent requirement for ordering of messages in multi-party communication systems is given in Birman's paper (1991). A unicast packet delivery may be used to build up a replicated application. However, if the application requires most stringent consistency, it may be that each transaction from each client must be ordered with respect to all other client transactions, as well as with respect to each replicant server. This ordering can be achieved (to a required level of reliability at least, as with all distributed programs) by timestamping requests, and using a receive queue in all hosts within which messages are only allowed to the server in monotonically increasing order after a global synchronization step.

If clocks are synchronized, these protocols may be relaxed, since a message received from source A can be ordered with respect to a message from source B purely by source timestamp. Care must be taken that we can still detect failure of clock synchronization so that these protocols fail to safe.

Again, with atomic broadcast protocols, a level of optimization may be achieved by actually using network-level multicast (and presumably transport-level multicast). Here, a packet that must be sent to more than one destination may be simply multicast.[5]

Messages have the following control information:
• source address (always individual process/host or unique port)

---

5. A message may consist of many packets; we assume these are subsequence-numbered, and can be delivered in required order and so forth. The message arrival (time/event) can be construed as the arrival of the final packet of the message.

237

- destination address (process group address or individual process)
- send time
- and on reception, receive time

As in Lamport (1978), assume systems advance at least one tick per send or receive message. Given a particular protocol, we would like to establish whether a version using multicast and/or timestamps with synchronized clocks can be shown to have the same semantics, but fewer packets exchanged. The most common failure is the channel, especially in wide-area networks. This means that using multicast will result in the simplest failure mode (no answer from anyone).

Real-time delivery can be optimized using network-level multicast, as the message will be delivered at almost the same time (when compared with successive unicasts: of course we cannot ignore things like propagation delay). Thus the buffer time will be less and this in turn saves buffer space and end–end delay. Considering dynamically changing groups, if we can make group join/leave message to be ordered, then multicast groups can avoid the problems of different processes having different views of group membership. Such problems include the fact that this makes it harder to determine consistently the nature of a majority in a vote, for example.

Multicast packet delivery is a useful facility for optimizing network efficiency of multi-party distributed applications. However, the interactions between the applications and a multicast system are more complex than is obvious at first sight. One consequence of the high bandwidth requirements of multi-party multimedia communication is that we will need an interaction between multicast routeing and the application. This may need rapid switching of forwarding paths on and off. It is clear that if we are to make effective use of multicast in the WAN, we are going to need a large-address, flexible multicast address space.

8.4 Classical IPC usage for multimedia conference control

8.4.1 CAR conferencing system components

The CAR conferencing system has many components in common with the architectures described in Nicolaou (1990) and (Schooler 1993). These components are shown in Figure 8.4. The components all communicate using remote procedure call, with the exception of the channel between the Notification Service and CAR library, which uses a Unix pipe.

The system's clients and servers have the following roles:

- The *Switch Controller* acts purely as a service that exports an interface only to the Switching Server. The former runs on a machine attached to any hardware specific to providing switched video or audio services. These include a digitally controlled analogue video switch and a codec hub, providing multiplexing and demultiplexing of video streams.
- The *Switching Server* is a client of the Switch Controller and can run on any host in the system. It exports an interface that is used by the Conference Server.

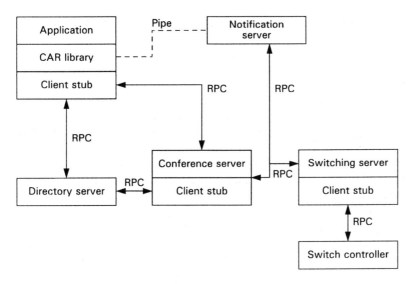

Figure 8.4   The CAR conference system architecture.

- The *Directory Server* is purely a server, and provides user and multimedia workstation location information for a site. This is used by the Conference Server.
- The *Conference Server* primarily provides a service for the applications interface via the standard CAR library. The Conference Server is also a client of the Directory Server, the Switching Server and the Notification Server.
- Applications are clients of the Conference and Directory Server, but are linked with a standard CAR library to hide this communication and to hide their dependence on the Notification server described next.
- Every application is run alongside a *Notification Server*, which is called by the Conference Server as a result of the actions of other applications. The interface between the Notification Server and the application is via a pipe. This is implemented inside the CAR library, so that it is largely transparent to the application.

For a given CAR set of conferences, there is only one Switch Controller, one Switching Server, one Directory Server and one Conference Server. These are run as daemons by the system (possibly on a variety of different machines, but quite possibly on a single machine). Due to the blocking synchronous nature of the version of the RPC system used, and the choice to import interfaces immediately at startup of each client, the servers must be started in the correct order: Switch Controller, then Switching Server in parallel with the Directory Server, then Conference Service, and finally conferencing applications.

There is another level of indirection and cause of unreliability, to paraphrase Dijkstra: there is a trader, in our case the RPC binder, which is required by clients to locate servers, as they do not make use of well-known ports: a restart of part of the system results in deadlock because new services' locations are no longer known to old clients. This is because there is state in the client that reflects the old locations.

8.4.2 Applications

The user may run a variety of applications. For example, the user usually runs a Conference Manager application, which lets the user control and know what is going on in a conference. A user can also run two other distinguishable types of application, called "*conference-aware*" and "*conference-transparent*". Conference-aware applications have been explicitly implemented as conferencing applications for the CAR system, such as a purpose-written shared editor. Conference-transparent applications are ones that have been implemented either as stand-alone, or else as distributed, but unaware of possible interactions with other distributed applications. In both these cases, a so-called *Nest* program is used to encapsulate the application and map CAR Conference Library calls and Notifications into meaningful application-specific actions. A Nest program must be written for each new type of conference-transparent application to implement these mappings. Examples of conference-transparent applications currently fall into three types:

1. *X-Windows-based applications*

    These are conferenced by using a CAR version of Shared X, and a Nest for Shared X to provide application inclusion/termination or exclusion, floor control and other CAR functions (Handley & Wilbur 1992).

    Shared X is a mechanism for replicating the window of an X-Windows client program on a number of servers' displays. The model is illustrated in Figure 8.5.

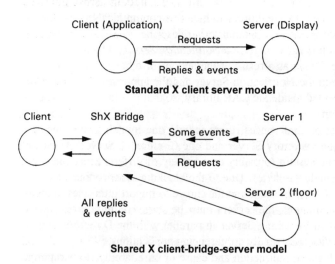

Figure 8.5 Shared X-Windows.

Other shared-window paradigms are feasible, as long as they allow single-user applications to produce replicated bitmap display output, and have modest control mechanisms for the workstation providing input at any one time.

2. *Conventional Interactive Applications*
These include applications that are normally run on a workstation interactively by a single user. For instance, editors (whether text or graphics) fall into this category. Each of these requires a special-purpose Nest.

3. *Simple (mono-media) Conferencing Applications*
These use a multicast network address as their means of identifying a conference as well as transmitting their media data. These include the LBL vat (Jacobson 1991) program and the INRIA ivs program (Turletti & Huitema 1992). They need to have multicast addresses allocated per conference. Floor control, restricting which source can send at any one time, can be applied through the Notification Service and a vat- or ivs-specific Nest.

8.4.3 Inter-process communication

The CAR conferencing system used RPC because the system designers were familiar with RPC, and not so familiar with lower-level network programming tools. The modularization that we chose lent itself to separate implementation and testing. Different programmers were able to carry out these tasks, even though several of the programmers had no previous experience with networks. Testing could take place without the need for a network at all, since RPCs could be called in the same system. The benefit was that the complete system was produced in a matter of months.

It was expected that conferences would be small and tightly controlled so that a single, centralized Conference Server would be adequate. Networks were believed to be reliable. Our experience of running the system across European sites, interconnected by IP routers across the narrow-band ISDN, was that demand for wide-area conferences amongst larger groups exceeded our expectations. We also found that network failures were common.

Points of failure will cause the entire system to fail:

* If any of the Switch Controller, Switching Server, Directory Server or Conference Server fails, the entire system fails.
* If the servers above are distributed across a network, then if any link between them fails, then the entire system blocks until that link recovers.
* Worse still, the nature of synchronous blocking RPC is such that if a link fails between the Conference Server acting as a Notification Client and a Notification Server, the entire system blocks until that link recovers.

Of course, the programmer using an RPC system can always set a finite timeout. However, the programmer then has two problems: determining a valid timeout without access to underlying communicatons code (e.g. round-trip time estimations in the transport protocol) is hard; in the event of a failure (whether the call was received and acted on or not) the caller must handle the exception. One might prefer to use a messaging system from the start.

Since the Conference Server is central to a conference, it is also a performance bottleneck for the system. Recent experience broadcasting the Internet Engineering Task Force Meeting over the Internet in the USA (Casner & Deering 1992) using a more loosely structured system shows that it is not unreasonable to have 500 participants in a networked multimedia conference. However, there is little hope of the CAR conferencing system architecture scaling to 500. In the Internet, 500 sites rarely have full connectivity, and any single link outage will thus frequently block the progress of the entire conference. It may be that real-time multimedia chatlines will become as commonplace as Internet Relay Chat and Bulletin Board use – in this case, we may see many systems spread over the wide-area, and inevitably have to deal with partial availability.

We believe that our instantiation of components as processes, and the subsequent communications architecture, was a poor implementation strategy. To use open distributed processing terminology, from the information viewpoint we have reflected the right model, but from the engineering viewpoint we may not have.

Simple replication of the servers provides no solution to the lack of fault tolerance – an entire protocol must be developed to make any access to those replicated servers location-transparent, and map failures into the right application exceptions. In other words, the decomposition into services has done little more than basic software engineering would, and does not address the real distributed computing aspects of the problem. A classical approach consisting of replicated servers, timeout and relocation by client of a secondary server would rectify these problems but seems perhaps a bit ad hoc.

8.5 Weak RPC

During the task of porting the application to a newer RPC system, we learned that there are ways in which an RPC implementation permits the programmer more flexibility than a strict remote emulation of local procedure call implies. We call this "weaker" RPC. Its features are as follows:

- *Callback*

  A client calls an RPC and normally blocks until there is a response. Some systems permit servers to make calls to the client process while it is blocked awaiting their response. This role reversal may continue, providing mutual recursion of RPCs. This is called *callback*.

  Since many newer RPC systems support callback, we can dispense with the Notification Service as a separate process, and merge it in the Library. We simply replace reading the pipe between separate processes, by polling on the RPC socket, followed by the dispatch table call if any data is present. This makes the system simpler, more robust, and possibly more responsive.

- *Broadcast*

  Some RPC systems provide a form of broadcast. At the moment several of the servers, the Conference Server, Directory Server, Switch Controller and Switching Servers, are bound to particular hosts, and are found through global knowledge of their host location.

Broadcast (or better still, multicast) RPC could provide a discovery-based approach, where no bootstrapping information at all is required. A trader or intelligent dynamic (run-time) binding service could also play a role here.

- *Streaming*
  More recent RPC provides a streaming service, where RPCs do not block at the client, and a number of calls may be made successively without awaiting a response for each. This may be used to make the system robust in the face of link outages. For example, notifications can be streamed to applications, instead of the Conference Server blocking unnecessarily for responses.

ANSAWare 4.0 has many of these new mechanisms, based on a system of tokens that permit callback, streaming and so on. In addition, it provides a threads package, which permits lightweight concurrency within servers. These capabilities would permit a similar restructuring of the system, but would make the conferencing system further dependent on a less commonly available RPC system. We would also be more dependent on its annotation approach to enhancing C. This is felt to be inappropriate because the maintenance of the system would be greatly complicated by having to track ANSA releases as well.

In a related piece of work, we are designing a compiler for the GDMO language (Guidelines for the Definition of Managed Objects, an ITU standard) to produce C++ code to provide easy access to new managed objects in a large system. Programmers have reported that they were happier with a scripting approach than with an annotation approach to this type of problem. The script approach entails the programmer writing scripts that direct the actions of the stub compiler in a special-purpose compiler directive language, as opposed to adding notes in the actual RPC code in a hybrid language. Thus the distributed application is kept one step removed from the communications software.

8.6 Event-driven approaches

In the future, it is clear that a more object-oriented approach will enhance the system. This will remove redundancy in the code, eradicate most of the (trivial) annoyances in the current environment by further removing the scripts or annotation, and permit clean integration of networked data types with ordinary programming data types.

However, the CAR communications architecture is still flawed: it is inherently designed around a model of distributed processes that perform specialized tasks on behalf of the whole system. Any attempt to provide robustness (e.g. the broadcast for directory or the streaming of Notification RPCs) only alleviates some of the problems. There still exist centralized points of failure. This is in fact inevitable for a system designed this way. The CAR conference system was built initially in the original spirit of RPC, which is (Wilbur & Bacarisse 1987) to provide an "exactly once" semantics for remote procedure call that is as close to local procedure call as possible (Xerox 1981). Consequently, systems built this way are sequential programs running in multiple address spaces – when these are instantiated as separate processes on separate machines networked, such systems are far less reliable than a single process/on a single machine. In the extreme, pure RPC is an anathema to distributed algorithms.

In the case of the system discussed here, the requirements for consistency are weak in many components, thus it is not a strong case for RPC. In more interesting distributed computations, whether for increased concurrency and performance, or fault tolerance, we often find that divide-and-conquer or other approaches to the distribution again have little requirement for a response to messages coupled with associated processing. That this should appear attractive for conferencing is a consequence of the peer-wise nature of the application. Communications between components in a multi-party conference is much more akin to that of a collection of distributed routers, than to a client/server model.

Re-examining each of the basic CAR conference system services in turn, we can see that very few of them need the stricter requirements of pure RPC:

- The Switch Controller is attached to a physical resource that keeps permanent state, and therefore cannot be distributed. However, access to it may be distributed. Thus RPC is appropriate here.
- The Switching Server is, on the other hand, a deliberate attempt to remove the service from the location, and thus should be distributed. Indeed, we can foresee a system with multiple distributed servers, and the Switching Server should be aware of all these.
- The Directory Service, like any other directory service, need not be a central system, e.g. DNS (Mockapetris 1985), X.500 (Kille 1988). Since a directory is a read-only service, it needs weaker semantics than the normal *exactly once* RPC. Some information held by the Directory Server may be completely distributed with the application.
- The Notification Service is inherently asynchronous. Thus a message-passing system is sufficient. Given that notifications come from the Confer-

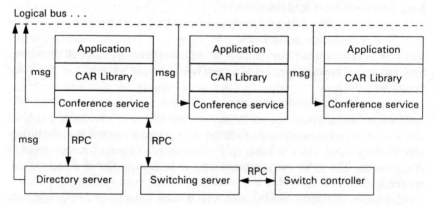

Figure 8.6 An event-driven conference system architecture.

ence Server largely as a result of other application actions it is possible that these can be sourced from each application, and directly multicast to all other applications' Notification Interface, using reliable delivery (if large notification messages are sent), but not awaiting any response.

- Lastly, the conference service is merely a coordinator of the system. If the steps outlined above are taken, it withers away and becomes redundant.

In Figure 8.6, we illustrate the components of a more distributed approach. Here, we have adopted a pure message-passing/event-driven model that incorporates the ideas above. Independent failure of a site is now feasible without delaying or halting an entire conference.

8.7 Related work

Recent years have seen a great deal of research and development in the area of multimedia conferencing.

Crowley (1990) describes *MMConf*, a system for building shared multimedia applications. Here, the actual protocols that control and coordinate the applications are based around extensions to the Diamond/Slate multimedia mail systems.

Arango et al. (1992) describes the *Touring Machine*, a system for moving the media around. The conference control architecture is not expounded in detail in that paper.

Schooler (1993) describes *mmcc*, a system for controlling largely tightly bound multimedia conferences, based around RPC.

The ITU standard, H.320 (ITU 1992), is a classical design for the signalling of messages between components in a telephony-style conference control system.

A different approach can be seen in the work at LBL (Lawrence Berkeley Laboratories)on a Session Directory and Visual Audio Conferencing tool (Jacobson 1991). This makes use of a distributed algorithm for conference identification and for session and conference announcements based on periodic multicasting of information in a similar way to beaconing in cell-based phone systems or station-identification protocols. This can replace a directory service, including session membership, and a fair portion of a conference management system, including floor control. The n-to-n use of multicast can lead to synchronized traffic unless care is taken. We have named this behaviour of distributed applications a "systolic tendency" from the original meaning of the word "systolic", meaning "heartbeat". It has been reported in distributed routeing algorithms (Floyd & Jacobson 1993).

If it is engineered properly, we believe that the approach using loosely coupled messages and events as espoused by these researchers forms a more robust scalable starting point. Work at UCL on the Conference Control Channel Protocol (CCCP) (Handley et al. 1995) is attempting to bring together all aspects of this approach.

The notion of *tightly coupled* conferences, with strict membership and floor control, has led some researchers to re-examine the more RPC-like approach.

However, the CCCP work shows that the semantics of conferencing are orthogonal to the way they are constructed from IPC mechanisms.

8.7.1 Practical use of ANSA RPC

ANSA RPC is used in a straightforward way to support the interfaces exported by each of the servers described in Section 8.4. The source code is divided into a set of subdirectories of a top-level source tree on a Unix development machine following normal "C and Unix" software engineering practice.

Each service is defined in a separate module, with the code that implements the service in one C module, the actual procedures in a second (separate from the bulk of the service just so that it might be possible later to cleanly replace one RPC mechanism with another). This latter module is in DPL which is a form of annotated C that an ANSA preprocessor parses and replaces the annotated sections with:

- calls to remote procedures from the correct interface
- calls to ANSA run-time support to do exception handling (a remote procedure invocation can result in more exceptions than a local one.

The definitions of the interfaces (global types and procedures) ("OPERATIONS" in ANSA terminology) are in a separate IDL module in the same subdirectory as the service source and DPL. These are parsed by another preprocessor to generate:

- Client-stub C modules – the client program(s) will be linked with these modules which marshal and unmarshal call and response messages and call ANSA run-time support and communications primitives to transmit and receive these to (remote) servers.
- Server-stub C modules – the server program(s) will be linked with these to provide the complementary tasks to the client stubs. At the server end, there is also the question of the main entry point to a program. This could either be in the stub, with a dispatch table to service calls, or else can be in the server DPL or C, in which case the dispatcher must be called from there. In the ANSA system as used in CAR, the former approach is used.
- C type definitions for the types referenced in the last two modules and in the DPL modules (and in the service C modules).

Since there are a number of types in common across all of the services, there is a subdirectory with both a C type definition module and an IDL type definition.

Each subdirectory has its own makefile (Unix 1990) This leads to an initial pair of problems – makefiles for clients now have to reference IDL files in the server subdirectories and many of the dependencies are heavily entwined to and fro across the subdirectories.

8.7.2 Porting to a less pure RPC

The experience we wish to emphasize is not that RPC cannot be changed. It is that RPC is represented in modellers' minds as providing a base communications paradigm, first and foremost, which is as like to local procedure as possible, by default, and only relaxed later. This, as we shall see, is what has caused problems.

First, we must answer the inevitable question relating to standards: why not CORBA (or some other)? The answer to this is non-technical, but stems from our original motivation in stopping using ANSA – it is not part of the installed/bundled system (i.e. the same reason we do not want to use TP4/CLNP instead of TCP/IP). Sun RPC is a widely available system with stub compilers in the public domain (Sun 1986).

The process of porting to Sun RPC was relatively straightforward, and consists of the following (semi-automated) steps:

1. Converting the IDL to XDR suitable for processing by the stub generator utility, rpcgen. This consists of:
   - conversion of IDL comment style to C
   - conversion of "INTERFACE/BEGIN/END" to program, etc.
   - conversion of TYPES to XDR, including constructors such as struct, enum
   - conversion of OPERATIONS to XDR procedures

   The conversion of operation parameter types involves merging call-and-return parameters into single call-and-return structures, since Sun RPC's XDR only supports a single parameter and return value in this way. The only difference that might have led to any problems is that both ANSA and Sun RPC provide variable-length arrays, and the CAR software makes extensive use of this type constructor (though not part of the base C language that the CAR system is written in). The stub generators in both cases convert this into a structure that has both a length and a value field, where the value is a pointer type and the length is a number of objects. In both cases, the same approach is taken. Thus storage allocation associated with parameters can be dealt with in the same way as we pass between the stub and the actual client and server application code.

2. Conversion of the DPL files to C with:
   - inclusion of appropriate header fields to be generated from appropriate XDR files
   - embedded calls to the relevant Sun RPC run-time support in place of the ANSA annotations
   - conversion of exception-handling code to Sun RPC exception handling (instead of annotation, a return value of NULL pointer is used to indicate an RPC protocol problem, at which point an external global variable is available for testing what particular error has occurred) together with appropriate actions and error messages

3. Conversion of the Actual Server (called) C Code to match the stub declarations.

4. Conversion of Actual Client C (calling) Code to match stub declarations.

   This last step entails care, since the ANSA DPL annotation language provides a primitive attempt at object-orientedness, by tagging procedure calls with the interface name. This means that there could in principle be name clashes. However, in well-engineered software, as the CAR system is, this turned out to be rare.

5. Finally, references to interfaces, which are passed around between clients and servers to build more flexible distributed programs (i.e. provide an extra level of indirection, for instance in the Notification Service), must be changed to refer to an instance of a Sun RPC server – in our case, this is bound to a "host/port" pair, so can readily be implemented as a string or as a Unix sockaddr structure.

The only step that entails some complexity is in dealing with the inclusion of global definitions in XDR, in local XDR code. The problem is this: given

```
global/g.x      some global XDR definitions
s1/s1.x         server 1 XDR definitions
s2/s2.x         server 2 XDR definitions
```

a stub generator produces

```
global/g.h
s1/s1.h s1_svc.c s1_clnt.c s1_xdr.c
s2/s2.h s2_svc.c s2_clnt.c s2_xdr.c
```

where xxxclnt.c and xxxsvc.c are the client and server stubs, respectively. For these to compile, they must all include g.h, or, more cleanly, s1.x and s2.x must include g.x, and the stub generator program uses the C preprocessor to achieve the same thing.

The problem here lies in where a program that is a client of both services needs to include the C definitions, s1.h and s2.h, there is a repeated definition, which cannot be parsed.

The solutions are either to change the stub compiler so that it generates unique include guarantees (ifndef filenameIncluded followed by define filenameIncluded), or not to include the g.x in s1.x and s2.x, and to postprocess the client and server stub modules to include the global C definitions. All of this is unnecessary in the ANSA RPC system, through its pseudo-object-oriented approach. A system built on C++ could avoid this mess completely (indeed, the entire IDL/DPL, XDR support would then become unnecessary), since inheritance could be used to carry out a lot of what is implemented using preprocessors here.

8.7.3 Source changes – sizes

The source changes to the system are largely the translation from IDL to XDR (the names correspond roughly to the interfaces and object modules that are described in the CAR system above): see Tables 8.1 and 8.2. The changes in sizes of executables were more noteworthy: see Tables 8.3 and 8.4.

Table 8.1 The ANSA interface definition language (IDL) modules.

Lines of source	Module
452	cl/Cl.idl
1016	cnfserv/Cs.idl
304	dirserv/Ds.idl
196	global/car-type.idl
170	sc2/Sc.idl
663	sw/Sw.idl

Table 8.2 The Sun external data representation (XDR) modules.

Lines of source	Module
370	cl/Cl-sun.x
852	cnfserv/Cs-sun.x
256	dirserv/Ds-sun.x
224	global/car-type-sun.x
158	sc2/Sc-sun.x
566	sw/Sw-sun.x

Table 8.3 ANSA module, object sizes.

Text (bytes)	Data (bytes)	Module
122880	16384	dirserv/dirserv
221184	32768	cnfserv/cnfserv
155648	24576	sw/sw
122880	16384	sc2/scs
229376	57344	cl/clnfs
1220608	294912	mn/x-car

Table 8.4 Sun RPC module, object sizes.

Text (bytes)	Data (bytes)	Module
24576	8192	dirserv/dirserv
98304	24576	cnfserv/cnfserv
49152	16384	sw/sw
24576	8192	sc2/scs
24576	8192	cl/clnfs
1105920	294912	mn/x-car

8.7.4 RPC types and buffering changes

Sun RPC and ANSA RPC introduce variable arrays, which are not a base type of the C language. There are two important consequences of the introduction of RPC type constructors beyond those available in the base programming language:

- *Type conversion*

  The programmer is now obliged to manage type conversion between the IDL or XDR type, and whatever is available in run-time support (e.g. alloc/ free) for such a function. Since there may be more than one choice here, this leads to possible divergence in the internal representations of the external data type (in a non-type-safe way, so programs may crash). In C terms, this forces the programmer to use a *cast*, which actually hides any error of type conversion from the meagre checking provided in many compilers. Of course, a ubiquitous standard IDL would avert this problem a priori.

- *Buffer-allocation strategy*

  A client or server may receive a response or request containing variables whose storage requirements cannot be known at compile or initial run time, but only at actual call time. This means that dynamic storage allocation is required. In the server, any storage associated with the call or response parameters can be freed by the RPC dispatcher. However, in the client, either the user is obliged to provide the storage or they must be given a standard handle for freeing the RPC reply parameter storage. (They cannot just assume they can use a standard free function as, for efficiency reasons in protocol layering implementation, the result parameters may be part of a larger piece of dynamically allocated storage with preceding header information.) In fact, this last problem arises even for existing data types, such as strings, in any case.

There is also a storage management problem since the space required for the data type in machine native format may be more than network buffers provide, so the presentation decoding may not be done in place (even though it should be done inline with the network receive-buffer copy-code).

8.8 The MICE design of conferencing communications channel

In this section, we will discuss some of the lessons that we have garnered from previous work involving computer-based multimedia conferencing, and use these as a basis for developing an architecture for the next generation of conference-control applications, suitable for conferencing over wide-area networks. We show that a simple protocol acting over a conference-specific communications channel, named the Conference Control Channel or CCC, will perform all tasks within the scope of conference control.

The previous generation of conferencing tools, such as CAR, MMconf (Crowley 1990), the Touring Machine (Arango et al. 1992), mmcc (Schooler 1993) and H.320 (ITU 1992) were based on centralized architectures, where a central application on a central machine acted as the repository for all information relating to the conference. Although simple to understand and simple to implement, this model proved to have a number of disadvantages, the most important of which was the disregard for the failure modes arising from conferencing over the wide-area.

An alternative approach to the centralized model is the loosely coupled model promoted by Van Jacobson and exemplified by the vat (Jacobson 1991) and wb (Floyd et al. 1995) applications. In the "loose session model", the network is regarded as inherently unreliable. Our observations of the Mbone (Casner & Deering 1992) show that humans can cope with a degree of inconsistency that arises from partitioned networks and lost messages, as long as the distributed state will tend to converge in time. This model makes less demands on the network, and recognizes the possibility of failure modes up-front. We have taken these and the other lessons we have learned from experience with conferencing tools, and derived two important aims that any conference control architecture should meet:

1. The conference architecture should be flexible enough that any mode of operation of the conference can be used and any application can be brought into use. The architecture should impose the minimum constraints on how an application is designed and implemented.

2. The architecture should be scalable, so that "reasonable" performance is achieved across conferences involving people in the same room, through to conferences spanning continents with different degrees of connectivity and large numbers of participants. To support this aim, it is necessary explicitly to recognize the failure modes that can occur, and examine how they will

affect the conference, and then attempt to design the architecture to minimize their impact.

We model a conference as composed of a (possibly unknown) number of people at geographically distributed sites, using a variety of applications. These applications can be at a single site, and have no communication with other applications or instantiations of the same application across multiple sites. If an application shares information across remote sites, we distinguish between the cases when the participating processes are tightly coupled[6] – the application cannot run unless all processes are available and contactable – and when the participating processes are loosely coupled, in that the processes can run when some of the sites become unavailable. A tightly coupled application is considered to be a single instantiation spread over a number of sites, whilst loosely coupled and independent applications have a number of unique instantiations, although they possibly use the same application-specific information (such as which multicast address to use).

The tasks of conference control break down in the following way:

- application control – applications as defined above need to be started with the correct initial state, and the knowledge of their existence must be propagated across all participating sites; control over the starting and stopping can be either local or remote.
- membership control – who is currently in the conference and has access to what applications.
- floor management – who or what has control over the input to particular applications.
- network management – requests to set up and tear down media connections between endpoints (no matter whether they be analogue through a video switch, a request to set up an ATM virtual circuit, or using RSVP (Zhang 1993) over the Internet), and requests from the network to change bandwidth usage because of congestion.
- meta-conference management – how to initiate and finish conferences, how to advertise their availability, and how to invite people to join.

We maintain that the problem of meta-conference management is outside the bounds of the conference control architecture, and should be addressed using tools such as traditional directory services, or through external mechanisms such as email. The conference control system is intended to maintain consistency of state amongst the participants as far as is practical and not to address the social issues of how to bring people together and coordinate initial information such as encryption keys.

We then take these tasks as the basis for defining a set of simple protocols that work over a communication channel. We define a simple class hierarchy, with an application type as the parent class and subclasses of network manager, member

---

6. We define a tightly coupled system as one that attempts to ensure consistency at all sites. By contrast a more loosely coupled system tolerates inconsistencies, though it should attempt to resolve them in time. A very loosely coupled system will not even know the full list of conference members.

and floor manager, and define generic protocols that are used to talk between these classes and the application class, and an inter-application announcement protocol. We derive the necessary characteristics of the protocol messages as reliable/unreliable and confirmed/unconfirmed (where "unconfirmed" indicates whether responses saying "I heard you" come back, rather than indications of reliability). It is easily seen that both tightly and loosely coupled models of conferencing can be encompassed if the communication channel is secure. We have abstracted a messaging channel, using a simple distributed inter-process communication system, providing confirmed/unconfirmed and reliable/unreliable semantics. The naming of sources and destinations is based upon application-level naming, allowing wildcarding of fields such as instantiations (thus allowing messages to be sent to all instantiations of a particular type of application). Finally, we briefly consider the design of the high-level components of the messaging channel (named variously the CCC or triple-C). Mapping of the application-level names to network-level entities is performed using a distributed naming service, based upon multicast once again, and drawing upon the extensive experience already gained in the distributed operating systems field in designing highly available name services.

8.8.1 Multicast Internet conferencing

Since early 1992, a multicast virtual network has been constructed over the Internet. This multicast backbone or Mbone (Casner & Deering 1992) has been used for a number of applications including multimedia (audio, video and shared workspace) conferencing. These applications include vat (LBL's Visual Audio Tool), ivs (INRIA Videoconferencing System (Turletti & Huitema 1992), nv (Xerox's Network Video tool (Casner & Deering 1992) and wb (LBL's shared whiteboard) amongst others. They have a number of things in common:

- They are all based on IP multicast.
- They all report who is present in a conference by occasional multicasting of session information.
- The different media are represented by separate applications.[7]
- There is no conference control, other than each site deciding when and at what rate it sends.

These applications are designed so that conferencing will scale effectively to large numbers of conferees. At the time of writing, they have been used to provide audio, video and shared whiteboard to conferences with about 500 participants. Without multicast[8] this is clearly not possible. It is also clear that, with unreliable networks, these applications cannot achieve complete consistency between all participants, and so they do not attempt to do so. The conference control they support usually consists of:

---

7. Actually ivs does support audio, but it has also been widely used as a pure video codec with vat as the audio tool.

8. Also without broadcast, but that is outside the scope of this document, as it does not usually provide a reverse path from receiver to sender.

- periodic (unreliable) multicast reports of receivers
- the ability to locally mute a sender if you do not wish to hear or see them (however, in some cases stopping the transmission at the sender is actually what is required)

Thus any form of conference control that is to work with these applications should at least provide these basic facilities, and should also have scaling properties that are *no worse than the media applications themselves*.

The domains these applications have been applied to vary immensely. The same tools are used for small (say 20-participant) highly interactive conferences, as for large (500-participant) disseminations of seminars, and the application developers are working towards being able to use these applications for "broadcasts" that scale towards millions of receivers.

It should be clear that any proposed conference control scheme should not restrict the applicability of the applications it controls, and therefore should not impose any single conference control policy. For example, we would like to be able to use the same audio encoding engine (such as vat), irrespective of the size of the conference or the conference control scheme imposed. This leads us to the conclusion that *the media applications (audio, video, whiteboard, etc.) should not provide any conference control facilities themselves, but should provide the handles for external conference control and whatever policy is suitable for the conference in question.*

8.8.2 The MICE project requirements

The MICE project has slightly unusual requirements, needing to support:

- multicast-based applications running on workstations where possible
- hardware codecs and multiplex their output
- sites connecting into conferences from ISDN
- interconnecting all the above

These requirements have dictated that we build a number of conference management and multiplexing centres (CMMCs) to provide the necessary format conversion and multiplexing to interwork between the multicast workstation-based domain and the unicast (whether IP or ISDN) hardware-based domain.

Traditionally such a multiplexing centre would employ a centralized conference control system (such as the CAR system or a number of others mentioned above and later), but for MICE that is not possible as we wish the users of our CMMC to participate in large multicast-based conferences. Also we do not wish to change the multicast media applications when they switch from an entirely multicast-based conference to one using a CMMC for some participants.

We believe that these requirements are more general than just for the MICE project. It is inevitable that translators, multiplexors, format converters and so forth will form some part of future conferences, and that large conferences will be primarily multicast-based. Thus although CCCP (CCC protocol) has originated from the needs of the MICE project, it has done so from a process of generalization that we should make it widely applicable.

8.8.3 Where current systems fail

The sort of conference control system we are addressing here cannot be:

- Centralized. This will not scale.
- Fixed-policy. This would restrict the applicability. The important point here is that only the users can know what appropriate policies a meeting may need.
- Application-based. It is very likely that separate applications will be used for different media for the foreseeable future. We need to be able to switch media applications where appropriate. Basing the conference control in the applications prevents us changing policy simply for all applications.
- Heterogeneity. Most existing systems have been fairly homogeneous. An increasingly important requirement is for different systems to interwork. There needs to be some basis for this interworking, at both the media data-stream level and at the conference-control level.
- Difficult to get right. Writing distributed group applications that interwork and tolerate network failures is difficult to get right. Generally application writers either start from scratch, which means reimplementing stock algo-rithms, or base their applications on a scheme that promises to do every-thing, but in practice turns out to be too inflexible.

8.8.4 Specific requirements

Modularity

Conference-control mechanisms and conference-control applications should be separated. The mechanism to control applications (mute, unmute, change video quality, start sending, stop sending, etc.) should not be tied to any one confer-ence-control application in order to allow different conference-control policies to be chosen depending on the conference domain. This suggests that a modular approach be taken, with, for example, a specific floor-control module being added when required (or possibly choosing a conference manager tool from a selection of them according to the conference).

A unified user interface

A general requirement of conferencing systems, at least for relatively small con-ferences, is that the participants need to know who is in the conference and who is active. Vat is a significant improvement over telephone audio conferences, in part because participants can see who is (potentially) listening and who is speaking. Similarly if the whiteboard program wb is being used effectively, the participants can see who is drawing at any time from the activity window. However, a partici-pant in a conference using, say, vat (audio), ivs (video) and wb (whiteboard) has three separate sets of session information, and three places to look to see who is active.

Clearly any conference interface should provide a single set of session and activity information. A useful feature of these applications is the ability to "mute" (or hide or whatever) the local playout of a remote participant. Again, this should be possible from a single interface. Thus the conference-control scheme should provide local inter-application communication, allowing the display of session information, and the selective muting of participants. Taking this to its logical conclusion, the applications should only provide media-specific features (such as volume or brightness controls), and all the rest of the conference-control features should be provided through a conference-control application.

Flexible floor-control policies
Conferences come in all shapes and sizes. For some, no floor control, with every-one sending audio when they wish, and sending video continuously is fine. For others, this is not satisfactory because of insufficient available bandwidth or a number of other reasons. It should be possible to provide floor-control functional-ity, but the providers of audio, video and workspace applications should not specify which policy is to be used. Many different floor-control policies can be envisaged. A few example scenarios are:

- Explicit chaired conference, with a chairperson deciding when someone can send audio and video, and some mechanism equivalent to hand raising to request to speak. Granting the floor starts video transmission, and enables the audio device. Essentially this is a schoolroom-type scenario, requiring no expertise from end-users.
- Audio-triggered conferencing. This has no chairperson and no explicit floor control. When someone wants to speak, they do so using "push to talk". Their video application automatically increases its data rate from, for exam-ple, 10kb/s to 256kb/s as they start to talk. Twenty seconds after they stop speaking it returns to 10kb/s.
- Audio triggered conferencing with a CMMC (Handley & Wilbur 1992) – essentially one or more points where multiple streams are multiplexed to-gether for the benefit of people on unicast links, ISDN and hardware codecs. The CMMC can mix four streams for decoding by participants with hard-ware codecs. The four streams are those of the last four people to speak, with only the current speaker transmitting at a high data rate. Everyone else stops sending video automatically.
- A background Mbone engineering conference that's been idle for 3 hours. All the applications are iconized, as the participant is doing something else. Someone starts drawing on the whiteboard, and the audio application plays an audio icon to notify the participant.

Scaling from tightly coupled to loosely coupled conferences
CCCP originates in part as a result of experience gained from the CAR Multime-dia Conference Control system (Handley & Wilbur 1992). The CAR system was a tightly coupled centralized system intended for use over ISDN. As described earlier in this chapter, the functionality it provided can be summarized by listing its basic primitives:

- create conference
- join/leave conference
- list members of conference
- include/exclude application in conference
- take floor

In addition, there were a number of asynchronous notification events:
- floor change
- participant joining/leaving
- application included/excluded

CAR's application model was modelled around applications that could replicate either themselves or their display onto remote machines if they were given a list of addresses or displays, hence the include/exclude functionality. However, these are the basic primitives required to support a tightly coupled conference, although for some uses others may be added. Any conference-control system that claims to be fairly generic must be able to support these primitives with reasonable reliability. (Absolute consistency is not really a feasible option in a multi-way conference.)

Loosely coupled conferences put less constraints on the protocols used, but must scale to much larger numbers and must be very tolerant of loss and network segmentation.

Taking the modular approach described above, we would expect to change conference controllers when moving from one regime to another, but we do not wish to change the media applications too.[9]

8.8.5 The conference control channel (CCC)

To bind the conference constituents together, a common communication channel is required, which offers facilities and services for the applications to send to each other. This is akin to the inter-process communication facilities offered by the operating system. The conference communication channel should offer the necessary primitives upon which heterogeneous applications can talk to each other.

The first attempt would appear to be a messaging service, which can support one-to-many communication, and with various levels of confirmation and reliability. We can then build the appropriate application protocols on top of this abstraction to allow the common functionality of conferences.

We need an abstraction to manage a loosely coupled distributed system, that can scale to as many parties as we want. In order to scale we need the underlying communication to use multicast. Many people have suggested that one way of thinking about multicast is as a multifrequency radio, in which one tunes into particular channels in which we are interested. We extend this model to build an inter-process communications model, on which we can build specific conference management protocols. Thus we define an application control channel.

What do we actually want from the system?

---

9. Actually many shared workspace tools will not scale anyway, but we shall concern ourselves here with those that will.

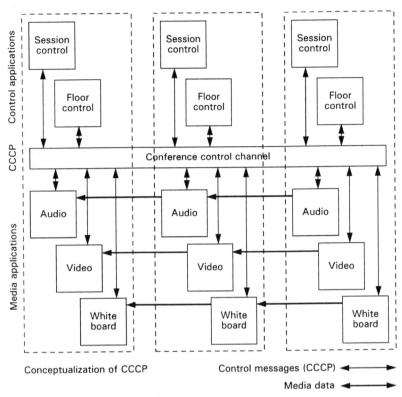

Figure 8.7 CCCP conceptual design.

- We want to ask for services.
- We want to send requests to specific entities or groups of entities and receive responses from some subset of them with notifications sent out to others.

CCCP originates in the observation that *in a reliable network*, conference control would behave like an Ethernet or bus – addressed messages would be put on the bus, and the relevant applications will receive the message and if necessary respond. In the Internet, this model maps directly onto IP multicast. This is illustrated in Figure 8.7. In fact, the IP multicast groups concept is extremely close to what is required. In CCCP, applications have a tuple as their address: (instantiation, application type, address). We shall discuss exactly what goes into these fields in more detail later. In actual fact, an application can have a number of tuples as its address, depending on its multiple functions. Examples of the use of this would be:

```
Destination Tuple Message
----------------- -------
(1, audio, localhost) <start sending>
(*, activity_management, localhost) <receiving audio from host:>
  ADDRESS
```

```
(*, session_management, *) <I am:> NAME
(*, session_management, *) <I have media:> {application list}
(*, session_management, *) <Participant list:> {participant list}
(*, floor_control, *) <REQUEST FLOOR>
(*, floor_control, *) <I HAVE FLOOR>
```

and so on. The actual messages carried depend on the application type, and thus the protocol is easily extended by adding new application types. In keeping with the underlying multicast message reception paradigm, a CCC application needs to register its interest in messages before it will receive them. Where possible, a CCC system uses the underlying multicast delivery to optimize where messages are filtered.

8.8.6 CCC names

Our model of the CCC is a broadcast bus, where the receivers filter the messages according to what information and which protocols they need to receive and participate in. Using this model, we based our naming scheme upon the attributes of an application that could be used in deciding whether to receive a message. We thus build a name tuple from three parts:

```
(instantiation, type, address)
```

An application registers itself with its CCC library, specifying one or more tuples that it considers describe itself. Note that there is no conference identifier currently specified as part of the tuple, but this is liable to change, since a conference identifier may be useful in unifying conference management and conference meta-management, and considerably simplifies the design of applications that may be part of several conferences simultaneously. In the current prototype design, a control group address or control host address or address list is specified at startup, and that meta-conferencing (i.e. allocation and discovery of conference addresses) is outside the scope the CCC itself. The parts of the tuple will now be described.

Address

In our model of a conference, applications are associated with a machine and possibly a user at a particular machine. Thus we use a representation of the user or the machine as a field in the tuple, to allow us to specify applications by location. The *address* field will normally be registered as one of the following:

- `hostname`
- `username@hostname`

When the application is associated with a user, such as a shared whiteboard, the `username@hostname` form is used, whereas applications that are not associated with a particular user, such as a video switch controller, register simply as `hostname`. For simplicity, we use the domain naming scheme in our current implementation, although this does not preclude other identifiable naming schemes. When other applications wish to send a message to a destination group (a single application is a group of size 1), they can specify the *address* field as one of the following:

- `username@hostname`
- `hostname`
- `*@hostname` – note that the `hostname` is shorthand for `no-user@hostname`, so that this matches all applications on the given host
- `*` – this is used to address applications regardless of location

The CCC library is responsible for ensuring that a suitable multicast group (or other means) is chosen to ensure that all possible matching applications are potentially reachable (though depending on the reliability mode, it does not necessarily ensure the message got to them all).

It should be noted that in any tuple containing a wildcard (*) in the address, specifying the instantiation (as described below), does not guarantee a unique receiver, and so normally the instantiation should be wildcarded too.

Type

The next attribute we use in naming applications is based on hierarchical typing of the application and of the management protocols. The type field is descriptive both of the protocol that is being used and of the state of the application within the protocol at a particular time. For example, a particular application such as vat may use a private protocol to communicate between instantiations of the application, so a vat type is defined, and only applications that believe they can understand the vat protocol and are interested in it would register themselves as being of type **vat**. An alternative way of using the type field is to embed the finite-state machine corresponding to the protocol within the type field – thus a floor-management protocol could use types `floor.management.holder` and `floor.management.requester` in a simple floor-control protocol that can cope with multiple requests at once. A final way of using the type field is to allow extensions to existing protocols in a transparent fashion, by simply extending the type field by using a version number. Some examples of these techniques can be found in the examples given. Some base types are needed to ensure that common applications can communication with each other. As a first pass, the following types have been suggested:

- `audio.send` – the application is interested in messages about sending audio
- `audio.recv` – the application is interested in messages about receiving audio
- `video.send` – the application is interested in messages about sending video
- `video.recv` – the application is interested in messages about receiving video
- `workspace` – the application is a shared workspace application, such as a whiteboard
- `session.remote` – the application is interested in knowing the existence of remote applications (exactly which ones depends on the conference and the session manager)

- `session.local` – the application is interested in knowing of the existence of local applications
- `media-ctrl` – the application is interested in being informed of any change in conference media state (such as unmuting of a microphone)
- `floor.manager` – the application is a floor manager
- `floor.slave` – the application is interested in being notified of any change in floor, but not (necessarily) in the negotiation process

It should be noted that types can be hierarchical, so (for example) any message addressed to audio would address both **audio.send** and **audio.recv** applications. It should also be noted that an application expressing an interest in a type does not necessarily mean that the application has to be able to respond to all the functions that can be addresses to that type. Also, (if required) the CCC library will acknowledge receipt on behalf of the application.

Examples of the types existing applications would register under are:

- vat – `vat, audio.send, audio.recv`
- ivs – `ivs, video.send, video.recv`
- nv – `nv, video.send, video.recv`
- wb – `wb, workspace`
- a conference manager – `confman, session.local, session.remote, media-ctrl, floor.slave`
- a floor-control agent – `flooragent, floor.manager, floor.slave`

In the current implementation, the type field is text-based, so that debugging is simpler, and we can extend the type hierarchy without difficulty.

Instantiation

The instantiation field is purely to enable a message to be addressed to a unique application. When an application registers, it does not specify the instantiation – rather this is returned by the CCC library such that it is unique for the specified *type* at the specified *address*. It is not guaranteed to be globally unique – global uniqueness is only guaranteed by the triple of (`instantiation, type, address`) with no wildcards in any field. When an application sends a message, it uses one of its unique triples as the source address. Which one it chooses should depend on to whom the message was addressed.

8.8.7 Reliability

CCCP would be of very little use if it were merely the simple protocol described above, because of the inherently unreliable nature of the Internet. Techniques for increasing the end-to-end reliability are well known and varied, and will not be discussed here. However, it should be stressed that most (but not all) of the CCCP messages will be addressed to groups. Thus a number of enhanced reliability modes may be desired:

- None. Send and forget. (An example is session-management messages in a loosely coupled system.)
- At least one. The sending application wants to be sure that at least one mem-

ber of the destination group received the message. (An example is a request-floor message which would not be acknowledged by anyone except the current floor folder.)

- *n* out of *m*. The sending application wants to be sure that at least *n* members of the destination group received the message. For this to be useful, the application must have a fairly good idea of the destination group size. (An example may be joining a semi-tightly coupled conference.)
- All. The sending application wants to be sure that all members of the destination group received the message. (An example may be "join conference" in a very tightly coupled conference.)

It makes little sense for applications requiring conference control to reimplement the schemes they require. As there are a limited number of these messages, it makes sense to implement CCCP in a library, so an application can send a CCCP message with a requested reliability, without the application writer having to concern themselves with how CCCP sends the message(s). The underlying mechanism can then be optimized later for conditions that were not initially foreseen, without requiring a rewrite of the application software.

There are a number of "reliable" multicast schemes available, such as Crowcroft & Paliwoda (1988) and Kanika & Cheriton (1988), which can be used to build consensus and agreement protocols in asynchronous distributed systems. However, the use of full agreement protocols is seen to be currently limited to tightly coupled conferences, in which the membership is known, and the first design of the CCC library will not include reliable multicast support although it may be added later as additional functionality. Unlike distributed databases or other automated systems that might exploit causal ordered multicast as discussed in Chapters 2 and 3, communications systems for humans can exploit the users' tolerance of inconsistency.

We believe that sending a message with reliability "*all*" to an unknown group is undesirable. Even if CCCP can track or obtain the group membership transparently to the application through the existence of a distributed nameserver, we believe that the application should explicitly know who it was addressing the message to. It does not appear to be meaningful to need a message to get to all the members of a group if we can't find out who all those members are, as, if the message fails to get to some members, the application can't sensibly cope with the failure. Thus we intend to only support the all-reliability mode to an explicit list of fully qualified destinations (i.e. no wildcards). Applications joining a secure (and therefore externally anonymous) conference can always send a message to the group with "at least one" reliability. Then an existing group member initiates a reliable vote and returns the result to the new member.

8.8.8 Ordering

Of course loss is not the only reliability issue. Messages from a single source may be reordered or duplicated and because of differing delays, messages from different sources may arrive in an "incorrect" order.

Single-source reordering

Addressing reordering of messages from a single source first, there are many possible schemes, almost all of which require a sequence number or a timestamp. A few examples are as follows:

1. Ignore the problem. A suitable example is for session messages reporting presence in a conference.
2. Deal with messages immediately. Discard any packets that are older than the latest seen. Quite a number of applications may be able to operate effectively in this manner. However, some networks can cause very severe reordering and it is questionable whether this is desirable.
3. Using the timestamp in a message and the local clock, estimate the perceived delay from the packet being sourced that allows (say) 90% of packets to arrive. When a packet arrives out of order, buffer it for this delay minus the perceived trip time to give the missing packet(s) time to arrive. If a packet arrives after this timeout, discard it. A similar adaptive playout buffer is used in vat for removal of audio jitter. This is useful where ordering of requests is necessary and where packet loss can be tolerated but delay should be bounded.
4. Similar to the above, specify a fixed maximum delay above minimum perceived trip time, before deciding that a packet really has been lost. If a packet arrives after this time, discard it.
5. A combination of 3 and 4. Some delay patterns may be so odd that they upset the running estimate in 3. Many conference-control functions fall into this category, e.g. time-bounded, but tolerant of loss.
6. Use a sliding window protocol with retransmissions as in TCP. This is only useful where loss cannot be tolerated and where delay can be unbounded. Very tightly coupled conferences may fall into this category, but will be very intolerant of failure. This method should probably only be used along with application-level timeouts in the transmitting application.

It should be noted that all examples except 1 require state to be held in a receiver for every source. As not every message from a particular source will be received at a particular receiver because of CCCP's multiple destination group model, receiver-based mechanisms that require knowing whether a packet has been lost will not work unless the source and receiver use a different sequence space for every (source, destination group) pair. If we wish to avoid this (and I think we usually do!), we must use mechanisms that do not require knowing whether a packet has been lost. Thus the above list of mechanisms becomes:

1. Have CCCP ignore the problem. Let the application sort it out.
2. Have CCCP pass messages to the application immediately. Discard any packets that are older than the latest seen.
3. As above, estimate the perceived delay within which (say) 90% of packets from a particular source arrive, but delay *all* packets from this source by the perceived delay minus the perceived trip time.

4. As above, calculate the minimum perceived trip time. Add a fixed delay to this and buffer all packets for this time minus their perceived trip time.
5. A combination of 3 and 4, buffering *all* packets by the smaller of the two amounts.
6. Explicitly acknowledge every packet. Do not use a sliding window.

Note that just because CCCP cannot provide more elaborate mechanisms, this does not mean an application itself (with some semantic knowledge) cannot build a more elaborate mechanism on top of any of 1–5. However, it does mean that *message timestamps and sequence numbers must be available at the application level.*

Multiple-source ordering

In general we do not believe that CCCP can or should attempt to provide ordering of messages to the application that originate at different sites. CCCP cannot predict that a message will be sent by, and therefore arrive from, a particular source, so it cannot know that it should delay another message that was sent at a later time. The only full synchronization mechanism that can work is an adaptation of 3–5 above that delays all packets by a fixed amount depending on the trip time, and discards them if they arrive after this time if another packet has been passed to the user in the meantime. However, unlike the single-source reordering case, this requires that clocks be synchronized at each site.

CCCP does not intend to provide clock synchronization and global ordering facilities. If applications require this, they must do it themselves. However, for most applications, a better bet is to design the application protocol to tolerate temporary inconsistencies and to ensure that these inconsistencies are resolved in a finite number of exchanges. An example is the algorithm for managing shared teleconferencing state proposed by Shenker & Weinrib (1989) and Schooler (1993).

For algorithms that do require global ordering and clock synchronization, CCCP will pass the sequence numbers and timestamps of messages through to the application. It is then up to the application to implement the desired global ordering algorithm and/or clock synchronization scheme using one of the available protocols and algorithms such as NTP (Birman 1991, Lam 1991, Feldmeier 1993).

8.8.9 A few examples

Before we describe what CCCP should comprise, we will present a few simple examples of CCCP in action. There are a number of ways each of these could be done – this section is not meant to imply these are the best ways of implementing the examples over CCCP.

Unifying user interfaces – session messages in a "small" conference

We illustrate how services and applications are unified using CCCP in Figures 8.8 and 8.9.

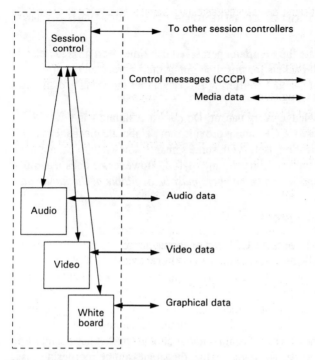

Figure 8.8 Unifying services with CCCP.

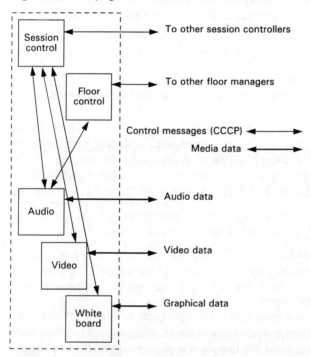

Figure 8.9 Unifying floor control with CCCP.

Applications include:
- an audio tool (at), registers as types: `at`, `audio.send`, `audio.recv`
- a video tool (vt), registers as types: `vt`, `video.send`, `video.recv`
- a whiteboard (wb), registers as types: `wb`, `workspace`
- a session manager (sm), registers as types: `sm`, `session.local`, `session.remote`

The local hostname is x. There are a number of remote hosts, one of which is called y. A typical exchange of messages may be as follows:

From	To	Message

The following will be sent periodically:

(1,audio.recv,x)	(*,sm.local,x)	KEEPALIVE
(1,video.recv,x)	(*,sm.local,x)	KEEPALIVE
(1,wb,x)	(*,sm.local,x)	KEEPALIVE

The following will be sent periodically with interval:

(1,sm,x)	(*,sm.remote,*)	I HAVE MEDIA text user name audio.recv video.recv wb

An audio speech burst arrives at the audio application from y:

(1,audio.recv,x)	(*,sm.local,x)	MEDIA STARTED

Audio y session manager highlights the name of the person who is speaking.

Speech burst finishes:

(1,audio.recv,x)	(*,sm.local,x)	MEDIA STOPPED

Audio y session manager de-highlights the name of the person who was speaking.

Video starts from z:

(1,video.recv,x)	(*,sm.local,x)	MEDIA STARTED video z

Periodical reports:

(1,audio.recv,x)	(*,sm.local,x)	KEEPALIVE
(1,video.recv,x)	(*,sm.local,x)	MEDIA ACTIVE video z
(1,wb,x)	(*,sm.local,x)	KEEPALIVE

Someone restarts the session manager:

(1,sm,x)	(*,*,x)	WHOS THERE
(1,audio.recv,x)	(*,sm.local,x)	KEEPALIVE
(1,video.recv,x)	(*,sm.local,x)	MEDIA ACTIVE video z
(1,wb,x)	(*,sm.local,x)	KEEPALIVE

and so on.

A voice-controlled video conference

In this example, the desired behaviour is for participants to be able to speak when they wish. A user's video application should start sending video when their audio application starts sending audio. No two video applications should aim to be sending at the same time, although some transient overlap can be tolerated.

Applications include:
- an audio tool (at), registers as types: `at, audio.send, audio.recv`
- a video tool (vt), registers as types: `vt, video.send, video.recv`
- a session manager (sm), registers as types: `sm, session.local, session.remote`
- a floor manager (fm), registers as types: `fm, floor.master`

There are hosts x and y, amongst others. It is assumed that session control messages are being sent, as in the example above. A typical exchange of messages may be as follows:

From	To	Message

The user at x starts speaking. Silence suppression cuts out, and the audio tool starts sending audio data:

```
(1, audio.send, x)    (*,sm.local,x),       MEDIA STARTED audio x
                      (*,floor.master,x)
```

This causes the sm to highlight the "you are sending audio" icon. It also causes the floor manager to report to the other floor managers:

```
(1, floor.master,x)  (*, floor.master, *)   MEDIA STARTED audio x
```

It also requests the local video tool to send video:

```
(1, floor.master,x)  (*, video.send, x)     START SENDING video
```

This causes the video tool to start sending:

```
(1, video.send, x)    (*, sm.local, x),     MEDIA STARTED video x
                      (*.floor.master, x)
```
which, in turn, causes the sm to highlight the "you are sending video" icon.

The user at x stops speaking. Silence suppression cuts in, and the audio tool stops sending audio data:

```
(1, audio.send, x)    (*,sm.local,x),       MEDIA STOPPED audio x
                      (*,floor.master,x)
```

This causes the sm to de-highlight the "you are sending audio" icon. The session manager starts a timeout procedure before it will stop sending video. A user at y starts sending audio and video data. The local audio and video tools report this to the session manager:

```
(1,audio.recv,x)      (*,sm.local,x)        MEDIA STARTED audio y
(1,video.recv,x)      (*,sm.local,x)        MEDIA STARTED video y
```

As in the previous example, sm highlights the sender's name. Also y's floor manager reports what's happening:

```
(1, floor.master, y) (*, floor.master,*)    MEDIA STARTED audio y
(1, floor.master, y) (*, floor.master,*)    MEDIA STARTED video y
```

The local floor manager tells the local video tool to stop sending

```
(1, floor.master,x)  (*, video.send, x)     STOP SENDING video
```

This causes the video tool at x to stop sending.

```
(1, audio.send, x)    (*,sm.local,x),       MEDIA STOPPED video x ...
                      (*,floor.master,x)
```

The CCCP message is:

```
(SRC triple){list of (DST triple)s} FUNCTION parameter list
```

8.8.10 More complex needs

Dynamic type-group membership
Many potential applications need to be able to contact a server or a token holder reliably without necessarily knowing the location of that server. An example might be a request for the floor in a conference with one roaming floor holder. The application requires that the message gets to the floor holder if at all possible, which may require retransmission and will require acknowledgement from the remote server, but the application writer should not have to write the retransmission code for each new application. CCCP supports "at least one" reliability, but to address such a `REQUEST_FLOOR` message to all floor managers is meaningless. By supporting dynamic type-groups CCCP can let the application writer address a message to a group that is expected to have only one or a very small number of members, but whose membership is changing constantly.

In the example above, the application requiring the floor sends:

```
SRC Tuple              DEST Tuple                  Message
---------              ----------                  -------
(1, floor.master, x)   (*, floor.master.holder, *)  REQUEST_FLOOR
```

with "at least one" reliability. Retransmissions continue until the message is acknowledged or a timeout occurs.

When the floor holder receives this message, it can then send either a grant-floor or a deny-floor message:

```
SRC Tuple              DEST Tuple                  Message
---------              ----------                  -------
(1, floor.master, y)   (1, floor.master, x)        GRANT_FLOOR
```

This message is sent reliably (i.e. retransmitted by CCCP until an ack is received). On receiving the `GRANT_FLOOR` message, the floor manager at x expresses an interest in the type-group `floor.master.holder`. On sending the `GRANT_FLOOR` message, the floor manager at y also removes its interest in the type-group `floor.master.holder` to prevent spurious acking of other `REQUEST_FLOOR` messages. However, if the `GRANT_FLOOR` message retransmissions timeout, it should re-express an interest. See Section 8.8.11 on the Naming Service for more details of how dynamic type-groups work.

Need to know

When an application sends a message, it is up to the sending application to choose the reliability mode for the message. For example, in a large loosely coupled conference, a floor-change announcement may be multicast in an unreliable mode. However, there may be a number of applications that really do require to see that information. In the floor-control example, the existing floor-holding applications need to see the floor-change announcements. We propose allowing a receiving application to modify the reliability with which other applications send specific messages by allowing messages of the form:

```
(SRC triple)(*, floor.manager, *) NEED_TO_KNOW (*, floor.slave, *)
{list of fns}
```

In this case the application specified by the source triple is telling all `floor.manager` applications that when they send one of the specified functions to (*, `floor.slave`, *), this application would like reliable delivery of the message.

`NEED_TO_KNOW` messages should be sent periodically, and will timeout if one hasn't been received in a set amount of time. `NEED_TO_KNOW` requests will also timeout at a particular application if that application ever fails to reliably deliver a message to the specified address. Clearly `NEED_TO_KNOW` messages should be used sparingly, as they adversely affect the scaling properties of the CCC. However, there are a number of cases where they can be useful. The same effect could be achieved by declaring another type (for example, `floor.holder`, which may be desirable in some cases), but `NEED_TO_KNOW` also has the benefit that it can be used to modify the behaviour of existing applications without a requirement to access the source code.

8.8.11 The naming service

CCC can be run on the bus model, passing all messages around a single multicast group per conference. This will scale reasonably, since it scales with the number of participants in the conference. Name resolution occurs at each host, matching the destination-naming tuple in the message against the list of tuples that are registered at this particular host. However, it does not scale indefinitely, because the load on each host and the network increases with the complexity of the conference and the number of messages. To improve scaling, the communications should be optimized so that messages are only propagated to the machines that are interested. Thus we need a service that maps the naming tuples to locations, so that intelligent mapping of message paths to locations can be performed (this is also called "intelligent routeing and placement of multicast groups"). This name-location service (or "naming service" as it is more generally known) has a number of properties that differentiate it from other naming services such as X.500 and the DNS (see Section 2.11.7):

- dynamic and frequent updates
- fast propagation of changes
- ability to fall back to broadcast to interested parties when uncertain about the consistency of a refined addressing group, since names are unique per conference and are included in each message

The last property is important, since it allows a relaxed approach to maintenance of consistency amongst the naming servers, saving greatly in the messages and complexity of the internals of the service.

We intend to implement a nameserver suitable for loosely coupled conferences as the default in the CCC library. However, CCCP will also allow the use of an external nameserver to supplement or replace the internal nameserver behaviour, which will allow much greater use of the nameserver to made in more tightly coupled conferences, for instance by using the nameserver to keep an accurate list of members.

8.8.12 Security

CCCP will implement two levels of security – a very simple host access model similar to the xhost mechanism in the X-Windows system (X security, X11 Release 5 manual page), and encryption of all CCCP packets with a key provided.

Host access security

The application is started with an access-control string, which is a list of hosts it is prepared to accept commands from. It passes this to the CCC library, and the CCC library then filters all messages whose source is not in the access-control list.

This very simple level of security is intended primarily to prevent external attacks such as switching media tools transmission on or off, and thus compromising the privacy of users. Note that the X magic-cookie mechanism is not too useful here, as the cookie would have to be carried in CCC packet, which lays it open to attack from anyone who can capture multicast packets.

Encryption

We recognize that the only way for CCCP to be really secure is to use encryption of all CCC packets, and CCCP will support an encryption scheme. The key distribution problem is considered to be outside the scope of CCCP itself, and CCCP will require the application to pass the key to it. After this, all CCCP messages from this library will be encrypted, and non-encrypted messages will be ignored.

CCCP will allow an encryption key per conference id, and a key for messages not associated with any conference. Which encryption key to use for outgoing messages is chosen by the CCC library according to the conference id. Once the application has passed the set of keys to the CCC library, it no longer has to concern itself with encryption.

Encryption and host access can be used simultaneously.

8.8.13 Conference membership discovery

CCCP will support conference membership discovery by providing the necessary functions and types. However, the choice of discovery algorithm, loose or tight control of the conference membership, and so forth, are not within the scope of CCCP itself. Instead these algorithms should be implemented in a session manager on top of the CCC.

8.8.14 CCCP implementation

The authors always had an implementation based on IP multicast in mind. However, every effort has been made to ensure there is nothing in CCCP that precludes implementation over unicast IP. However, CCCP does make the assumption that the Conference Communication Channel (however implemented) is always available. On systems based over circuit-switched channels, such as ISDN, this may not be the case.

8.9 Summary

In this chapter, we have looked at an extended example of a distributed application, namely a multimedia conference-control system. It has evolved from a simple classical RPC design to a subtle fully distributed multicast message-based system. In an environment where consistency and correctness are not primary requirements, but performance and scaling are, we have found that a more loosely coupled approach is superior for controlling such distributed applications.

8.10 Exercises

1. How would our final system differ if the underlying communication was virtual-circuit-based instead of employing multicast datagrams?
2. What kind of name/directory service would best suit the CCCP hierarchical naming system?
3. What security risks are there in a multimedia conferencing system as presented here?
4. How might CCC relate to a group-based RPC approach? Are they in some senses duals? What if the programmer is allowed control over the invocation distribution and reply collation policies? (Examples of the latter would be none required, one required, majority, all.)

CHAPTER 9

Applications to network management

with David Lewis, University College London

9.1 Introduction

In this chapter, we use the very high-level approach of open distributed systems modelling to look at network management. We choose this high-level approach here since there is a great deal of material available on the lower-level aspects of network management. In other chapters, we have already looked more closely at lower-level, engineering aspects of other applications of distributed systems. For example, network-management standards cover the definition of managed objects, and the standard interfaces to management agents (or servers) through SNMP (Simple Network Management Protocol) or CMIP (Common Management Information Protocol), and using ASN.1 (see Ch. 7). Many network-management standards include mechanisms to deal with heterogeneity, such as *proxy* servers and remote access to different protocols through translating gateways such as the remote monitoring. What is not specified by network-management standards is precisely the nature of the distribution of functionality. In fact, from all the standards it would appear that a first try at building a management application would be essentially centralized.

There is a clear need for an open network management architecture. Networks are becoming very widespread and heterogeneous, and it is becoming vital to control them and make them useful as they evolve.

The model of an open network that admits of multiple providers and multiple subscribers, arbitrarily nested, provides virtual private networks. The Internet is a very good example of a VPN. Another type of VPN commonly found is the so-called Enterprise Network, used by many large corporations to connect together different services (ranging from telephony through to data) at different sites, but drawing transmission capacity (and switching, and possibly other services) from public network operators.

There are two ways that ODP can inform network managements. First, ODP modelling can be used to design the management functions. We look at this when applied to VPNs in the first part of this chapter. Secondly, we can use ODP (for example through CORBA) to implement service management directly. This has several advanatages over simply enhancing existing network-management platforms that are based on CMIP or SNMP, especially when applied to telecommunications networks such as the Plain Old Telephone Service or the ISDN. In particular, the creation of new services becomes a matter for software, and is not the tremendously complex task that it is now. To see how hard it is in monolithic systerms, you need only look at the complexity of adding the simplest services in the so-called "intelligent networks" that are being slowly provided in telephone systems – the effort needed to deploy something as easy as call forwarding or number portability across providers is astounding.

An open network management architecture must address the following requirements:

- *Flexibility*
  It must be flexible enough to be applied effectively to the management of large or small communications networks that consist of a variety of equipment types and that provide a variety of services. It must accommodate change.

- *Extensibility*
  It should be able to follow trends in technology and systems. At the simplest level, this means accommodating new transmission technology and new performance ranges. At the extreme, we might ask that a network management system admit of new network architectures (e.g. B-ISDN as well as OSI and TCP/IP, for example).

- *Scaling*
  It must scale so that it can be applied to real systems and with realistic performance. The design should make clear where there are limits to scaling that constrain the applicability of particular components.

- *Interoperability and interworking*
  The primary goal is to provide a framework for network-management products and services from different suppliers to work together to manage communications and computer networks. For example, a system from one supplier must be able to manage or be managed by a system from a different supplier, or act in both of these roles.

  An open architecture should be able to interwork with other network-management architectures if possible. In other words, it must be a superset of all possible, sensible network architectures.

- *Generic model*
  When network-management systems interoperate, it is necessary for each system to be able to call meaningfully on the management functions supported or required by the others and the underlying physical or logical components on which they operate. This is provided by an object-oriented paradigm, and the facilities are provided by *genericity*. Of course, the overall system model may differ markedly from the internal operation of any or all of the management systems.

- *Implementation freedom*
  It must not unduly put limits on the internal design or implementation of a management system. In the commercial world, an open system will only gain acceptance if it also ensures that there are always opportunities for competitive differentiation of network-management products that conform

to implementors' agreements.

This objective must be balanced with the previous objectives: the architecture must be described in enough detail to allow interoperability and interworking, but not so much that all conformant systems must be identical, and that a particular implementation cannot add value.

- *Performance*
  It should allow for stripping of all unnecessary functionality to permit new levels of performance and simplicity.

The working definition of an architecture (Herbert 1994) is an engineering discipline of design with a *common framework* and a consistency of style. The following is a review and a synthesis of the description of the functions and conceptual architecture that fully identify the problem space.

9.2 Functions

We relate the management aspects to the network by the definition of two kinds of service. These are telecommunications services which manage the network itself and telecommunications management services which support these management functions. The latter are very similar to application services.

9.2.1 The agents of a management system

Taking the enterprise view of a management system we see that it consists of three components: people, procedures and tools. In this view, the people perform the required functions by following the appropriate procedures. In so doing, they may use any tools that are made available to them.

This approach is also consistent with the information view, which can categorize the processes into three phases: awareness creation, decision making and implementation. A fully manual system would involve all decisions being taken by a human, who is also responsible for identifying a situation and taking corrective action. This corresponds to a situation in which no tools are provided.

In the ideal, subject to careful control, all the procedures needed have been automated and no human intervention is needed. Most systems involve a mix of human intervention and automation. The balance of the mix will vary in different systems. As technology improves, systems will be more automated. An open architecture should support this flexibility.

9.2.2 Reference configurations

When defining open models of anything, it is important to give examples, which clarify the model without tying down any particular vendor to any particular approach. Such examples are called "reference configurations".

9.2.3 Classification of functions

Network-management functions have been classified by the ISO into five categories:

1. fault management
2. configuration management
3. accounting management
4. performance management
5. security management

This classification has been adopted by CCITT in Recommendation M.30.

9.2.4 Non-functional requirements

Non-functional requirements are used in all fields of application of software engineering to capture the difference between design and implementation. In an open network-management design, we want to avoid specifying the engineering elements that are actually part of a particular vendor's design freedom.

- *Performance*
  A contract for a service such as a communications system will often state desired and required performance levels. Hence it is paramount to manage this aspect of the system.

- *Data volumes*
  The size of files, length of terminal sessions, quantity of video/audio information, etc.,

- *Throughput*
  The dynamics of the flow of data determine the needs of a function for processing power. If, for some reason, that function cannot be replicated or distributed then the total throughput may have to be handled at one point. It is possible that a bottleneck which limits total system performance may result.

- *Response time*
  Interactive systems must have a respectable response time. Systems that involve process control must have very timely performance. Matching such a need to an appropriately reduced processing capability may result in significant cost reduction of the system.

- *Error rates*
  Errors are inevitable. The failure of a system to produce correct results must be matched to the importance of the result and the impact of the error. The probabilities and sources of error must be known so that proper account of them may be taken in the system design. Managing error rates is less dynamically important in modern networks, but is still key in some critical situations.

- *Availability*
  The percentage of time that a system is actually available (rather than just perceived by a manager to be available) must be managed. Very high availability has an exponentially increasing cost. The cost must be balanced with the requirements of the enterprise.

- *Location*
  It will often be a requirement that certain functions be located at specific sites. This may be for reasons of performance, particularly if remote access

would mean, for example, the transfer of very large volumes of data, or of security, minimizing the risks that key information is not tampered with or accessed without authority.

- *Autonomy*
  Ensuring that a subsystem that performs a specific set of functions can stand alone if it should ever become isolated can be advantageous. Again, robustness of the total system can be improved, upgrades made simpler and security enhanced. The Internet, for example, owes a great deal of its success to the relatively large degree of autonomy in its subsystems.

- *Human–computer interaction requirements*
  Different functions support different human roles. The requirements for the interaction between the users and the function must therefore be specified along with the function itself. This can then be translated into an appropriate man–machine interface design, taking into account the related functions, the skill base of the staff and the ever-present factor of cost.

- *Security of the management system*
  The information held within a system could be misused in a number of ways. Knowledge of the equipment configurations could be of commercial value to competitive suppliers. There is also the obvious risk of malicious changes to customer files. Control of access to functions is one aspect of security, but authentication of users, tamper-proofing of data and physical security are others. Where the management subsystem relates to charging, the requirement for security is obvious.

- *Physical environment*
  It may often be necessary to locate subsystems in particular sites. For example, first line maintenance tools may best be co-located with the exchange equipment being supported. For these reasons and many others the environment of the equipment hosting the functions may be constrained. This must be known to the designers.

- *Support*
  All subsystems will require some degree of support. This applies to hardware, software and data (including knowledge). Some forms of support will be routine, others unpredictable, for example to correct a malfunction or to update a capability. Both the general requirements for and any special provisions to be made for support must be stated.

- *Rate of system change*
  It may be important to know that some functions will be updated or reviewed frequently. Specific provision for this could significantly reduce the lifetime of the system.

- *Legislation*
  It is quite possible that legislation may dictate the way in which certain management functions are presented and made available. It may not be permitted to combine certain functions in order to ensure the adequate protection of data while making access available to information to meet mandatory

requirements.

- *Business constraints*
  The way in which the organization that owns the network or offers the service is structured and operated may affect the way in which functions are presented and combined. For example, access by sales staff, where permissible, may be needed. A help desk would require wide access to information, but the business may dictate that a support system treat data as read-only.

- *Existing investment*
  New systems may be required to work with older systems or to re-use hardware that has been released by system changes and upgrades so that investment is preserved. This would impact the design and potential capability of the desired management functions.

- *Migration*
  It is rarely feasible to install major management systems from scratch. They have to coexist with older systems. They may have to take over some but perhaps not all of the functionality of those existing systems in such a way that impact on the operation of the organization is minimized. This will impact both the choice of equipment and the way in which the system is designed in order to interface more easily with older systems that are to remain in operation.

- *Cost*
  The cost of implementing features and functions has been mentioned repeatedly. Clearly cost/performance tradeoffs will always have to be made. If any specific limits on the cost of a particular subsystem exist this is vital information for the designer.

9.3 Conceptual architectures

An architecture is a means of organizing and representing knowledge within a given field of application. Typically, it provides a common model that identifies the major system components and the interactions between them. The architecture addresses the problem of interoperable network management and presents a framework for describing the various aspects of the problem and the solutions.

The architecture consists of the following building-block concepts and components. These components may be either physical or logical, depending on the context in which they are used. Other components of the architecture are identified in the individual perspectives.

- *Interoperable interface*
  The interoperable interface is the formally defined set of protocols, procedures, message formats and semantics used to communicate management information within an object-oriented paradigm.

- *Operations systems (OS)*
  An OS is a real open system that supports the defined interoperable interface. Thus, two OSs communicate across the interoperable interface.[1]

- *Management network (MN)*
  A management network is a network through which OSs communicate for the purposes of network management. It is modelled as a separate network from the communications network, although it may actually use elements of the managed network.
- *Management solution (MS)*
  The management solution is the complete set of network-management systems, procedures and facilities used by an organization. (This includes management users, OSs, other management systems, and the management network.)
- *Managed elements (MEs)*
  Managed elements are physical or logical resources that are to be managed, but that exist independently of their need to be managed. Managed elements include resources within the communications network that provide communications services and systems resources that make use of the communications network. (Aspects of the communications network must be modelled to achieve a common understanding of the elements being managed; however, this modelling task is treated as an early part of the managed object design process.)
- *Managed object (MO)*
  A managed object is the destination of management directives and the sources of management event reports. A managed object may be a physical item of equipment, a logical component, some abstract of information, a combination of any of these, a part of any of these, or a combination of such parts.
- *Management domains (MDs)*
  A management domain is composed of a managing process or system and all the managed objects that are under control. The collection of managed objects will be called the management domain.

9.3.1 General model of a TMN architecture

Here we explore a general architectural model of a telecommunications management network (TMN) based on the components listed above and the relationships between them.

Figure 9.1 shows an OS that may be accessed through the interoperable interface for the purpose of managing resources. These managed resources (which may be parts of managed elements or of the management solution) are visible through the OS. The management network, not shown in this figure, is the means for allowing OSs to communicate via the interoperable interface.

Since the TMN's scope is limited to interoperability in network management, the area outside the management network is beyond the scope of this document. However, this architecture models some aspects of this outer area in an abstract way in order to better understand the interactions between OSs:

---

1. Note that "OS" is used in a special way in network-management standards – it is the *operations system*, not the operating system.

Underlying VPN service

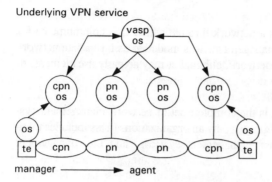

manager —————————→ agent

- management of: end user, terminal equipment (te)
  CPN (customer premises network) & PN resources, closed user groups
- management plane signalling: end-to-end user streams

Figure 9.1   An open network management architecture.

- The human users of network management are shown.
- The management solution is shown as the second circle, which encompasses management users, OSs, other management systems, the management network, and other aspects of the solution.
- The managed elements made available for management by the various OSs are shown as the outer ring in the diagram. This is treated as a simple set of elements; the structure or topology of these elements is not modelled in this architecture.

9.4 Viewpoints of the architecture

This architecture provides the common model required for interoperable network management. It is presented as a number of viewpoints, each of which provides a different abstraction of the system and examines some aspects of the general model presented above. Each viewpoint describes the major components and the interactions from different points of abstraction. Viewpoints are simply different views of the same overall problem, with a focus on a particular aspect. This very much follows on from the model we presented in Chapter 1.

The presentation of architectural issues through a number of viewpoints is intended to give a clearer understanding of the issues and how they relate to each other. This approach also helps in placing priorities on issues and identifying areas of neglect. Considering each of the viewpoints in turn may be helpful in the process of designing a management solution.

The viewpoints in this architecture are as follows:

1. *The enterprise viewpoint*

   This viewpoint focuses on requirements of management and manageability, policies and interoperability. The intent is to represent the user's view of the architecture, and the overall goals of the architecture. An enterprise model describes the overall objectives of a system in terms of roles (for people), actions, goals and policies. It specifies the activities that take place within the organization using the system, the roles that people play in the organization, and the interactions between the organization, the system, and the environment in which system and organization are placed.

2. *The information and computational viewpoint*

   The purpose of the information viewpoint is the identification and location of information, and the description of information-processing activities. An information model describes the structure, flow, interpretation, value, timeliness and consistency of information held within the system. The purpose of the computational viewpoint is to describe the system as a set of linked applications programs. A computational model provides programmers with a description of a system that explains how distributed application programs may be written for it. The two viewpoints consist of:

   • *The single-managed-object view*

     A managed object is the view of a resource for the purposes of management. This view examines the characteristics of a single managed object in isolation.

   • *The managed-object relationships view*

     Managed objects participate in a number of relationships. This viewpoint describes various relationships between managed objects.

   • *The logical distribution view*

     Managed objects and OSs that manage them are distributed about the network. This view considers aspects of this distribution and how knowledge of that distribution is managed.

3. *The engineering viewpoint*

   The purpose of the engineering viewpoint is to describe the system in such a way that designers can reason about the performance of the system built to their designs. This viewpoint discusses the realization of the common model as physical communication, and addresses the requirements that arise from physically separating OSs and managed objects. This includes communication techniques, conformance, and supplier-specific extensions.

4. *Conformance*

   It is envisaged for a system to conform in any number of viewpoints and conformance to each viewpoint brings different benefits. The enterprise and information viewpoints can be used to establish a design model of information sources and processes that meet the requirements of the enterprise that requested the system. Conformance requirements in these viewpoints identify constraints on the conceptual schema of the system information base and on system-management policies necessary to enable the system to operate.

   The computational viewpoint can be used to transform an information model into a network of interacting computer programs. Conformance requirements at this level identify constraints on programming language structures to enable the system to operate.

The engineering viewpoint can be used to transform a computational viewpoint model into a model in terms of processing, memory and communication functions. The conformance requirements at this level identify constraints on system that independently conform to the architecture necessary to enable their interconnection.

9.5 The enterprise viewpoint

The enterprise viewpoint of network management is concerned with user requirements, policies, and the broadest level of interoperability modelling. This viewpoint focuses on the primary aim: to provide interoperable network management. An enterprise is an organization working towards common business objectives. In the context of network management, an enterprise includes:

- the scope of the organization's policy and objectives to provide a management solution
- the users in its management solution
- the elements managed by the solution

A management solution is the total set of network-management systems, procedures and facilities that are used by an enterprise or cooperating group of enterprises. Management users are part of this solution.

The management solution is introduced to the architecture to model both the standardized communications aspects and the non-standard aspects of network management. Other than the standardized communications aspects, the internal structure of the management solution is not modelled or specified in any way. To help clarify this modelling concept, we give a number of examples of possible parts of a management solution:

- applications and communications hardware and software
- database functions
- user interface
- interaction with managed elements

When the management solutions of two or more enterprises begin to communicate, this results in a single combined management solution for the enterprise that arises from the common business objectives of the cooperating group of enterprises. Various groups (ISO, CCITT, ITEM, etc.) are gathering consensus on the application of these standards for managing resources such as modems, (N)-layers and end-systems. The same standards are being applied towards management interoperability.

9.6 Aspects of interoperability

Four areas of interoperability are considered in the enterprise viewpoint: an interoperable management interface, a collective management network, a shared conceptual schema, and negotiated interworking policies. In order for two or more systems to be able to exchange management information they must each support one or more interoperable interfaces.

9.6.1 Shared conceptual schema

Information exchanged between enterprises may range from highly processed to very elemental data. Consequently, the effect of the exchange may range from widespread to very narrow impact. In any case, effective interoperability can only be achieved if the enterprises share a common understanding of the structure and meaning of management information – a shared conceptual schema. Adopting the approach suggested by OSI management standards we use managed objects as the basis of its schemata. (See Section 9.7) Managed objects are considered open by virtue of their registration. Any such managed objects (not only those registered by the TMN) are included as managed objects open to access across the interoperable interface.

An enterprise is an organization or group of organizations together with the communications equipment they use and the management solutions that manage it. The goal is to allow different management solutions to interoperate to manage a communications network. Interoperability is achieved using the interoperable interface across a management network, and is subject to negotiated interworking policies.

Human network-management users have the responsibility of specifying network-management requirements, and a functional client/server approach can be taken to analyse these requirements.

9.7 The single managed-object view

This view defines and describes the characteristics of a single managed object, treated in isolation. Managed objects are made visible through the OS and are abstractions of managed elements or of parts of the management solution.

A managed object presents a view of a resource or set of resources for the purposes of management. A managed object contains attributes and may be capable of performing operations and emitting notifications. These classes are specified using a template and registered with globally unique identifiers.

9.7.1 Principles of managed objects

Information that is exchanged between management systems is modelled in terms of managed objects. Managed objects are views of resources; these resources may exist independently of management concerns, or may exist to support the management of other resources. A managed object may represent, for example, a modem, a log, or a circuit.

In order to allow effective definition of a growing set of managed objects, we use object-oriented design principles. Object-oriented design is characterized by the definition of objects, where an object is an abstraction of a physical or logical thing.

There is not necessarily a one-to-one mapping between managed objects and real resources. A managed object may represent one or more resources. These resources can be managed elements or parts of the management solution. Likewise, a resource may be represented by zero, one, or more managed objects. If a resource is not represented by a managed object, it cannot be managed across the interoperable interface.

A managed object may provide an abstract view of resources that are represented by other managed object(s). A managed object is defined by:

- the attributes visible at its boundary
- the management operations that may be applied to it
- the behaviour exhibited by it in response to management operations
- the notifications emitted by the object

A managed-object class defines a "type" of managed object, and a member of a managed-object class is called a "managed-object instance". All managed-object instances in the same class have the same attributes, operations, behaviour and notifications. The term "managed-object" is used to mean "managed-object instance" if this meaning is clear from the context.

Although managed-object classes may be defined for anything that needs to be managed, it is useful to give some examples of managed-object classes to help in understanding this wide variety. These examples show that managed-object classes can be defined for physical and logical components, or to represent some other aspect of management.

A facet of object-oriented design is that of encapsulation. Encapsulation is a form of information hiding, in that all implementation details, internal data structures, algorithms, local interprocess communications, etc. are known only to the implementation of the object. For any object, only the properties defined for it are visible. That is, the internal operation of a managed object (or its mapping to a real resource) is not visible at the object boundary unless attributes, operations, behaviour or notifications are defined to expose this information. How operations are performed and enforcement of any appropriate consistency constraints are determined by the definition of the managed-object class.

9.7.2 Attributes

Attributes are properties of managed objects. An attribute has one or more associated values, each of which may have a simple or a complex structure. When an attribute has more than one value, no ordering of the values is implied.

The value of an attribute is, in general, observable (at the managed-object boundary). It may determine or reflect the behaviour of the managed object.

The value of an attribute is observed or modified by requesting a managed object to read or write the value. Additional operations are defined for set-valued attributes; these are attributes of a given data type whose value is a set of elements of variable size, which may be empty. Operations on attributes are defined to be performed on the managed object that contains the attributes, and not directly upon the attributes. The managed object is able to enforce constraints on attribute values to ensure internal consistency or to enforce access limitations. The definition of a managed-object class may specify relationships between the values of its individual attributes.

Attributes of a managed-object class may be mandatory (they must be always appear in an instance of that class) or optional (they may appear). An attribute may be defined to disallow reading or writing of its value(s).

9.7.3 Operations on attributes

The following operations can be performed on a managed object to manipulate the values of its attributes:

- get attribute value: reads and returns the requested attribute values
- set attribute value: sets values of specified attributes to the supplied values
- derive attribute value: sets the values of the specified attributes in accordance with a specified derivation rule (e.g. set to default)
- add attribute value: adds additional values to a set-valued attribute
- remove attribute value: removes values from a set-valued attribute

The following operations apply to managed objects as a whole and their impact is generally not confined to modifications of attribute values:

- create: creates a new managed object
- delete: deletes an existing managed object
- action: performs a task that is defined by the managed-object class

9.8 Notifications

Managed objects may emit notifications when some internal or external event occurs. Notifications are specific to the class of the managed objects that emit them. The information contained within a notification is part of the definition of the managed-object class. The information in a notification may be used to generate event reports, which are sent across the interoperable interface. Event handling in programming is a classic problem in user-interface systems and in network-management systems. In fact, a very common practical problem for engineers building network-management tools is reconciling different mechanisms for interfacing programs to asynchrony.[2]

9.9 Behaviour

The behaviour of a managed object includes:

- the effect of operations that are performed on the managed object
- any constraints that are placed on operations or attributes in order to satisfy consistency rules, and in particular, the rules under which creation and deletion of managed objects may be performed and the consequences of these operations
- the nature of any relationships between attributes
- a complete definition of any other aspects of the behaviour of the object class

---

2. If I had a pound for every time I had had to choose how to merge a GUI system that has its own callback structure with a communications API that has *its* own, I would be very wealthy.

This definition may be documented by use of English text or by the use of formal description techniques (a subject of current research).

9.9.1 Generic attributes, actions, and notifications

There are aspects of managed objects that are not specific to a single class. It is useful for these cases to define generic attributes, actions or notifications that may be used in many managed-object classes. This provides consistency and efficiency in both specification and implementation of managed-object classes and the applications that use them.

The generic definitions of attributes, notifications and actions may well not be complete unto themselves. Generally, the full definition can be obtained only by examining the definition and any modifications to it contained in the specification of the managed-object class in which it is used.

Examples of generic attributes are: administrative state and connected objects. An alarm message to report a fault is an example of a generic notification.

9.10 Specification of managed-object classes

Managed-object classes must be specified in a structured way in order to be consistently implemented to allow interoperability. The most common specification tool for managed-object classes is a template: a form that is filled in with details about the managed-object class, attribute, or whatever is being defined.

9.11 Registration

The final step in completing the specification of a managed-object class is the assignment of globally unique identifiers to the ASN.1 productions. These identifiers will be used in CMIP messages to reference specific properties of a managed object. Development of OS software to deal with instances of a managed-object class requires the knowledge of these identifiers. Furthermore, the stability of software development is assured by the fact that, once assigned, these identifiers retain their association with the properties of a specified managed-object class forever (i.e. the identifiers are never reassigned). To ensure global uniqueness, the identifiers are arranged in a tree by authorized organizations.

We will need to register objects in the course of completing our development goals. An established procedure will be necessary to facilitate registration of the managed-object classes that are specified. In establishing this procedure, consideration must be given to record keeping, experimental developments, retiring identifiers, and the possibility of online access to the library of managed object-class definitions including their assigned identifiers. Formal guidelines governing the responsibilities of authorities assigning identifiers is forthcoming from ISO.

9.12 The managed object relationships view

This view describes how managed objects can be considered in terms of their relationships to each other. Managed-object classes and instances do not exist in isolation; they always have some bearing on other objects. The purpose of this view is to describe the relationships that can exist between managed resources and how the corresponding managed objects represent these relationships.

Managed-object relationships are normally described as applying to instances. However, for each relationship between instances, there may be a corresponding relationship between classes that specifies a general rule for relating instances. For example, managed-object instances may be related by the "is-connected-to" relationship, and there may be rules defining which classes are allowed to have instances related in this way (i.e. be connected together).

Just as managed objects are abstractions or views or resources, managed-object relationships are views of relationships between resources. Therefore, a managed-object relationship reflects the significant aspects and leaves out the unimportant (from a management standpoint) aspects of a relationship. The variety of managed-object relationships mirrors the variety of real-world relationships between resources.

9.13 Relationships

There are very many possible relationships. Two kinds of relationships merit special discussion, because of their importance: inheritance and containment.

9.13.1 Inheritance

Inheritance is a special relationship between classes that exploits the commonality in managed-object class definitions. Managed-object classes are arranged in a hierarchy known as the "inheritance tree" (or "object-class hierarchy" or "class tree"). A class in this tree is known as a subclass of its parent in the tree (its superclass). A subclass inherits all characteristics of all of its subclasses. There is one basic managed-object class, *top*, and all other classes are subclasses of top. The classes are more specialized going down the inheritance tree.

Inheritance is used in specifying object classes. A new object class is specified as a subclass of a defined class. Only additional characteristics (attributes, operations, behaviour, and/or notifications) are specified.

The refinement method uses strict single inheritance (inheritance of all characteristics from a single superclass). A complementary approach is the construction method, which uses strict multiple inheritance (inheritance of all characteristics from each of several superclasses).

Once a class has been designed and formally specified, the class is given a globally unique registered identifier which is used in communications.

The instance behaviour that corresponds to this superclass–subclass relationship is that an instance of a particular managed-object class has the ability to act as either its defined class or any of its superclasses (since the superclasses' characteristics are inherited). This capability is known as "polymorphism". For example, the class "modem" could be defined as a subclass of "equipment", so that an instance of "modem" could also behave as an instance of "equipment". In some cases, it may be necessary for implementation reasons to restrict the set of super-classes that an instance can imitate.

9.13.2 Containment relationships

Containment is a special kind of relationship that must observe special rules, and is used to name managed-object instances. All relationships used for naming are containments, but not all containment relationships are used for naming.

Every containment relationship is by nature hierarchical – managed-object instances are contained in other instances which may in turn be contained in other instances. This characteristic does not necessarily apply to other relationships.

Containment may be physical or logical, but may generally be described with the phrase "is part of". The following are examples of containment relationships:

- line-card A is part of multiplexer B
- circuit C is part of circuit D
- circuit E is part of network F
- customer G is part of enterprise H
- enterprise I is part of enterprise J

A managed object contained in an object that is itself contained in a third object is considered to be contained in the third object. That is, containment relationships are transitive.

9.13.3 Group, service and other relationships

In addition to containment, other relationships between managed objects can be defined (e.g. is connected to, backs up, uses, etc.). Some may be symmetric, in that the relationship is the same from the viewpoint of either managed object. Others may be asymmetric where the roles of the managed objects cannot be interchanged. Relationships are not limited to a pair of managed objects (one-to-one), but may also be one-to-many, many-to-one, or many-to-many.

Group relationships are those that allow managed objects to be members of some particular set or grouping. That grouping may be for any management purpose, but must be defined as part of the managed-object class definitions.

One of the relationships mentioned above is the "uses relationship". One managed object may make use of another managed object (on the same or a different OS) in order to provide its management or service-providing capability. This relationship is known variously as a "service relationship", a "uses relationship", a "client/server relationship", or a "service-user/service-provider relationship". Service relationships are by nature asymmetric – one managed object is the service provider and the other is the service user. This gives rise to two different viewpoints on the relationship. The service-user managed object knows only the characteristics of the managed object that provides the service, and not how the service is being provided (including whether the service provider in fact uses any other managed objects(s) to provide its service). On the other hand, the service provider knows how it is providing the service, but doesn't know about the service user, beyond its identity for security reasons.

Rules for service relationships may be defined, but are limited to those aspects that are necessary for management. Other rules regarding service relationships are left to the implementation of the underlying services.

9.14 Relationship definition and representation

Relationships between managed objects can be shown either explicitly or implicitly. In either case, names of managed objects are used to identify the participants in a relationship.

Explicit relationships are part of the definition of the managed objects making up the relationship. For each such relationship, a specific attribute is defined (e.g. "backedUpObjectInstance"). The value(s) would be the name(s) of the other managed objects(s) participating in the relationship. Each managed object participating in a relationship will have an attribute that names all of the other managed objects in that relationship. For example, in a one-to-one relationship, each managed object will have an attribute whose value is the name of the other managed object. This allows the relationship to be identified from either managed object. Changes to the relationship, that is, adding, removing, and/or changing members, are accomplished by simply changing the values of the appropriate relationship attribute.

Implicit relationships are shown with special relationship objects. A relationship object is a managed object that is defined with attributes that name all of the managed objects making up the relationship. For example, a relationship object might be used to identify all of the managed objects associated with providing service to a particular user. Such an object would then have attributes values naming all of the appropriate managed objects. This approach allows new relationships to be defined and related managed objects created, without any impact on the other participating managed objects. The disadvantage is that the relationships a managed object participates in cannot always be easily determined.

Relationships between managed objects are not limited to a single OS, but can extend across multiple OSs. The way relationships are defined needs to reflect this fact. To a large extent, interoperability has to do with those relationships that span OSs.

9.15 The logical distribution view

The previous view described relationships between managed objects, without considering their distribution. This view deals with issues arising from the relationships between parts of the management solution behind interoperating OSs and regarding the logical distribution of managed objects and the applications that manage them.

In the following sections are presented a number of techniques that may be used in a distributed management network (e.g. abstraction, hierarchies, authority domains). The process of designing a management network includes deciding which, if any, of these techniques are appropriate.

9.15.1 Managed objects and relationships to an OS

Managed objects are made visible over the interoperable interface. All of the managed objects made visible by one OS to one other OS make up a set called the "management information base" (MIB). As seen by another OS, the managed objects in an MIB appear to be inside the OS that "owns" the MIB. Since managed objects make up the total management view provided across the interoperable interface, the MIB is the repository of all management information in an OS.

In the context of managed objects, the phrase "make visible" is not limited to a passive role, but includes both observation and manipulation of a managed object. Stating that a OS makes a managed object "visible" means that the OS will allow other OSs to know the managed object's name (thus acknowledging the existence of the managed object), and may allow other OSs to manage the managed object.

The contents of an MIB is dynamic and reflects only those managed objects which exist at any point in time. In addition, an OS may make different sets of managed objects visible to different OSs, for security or other reasons.

The set of managed-object classes that an OS can support is a part of the shared conceptual schema. An OS is said to "support" a managed object if it can perform either or both of the following:

- It can perform operations (create, get, etc.) on instances of the class or receive notifications (event reports) from instances of the class (i.e. it can manage instances of the class). This includes a semantic understanding of the definition of the managed-object class.
- It can make instances of the class visible to other OSs.

9.15.2 Authority relationships

An authority relationship identifies a specific managing process as having the authority to manage a specific managed object.

To participate in authority relationships, an OS has to be capable of performing the role of a managing process or an agent process, or both. In the context of the architecture, an OS performing the role of a managing process issues operations on and receives notifications from managed objects in another OS. An OS performing the role of an agent process makes managed objects visible to other OSs. To accomplish this, an agent OS has to map its managed objects to corresponding real resources or other managed objects. That mapping is not subject to specification. An OS may participate as a manager in several authority relationships. Likewise, a managed object may be managed by several OSs.

Authority relationships may be grouped in "authority relationship sets", where the sets correspond to divisions based on one or more of the following methods of allocating management responsibility:

- organizational
- administrative
- functional
- geographical
- technological
- other

A management network may make use of several authority relationship sets to reflect different aspects of network management.

9.16 Peer-to-peer OS relationships

When two OSs manage objects in each others' MIBs, these OSs are said to "interoperate as peers", or be in a "peer-to-peer mode". This is the case when there is at least one authority relationship in each direction between the two OSs. Each OS in such an arrangement performs both managing and agent roles.

9.17 Abstraction

One way to handle the complexity in a large system of any kind is by abstraction – the ability to suppress detail that is irrelevant at a particular level. This concept is discussed in the preceding two views. The single managed-object view describes the managed object as an abstract view of a resource or set of resources. An MIB is defined above as the set of managed objects made visible by an OS – thus, the MIB is an abstraction of the physical and logical resources that are accessible through that OS. This section discusses abstraction across multiple OSs and multiple MIBs.

The abstraction provided by a managed object may consist of aggregating, summarizing, partitioning, or otherwise abstracting aspects of a set of resources. The resources that are being abstracted may be distributed around the network, and they may themselves be represented by managed objects on the same or different OSs. This abstraction is invisible to the user of the managed object that provides the abstraction. Regardless of whether a managed object is an abstraction of other managed objects, it is fully defined at the interoperable interface by its class. One implementation of a particular class may call upon managed objects in other OSs, and another implementation of the same class may use other means to provide the required behaviour. (This mapping is a part of the management solution provided by the OS.) It will often be the case that a managed object provides an abstraction of some other managed objects but appears as a single component to a manager of the object. For example, a "circuit" managed object coordinates and abstracts the components that make up the circuit, but it appears to be a simple component to the manager of the circuit.

As we have described, a managed system may provide a managed object in its MIB that provides an abstract view of one or more lower-level managed objects. The degenerate case of this technique is where a managed system provides an exactly identical view of a managed object on another OS (i.e. no abstraction is done). Requests relating to this managed object are simply passed on to the OS holding the other managed object. The "intermediate" OS does not deal with the real resource and does not hold attribute values.

An OS may choose to allow this kind of "pass-through" access to other managed objects for another entire OS. In this case, all the managed objects in the MIB of one OS will appear in the other OS's MIB – possibly as a subtree.

9.18 Management hierarchies

Authority relationships can be applied recursively (possibly in combination with abstraction), resulting in a range known as "management rank". An OS's or managed object's management rank is determined by its span of control and by the level of detail that it understands in contrast to the level of abstraction. OSs near the top of the hierarchy are responsible for controlling a large span of managed objects (directly or indirectly), but in an abstract (not detailed) way, and OSs near the bottom are responsible for a small set of managed objects at a higher level of detail.

The general principles of abstraction and nested authority can be applied to whatever degree is required in a particular management network. A small network may have only one level of managers or just one manager. A large network may need many levels of management rank.

9.19 Authority domains

An authority domain is the set of managed objects managed by a managing process in the context of a particular authority relationship set. Other types of domain exist and are subjects for further study. The concept of authority domains is important to this architecture because it may be necessary for OSs to communicate about authority domains, for example to query or change the membership of an authority domain or to manage properties of the authority domain as a whole.

9.20 The engineering viewpoint

This viewpoint covers mechanisms, structures and rules required when managed objects and management solutions are embodied in a physically distributed set of information processing systems. Conformance testing extensions to the implementors' agreements are also included in this viewpoint.

9.21 The interoperable interface and the OS

The interoperable interface is the physical counterpart of the shared conceptual schema (Section 9.6.1). It is the formally defined set of protocols, procedures, messages and formats and semantics used to communicate between management systems. The interoperable interface reflects all aspects of the shared conceptual schema that are necessary for meaningful communication. Any real open system that is capable of communicating using this interoperable interface is known as a "conformant management entity OS". Any OSs wishing to communicate must have a shared conceptual schema, and they interoperate across the interoperable interface.

It is important to note that, although the shared conceptual schema (in particular, definitions of managed-object classes) may appear to describe aspects of a management system that are "beyond" the interoperable interface, it is the interoperable interface itself (e.g. the messages about the managed objects) that determines conformance. Thus, implementors are not constrained to implement any aspect of the shared conceptual schema in their systems, as long as they provide the appropriate image of the schema in the interoperable interface.

As described in the other viewpoints, the shared conceptual schema is centred around the concept of the managed object. The interoperable interface consists of two components that enable communication between OSs about these managed objects:

- a "P" component, which represents a set of management-specific OSI functional profiles
- an "M" component, which represents the complete range of messages necessary to carry management information between OSs

Note: the interface between two OSs is physically provided by the "P+M" interface. The messages that flow across this interface refer to managed objects. The definition of each message is a part of the definition of a managed-object class although there are generic messages that are used identically in many managed-object classes.

An OS must conform to the interoperable interface, but is otherwise unconstrained in design. The hardware and software that implement the interoperable interface may be combined with other aspects of the management solution or may be separate.

A management solution may be provided in one or more discrete physical units, depending on the size of the managed network, existing configurations, or other design factors.

9.22 Communication protocols

The TMN has agreed to use OSI protocols as the basis for interconnecting conformant physical systems. This specification provides, among other capabilities, a service for communicating messages from a managing process to the agent process of a managed object and vice versa.

An OS must operate in one of three modes:

1. agent: the OS only makes managed objects visible to other OSs, and does not manage any managed objects in other OSs
2. managing: the OS manages managed objects in other OSs, but does not

make any managed objects visible
3. agent/managing: the OS both makes managed objects visible, and manages managed objects made visible by other OSs

9.23 Management information

When two or more OSs exchange management information, it is necessary for them to understand the shared conceptual schema used within the context of this exchange. Some form of context negotiation is required to establish this common understanding within each OS.

9.23.1 Shared conceptual schema

In order to perform interoperable management activities, communicating OSs must share a common view or understanding of the following information:
- supported management functions
- supported managed-object classes
- available managed-object instances
- authorized capabilities

Understanding management functions (e.g. event management and state management) includes an understanding of what options and which roles (e.g. manager or agent) are supported for each function. While trial and error is one method of gaining this understanding the need for a more efficient mechanism is appreciated.

It is necessary to understand which managed-object classes are supported by each OS. Since CMIP scoping is only capable of discovering instances of managed-object classes, a more comprehensive mechanism is needed to understand the complete set of managed-object classes supported including those for which there is not presently an instance available. There may also be relationships (e.g. possible superior–subordinate pairs for naming) between managed-object classes. If so, the negotiation mechanism needs to support the development of this understanding as well.

The actual instances of managed-object classes that are available in an OS forms the most significant base of understanding needed by communicating OSs. CMIP scoping is a reasonable mechanism to provide most of this understanding. As with managed-object classes, managed-object instances may also be participating in relationships that need to be understood by communicating OSs.

Beside understanding what functions and managed objects are supported, the shared conceptual schema also includes an understanding of authorized management capabilities (e.g. permission to modify configurations, adjust tariffs, create or delete managed objects, run destructive tests).

The interoperable interface specifies the protocols that are used for communication between OSs. OSs must implement this interface and perform either the role of a managing process, an agent process, or both; OS design is otherwise unconstrained. OSs wishing to communicate must agree (either offline or online) on a shared conceptual schema. Where necessary, supplier-specific information may be carried within the framework of standard interactions. Finally, OS implementations evolve over time and must be tested for conformance with the interoperable interface.

9.24 Mapping the service onto the architecture

Figure 9.2 illustrates how we map a collection of applications to the service and then to the management system.

Service specification

• Representations of configuration and resources for Multimedia Terminal Equipment (MTE) and CMMCs
• Media channels represent media data paths between user and network, e.g.:

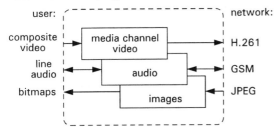

• user replaced by multiplexing unit for CMMC

Figure 9.2 Multimedia application streams over managed system.

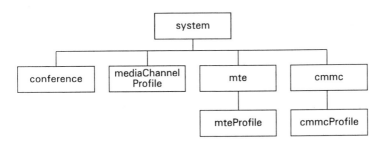

Figure 9.3 Containment tree.

9.25 Management protocols

Most access to managed systems is carried over the Simple Network Management Protocol (SNMP).[3] Suffice it to say that this is simple, providing get and set

3. The ISO protocol CMIP, the Common Management Information Protocol, is also used and has a richer set of primitives including the ability to scope access to levels of the hierarchy of management objects.

operations and a get-next operation to traverse a table of information. It is not so much the access, as what information there is to access and what is then done with that information, that is interesting and difficult about network management.

While tools such as the MIB help deal with the data dictionary for the management system, this only defines the types of managed objects. The names/ addresses of instances of these objects need to be stored in a database, and this can be distributed and accessed through a conventional distributed system.

9.26 Applying ODP and CORBA directly to management

Network management systems are very large, but are easily decomposed into many separate functions (or objects). From this, it is clear that one can distribute the management systems, and connect these together using CORBA (for example) for inter-process communication. One can also take advantage of the other facilities in distributed systems to help scale the management system, for example:

- The use of naming services permits components to be location-independent. This leads to the potential for replication of services, which has consequences for improved availability and performance.
- Distributed platforms provide a number of other standard facilities which are all useful for management functions. For example, concurrency in servers and clock syncronization are useful for managing the managers. Authentication and privacy are all-important for billing and auditing as well as preventing denial of service attacks through the management systems.

By making the access between management components part of a set of standard objects, we can use inheritance to implement the common functions across the different management functions – for example performance, fault and billing management may all need to access very similar objects in various databases that log counters from various MIBs (e.g. call durations, packet counts, errors logged, and so forth).

An important data type that might be stored in a distributed management system is the *map*. This is a description of the topological relationship between a number of managed entities (for example, a cable plant map, a routeing table, or even a protocol stack or collection of them. Maps can describe connections, sets of connections and so on; so we can model many of the real-world systems that exist in networks.

These maps too will be in some conceptual database. It will be created at configuration time, and can be used by the distributed management system to discover where things are and may implement policies for any management mechanisms through further configuration.

9.27 Distributed systems for managing networks

One advantage of using a system like CORBA to manage a network is that this in the long run will lead to several advances in networks:

- Systems management (which is often distributed already) can be usefully combined with network management, and save on resources and expertise.
- Distributed systems can provide common interfaces for applications to some communications functions such as signalling and bandwidth management.
- Distributed systems are the basis for the applications themselves, and so new network services that require distributed functionality can be added more easily when the network management system is a distributed system.

9.28 Embedded management functionality

It is not always clear when something is best managed through a management application and agent approach and when it is best embedded in the distributed system itself. For example, name services, routeing and time services are not usually implemented through management systems, even though aspects of them will be managed. Name, time and route service configuration, performance and errors might all be stored and accessed through an MIB. However, it would be most inefficient to invoke the whole structure of an application to actually build name-to-address mappings, or to exchange link and node status and calculate the topology, or to carry out clock synchronization services. These are all low-level functions higher-level management (and distributed systems themselves) rests upon, rather than implements!

9.29 Summary

Ⓘ Reality checkpoint   Network management is possibly one of the most important, least interesting (to the author) distributed applications in existence. Luckily, its economic importance has led to a great deal of excellent work being done to design reasonable systems that permit multivendor networks to be managed.

9.30 Exercises

1. What aspects of network management should be secured, and from what attacks?
2. How would you apply the management model presented here differently to distributed systems and to networking entities?

CHAPTER 10

Distributed file systems

with Nermeen Ismail, University College London

10.1 Virtual file system model

File systems hold persistent data (that survives power outages). Networked file systems make that data available across a network. Distributed file systems make the data more available, perhaps with higher performance. See Figure 10.1.

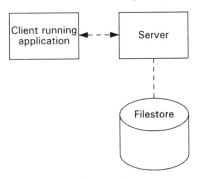

Figure 10.1   Remote file access.

Distributed file systems exist because of certain cost/performance tradeoffs. At various points in history, the relative costs of diskstore compared with monitor, CPU and memory, as well as network costs, together with the reasonable performance of local-area networks, have meant that it is easier to put mass storage on centrally managed servers than on all the workstations in a site. The main gain has been one of manageability, but with replication of disks there are also increases in fault tolerance and in performance.

ⓘ Reality checkpoint   However, the economics of such systems are by no means fixed. Indeed, many sites in the 1980s and early 1990s have had disks on all machines, and have distributed executable files (typically a large proportion of filestore requirement) to those disks periodically, and only kept the rapidly changing priceless user files on centrally managed filestores. With a clean replication system, the central servers would shrink to nearly nothing, merely existing as caches for replicas to changes, before they were stored on safer media such as tape or writable optical storage.

To start with, let us outline a taxonomy of a networked file system:

- disk
- server machine
- server software
- network
- client software
- client machine
- client application

Note that there are a number more components than with local file access. This means that extra mechanisms must be introduced to improve availability, even just to the level of local access.

Note, as illustrated in Table 10.1, that there are several places where protocols are involved: between the client and server machines, between the client application and the client file-system access code, and between the server and the filestore. Typically, the client and server protocols are made as similar to local access as possible (for example, by using remote procedure calls that are nearly the same as the system procedures for accessing local files).

However, there are more modes in which the system can fail, and so the failure semantics are changed. There are also more opportunities for concurrency, and therefore chances of inconsistency, since a server cannot tell what a client application is doing with data once it has given that data over, and there may be multiple clients of a given server (and of a given file on that server).

Since disks are relatively slow, even local access is typically cached in memory. When file access is remote, this leads to the further choice of whether there is caching at the server, at the client, or at both. The choice is dependent on the semantics of remote file access, as shown in Table 10.2.

When designing a network or distributed file-system, performance is a key parameter. To select the right paradigm, first we must look at the underlying access patterns for local file access. Then we try and predict if this access will remain the same for remote access, and if not, how it will change.[1]

Table 10.1 Changing from local to remote access.

Local protocol	Remote protocol
Local service	Remote service
Local API	Remote API
Local semantics	Remote semantics

Table 10.2 Examples of choice.

	Exactly-once RPC	Idempotent RPC
Semantics	y	n
Client cache	n	n
Service	y	n

There have been many studies of file-access patterns, though most have been on the same kinds of system (Unix). They have mainly found that there is a very high degree of what is called "locality of reference, both in time and space". Put simply, if you access a part of a file you are much more likely to access the next part of the file, and soon, than some other part of the file, or another file, at some far-off time in the future (through symmetry arguments, the past behaviour resembles the future).

Another part of the picture is that the majority of files are opened for reading only, and rarely for writing. This is very important when considering how expensive a concurrency-control scheme one should use since there's no need to invoke it for read-only file access.

When looking at the service used to access the file, we should distinguish between the service seen by the application and that actually carried out by the system. This is no different from local access: local file access in many systems is provided by a *stream* abstraction. In fact, hardware access to the file consists of a possibly arbitrary scattering of blocks across a disk, but layers of software con-

---

1. Early World Wide Web access did not include caches or replicas – this led very rapidly to saturation of world-wide networks. In contrast, archive servers in the Internet are heavily based around replication, and consequently they reduce the traffic.

spire to hide this. A remote-file access protocol may well preserve the stream appearance of access, while actually translating it into unique accesses to blocks (NFS works in approximately this way). Alternatively, it may provide a lower-layer *side-effect*, whereby the entire file is moved from server to client as a stream, and access at the client is mapped into access to the copy (AFS works roughly like this).

10.2 Consequences of the open model

Replication is an area where there is a lot of room for competition between different algorithms. Unfortunately, this means that it may be hard to provide an open system.

A key problem is whether a server has to keep state about clients. Depending on a number of design decisions, different distributed file-systems require more or less server state. An open system would imply that all servers must keep state about all clients irrespective of the protocol, since they cannot tell if the client (or other servers) is conspiring to produce the right reliability of service.

10.3 File (system) naming

Any good networked or distributed file system will hide the locality of a file from the application (user), to some extent. But in doing this it must still provide the user with a way of navigating the file-system. Typically, this is done by extending the idea of physical or logical disks or disk partitions that are present in many operating-system views of files. For example, DOS has a notion of *drive*, and many distributed file-systems for DOS simply allocate *network drives* as the names for file systems on a server.

On the other hand, Unix has a more general mechanism for building a view of a set of file-systems into a tree structure, using points in the file-system called *mount points* where entire new file-systems can be *found*. Many networked file-systems have used this hierarchical naming system to place a server's file-system(s) in the view of a client machine. There is a choice here, as to whether all servers are seen by all clients in the same place in the same tree, or each client can carries the mapping wherever it likes. The latter approach is more common, as it is more open.

Basically, initial access to a file is seen by the client operating system as some call to a system function that names this mount point or network drive, explicitly or implicitly (e.g. with respect to the current working directory). The system simply intercepts this and further access calls to the file and redirects them to the client protocol code. This is an ideal job for remote procedure call.

10.3.1 Access protocols

There are three main approaches to remote file access:

1. remote disk

2. remote calls to file access
3. whole-file copy

Which is used depends largely on how much operating-system code re-use is required, and also what level of fault tolerance is needed.

10.4 Replication

File replication systems are really just one manifestation of replicated persistent data. We will talk about replicated files in the rest of this section, but the concepts are generally applicable to other objects, including parts of files. There are a number of techniques that are used to provide replication, and they each have their costs and benefits.

Replication is used to provide a number of transparencies:

- Fault transparency or tolerance – components in a distributed system can fail independently. A file may be made more available in the face of failures of a fileserver if it appears on more than one fileserver. Availability is one of the main measures of the advantage of a replication algorithm.
- Performance – if a file is "nearer" a user, access will generally be faster. Files may be replicated across local storage devices at creation time, or they may be "cached" when first accessed. Such caching may be on the basis of a few blocks of the file (NFS), the whole file (AFS 1), or as much of the file as possible (AFS 3).
- Portability – file access should be possible after a workstation is detached from the network if portability is required.

Replication carries with it several overheads. These include:

- Storage costs: whole-file copies are relatively expensive.
- Consistency of updates: there is cost in coordinating the update of a replicated file so that further accesses perceive a consistent object. This has an associated execution and communication cost.
- Complexity: some replication schemes may require complex software to implement them. This has an associated implementation and maintenance overhead.

Replication techniques to provide consistency can be divided into two main classes:

- *Optimistic*
  These schemes assume faults are rare and implement recovery schemes to deal with inconsistency.
- *Pessimistic*
  These schemes assume faults are more common, and attempt to ensure consistency of every access. Schemes that allow access when all copies are not available use voting protocols to decide if enough copies are available to proceed.

10.4.1 Update algorithms

1. *Basic update algorithms*

   The following two algorithms show the basic idea of replicated files. They fail to provide availability in the face of network partitioning (a common failure mode in large distributed systems).

   - *Unanimous update*

     An update must succeed on all copies or none. A read can succeed from any one copy. Writes use 2-phase commit.

   - *Available copy*

     Updates succeed on all available copies. If a server is down, it is excluded as a copy. The problem is the difference between detecting a server down and a server not reachable.

2. *Voting algorithms*

   Voting algorithms include a mechanism for deciding if enough copies of a file are available to proceed with updates safely.

   - *Majority voting*

     This scheme simply assigns votes to each copy, together with version numbers. Reads now use two phases: a first phase collects the latest version's votes, the second commits to the read on the latest version. Writes collect votes and request to write on all versions. When a majority of votes is read, the write can be committed (otherwise it is rolled back).

   - *Weighted voting*

     The availability of the replicated file may be tuned to deal with different kinds of failures by associating weights with votes at particular sites.

   - *Quorum consensus*

     In general, objects are often complex, with different operations affecting the state of the object differently. This can be exploited by generalizing the idea of weighted votes on copies to quorum consensus voting.

     In this scheme, an object's state is represented as a sequence of time-stamped operations on the state. Depending on the semantics of each operation (read or write), we can adjust the availability versus cost by setting a quorum for starting each operation and another for finishing.

10.5 Management

The distributed file system will have to support diverse file systems, some sooner than later. These will include:

- PC-NFS/DOS file systems – these will be essential for safe software availability (since distribution to pure DOS machines could be a disaster area). It is probably best not to allow DOS machines to hold user files if possible.

- Andrew AFS – a vastly superior distributed file system to NFS, but not in widespread use. It is probably ideal for teaching since cached files used in teaching are relatively small. It is known to coexist with NFS. How it interacts with naming/mounting/access control is not known.

- The Coda file system extends the AFS (see Section 10.8) to add a cache-coherence algorithm. Basically, a Coda client has a cache of a file. Since most files are read-only, network partitioning or even server crash are not problems. If a client opens a file for write, Coda is optimistic, and simply assumes that statistically it is unlikely two clients will open the same file to write. If they do, then on writing the cache back to the server there is a rollback and re-integration scheme that is invoked. Unfortunately, for many common file-systems, a file is a stream of bytes (cf. Unix/DOS), and integration of two sequences of changes is not meaningful. This has led to the next generation of file-system designs, where all files are kept in a series of updates of their contents. With decreasing storage costs, such *log-structured file-systems* are becoming increasingly attractive, since they simplify a number of error recovery procedures outside distributed systems as well as inside.[2]

10.6 The network file system (NFS)

Authentication and naming facilities
NFS is simplistic in its notion of "naming" and permissions. By default (and in many implementations) it requires a flat "uid" (user identity) space across the set of machines sharing the file systems (except for the root or superuser privileged user whose ownership vanishes across an NFS mount). This means simply that two different users could have read/write permissions over each other's files on different servers if they mounted each other's filestores. Note that this can be stopped by controlling who may mount a filestore with the "exports" file.

This causes problems when adding existing systems to the consortium filestore (without some gateway/uid-mapping service). For instance, UCL uses uids 0–7999 already (most systems support 2^{15} or 2^{31} uids).

NIS (Kille 1988) provides a way of distributing the user names/uids without having multiple stored copies, but does not provide a uid-mapping service.

Hesiod (Kille 1988) provides a similar service to NIS.

Other facilities
There are a number of other facilities that must be considered in the context of distribution of file services, including

- *Quotas*
  BSD (Berkeley standard definition) quotas on file systems work independently of NFS. As mentioned above, separation of user communities onto separate file systems has a benefit in that it provides coarse-grained quota-ing of each community (with the drawback that file-free blocks are not shared – the usual engineering trade off).

---

2. Log-structured file systems were designed to optimize or eliminate seek times for disk access, but they can also be extended to optimize concurrent, distributed access.

- *Distributed execution*

  Some views or architectures may impose certain hierarchies or structures from the server (e.g. TCF (transparent computing facility; see AFS, Section 10.7) works in clusters of up to 31 workstations).

- *Performance/reliability considerations*

  When a filestore is not mounted, NFS fails exactly as required: the application gets an open/read/write error. If a filestore is already mounted, but fails, NFS fails in different ways depending on mount options: if hard-mounted, it retries for ever (using the -intr, or interruptable option in which case an interrupt to the application terminates the NFS call); if soft-mounted, it can fail after some number of retries (and it can fail silently, as in "write behinds").

Consider an NFS setup with N fileservers with some availability x. If the average utilization of a filestore is y, then mean chance of hanging an application is $N(1 - x)$ assuming machines run much longer than the MTBF.

With automount, each filestore has a chance y of being mounted when the server crashes. Then we get $N(1 - x)y$, assuming all filestores roughly the same.

But if the filestore mount map is flat, there are some operations that systematically do badly (e.g. the find operation). The same effect will also be seen if finding the current working directory uses the top-down approach to finding the correct working directory rather than looking at the parent directory (. .).

Luckily, such broad file-tree activities are rare. If sufficiently rarer than the fileserver failures, they won't cause broken filestores to stay mounted.

By contrast, there is an overhead associated with opening a file in a deeply nested filestore of a readdir per level. It is known that a great many Unix applications open a file, read a block, and close the file. For each level of the file system the number of resulting NFS calls increases by at least one.

10.6.1 Details of the network file system

Sun NFS is one of the most widely used network filespace access systems. NFS uses RPC to provide the access primitives from client to server. Sun has devised its own RPC protocol, together with its own external data representation language called XDR.

The NFS model of the world is of stateless servers. Servers keep no track of whether any clients exist, or who they are if they do. Instead, client retry is relied on to provide reliability. The RPC is an at-most-once time, so the defined operations are all idempotent, as far as possible (i.e. assuming the actual file data doesn't change, repeating the operation produces the same client and server state change).

Since NFS is usually used for access from or to Unix systems, this means that there is a level of indirection, since the Unix file-access primitives are by no means idempotent (a read operation moves an implicit pointer through a file, while an NFS read references an absolute offset in a file).

The model of the actual file system is that of Unix. The name space is a hierarchy that consists of directories or files. Directories are everything except the leaf nodes.

Location transparency is provided by permitting any point in the tree to be a link to a (possibly) remote file system (a "mount point"). Thus, NFS looks up one component of a pathname at a time. A table is kept that maps mount points to remote server machine names, and thus provides the location service.

The collection of server procedures is fairly simple, and a subset of these is reproduced in Figure 10.2 from the NFS standard:

- NFSPROC_NULL(void) = 0;
  This procedure does no work. It is made available in all RPC services to allow server response testing and timing.
- attrstat NFSPROC_GETATTR (fhandle) = 1;
  If the reply status is NFS_OK, then the reply attributes contains the attributes for the file given by the input fhandle.
- attrstat NFSPROC_SETATTR (sattrargs) = 2;

```
struct sattrargs {
  fhandle file;
  sattr attributes;
};
```

The "attributes" argument contains fields that are either –1 or are the new value for the attributes of "file". If the reply status is NFS_OK, then the reply attributes have the attributes of the file after the "SETATTR" operation has completed.

Note the use of –1 to indicate an unused field in "attributes" is changed in the next version of the protocol.

- diropres NFSPROC_LOOKUP(diropargs) = 4;
  If the reply "status" is NFS_OK, then the reply "file" and reply "attributes" are the file handle and attributes for the file "name" in the directory given by "dir" in the argument.
- readlinkres NFSPROC_READLINK(fhandle) = 5;

```
union readlinkres switch (stat status) {
case NFS\_OK:
  path data;
default:
  void;
};
```

If "status" has the value NFS_OK, then the reply "data" is the data in the symbolic link given by the file referred to by the fhandle argument.

Note since NFS always parses pathnames on the client, the pathname in a symbolic link may mean something different (or be meaningless) on a different client or on the server if a different pathname syntax is used.

```
program NFS_PROGRAM { version NFS_VERSION { void
   NFSPROC_NULL(void) = 0;

   attrstat
   NFSPROC_GETATTR(fhandle) = 1;

   attrstat
   NFSPROC_SETATTR(sattrargs) = 2;

   void
   NFSPROC_ROOT(void) = 3;

   diropres
   NFSPROC_LOOKUP(diropargs) = 4;

   readlinkres
   NFSPROC_READLINK(fhandle) = 5;

   readres
   NFSPROC_READ(readargs) = 6;

   void
   NFSPROC_WRITECACHE(void) = 7;

   attrstat
   NFSPROC_WRITE(writeargs) = 8;

   diropres
   NFSPROC_CREATE(createargs) = 9;

   stat
   NFSPROC_REMOVE(diropargs) = 10;

   stat
   NFSPROC_RENAME(renameargs) = 11;

   stat
   NFSPROC_LINK(linkargs) = 12;

   stat
   NFSPROC_SYMLINK(symlinkargs) = 13;

   diropres
   NFSPROC_MKDIR(createargs) = 14;

   stat
   NFSPROC_RMDIR(diropargs) = 15;

   readdirres
   NFSPROC_READDIR(readdirargs) = 16;

   statfsres
   NFSPROC_STATFS(fhandle) = 17;
   } = 2;
} = 100003;
```

Figure 10.2   The NFS remote procedure interface.

- readres NFSPROC_READ(readargs) = 6;

```
struct readargs {
   fhandle file;
   unsigned offset;
   unsigned count;
   unsigned totalcount;
};
union readres switch (stat status) {
case NFS_OK:
   fattr attributes;
   nfsdata data;
default:
   void;
};
```

Returns up to "count" bytes of "data" from the file given by "file", starting at "offset" bytes from the beginning of the file. The first byte of the file is at offset zero. The file attributes after the read takes place are returned in "attributes".

Note the argument "totalcount" is unused, and is removed in the next protocol revision.

- attrstat NFSPROC_WRITE(writeargs) = 8;

```
struct writeargs {
   fhandle file;
   unsigned beginoffset;
   unsigned offset;
   unsigned totalcount;
   nfsdata data;
};
```

Writes "data" beginning "offset" bytes from the beginning of "file". The first byte of the file is at offset zero. If the reply "status" is NFS_OK, then the reply "attributes" contains the attributes of the file after the write has completed. The write operation is atomic. Data from this "WRITE" will not be mixed with data from another client's "WRITE".

Note the arguments "beginoffset" and "totalcount" are ignored and are removed in the next protocol revision.

- diropres NFSPROC_CREATE(createargs) = 9;

```
struct createargs {
   diropargs where;
   sattr attributes;
};
```

The file "name" is created in the directory given by "dir". The initial

306

attributes of the new file are given by "attributes". A reply "status" of NFS_OK indicates that the file was created, and reply "file" and reply "attributes" are its file handle and attributes. Any other reply "status" means that the operation failed and no file was created.

Note this routine should pass an exclusive create flag, meaning "create the file only if it is not already there".

- stat NFSPROC_REMOVE(diropargs) = 10;
  The file "name" is removed from the directory given by "dir". A reply of NFS_OK means the directory entry was removed.

  Note this is possibly a non-idempotent operation.

10.7 The Andrew file system (AFS)

The Andrew File System was developed at Carnegie Mellon University (and named Andrew after the founder's first name), as part of a large project in next-generation distributed systems in the mid-1980s. It has two main components; Vice and Venus:

- Vice provides the shared file system
- Venus provides the redirector function for clients

AFS has two main advantages over some other systems in terms of scaling:

1. prefix naming – pathname prefixes are used to provide location
2. whole-file caching – the first access to a file causes it to appear in its entirety on the client machine's local disk

The development of the three versions of AFS is an instructive lesson in good distributed systems design, since the later phases solved problems that were preceived in the earlier versions by a series of refinements were not precluded in any way by earlier designs. The initial design of AFS was based around the client–server paradigm. However, unlike (at least the original) NFS, the system addressed *scaling* as a base requirement. The goal was to maximize the number of clients that could be served from one machine. To this end, the clients cached whole files, so that a series of passes through the file only resulted in a single access. Even a single pass over the file (a very common pattern of access, for example on DOS and Unix systems) could take advantage of streamed requests from the client to the server to fill the cache, which can scale to long-haul networks (with a large bandwidth/delay product) better than the stop-and-wait performance of an RPC per block of a file.

The problem with whole-file caching is that it increases the probability of concurrent accesses to a file, creating an inconsistent view at the server. In fact, concurrent accesses to write files are rare in many environments, but some (e.g. workgroup environments) do have many writers of a given file.

Hence we need a mechanism for maintaining consistency, either at the server or to inform clients that their cache is invalid. There are two points on a spectrum of design at which to do this: one extreme is that we are *optimistic* and the server informs clients in the hopefully "rare" event of intervening writes; the other extreme is that clients check each time they try to carry out any action.

The first modification to the AFS (going from AFS 1 to AFS 2), was an optimization of the cache consistency in two ways. First, the servers had an RPC *callback* to clients to carry out cache invalidation. This eliminates the cache validation traffic that was present in the pessimistic AFS 1 (directories are still written through to the server because directory integrity is vital, and the costs are low for this). Secondly, the internal implementation of the client and server was enhanced to include *threads*, which makes handling callbacks more straightforward.

Notice that the decision to move from cache validation to cache invalidation is based on a move in the view of the likelihood of incoherence from being pessimistic to being optimistic. This is based on actual measurements of typical behaviour (i.e. it is an engineering viewpoint change, in ODP modelling terms).

The next phase of development of AFS (from AFS 2 to AFS 3) was to deal with another step in scaling. To achieve this, a hierarchy of systems was introduced, called "administrative cells". A cell contains a set of clients, servers, users and system administrators, and is also the unit of security management. To work between cells, as well as providing internal security, authentication servers are used. The overall system provides access-control lists for protecting files, and groups for aggregating users' permissions. This set of enhancements is possible almost as a layer on top of the previous version of AFS. A refinement of the whole-file caching was introduced, based (again) on performance analysis of actual usage. This led to a compromise whereby clients can cache files from servers in 64-kbyte chunks rather than the whole file. This accommodates many typical files (e.g. documents) while also recognizing that client machines may not have (effectively) infinite local diskstore. It can also help with the startup performance (latency) for initial file access, although concurrency in the client code could also help this by allowing early completion of a call to open a file and permitting the client to start reading the file before it has all arrived.

The last phase in the evolution of AFS has been to accommodate "disconnected" operation. Many users are starting to use workstations that are wireless. Laptop PCs and handheld computers should be able to use AFS, and continue to let a client work on a file even when network access to the server is no longer available, restoring cache consistency when the network is reconnected. This can also support access in less reliable networks. The Coda file system is an extension of AFS 2 (and not 3) to provide two main functions: server replication permits operations to continue in the event of a link outage; disconnected operation is provided by introducing a new notion of a directory of files that a mobile client may wish to carry around.

Replication in Coda is provided through a simple model in which a client reads data from a preferred server, but writes data back to all servers. The fact that this is client-driven again takes load (and complexity) away from the servers. The many-update protocol uses a two-phase scheme. The first phase attempts to write the data optimistically to all the servers. In the second phase, which operates asynchronously, the client carries out any consistency check by updating version information at the servers. A neat optimization is that the second phase of the update protocol can be piggybacked on requests to read (or write) new files.

Disconnected operation is based on profiling the set of files that a user wishes to hoard, on their laptop. The client access code switches from normal server access to accessing the local copy as the client machine loses connectivity. When server access is regained, the client goes through a reintegration phase to update the server(s). At this stage, a similar conflict resolution to that described for partial write fails above might be used.

10.8 Media file system

The digital multimedia server (DMS) allows multiple remote clients to store, structure and retrieve multimedia objects. Multimedia objects can contain any combination of video sequences, audio clips, still images and text.

10.8.1 The server

The DMS offers two level of services, the low-level storage service (LLSS) and the high-level storage service (HLSS).

The low-level storage service is responsible for the storage, retrieval and synchronization of multiple streams of monomedia objects. It deals with the hardware and the low-level aspects of the system such as managing the physical storage devices as well as the communication media and protocols.

The high-level storage service is responsible for the construction of structured multimedia objects out of the monomedia ones already stored by the low-level storage server. It also performs an admission policy allowing only requests with real-time constraints that can be guaranteed without affecting the already-being-served requests being admitted. The high-level storage server is designed to be able to manage more than one low-level storage server, though at the moment it is just managing one.

A DMS library is provided to allow application programs an easy way to access the DMS and shield them from the underlying communication protocols. A DMS client is built on top of the library to allow end-users a simple access to the server.

10.8.2 Low-level storage server

The low-level storage server is responsible for

1. the storage and retrieval of synchronized digital data streams to and from the physical devices of the system
2. providing random access to the stored monomedia objects based on different criteria (at the moment random access is just provided on video and audio objects and is based on time)
3. the conversion between the format of the stored objects and that that is required by, or more suitable to, the client
4. choosing which communication medium to use for data transmission accord-

ing to the client's available resources

The LLSS uses the notion of context to determine the physical location of the objects. In Unix jargon, a context can be mapped on a Unix directory. Every object does have a context id associated with it that determines the category this object belongs to. The context can be determined either by the end-application or by the IR (information retrieval) database.

The video objects are stored as an H.261 (ITU 1992) compressed stream of data. The audio objects are stored as an G.722 (Jayant 1990) compressed stream of data. With each video or audio stream an indexing file is generated and stored. The indexing information is used to provide a quick random access to the video and audio objects.

The LLSS can receive/transmit the audio and video objects using one of two protocols:

1. *RTP protocol*

   This protocol is used when transmitting real-time data over PSDN (packet-switched data networks). It specifies timestamps and sequence numbers with each packet (Crowcroft & Paliwoda 1988). The LLSS is using the same protocol as the Inria Video System (Turletti & Huitema 1992), which is a software installation of an H.261 codec, thus allowing clients with no access to hardware codecs to use IVS instead.

2. *H.221 protocol*

   This is a framing protocol for audiovisual data transmission over serial lines (such as ISDN). A lot of hardware codecs (including the one we use) generate a stream of H.221 frames (ITU 1992).

   To store the data, the LLSS first strips off the H.221 control data, then it separates the video data stream from the audio data stream (if both exist). The audio data is then divided into access units and a timestamp is allocated for each unit. The error-correction framing data is stripped off the H.261 video data the raw H.261 data is analysed and a timestamp is allocated for each picture.

   During data retrieval the reverse process takes place. The H.261 error-correction frames have to be constructed and mixed with the audio data. The H.221 control data will be added after that.

10.8.3 High-level storage server

The high-level storage server is responsible for building structured multimedia objects and applying an admission control policy to guarantee the real-time requirements of new as well as already-being-served requests.

A structured multimedia object consists of a group of monomedia objects along with a set of constructors to glue them into units, a time frame to determine the time relationship (temporal synchronization) between the monomedia objects, and a layout to determine the space relationship between them. The monomedia objects are those supported by the LLSS: video sequences, audio clips, still images and text.

10.8.4 Object constructors
The object constructors are operators that glue monomedia objects into multimedia units. Two types of constructors are defined:
1. *Record*: a group of different monomedia objects or multimedia units that together form a new multimedia unit. The retrieval of a record results in the retrieval of all its elements.
2. *Union*: one of different monomedia objects or multimedia units. The retrieval of a union results in the retrieval of just one of its elements.

The union constructor is particularly useful for the association of more than one audio stream, all in different languages, with the same video clip.

10.8.5 Object time frame
The object time frame determines how the elements of a structured object are related to each other with respect to time (temporal synchronization). Two kinds of synchronization can be distinguished: loose and tight synchronization. The first deals with the sequence in which objects should be displayed, i.e. it determines when to start displaying/transferring a certain monomedia stream. Tight synchronization maintains a more continuous relation between two or more streams of data, e.g. lip synchronization.

For each time frame, a monomedia object is chosen as the origin of the time frame, i.e. the first object to be displayed. Relative to this object the playing time of the rest of the objects is determined. For tight synchronization the two streams must have a colliding period on the time frame and a synchronization granularity is associated with each relation.

10.8.6 Object layout
The object layout determines the space relationship between the various elements of a structured object. For every monomedia object, a reference object will be defined along with a space operator. Both the reference object and the space operator determine the position of the object. For each structured object, an absolute object that has no reference to any other object is assigned. The place of the absolute object is either determined during storage time or is chosen by the retrieving application. Space operators that are defined are overlay, concatenate and locate. Layout definition is only applicable to visual objects.

10.8.7 DMS client environment
For multimedia data *storage*, the client site should be capable of converting the analogue signals needed to be stored within the DMS into digital streams that can be understood by the DMS. For data *retrieval*, the client should be able to decompress the digital streams received from the DMS if they are compressed, convert them into analogue signal if required, and display them. On the other hand the server would receive digital data streams from clients, process them if necessary, and store them in its physical storage devices. It will load the digital streams from the physical devices, process them if necessary, and transmit them back to clients.

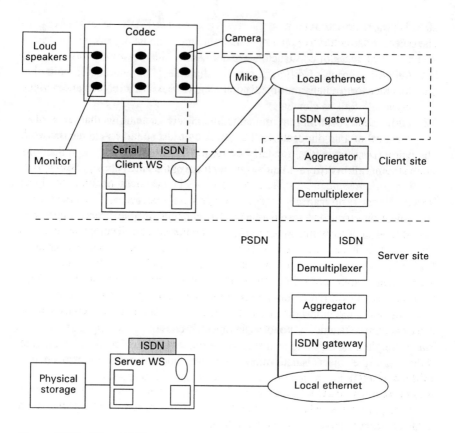

Figure 10.3 Client–DMS environment.

Figure 10.3 shows a typical client environment (the one used at the moment) and how multimedia data can be transmitted to the DMS and back.

In the diagram the client site is equipped with a codec (GPT H.261) that digitizes video and audio signals and compresses them. The codec is connected to the client machine via an RS449 serial interface which receives the digital data, packetizes them and sends them over the local client Ethernet to the ISDN gateway. The ISDN gateway receives the data packets addressed to the server, encapsulates them in ISDN frames, initiates an ISDN connection to the server gateway, and starts sending the data over ISDN.

The packetized data can also be sent over PSDN if a high-bandwidth link between the client and the DMS is available (e.g. SuperJANET).

Alternatively the codec can be connected to the client machine via an ISDN board. In this case data would be sent directly to ISDN, not through the ISDN gateway. The server ISDN gateway on the other hand receives the ISDN data addressed to the server, strips off the ISDN headers, and sends the data packets to the server machine. To retrieve data from the server, the same process happens in the reverse order. The server can have direct access to ISDN via an ISDN board instead of using the ISDN gateway.

The Codec constitutes the most expensive part of the scenario. It has two main functions:

1. analogue-to-digital and digital-to-analogue conversion of the audio/video signals
2. compression/decompression of the audio/video signals so that the size of data needed to be transmitted and stored is suitable for the network resources (bandwidth) used at the moment

The compression process is usually more expensive than the decompression process. The compression process is needed just once by the client initiating the object storage request whereas the decompression process is needed by each client wishing to retrieve the compressed object. Development in the processing power available to end-users makes it possible to compress and decompress audio in software and to decompress low-quality video data using software instead of hardware. This means that one of the most expensive elements in the above scenario would just be needed for clients wishing to store data within the DMS or retrieve high-quality video data. With more and more processing power being available at the client end and more efficient frame grabbers, the codec can be completely exchanged with a software replacement.

10.9 Security

Adding security to remote file access is merely a matter of taking the various secure requirements and the technology presented in Chapter 4 and applying them to the particular file-access protocol in hand.

One existing example of this is the multi-level secure version of the Network File System. This includes discretionary access control (DAC), subject and object security labelling, mandatory access control (MAC), authentication, auditing and documentation.

NFS provides authentication in a range of ways and by extending the credentials required one can provide multiple levels of access. For example, NFS adds:

-   audit id – immutable subject (user) identifier, not affected by modifications to either the real or effective user or group identifiers
-   sensitivity label – used with a MAC policy; a subject generally has a static, top-level clearance, but is permitted to execute processes at a sensitivity level different from (i.e. lower than) their actual clearance
-   information label – used with a dual-level labelling policy; dynamically adjusted based upon the information content associated with the subject (or object)
-   integrity label – used with commercial, multi-party security policy (e.g. Clark–Wilson)
-   privilege mask – used to identify privileges (e.g. chown, chmod) or "rights" granted to a given subject, generally to override an existing security policy

313

10.10 Summary

This chapter has looked at some practical aspects of distributed file systems, and in particular at supporting access to multimedia data in a file system.

10.11 Exercises

1. Classify NFS and AFS according to the taxonomy earlier in this chapter.
2. How would you add file replication to NFS?

CHAPTER 11

Load balancing

with S. Hailes, University College London

11.1 Introduction

One of the potential benefits of a distributed system is the ability to reduce overall response time by effectively utilizing the concurrency inherent in distributed systems in order to make the best use of computational resources

- *monitoring* – determining the current state of a system in terms of network load, processor load and resource availability
- *migration* – transparently transferring an executing computation from one physical node to another
- *load balancing* – actually a specific instance of a general problem, that of distributed scheduling (distributed scheduling includes both static and placement whereas load balancing implies a totally dynamic system)

11.2 ODP/ANSA migration

Both ODP and ANSA have the concept of relocation service: if you have an interface reference (that appears to be broken) go to an appropriate relocation service and this will update it for you. Interface references in ANSA (and ANSAware) consist of a sequence of end points at which the service may be found.

In addition, ANSA interface references for a service contain a sequence of interface references for relocators responsible for that service. When an object is moved it is responsible for updating the relocators associated with any interface references it exported. When a client's binding breaks because it can no longer find the service at any of the end points in the interface reference, the client consults one of the locators to get an updated interface reference.

Relocation of relocators can be handled by making them a group responsible for providing a relocation service for each other. This will work provided they only relocate infrequently. All this can be made completely transparent to the application program.

11.3 Monitoring distributed systems

Any monitoring of distributed systems must be based on what classes of information are available through monitoring on each separate component system. This will then be disseminated throughout the system by some means. The ways the information is gathered and disseminated both affect the accuracy of the information in terms of correctness and timeliness.

11.3.1 Class of information

There are three broad classes of information gathered for load balancing. The configuration of a system (see Figure 11.1) must be known so it can be compared meaningfully with other systems. The system state is monitored periodically. The processes that run may be characterized so that they can be scheduled – this can be done short-term as they run, based on very recent history, or long-term-based over a number of runs – this is especially true of embedded and real-time systems.

```
configuration -
    machine type,
    operating system version
    memory
    disk I/O systems
    etc.

system state
    processor load
    I/O load (disk/terminals/graphics/devices)
    network load (if separate from above)
    filesystem activity

process characteristics
    I/O versus CPU bound
    # files accessed
    # pages/swapping statistics
```

Figure 11.1   Typical system configuration information.

In addition, in a distributed system, it is necessary to have other configuration information – in particular the relative proximity of processes, processors and data. In a large system this may involve interacting with routeing/topological information (e.g. bandwidth and delay/latency and error rates of lines between systems – for instance FDDI (fibre-distributed data interface) may be faster than bus access for some systems, or in other words remote file access is faster than data migration to a slower disk).

11.3.2 Dissemination

Information may be disseminated unsolicited, or it may be requested. It may be stored in a central broker or trader which acts as a go-between to place processes based on load information, or else it may be fully distributed. There are two basic protocol approaches to distributing this information:
- broadcast/multicast from each server to all others
- requested from each server by each client

The former approach is used for fault tolerance fully distributed (client-driven) load-balancing systems. The latter might be coupled with the nameservice or trading service to provide unified location and load information.

Periodic broadcasts are a powerful way of disseminating any information, but one must be aware of the danger of systems becoming synchronized and causing a "spike" of traffic (this tendency must be counteracted by specific randomizing of the broadcasts over the interval). It can also be coupled with solicited information, as in the Address Resolution Protocol, where the solicitor broadcasts a request for information, but also includes their own statistics in the request so that everyone else is informed for free.

11.3.3 Accuracy

The accuracy of monitoring information in a distributed system depends on the frequency with which it is gathered and the frequency with which it is disseminated. It also depends (as does any measurement) on the effect of monitoring on the system being examined itself.

11.3.4 Problems inherent in monitoring computing systems

There is a tradeoff, using an analogy drawn from quantum mechanics, of a Heisenbergian nature, between load and timeliness/accuracy. Basically, the more you monitor, the more it costs in gathering, loading the network or I/O systems and storage, and the more processing you have to do to make a choice. There is also more and more interference in your systems, so that the information loses accuracy as it becomes more up to date as the system's load increases because of the extraction of the load information. The less you monitor, the less timely is your information.

All this is circumvented by providing statistical metrics rather than details of system activity all the time – typically, run queue information and average I/O over various sample periods are sufficient for distinguishing trends and basic differences.

11.3.5 Overview of existing systems and Unix specifics

There are so few systems that provide dynamic load-balancing that little has been done to enhance the basic monitoring present on each central system by providing remote access to each system's load monitoring through remote procedure call service to that system.

Unix/Solaris tools for local performance monitoring include:

- ps – process status listing (related public-domain programs such as top and mon provide continual versions of the same information – usually by reading /dev/kmem)
- vmstat – virtual memory statistics, see for example Figure 11.2

procs			memory		page							disk faults					
r	b	w	swap	free	re	mf	pi	po	fr	de	sr	s0	s1	s2	s3	in	sy

Figure 11.2 Virtual memory usage example output.

disk	name of the disk
r/s	reads per second
w/s	writes per second
Kr/s	kilobytes read per second
Kw/s	kilobytes written per second
wait	average number of transactions waiting for service (queue length)
actv	average number of transactions actively being services (removed from the queue but not yet completed)
svc_t	average service time, in milliseconds
%w	percent of time there are transactions waiting for service (queue non-empty)
%b	percent of time the disk is busy (transactions in progress)

Figure 11.3 Input/output example.

- iostat – input/output statistics, typically as in Figure 11.3.
- netstat – can show configuration, status and simple statistics
- lpstat – uptime (the BSD version) shows the first line of "w" output, including the average number of jobs in the "ready" queue over the last sample periods of 1, 5 and 15 minutes (this is in fact one of the *most* useful characterizations of a system that is available)

Network versions of some of these are available through Sun RPC servers:

- ruptime – retrieves the process statistics from remote systems
- rup – retrieves system load characteristics
- rusers – returns information about users' processes
- rstat/statd – returns statistics from remote load server

For process and system characterization, there are tools for user and system profiling:

- user-space profiling – prof/gprof monitor via the trace system call etc.
- kernel profiling – through system administrators' interfaces such as sad

11.3.6 Solaris SunOS 5.1 specifics

Solaris provides automatic data-collection tools, for system activity, in addition to the normal set of Unix performance-monitoring facilities mentioned above.

They all work to provide reports on accumulated statistics including: CPU utilization, buffer usage, disk and tape I/O activity, tty device activity, switching and system-call activity, file-access, queue activity, inter-process communications, paging, and remote file sharing.

There are added complications in Solaris because of processes consisting potentially of lightweight processes and threads. This means that their behaviour could be more complex and will depend on the number of processors on even a single system. This needs further study.

For programmatic access to process status, Unix has traditionally relied on the kernel symbol table and read access to /dev/kmem through the kvm routines:

```
kvm_open, kvm_close
kvm_t *kvm_open(namelist, corefile, swap file, flag, errstr)
int kvm_close(kd)
kvm_getu, kvm_nextproc,
kvm_nlist, kvm_read
```

AT&T Unix introduced the "/proc" abstraction, which permits more portable access to process status through a special file system. Solaris provides access to process and LWP information through I/O controls to /proc, for instance returning the C structure illustrated in Figure 11.4.

```
typedef            struct            prstatus {
long               pr_flags;         /* Flags */
short              pr_why;           /* Reason for stop (if stopped) */
short              pr_what;          /* More detailed reason */
id_t               pr_who;           /* Specific lwp identifier */
u_short            pr_nlwp;          /* Number of lwps in the process */
short              pr_cursig;        /* Current signal */
sigset_t           pr_sigpend;       /* Set of process pending signals
sigset_t           pr_lwppend;       /* Set of lwp pending signals */
sigset_t           pr_sighold;       /* Set of lwp held signals */
struct siginfo     pr_info;          /* Info associated with signal or
struct sigaltstack pr_altstack;      /* Alternate signal stack */
struct sigaction   pr_action;        /* Signal action for current */
struct ucontext    pr_oldcontext;    /* Address of previous ucontext */
caddr_t            pr_brkbase;       /* Address of the process heap */
u_long             pr_brksize;       /* Size of the process heap, in bytes */
caddr_t            pr_stkbase;       /* Address of the process stack */
u_long             pr_stksize;       /* Size of the process stack, in bytes */
short              pr_syscall;       /* System call number (if in syscall */
short              pr_nsysarg;       /* Number of arguments to this system call */
long               pr_sysarg;        /* Arguments to this syscall */
pid_t              pr_pid;           /* Process id */
pid_t              pr_ppid;          /* Parent process id */
pid_t              pr_pgrp;          /* Process group id */
pid_t              pr_sid;           /* Session id */
timestruc_t        pr_utime;         /* Process user cpu time */
timestruc_t        pr_stime;         /* Process system cpu time */
timestruc_t        pr_cutime;        /* Sum of children's user */
timestruc_t        pr_cstime;        /* Sum of children's system */
char               pr_clname;        /* Scheduling class name */
long               pr_instr;         /* Current instruction */
prgregset_t        pr_reg;           /* General registers */
} prstatus_t;
```

Figure 11.4 Process state information.

Clearly, accessing this information across all processes would provide an *extremely* detailed view of the load characteristics of the system – it remains to be studied in practice how expensive this would be, and what sampling techniques could be applied to reduce the overhead while minimizing inaccuracies.

11.4 Migration

11.4.1 Introduction

What is migration? In systems without objects there are two forms of migration:

- *Data migration*

  Passive data, for example files, are transferred, in whole or in part, to a node at which they are used in some computation. The advent of NFS has meant that data migration is largely transparent to programmers.

- *Computation migration*

  The computation migrates to the data. This is the more difficult "process migration". The act of process migration involves the dynamic transfer of an executing process from one node in a distributed system to another. This involves the transfer of state (typically an address space in the context of process migration), references to other processes (e.g. sockets, pipes), code (may form part of the address space), and execution state (e.g. registers, stack). In addition to this, the original process must be disposed of in such a way that all references to it are relinked to the new copy; otherwise migration is not seamless and may lead to errors. Clearly, the whole process must be atomic to avoid either the process disappearing or there being two copies.

In a uniform object-based system the dichotomy is removed. All entities are represented by objects, so there is only one form of migration, object migration, in which objects, possibly containing threads, migrate around the system and perform work. One notable difference between some of the object-migration mechanisms and process migration is the question of granularity. Processes are typically rather large; objects can be of any size, down to single integers.

The need for process migration was identified in the late 1970s by Solomon and Finkel (1979) but only relatively few successful implementations have been reported. Amongst them are the Eden system (Lazowska et al. 1981), its successor the Emerald system (Jul et al. 1987), Accent (Rashid & Robertson 1981), Demos/MP (Powell & Miller 1983), LOCUS (Walker et al. 1983), the V-system (Theimer et al. 1985), Charlotte (Artsy & Finkel 1989), Sprite (Douglis & Ousterhout 1987, 1991), SPICE (Zayas 1987), and Chorus/COOL (Habert & Mosseri 1990). A selection of these mechanisms will be examined in more detail in Section 11.4.5.

Various attempts have been made to migrate Unix processes. These deserve some attention and will be addressed in more detail in Section 11.4.4, largely because they demonstrate the difficulties inherent in such an approach.

Smith (1988) and Jul (1989) identify a number of primary reasons as to why migration is desirable in a distributed system:

- *Communication performance*
  Objects that communicate heavily can be co-located during the period in which they interact, in order to minimize communication costs. Since "remote communication can be three orders of magnitudes as costly as local communication" (Jul 1989) co-location can be extremely significant in ensuring acceptable performance.
- *Load balancing*
  Moving processes may serve as a tool for balancing the load in a distributed system. It is necessary to trade off the possibly increased communication costs added to the cost of migration, against the increase in parallelism. If suitable algorithms are used, it has been demonstrated empirically that a large gain in performance can be achieved.
- *Reconfiguration*
  Long-running processes may need to migrate in order to provide fault tolerance in the face of a certain class of faults about which advance notice can be given.
- *Data reduction*
  Whenever the process performs data reduction on some volume of data larger than its size, it may be advantageous to move the process to the data. Such operations may include the creation of summaries of large distributed databases (e.g. telemetry databases). This follows directly from the facts that large amounts of data are expensive to move and that heavily communicating processes operate most efficiently when co-located.
- *Inaccessibility*
  The desired resource is not remotely accessible. This is particularly true of special-purpose hardware devices, for example array processors, or situations in which guaranteed real-time response is critical.
- *Weakness in facilities*
  Existing facilities may not provide sufficient power. For example, in cases where the semantics for remote access of a resource are different from those for local access, it may be expedient to migrate objects in order to achieve the desired effect.
- *User mobility*
  If users move from one machine to another it may be useful to them if they are able to migrate objects to their current location without disruption.
- *Efficient garbage collection*
  It may be possible to improve the efficiency of garbage collection if objects can be migrated to machines that contain references.

11.4.2 Policy matters
Process-migration mechanisms have been implemented at two different levels:
- as part of the operating system, regardless of whether this is within the kernel or as a user-level process executing outside a microkernel
- embedded in a compiler and run-time system

Both approaches have benefits and limitations. For example, language-based migration mechanisms allow the system to use contextual information in an intelligent way. However, they are based around a language that may not be appropriate in given circumstances.

Language support for migration

Almost all language-based migration mechanisms form an integral part of an object-based system. Within such systems, there are two approaches to the provision of support for mobility, depending on the degree of autonomy given to the object in deciding whether or not to move: non-autonomous objects and autonomous objects.

Non-autonomous objects

Emerald has several primitives that can be used to move objects without obtaining their consent. These are:

- *Move*

  The syntax for a move operation is: `move Obj to Loc`. The semantics are weak in that the move operation is a hint to the system that an object can be moved; it does not guarantee that the move will occur. Furthermore, the system can move objects as it sees fit. Note that anybody with a reference may attempt to move an object. The only veto that can be exercised is that of the kernel; the object itself has no say. This may make the implementation of user-defined security and load balancing problematical, and is incompatible with the idea that an object be an autonomous self-protecting entity.

- *Fix*

  In order to lock objects onto particular nodes the operation `fix Obj at Loc` is provided.

- *Unfix*

  The corresponding operation to release the lock is `unfix`.

- *Refix*

  In order to provide a mechanism to enable a fixed object to be moved to another node and fixed there, the `refix` operation atomically performs an `unfix` followed by a `fix`.

ODP includes the idea of the state of *activation* of an object, which describes the state of execution of its code portion. An autonomous object should be in a safe or quiescent state before it is migrated. Otherwise, inconsistencies can arise (e.g. migrating in the middle of an operation). Emerald does not support the notion of marshalling, more often seen in the context of RPC systems. In other words, objects are always moved as they are, rather than allowing them to transform themselves into a more suitable state.

Consider the example of a sparse array. In order to enhance efficiency, some sparse arrays may be maintained using a non-sparse representation in memory. Using the Emerald approach, no option would be given to the object to convert itself to a sparse representation for transmission, followed by a reconversion into a non-sparse array at the receiving end. Since the cost of transmitting large quantities of unnecessary data over the network is likely to be much higher than that of marshalling and unmarshalling, this approach must be considered to be seriously flawed.

A marshalling mechanism could be supported within the Emerald model by requiring that each object to be moved support `marshal` and `unmarshal` operations, which are invoked by the system as part of a move. However, this does not permit differentiation between different uses of the `move` primitive; different compaction strategies might be appropriate when moving objects over different networks, say.

Autonomous objects

A different approach to the provision of a migration primitive is to restrict the Emerald-style `move Obj to Loc` by only allowing objects to move themselves, as, for example, with a `moveto Loc` primitive (Hailes 1991). Somewhat surprisingly, imposing this restriction gives rise to several significant advantages over the more general case:

- The object may vet, and if necessary veto, a request to move, simply by not executing the `moveto` primitive should a security constraint be violated. This ties in with the general ethos that objects should be allowed to be self-protecting.
- No extra primitives in the way of `fix`, `unfix`, or `refix` are required. If suitable locking is employed, these can easily be achieved as a side effect of the fact that all move operations are contained within the object. More complex compound operations can obviously be built if required, in a manner that would be difficult to police in Emerald.
- There is no need for separate marshalling procedures. Since the object knows when it is about to move, it can perform whatever marshalling and unmarshalling it requires immediately before and after the move operation. Moreover, the marshalling procedure has more information available to it than is the case with non-autonomous objects.

Perhaps the major disadvantage is that only objects that export an operation that causes a move are mobile.[1] In the Emerald scheme all objects are potentially mobile; it is merely necessary to possess a reference to enable a move to take place. However, this is merely the price to be paid for the benefits outlined above; objects that are intended to be mobile must be designed with such an eventuality in mind, compelling the designers to consider the circumstances under which a move should be permitted.

The semantics of the `moveto` primitive were not addressed in the above discussion. It is, therefore, necessary to decide whether the system is compelled to

---

1. Clearly, it would be possible for the system to support a backdoor primitive that would cause objects to move without the need to consult them. However, this is dangerous, and great care would have to be exercised in determining who had the right to invoke it.

move an object when the `moveto` primitive is executed[2], or whether it is merely a hint to the system that a move might be desirable. The former approach implies that every object with security requirements has sole responsibility for its own security, which, in turn, means that it must maintain information about which nodes are trusted or not. Arguably, this places too much security responsibility onto the objects. The second approach means that higher-level security requirements can be imposed by the system; for example, migration to a node that is not trusted by the current node can be prevented.

A further question is whether the system may perform moves without the consent of the objects involved, in order to allow for load balancing and autonomy of nodes. If this is allowed, then the object must be moved as it is; there is no opportunity for marshalling.

Immutability

Within CLU there are two forms of object: mutable and immutable. Mutable objects exhibit time-dependent behaviour through changes in internal state in response to routine invocation. For immutable objects, behaviour is fixed for all time. As a result, it is possible to replace a reference to an immutable object with a reference to a copy, without any perceived functional change. This is potentially a very useful observation in a distributed environment. Either when an immutable object is migrated or when it is passed as an argument to a routine call, a copy of the original object can be made whenever a remote reference would otherwise have been created. The result is that local copies of immutable objects can be used instead of remote references, increasing efficiency, but resulting in a larger overall cost in terms of space. If the generation of copies of immutable objects is allowed to proceed unchecked, then it is possible that large quantities of garbage will be generated. For a more detailed analysis see Dickman (1991).

Systems issues in migration

Interference

There is a possible problem, identified by Theimer et al. (1985), concerning the transfer of objects from one machine to another. The migration process requires that a copy of the state of an object be atomically transferred from one node to another. During the time that this transfer is in progress, all messages sent to the object must be queued, until such time as they can be redirected to the migrated copy. This queuing introduces a delay in the response time of the object and may cause the application that sent them to timeout and assume that the object is inaccessible.[3] As far as possible, therefore, it is desirable that such delays be minimized.

---

2. Clearly, there are some restrictions on the degree of compulsion; for example, it is not reasonable to expect the system to move an object to a protected node.

3. There are various schemes to avoid unnecessary timeout. For example, assuming that globally synchronized clocks could be implemented, the called object (or kernel on which it is cur

Residual dependencies

If an object continues to depend on the host from which it migrated, then it becomes doubly susceptible to failures. In particular, schemes that rely heavily on forwarding of messages, for example Demos/MP, suffer from such problems. As a result, it is desirable that residual dependencies be minimized. It is not, in general, possible to eliminate residual dependencies entirely. For example, objects may still require access to the screen and keyboard input on the node from which they migrated. Furthermore, they may have open files on the local disk of their former host, which must also theoretically be migrated in order to remove all dependencies. This may involve the transfer of an arbitrarily large amount of data, which introduces an arbitrary delay and is, therefore, not acceptable.

In any system that supports a uniform object model, medium- and coarse-grain objects contain a potentially large number of references to both fine-grain and other medium-grain objects. What this implies is that, after moving such objects, there are a potentially large number of residual dependencies.

Heterogeneity

The complexity of distributed systems is compounded by the presence of different forms of both hardware and software. For example, different machines may have different instruction sets and different word sizes, and may be big- or little-endian. Before objects can be migrated between different machines it is necessary to convert both the data representation and the code of the object into one that is comprehensible on the remote machine. The data may be transformed in one of two ways:

- All processors know how to translate from all other representations to their own. This is feasible in a system with few different machine types. However, in a large environment it requires a large amount of effort to add a new processor type to the system; it is necessary to add a translation to all the existing processor types. Since the existing processors might be geographically distributed throughout different administrative domains, this is problematical.

- There is an external data representation to and from which all processor types can translate. The introduction of a new processor only involves the writing of two translation procedures. However, this gives rise to a common problem with standardization: which standard is chosen? One aspect of this choice, the precision of floating-point representation, can be seen in Maguire & Smith (1988).

The second option has a natural counterpart in code migration. Either the code is recompiled from source on the remote machine, or, preferably, the compiler produces machine-independent intermediate code that can then be interpreted or compiled, depending, perhaps, on how often it is used and how busy the node is. The intermediate code (or source) may be attached to the object, along with the

---

rently located) could send a "stay alive" message to the caller when the call timeout was close to expiry. Clearly, this behaviour would have to be programmer-selectable.

currently compiled version. Alternatively, they may be accessible by contacting a specific service, which could also hold the binaries previously compiled for the different types of machine on which any instance of the object's class had resided.

Migration deadlock

In systems with the following properties it is possible for two forms of migration deadlock to occur:

- There must be some upper limit on the process number or load on each node.
- Blocking communication primitives must be used.
- The migration command must be mandatory and blocking.
- There is no mechanism other than explicit migration for moving processes (in particular, no load balancing).

If all four conditions are satisfied then it is possible for the system to deadlock:

- *Local migration deadlock*

  Consider a node with an upper limit of two processes. Assume that there are two processes on the node, P_1 and P_2. P_1 calls P_2, which then tries to migrate a third process, P_3, onto the node. At this point, P_1 is blocked calling P_2 and P_2 is blocked trying to migrate P_3, which cannot migrate because the node is full.

- *Global migration deadlock*

  Global migration deadlock is somewhat akin to communication deadlock and exists when every node is computationally full and at least one process on each node in the system wants to migrate to another node.

11.4.3 Communication issues

In a distributed system entities communicate in order to perform work. When one of the entities migrates to a different node, it is necessary that those things that have references to it still be able to contact it. In other words, when a process migrates from one node to another it is necessary to redirect messages sent to the process at its old location. There are two basic techniques for achieving this: message redirection and message-loss prevention.

Message redirection

When a process is moved from a source to a destination node its new location is saved on the source node. Initially, no information about the move is sent to the processes holding references to the migrated process. As a consequence, they continue to send messages to the old location, which forwards them to the new location. If a message reaches a node whilst a process's execution has been suspended pending the completion of migration, then they are buffered. After the execution of the suspended process is resumed on the destination computer, all buffered messages are forwarded.

If a process migrates several times, then a chain of forwarding pointers (or "proxies") exists. This is undesirable for several reasons. If any of the nodes holding a forwarding pointer in the chain fails, then the object becomes unreachable (i.e. there are residual dependencies). In addition, all messages to the migrated object must now be retransmitted several times before they are received. This increases the network load and increases the delay, potentially to the point at which message timeouts expire and the senders come to believe that the process no longer exists.

One way round this problem is to piggyback the new location of the object on the reply to (the first) messages sent by a process to the old location. At the same time, the whole chain of pointers is updated to point to the last known location. This means that after a move (or series of moves) a pointer chain is followed only once by a particular process; subsequent messages go directly to the last known location.

A second technique to reduce communications costs using this method is known as "short-circuiting". When a process migrates back to a node that already has a forwarding pointer for it (i.e. it has been there before) then the forwarding pointer is deleted. Any messages arriving at the node are not then propagated around the chain unnecessarily, but go directly to the object.

Message-loss prevention

Before a process migrates a message is sent by the source node to all reference holders indicating that the process intends to migrate. These processes then buffer messages to the migrating process until a second message is sent, passing the new address of the process. At all times each reference holder knows the exact location of a process.

Unfortunately this approach has significant drawbacks. First, it is more complex than message redirection. Secondly, it is necessary to contact all reference holders before effecting a move; this implies both that it is possible to determine which processes hold references (in general rather difficult) and that all such processes are contactable at the time of migration. If they are not, then the migration cannot take place.

A variant of this technique is one in which the initial message indicating intention to migrate is not sent. All messages to the process during migration are lost. Only when the process has successfully migrated does it contact all reference holders to update their addresses.

In ANSA/ODP, the techniques of redirection and loss prevention can be combined together so that a migrating node attempts to get clients to redirect their messages before it starts to move, but that its previous home will redirect messages from any clients who are still "using the old address".

11.4.4 Unix-based migration mechanisms

In the following section we discuss a range of different migration mechanisms, all of which rely on special features of either the operating system or the language in which they are embedded. Such features create a distributed environment and make it relatively easy for two machines to cooperate in moving a process from one machine to another. However, the Unix environment was not designed for distributed systems and lacks such features. This makes it significantly more complex to implement process migration.

In this section we will consider the Unix-based migration systems due to Mandelberg & Sunderam (1988), Alonso (1988), Hunter (1988), and Freedman (1991). Broadly, they appear to impose similar restrictions on the processes that can be migrated. From this it is not unreasonable to assume that such restrictions are fundamental and inherent in the design of Unix.

General considerations

Unix processes interact with the operating system, with other processes, memory, files, devices, and other resources. This means that there is a significant amount of location-dependent state associated with each process; file descriptors, IPC connections, device locks, etc. In a Unix context, a process image consists of:

- text, data, and stack segments, and auxiliary kernel data structures
- open files for the process along with current pointers and modes
- the state of its controlling terminal and any data in the terminal queues
- any other device-specific information

This state information must be migrated with the process and translated as required in order to ensure that it is valid in the new environment. Unfortunately, this is a far from trivial task:

- The state information must in general be considered to be dispersed throughout the process.
- It is not in general possible to decide what is state information and what is not; for example, Unix file descriptors are simply integers and may be stored anywhere in memory.
- Processes interact with the kernel through system calls. Most Unix system calls are either atomic or idempotent, or both. No special handling is necessary for such calls; however, certain calls are stateful, and the kernel table information must be reconstructed after the migration. If the migration system is external to the kernel, then a readable memory map of the kernel state is being accessed through /dev/kmem and/or system calls like `ptrace`.
- Information about processes may be held in device drivers. In systems with runtime-loadable device drivers neither the kernel nor the process can know where that information is.
- It is not generally possible to maintain the same process id when a process migrates from one node to another. This means that the behaviour of anything that utilizes the process id (e.g. in a file name) will be undefined after migration.
- The behaviour of processes that execute a Unix fork then wait for their children is not defined if the process is migrated. On migration, the process ceases to be the parent of its children; hence waiting for them has no meaning.

As a consequence of these difficulties almost all Unix process migrations schemes require quite severe limitations on the processes that can be migrated (although there is no way of checking compliance). To be migratable, processes should not:

1. perform I/O on non-NFS files
2. spawn subprocesses
3. utilize their pid or any other location-specific information
4. utilize pipes or sockets

As a general mechanism, then, the last restriction alone suggests that Unix process migration is not practicable in a general distributed system composed of communicating entities. In general, migrating an entire distributed system of application modules that shares state with the underlying system of communication support (kernel protocols) is close to impossible.

The Mandelberg and Sunderam approach

As an example of the implementation of a Unix-based approach we will consider the system due to Mandelberg & Sunderam (1988). This is broadly typical of the way in which processes and migration are handled.

The aim of the work undertaken by Mandelberg and Sunderam was to investigate the feasibility of supporting process migration on a network on independent Sun workstations running Unix 4.2 BSD and NFS, without any special support from or modifications to the kernel. There is a clear separation between policy and mechanism. The mechanism by which processes are migrated is distributed between cooperating software on source and destination nodes. However, the migration policy is made by a single agent, external to the migration mechanism; this allows changes in policy to be made easily and independently of already executing processes. The main features of the approach are as follows:

- *The terminal interface*

  Unix processes are "attached" to a terminal known as the "controlling tty" which normally serves as the standard input and output device for the process. One significant issue that must be addressed in any Unix-based process-migration mechanism is the maintenance of contact between a process and its controlling tty.

  The kernel maintains various queues for both input and output for each tty, which may contain partially processed data. It is not possible simply to sever the tty connection, as this results in the abnormal termination of the process and loss of data in the kernel queues. Consequently an alternative interface must be provided.

  In the Mandelberg & Sunderam system, this interface consists of two processes that communicate using a stream connection. The fe (front-end) process is a front-end that transfers data between the terminal and the stream connection. The agent process is connected to the other end of the stream and transfers data between the stream and the pseudo-tty (pty) that is set up between itself and the application. The agent also listens on a control port for migration-related requests. This scheme closely parallels that already used in remote logins.

- *The migration mechanism*

  When the migration procedure is initiated, a migration request is sent to the controlling agent of a process, specifying the hostname of the target machine. The controlling agent halts the process, generates a snapshot recording its state, and passes it to the remote node, where it is reinstated. The individual steps in this process are described in more detail below.

- *Obtaining the process image*

  Obtaining the process image is relatively straightforward. The data and stack areas are saved in a core file using a series of *ptrace* system calls, together with additional information obtained from the *proc* and *u* kernel data structures. In addition to the process image, it is necessary to record information about the interaction of the process with the external environment. Since no sockets or pipes are permitted this reduces to the problem of obtaining state information on disk files and the terminal to which the process is attached.

- *Process files*

  Open files have attributes such as access mode and current file pointer. In order to ensure transparency the file must be reopened at the destination node and these attributes restored. Fortunately, obtaining most of a file's attributes is a relatively simple matter of reading the right kernel data structures. Unfortunately, there is a more fundamental problem. Opening a file requires a pathname that is not recorded; all subsequent interaction with a file is done *via* a file descriptor. This means that deciding which files to open on the remote node is non-trivial, since there is no simple way of obtaining their names.

  The Mandelberg & Sunderam approach is to utilize the semantics of NFS. As part of the process of taking a snapshot, the NFS "filehandle" for each open file is extracted by traversing kernel data structures. Next, a *link* NFS call is executed to create a link to the file with a (known) special name that will be used as an indirection when the process is restored. Since links may not cross file-system boundaries, it proved necessary to create a special directory on each file system in which to hold the links. File system mount information was used to determine the appropriate file system for each file processed.

- *Terminal devices*

  Unix tty devices have three internal queues, the contents of which are dependent on the tty settings, type-ahead, program-controlled reads, writes, and flushes. Since it is not generally possible to empty these queues before migration their contents must again be recorded by reading kernel data structures. The tty modes and settings are also obtained and preserved.

- *Reinstating the process*

  Reinstatement of a process involves two basic elements. The first is creating a new process from the original object code file, and the second is superimposing the state held in the snapshot in order to make the continuation appear to be transparent.

  The agent on the destination node executes a *fork* instruction to make a

330

copy of itself, then opens the disk files that were open in the original process, setting modes and pointers appropriately. After this the process's stack and data areas and the machine registers are restored from the saved core image, again using *ptrace* system calls.

A *ptrace(TRACEME)* is used to pause the process prior to execution, which is initiated using an exec call. At this point, restoration continues as below.

- *Restoring tty queues*
  In order to ensure transparency it is necessary to restore the tty queues to their original state. Unfortunately, the kernel only allocates queue buffers when actual I/O is performed and these queues are created empty. Consequently, it is not possible to restore the saved values directly.

  The agent forces the creation of kernel buffers by a series of write and read operations on both sides of the pty with a particular combination of pty modes. Once the buffers have been allocated, the original queue data is written into them by writing to kernel virtual memory.

- *Process data area*
  After an *exec* system call, an object file is executed and the resulting process given a data area of a predefined size. Many large programs expand their data areas using *sbrk*. As a result, the data area of the reinstated process has to be expanded to the size it had before migration. This can only be done by the process itself. As a result, the controlling agent writes a section of code containing an appropriate *sbrk* call onto the process's stack, and forces the process to execute the code. Once this has been done, the data from the snapshot is written with a series of ptrace calls.

- *Signals and interrupted system calls*
  Since not all system calls (e.g. *read*, *write* (on slow devices), and *sigpause*) are atomic, it is possible that the process was executing a call when it was suspended. Correct reinstatement is only possible if the system call is redone. The controlling agent checks for such situations and adjusts the program counter as necessary to reissue the system call.

- *Cost*
  Mandelberg & Sunderam performed measurements on three different programs: a Unix shell, a compute-intensive combinatorics program, and a symbol-manipulation package. They came up with the following results on Sun 3 processors:

- *Shell*
  This was relatively small and mostly I/O bound. It required an average of 13 seconds to migrate – 8 seconds to obtain a snapshot and 5 to reinstate the process.

- *Combinatorics*
  This was a heavily compute-intensive program. It required an average of 23 seconds to migrate – 14 seconds to obtain a snapshot and 9 to reinstate the process.

- *Algebraic manipulation*

    This was a very large package, with a 5.5 Mbyte data space. It required an average of 650 seconds to migrate – 400 seconds to obtain a snapshot and 250 to reinstate the process.

In general Mandelberg & Sunderam found that the time to migrate processes was a linear function of their core image size. The costs of migration were approximately 14 seconds per 100 kbytes of core, the expense being due mainly to a file-system bottleneck. They have an alternative scheme that avoids creation of a file and seems to reduce the cost to about 3 seconds per 100 kbytes.

11.4.5 Existing non-UNIX mechanisms

The V system

Overview

The V system (Cheriton & Zwaenepoel 1983; Cheriton 1984, 1988; Theimer et al. 1985) was developed at Stanford, and was based on earlier work with Thoth (Cheriton et al. 1979). The designers wanted to prove:

- that a powerful system can be built on primitives that provide inexpensive process management and simple, fast IPC
- that synchronous message passing provides a simple interface and adequate efficiency for fast communication
- that common system problems can be solved with group communication primitives
- that a uniform interface and protocol, reasonably independent of particular physical devices and networks, can be defined to simplify the process of adding new services to the network
- that principles for distributed operating systems are applicable to operating systems for multiprocessors

A major feature of V is the particular division of responsibilities between the kernel and user-level processes, well in advance of its time. The V system consists of a distributed message-oriented kernel, primarily responsible for communication, together with a series of user-level server processes such as a file system, resource management and protection. A functionally identical copy of the kernel resides on each node and provides address spaces, lightweight processes that run within these address spaces, and network-transparent inter-process communication. Low-level process and memory management functions are provided by a kernel server executing within the kernel. In particular, there is a program manager on each workstation that provides program management for programs executing on that workstation.

V address spaces and their associated (lightweight) processes are grouped into *logical hosts* (somewhat akin to heavyweight processes). A V process identifier is globally unique, and structured as a (*logical-host-id*, *local- index*) pair. There may be multiple logical hosts associated with each workstation, but logical hosts cannot cross machine boundaries.

IPC

The V IPC system uses RPC-like semantics; messages are blocked, buffered and delivered reliably. The primitives are *send*, *receive* and *reply*. In addition, there are three types of message:

- *Message exchange* – since most communication involves relatively small amounts of data, V supports short (32-byte) fixed-length messages.
- *Data transfer* – since not all messages are small there is a need for a mechanisms for transferring larger amounts of data. Call parameters are passed *by reference*. Access to these is achieved by the execution of one or more *moveto* or *movefrom* data-transfer operations.
- *Group communication* – this is a form of multicast, used by the system for clock synchronization, for distribution of load information as part of load balancing, in transaction protocols, etc.

Migration

Three basic issues are addressed in the design of the migration mechanism (or "preemptable remote execution", as they term it):

1. Programs should execute in a network-transparent *execution environment*, where the names, operations and data with which the program can interact make up this environment.
2. Migration involves an atomic transfer of a process from one host to another. This involves suspension of the execution of the process for a period of time, and it is important that to avoid causing timeouts elsewhere in the system this time should be kept as short as possible. In other words, migration of a process should not introduce excessive *interference*, either to the progress of the process involved, or to the system as a whole.
3. A migrated program should not depend on its previous host; in particular, message forwarding is explicitly rejected.

When Theimer et al. (1985) was written, they were using Sun workstations based on 10 MHz 68010 processors, connected by a 10 Mbit/s Ethernet. Using this hardware setup, the time taken to copy address spaces was 3 seconds per megabyte. If a naive approach to process suspension were taken, this would lead to unacceptably large suspension times for even moderately sized logical host states. As a consequence, an alternative approach to the migration of logical hosts was taken by *precopying* the bulk of the logical host state before freezing it, thereby reducing the time during which it is frozen. The procedure to migrate a logical host is, then:

1. Locate another workstation (via IPC) that is willing and able to accept the migrating logical host.
2. Initialize the new host to accept the logical host.
3. Precopy the state of the logical host.
4. Freeze the logical host and complete the copy of its state.
5. Unfreeze the new copy, delete the old copy, and rebind references.

The initialization of the new host is performed by allocating it a different *logi-*

cal host id in order to allow it to be accessed from the original logical host in order to perform the precopying. When precopying is completed, the source logical host is frozen, and the destination logical host takes on the logical host id of the source, in order to facilitate transparent relocation. Precopying is implemented by the following algorithm:

```
repeat f
    transfer all state which has changed since the last copy
} until (changed state is small)
```

The first copy takes the longest time and provides the longest time for modification to be made to the state. The second copy moves only that state that was modified during the first copy and so, presumably, takes less time. This allows less time for modifications, and so the third iteration is even faster. When there is only a small amount of changed data, or until no significant reduction in the number of pages is achieved, the copy operation is completed thus:

- The logical host is frozen.
- Any remaining changed state is copied to the new logical host and it commences execution.
- The original logical host is deleted.
- Outstanding IPC requests to the old host are deleted, and the senders of them are prompted to retransmit to the new host.

As a consequence of the complete copy, residual dependencies are minimized. In the original V system, the workstations were diskless, so the question of the need to copy local files did not arise.

Accent/Spice

Accent (Rashid & Robertson 1981, Fitzgerald & Rashid 1986) was a communication-oriented operating system kernel built at Carnegie Mellon University to support distributed computing. In particular, it was designed to support the Spice environment (Zayas 1987).

In the Spice system it was perceived that the cost of moving the contents of a large virtual address space was the bottleneck in process migration, dominating all other costs and growing with the size of program. In order to attempt to overcome this the designers proposed to use the Accent copy-on-reference mechanism in order to restrict copying to a minimal amount of data and hence allow the very fast resumption of a process after migration. Their approach, with a claimed three-orders-of-magnitude speedup, was to perform a *logical* memory transfer at migration time, involving an immediate copy of the minimum set of pages needed to allow resumption of the process. Further pages were fetched remotely on demand. This gave significant savings in both the number of bytes actually transferred and the message-handling costs, because processes were shown to touch only a relatively small part of their memory whilst executing.

It proved possible to utilize the copy-on-reference approach within Spice because of the integration of IPC and virtual memory facilities within Accent.

The particular mechanism used was the *imaginary segment*, accessed not by direct reference to physical memory, but through the IPC system. Each imaginary segment has associated with it a *backing IPC port* that provides memory management services for the object. When a process touches a page associated with an imaginary segment a read request is sent to the region's backing port. The process with receive rights for this port interprets the request and returns the required page.

One unfortunate aspect of this system is the fact that there are inherently a great number of residual dependencies; the correct operation of a process may depend on the availability of more than one site. One possibility for increasing reliability would be to use the Spice approach to decrease interference but gradually to copy across all the pages making up the imaginary segments. Once this had been done, the dependency between new and old machine would have been broken.

Emerald

Emerald (Jul et al. 1987; Black et al. 1986, 1987; Raj et al. 1991) is a well-designed strongly typed distributed object-based language and system influenced by earlier work on Eden (Almes et al. 1985). One of its principal goals was to experiment with the use of *mobility* in distributed programming.

Objects

The Emerald object is fine-grained. This means that all entities in Emerald are notionally objects, from entire databases down to individual integers. Whilst different objects are implemented differently, they all exhibit the same semantics. An object (like any data abstraction) can only be accessed through invocation of its exported operations; no external access to the private data of an object is permitted. Objects can be invoked remotely (an object's location is transparent to the invoker) and can move from node to node.

Each object has four components:

1. A *name*, which uniquely identifies the object within the network.
2. A *representation state*, which consists of the private data stored in an object. The representation state of a user-defined object consists of a structured collection of references to other objects.
3. A set of *operations* which define the functions and procedures that the object can execute. Some operations are exported and may be invoked by other objects, while others may be private to the object.
4. An optional (lightweight) process, which operates in parallel with the invocations of the object's operations. An object with a process is said to be an *active object* and executes independently of other objects. An object without a process is *passive* and executes only in response to invocations. Thus Emerald objects can encapsulate both data and computation.

Emerald objects have two additional attributes: an object has a *location*, and it may be *immutable*. The former is useful in replication to ensure that two replicas

335

are not co-located, and the latter allows objects to be copied freely, as described in Section 11.4.2.

Emerald supports concurrency both between objects and within an object. Access control is provided by monitors and condition variables.

Mobility

Mobility differs from conventional process-migration schemes in two important aspects:

- Emerald is based on a *fine-grain object model* rather than heavyweight processes.
- The unit of distribution is the object.

The units of mobility are thus potentially much smaller for Emerald than for conventional systems. In addition, the mobility concepts are integrated into the language, allowing the possibility of cooperation and the exchange of contextual information between compiler and runtime system. This results in greater efficiency than is available in other systems. The primitives for mobility in Emerald have already been discussed earlier in this section. In addition to the move, fix, unfix and refix operations, there is a mechanism for object *attachment*. If a variable, a, is declared to be attached to another, b, then moving an object denoted by variable b also causes a (and any object attached to a) to be moved to the same node. Note that this relation is not symmetric; moving a does not cause b to move. The importance of attachment can be seen by noting that in object-based systems one of the largest costs is invocation, particularly remote invocation. If two objects are known to communicate heavily at some period of time, then it is possible to attach them, and so ensure that all communication between them remains local for the relevant period.

Parameter passing

In systems based on RPC there are two parameter-passing mechanisms in use: call by value and call by value/result. The former causes a copy of the parameter to be passed to the remote routine, the latter means that a copy is passed, changes are made to it, and it is copied back when the routine returns. Neither is entirely satisfactory for a variety of reasons.

In uniform object-based systems, and Emerald is no exception, all variables contain references to objects. Thus the natural parameter-passing mechanism is call by object reference. Unfortunately this has the potential to be unduly inefficient, since all references to a parameter would be remote. Emerald has three mechanisms for ameliorating this situation:

- Some objects may be declared as immutable, and hence copies of them can be passed to the remote node.
- The compiler can analyze the likely uses of parameters and decide which should be moved to the remote site on invocation.
- Application programmers can exercise control by using a new parameter-passing mechanism, call by move. When a parameter is passed by move it is

moved to the remote site, either permanently or for the duration of the call. Call by move is an optimization. Parameters could be moved explicitly using the *move* operation, but call by move allows them to be piggybacked on the original invocation message.

Location
Since there is no restriction on object movement, it is not in general possible to know the location of a given object. In order to retain location transparency the Emerald designers chose to implement a message-forwarding scheme with last known locations cached by reference holders.

Implementation
The implementation of the Emerald mobility primitives is not unduly complex, but it is involved, because of the existence of different types of reference and the need to segment stacks. All of this is hidden from the programmer who uses a small set of simple primitives which give great control over execution. More implementation details can be found in Jul et al. (1987).

11.4.6 Summary
In summary, the following are the important aspects distilled from the lessons learned by designers of migration mechanisms:

- *Policy–mechanism separation*
  As with many aspects of computing in general, and distributed computing in particular, the separation of policy and mechanism is of considerable importance. Policy is a matter of distributed scheduling: deciding which process to move and to where. The migration subsystem enables the policy to be effected. Maintaining a separation between the migration policy and the mechanism used to implement it has benefits both in easing the initial implementability of the system and in simplifying changes in policy made to cope with changed operational circumstances.

- *Mechanism–mechanism independence*
  The migration mechanism should be written so as to avoid interference between it and other kernel or run-time services. In the spirit of encapsulation this gives both comprehensible and easily modified software.

- *Transparency*
  Processes should be location-transparent. This means that any process holding a reference to a migrated process should be functionally unaware[4] of the change in location; such matters should be handled within the IPC mechanism.

  A migrated process itself should be unaware of any functional change in its environment. However, whether migration should be truly transparent to the process or object being migrated is a point of dispute.

---

4. It may of course notice that the response time of a process has increased or decreased.

- *Preemption*

  In a system with interactive workstations the owner of a workstation should have priority in its utilization over migrated processes. Thus when a user logs on, any migrated processes must be moved to other nodes in order to retain the interactive response time expected for today's highly interactive user interfaces.

- *Residual dependencies*

  As far as reasonably possible, residual dependencies should be avoided. For example, systems that rely on proxy chains for forwarding messages decrease the availability of the system as a whole because the failure of any node may mean that other processes are uncontactable although running and accessible. In addition, noting that remote communication is significantly more costly than local communication, residual dependencies (which are inherently remote) usually imply a degree of inefficiency. In certain cases (e.g. requiring input from the original host's keyboard), this is unavoidable.

- *Reliability*

  It is vital that the migration mechanism be atomic and reliable. There should be exactly one copy of the process active except whilst migration is in progress. Furthermore, should the destination computer crash whilst a migration is in progress, the migration should be aborted and the original copy reinstated.

- *Efficiency*

  It goes without saying that the time taken for migration to occur should be minimized as far as is allowed by the other design decisions. Furthermore, the time spent forwarding calls and rearranging communication links between the migrated process and others should be as short as feasible.

11.5 Scheduling

11.5.1 Introduction

Advances in processor design mean that the computing power available to users on their workstations is considerable. In general, users utilize only a fraction of the processing capacity of their workstations, and frequently leave them idle for significant periods of time; according to Mutka & Livny (1987) only 30% of the capacity of a group of workstations was used. Whilst this is the general case, there are occasions when a user wishes to execute jobs that exceed the effective capacity of their workstations. In this case they must either wait for excessive periods of time and suffer poor response times for interactive tasks or they must employ some form of distributed scheduling. There are two components in any scheduling policy (Krueger & Livny 1988):

- The local scheduling component: this determines how the local resources at a single node are allocated among the resident processes. Local scheduling is straightforward and well understood. Consequently it will not be discussed further.

- A load-distributing component: this allocates the system workload amongst the various machines in a distributed system through process transfer. Process transfer can be performed either non-preemptively through *process placement* or preemptively through *process migration*.

Process placement versus process migration

Process placement entails selecting a suitable node for a given process to execute. In other words, it is simply a remote execution facility. Migration involves interrupting a running process and restoring it on a different computer. Migration is rather more costly than placement, since the amount of state and the complexity of obtaining it increase significantly once a process begins execution. In addition, the whole process of migration involves a significant amount of computational overhead, so determining whether there is likely to be a performance improvement is non-trivial.

Krueger & Livny (1988) investigated whether the addition of a migration facility to a distributed scheduler already capable of process placement would significantly increase performance or not. They found that, whilst placement alone is capable of a large improvement in performance, the addition of migration achieves considerable additional improvement in many cases. The magnitude of the performance improvement is dependent on several conditions:

- There should be a high level of utilization over periods long enough to affect a user's perception of the performance of the system.
- Process initiation rates should be heterogeneous.
- The file system should store significant amounts locally, with little replication at other nodes.
- The overhead of migrating a process should be high relative to its service demand.

This conclusion is, however, contentious. According to Eager et al. (1988):

- There are probably no conditions under which migratory load-balancing could yield major performance improvements beyond those offered by process placement. This is particularly true with respect to the advantages of systems utilizing process placement over systems that do not provide any load balancing.
- Migratory load-balancing can offer modest additional performance improvements only under fairly extreme conditions. These conditions are characterized by high variability in both job service demands and the workload generation process.
- The benefits of migratory policies are not limited by their costs, but rather by the inherent effectiveness of non-preemptive load-balancing.

339

11.5.2 Load distribution

Given that it has been decided that process migration is useful, it is necessary to decide on a policy for load distribution. This is a question of deciding *which* process should be moved to *where* and *when* to move them, in order to achieve the maximum improvement in *performance*. Performance can be measured in a number of different ways: either as average throughput, delay, or response time of the overall system or for each individual process.

According to Eager et al. (1986) most load-distributing algorithms can be categorized as following one of two major approaches:

- *Load sharing*

  Load-sharing algorithms simply attempt to conserve the ability of the system to perform work by assuring that no node is idle while processes wait for service. The most notable feature of load sharing is that it is only when the computational capacity of a node is exceeded that processes from that node are migrated away (typically to totally idle nodes). Consequently, the algorithms are inherently local in that they only attempt to improve the performance of a small number of processes.

- *Load balancing*

  Load-balancing algorithms attempt to spread the workload amongst all the nodes in a distributed system. Processes are chosen from heavily loaded nodes and migrated to lightly loaded nodes, in order to try and achieve an equilibrium over the whole system. Thus, there is an attempt to improve performance globally, rather than for a relatively small number of processes as with load sharing. Unfortunately, the corresponding complexity both of implementation and of analysis is significantly increased. In the absence of near-to-idle processors (i.e. where there is little imbalance), there is little to be gained.

11.5.3 Load sharing

There are two aspects of load sharing: when to migrate processes to idle nodes and how to find which nodes are idle. The former is simple to decide: if the computational capacity of the node is exceeded, then the load-sharing algorithm attempts to migrate processes elsewhere. The second aspect is rather more involved, and there are various techniques:

- *Centralized approaches*

  A central node collects load statistics and details of processes and decides which should migrate to where at what time. As with all centralized approaches this is subject to three major drawbacks: the state information is always out of date, it is a potential bottleneck, and it is a single point of failure. This is not as critical as for some other distributed systems tasks, since load sharing is not a correctness criterion (so long as we have no timeliness constraints), merely a method of performance enhancement. In addition, techniques have been proposed for monitoring the state of servers and recovering them to other nodes in the event of failure (Lam 1991).

- *Distributed approaches*
  Workstations exchange information and cooperate in deciding which processes to move. Since there is true concurrency in distributed systems, there is a need for synchronization between different nodes. In view of the additional communications overhead and suboptimality this is less efficient than the centralized approach. However, it is rather more robust.

In the distributed approach, various different techniques exist for finding idle processors. Amongst these are (Goscinski 1991):

- a logical hierarchy of processors, as in MICROS (Wittie & van Tilborg 1980).
- a logical ring of processors
- no particular structure, as in Worms (Shoch & Hupp 1982)
- the Condor system (Litzkow et al. 1988)

Condor

The Condor system is one of the most advanced load-sharing systems to date. It operates in a workstation environment, aiming to maximize the utilization of workstations with as little interference as possible between the jobs it schedules and the activities of the people who own the workstations. It identifies idle workstations and schedules background jobs on them. When the owner of a workstation resumes activity at a station, Condor checkpoints the remote job running on the node and transfers it to another machine. It is claimed that the overhead needed to support remote execution is very low.

The Condor project has conducted work in three major areas:

1. the gathering and analysis of workstation usage patterns
2. The exploration of algorithms for the management of idle workstation capacity, which resulted in the design of the up–down algorithm (Mutka & Livny 1987) allowing fair access to remote capacity for light users of the system in spite of large demands from heavy users
3. the development of remote execution facilities, known as Remote Unix (Litzkow 1987)

In order to make the Condor system attractive to its potential users several issues requiring attention were identified:

- The placement of background jobs should be transparent to users. The system should be responsible for knowing when workstations are idle and the jobs should be location-transparent.
- If a remote site running a background job were to fail, the job should be restarted automatically at some other location.
- Access to remote cycles should be fair.
- The mechanisms for implementing the system should not consume sufficient resources to interfere with other activity.

Scheduling structure

Each workstation has associated with it a *local scheduler* and a *background job queue*. Jobs submitted by users are placed in the background job queue. There is one distinguished workstation that acts as a central coordinator and that periodically polls the other machines to determine whether they have any spare capacity. This capacity is divided and allocated to local schedulers on machines with background jobs awaiting execution. Those schedulers then decide which of the waiting jobs to execute in whichever part of the spare capacity it has been allocated.

Each local scheduler frequently checks to see whether a local user has resumed using the workstation. If they have, then the background job being executed is preempted in order to allow the user to have the full capacity of the workstation at their command.

Remote Unix

In order to allow jobs to be scheduled remotely, a remote execution facility was required. This led to the development of Remote Unix. The most significant feature of Remote Unix is the checkpointing facility, incorporated because of the need to preempt jobs when a user recommences activity on their workstation. If the state of the stopped job is discarded then all work accomplished is lost. Since the Condor system was specifically designed to accommodate long-running jobs, such a loss was considered to be highly undesirable.

Checkpointing is the act of saving the state of a process, including the text, data, bss and stack segments of the process, the machine registers, the status of open files etc. Typically this is done to the local disk of the workstation, which can prove problematical when that disk is almost full (generally the case in many systems because users tend not to manage their disk space carefully).

11.5.4 Load balancing

Load balancing has been shown to have the potential to provide better performance than load sharing if the overhead of load distribution is ignored (Krueger & Livny 1987). It is rather more equitable than load sharing and it addresses situations in which some processors are lightly loaded and some heavily loaded; it does not restrict migration to idle processors.

According to Goscinski (1991) there are a number of questions that must be answered in forming any load-balancing policy:

- When to migrate processes to balance the system workload?
- How to compare workloads of different computers to decide which should be offloaded first whilst others wait?
- Which process from a chosen computer should be moved?
- Which computer is the best destination for a process to be migrated?
- Which computer should be involved in searching for a lightly loaded (or idle) computer? Should it be the source computer for a given process, or should lightly loaded computers perhaps offer their services?

- When are the scheduling/load-balancing decisions to be made?
- Which parameters should be taken into consideration in making the decisions required by the above questions?
- What can happen when data is not available or is out of date?
- Should the data necessary to make these decisions be gathered and stored centrally or in a distributed manner?
- Should computers cooperate in making decisions or not? If so, what mechanisms are needed to update system state in relevant computers?
- What is the tradeoff between performance and overhead of making scheduling/load-balancing decisions?
- How can one avoid overloading a lightly loaded computer?
- How can one avoid starvation by constantly migrating the same processes between machines?

There are several different reasonable answers to all of these questions. Consequently there are tens if not hundreds of different approaches presented in the literature. This means that it would be impracticable to cover each in any detail. Fortunately, they can be separated into a relatively small number of different categories, which can be discussed separately. The taxonomy in general use is that due to Casavant & Kuhl (1988).

11.5.5 The Casavant–Kuhl taxonomy
The Casavant–Kuhl taxonomy (1988) is in two parts: there is a hierarchical classification together with a flat set of independent characteristics from which a subset can be chosen.

The hierarchical classification
The structure of the hierarchical classification is shown in Figure 11.5, minus the distinction between local and global scheduling, which was mentioned in Section 11.5.1.

Static versus dynamic scheduling
In static scheduling information about the mix of processes in the system is deemed to be available at the time that an object module is run. At that point a static assignment of process to processor is made, and this does not change over time. Static scheduling is effectively equivalent to process placement, discussed in Section 11.5.1. In general the assumption that information about the resource requirements or likely communication behaviour of a process can be determined statically is unreasonable. Dynamic scheduling uses process migration to take account of the time-varying behaviour of a system, and hence does not rely on a priori information about the behaviour of processes.

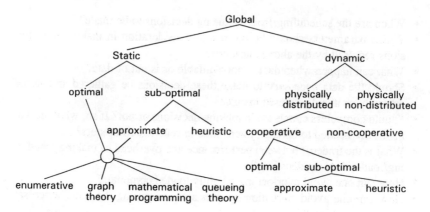

Figure 11.5 Hierarchical classification of non-local scheduling algorithms.

Optimal versus suboptimal scheduling
If sufficient up-to-date information is available about the requirements of processes and the state of the system, then it may be possible to make an optimal assignment of processes to processors. In order to decide what is optimal it is necessary to have a metric. This might be:
- minimal process-turnround time
- minimal response time
- maximal utilization of resources
- maximal overall system throughput

or, indeed, any combination of these. In general, it is not possible to obtain up-to-date information about executing processes, particularly where the scheduler is distributed. Furthermore, the number of processes in the system may make the calculation of an optimal solution sufficiently time-consuming that the answers arrived at would be so far out of date as to be effectively useless. Consequently in many cases suboptimal solutions may prove preferable.

Approximate versus heuristic scheduling
The suboptimal–approximate approach to scheduling utilizes the same metric as would an optimal approach, but the goal is merely to find a "good" solution as opposed to an optimal one. Unsurprisingly enough, it is non-trivial to define what is meant by "good". In general this approach is useful if the following constraints are satisfied:
- A function to evaluate a solution is available.
- The time required to evaluate a solution is small relative to the rate of change of load in the system.
- There is some metric for judging the value of an optimal solution.
- There is some mechanism for pruning the search space intelligently.

Heuristic schedulers make use of special parameters which are indirectly related to the performance metric chosen but are easier to measure. For example, if a scheduler were to co-locate groups of processes that are communicating heavily but to separate groups of processes that would benefit from parallelism, then it is not unreasonable to expect that the service provided to users would improve. However, such an effect is difficult to *prove* mathematically, and, indeed, there is a possibility that pathological cases could exist that would obliterate any potential benefits. It goes without saying that it would be effectively impossible to ensure that a heuristic system was free of pathological cases. That said, heuristic techniques are computationally inexpensive and are likely to provide significant benefits in most circumstances.

Distributed versus non-distributed scheduling
In dynamic scheduling it is necessary to determine whether the responsibility for scheduling should lie with a single processor or whether it should be distributed amongst all participants. As for load sharing (see Section 11.5.3), the centralized approach has a single point of failure, and is a potential bottleneck.

Cooperative versus non-cooperative scheduling
Cooperative algorithms involve collective decision-making amongst groups of processors all working towards the same goal. On the other hand, with non-cooperative approaches, processors make individual decisions independent of other nodes; consequently they aim only to maximize local performance. The result of all processors in the system attempting to maximize local performance may (and usually does) result in a reasonable overall performance for the system, but it is clearly suboptimal. On the other hand, in cases where there are many processors, particularly where those processors are in clumps, the communications costs of globally cooperative scheduling are prohibitive.

Flat characteristics
Some of the characteristics of scheduling systems do not fit uniquely under any particular branch of the hierarchical classification given above. However, they are still important because they represent valid design choices in particular implementations of schedulers.

Adaptive versus non-adaptive scheduling
An adaptive solution to the scheduling problem is one in which the algorithms and/or parameters used in implementing the scheduling policy change dynamically in response to the changing behaviour of the system. Such systems monitor the effects of their previous decisions on the behaviour of the system and change the way it responds in future on this basis; in some sense it is learning about how best to control the system.

Non-adaptive systems, as their name suggests, do not vary their behaviour on the basis of past system history. They are slightly easier to reason about, since it is difficult to determine ahead of time, exactly how adaptive systems will act over time; indeed, small variations in initial conditions may lead to widely differing strategies over time. In this sense the behaviour of adaptive systems may be said to be chaotic.

Load balancing

This is a series of techniques based on the premise that sharing the load of the system across the available hardware resources is good for the users of that system. The basic idea is to balance the load on all processors in the system in such a way that all processes on all nodes execute at approximately the same rate.

Note that the premise is not necessarily true. In particular, in object-based systems, one of the most significant costs is communication. Merely balancing system load takes no account of inter-node communication costs, and may result in a longer execution time than might have been expected from a system in which objects remained on the nodes on which they were created.

Bidding

In this approach, each node has a mechanism for announcing the existence of a task that requires remote execution, and a mechanism for generating a bid to perform work on behalf of another node. After a message has been sent to cooperating nodes indicating that there is a job requiring execution, each node that has spare capacity generates a bid for that job, based on some range of parameters. The bids are compared by the originating node and the "best" accepted.

Probabilistic

This approach is based on the observation that the number of possible assignments of processes to processors is generally so large that it is not possible to decide analytically on a suitable assignment within a reasonable period of time. Consequently, one possible method is to generate a sequence of processes to assign either randomly or using a biased random function. A relatively small number of such assignments are generated and analyzed, and the best chosen.

11.5.6 Overview of a scheduler

In general there are a small number of components in any load-balancing implementation, and these common elements are illustrated in Figure 11.7.

- *The information-gathering component*
  This exchanges information about processor load and communications patterns of entities with other information-gathering components.
- *The transfer component*
  This decides *which*, if any, of the processes on this node are eligible to run remotely.
- *The location component*
  This decides *where* the eligible processes should run.
- *The negotiation component*
  The negotiation component negotiates with negotiation components in other load balancers, either to try to have processes executed elsewhere or to indi-

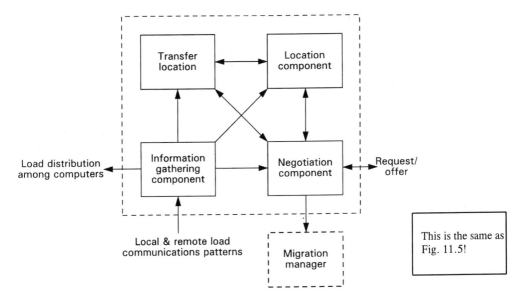

Figure 11.6 Block structure of a load balancer.

cate that capacity is available on this node. It indicates to the migration manager which processes are to be moved.

According to Goscinski (1991) there are certain desirable properties that should be possessed by any load-balancing strategy:

1. optimal overall system performance, defined as total processing capacity being maximized whilst retaining acceptable delays
2. fairness of service, defined as uniformly acceptable performance provided to jobs regardless of the source of the job
3. failure tolerance, defined as the robustness of performance in the presence of partial failures
4. accommodation ability, defined as the degree to which a strategy accommodates reconfiguration and extension
5. good performance of the system under overload

The overall efficiency of a scheduling system is defined by two factors:

- communication costs, in the exchange of load-estimation messages, synchronization of processes, negotiation messages, process transfer, and increased inter-process communication costs
- processor cost, for measuring current load and extracting and marshalling data

It is not easy to say which is the more significant cost; to a large extent it depends on the particular workstations and networks involved, and their utilizations.

11.5.7 Instances of load-balancing algorithms

It is impractical to consider all of the approaches presented in the literature. Instead we will examine two quite different approaches by way of illustration, and provide an annotated bibliography of those not already covered in Casavant & Kuhl (1988).

The Hać and Jin approach

The approach devised by Hać & Jin (1987) is a decentralized algorithm devised for homogeneous system, and utilizes both process and file migration. The overall strategy is that lightly loaded processors search for heavily loaded processors from which work may be transferred. The load-balancing algorithm consists of the following routines:

- *Local process queue*
  The local process-queue routine decides whether to execute a user process immediately or put the user job into the local process queue.
- *Local monitor*
  The local monitor routine performs process and file migration.
- *Distributed monitor*
  The distributed monitor on each host collects and updates the information about the state of the local host and broadcasts this information to all the remote hosts.

Terminology

The *capacity* of a processor is the maximum number of active processes allowed on it and is denoted C; clearly this is intended to prevent overflow. Each processor has the same capacity C, due to the system homogeneity. N_l and L_l are the number of active processes and the length of the local process queue respectively. N_r and L_r denote the total number of active processes and the sum of the lengths of the process queues respectively. P is the total number of processors in the system.

The number of *active processes* on a host at some time t corresponds to the number of processes present but not completed in the system at that time.

The *state of processor* H_i is determined by the number of active processes and the number of processes waiting in the queue on that processor, i.e. N_i and L_i.

The *system state* is determined by the number of active processes and the number of processes waiting in the queue on the local and remote processors in the system, i.e. N_l, L_l, N_r, and L_r.

The job *submission configuration* is the pattern that shows how the jobs are transferred from heavily loaded hosts to lightly loaded hosts by the decentralized algorithm.

The system load is *balanced* at some time t if a submitted job is transferred to the host where there is the least number of active processes.

The local process-queue routine
The local process-queue routine is available to all users on every processor in the system. Whenever the user submits a job to the processor the routine on that processor is invoked. The local process-queue routine uses a first-come first-served scheduling discipline. If the number of active processes N_l on the local processor is equal to or greater than the processor capacity C, then the routine appends the new process to the local process queue. Otherwise the routine calculates the dynamic threshold as the truncated ratio of the total number of active processes on all remote processors, N_r, to the number of remote processors $P - 1$. If the system is balanced, then the job is executed immediately, otherwise the routine checks to see whether the local processor is relatively heavily loaded, by comparing the number of local active processes with the dynamic threshold. If the processor is heavily loaded, then the routine appends the job to the end of the local process queue. Otherwise, the job is executed locally. The processes in the local queue may be transferred to lightly loaded remote processors or executed locally when the local processor becomes less loaded.

The algorithm is as follows:
1. Obtain the number of active processes N_l on the local processor
2. **if** N_l < processor capacity C **then**
3. **begin**
4.   Obtain the number of active processes on each processor in the system
5.   Calculate the threshold $T = \lfloor N_r/(P - 1) \rfloor$
6.   **if** $N \geq T$ **then**
7.   **goto** 10
8. **end**
9. Execute the user process locally and stop.
10. Append the user process to the end of the local process queue atomically and stop.

The local monitor routine
The local monitor routine is executed on each processor in the system. It searches for remote load to execute when it is idle, migrating processes to its local node and executing them. The algorithm it uses is as follows:
1. Obtain processor capacity, C
2. **while** true **do**
3. **begin**
4. Obtain N_l, L_l, N_r, and L_r
5. **if** $N_l > C$ **then**
6.   **sleep** for $f(N_l, L_l, N_r, L_r)$ seconds
7. **else** { We aren't saturated }
8. **begin**
9. Calculate the threshold $T = \lfloor N_r/(P - 1) \rfloor$
10. **if** $N_l > T$ **then** {We're heavily loaded }
11.   **sleep** for $f(N_l, L_l, N_r, L_r)$ seconds

12.   **else** { We aren't heavily loaded }
13.   **if** $L_l > 0$ **then** {the local process queue isn't empty }
14.   **begin**
15.   Remove first process from local process queue
16.   Execute this process (concurrently with the monitor)
17.   **end**
18.   **else** { the local process queue is empty }
19.   **if** H is the most heavily loaded remote processor **and** $L_l > 0$ **then**
20.   **begin**
21.   Remove first process from local process queue on H
22.   Migrate this process with local files to here
23.   Execute the process (concurrently with the monitor)
24.   Transfer the results back to H
25.   **end**
26.   **else** { there is no heavily loaded processor in the system }
27.   **sleep** for $f(N_l, L_l, N_r, L_r)$ seconds
28.   **end**
29. **end**

The distributed monitor routine

The distributed monitor routine collects and updates information about the state of the local host and broadcasts this information to all remote hosts. The distributed monitor is idle whenever the local host is heavily loaded or saturated. The algorithm given is as follows:

1. Obtain processor capacity C
2. **while** true **do**
3. **begin**
4.   Obtain N_l and L_l and broadcast this information to all remote hosts
5. Calculate the threshold $T = \lfloor N_l/(P-1) \rfloor$
6.   **if** $N_l > C$ **or** $N_l > T$ **then**
7.   **sleep** for $f(N_l, L_l, N_r, L_r)$ seconds
8. **end**

A microeconomic approach

This is a fairly atypical approach to load balancing largely because it is based on a pure supply and demand model (i.e. competition) as opposed to cooperation and consensus. Nevertheless, it is interesting and does appear to perform reasonably (Ferguson et al. 1988; also Waldspurger et al. 1992).

Assumptions

Assume that there are N processors in the system, $P_1, \ldots, P_N$. Each processor has associated with it a processing speed parameter r_i. This is defined as follows:

if a job requires μ seconds on a processor P_x with $r_x = 1$, then it takes μ/r_i on processor P_i. The processors are connected by a point-to-point network, defined by a set of edges:

$$E = \{(i, j, d) \mid (P_i \text{ and } P_j) \text{ are connected with delay } d \text{ s/byte}\}$$

Job parameters

Three parameters are associated with each job:

- μ – the CPU service time of the job on a processor with $r_x = 1$
- ReqBC – the size of the job in bytes. When a job migrates this many bytes must be moved.
- RspBC – the size of the result of executing the job in bytes. The result of executing a job is expected to return to the originating processor when the job completes.

It is assumed that all these are known (or at least can be estimated) when the job enters the system. This may or may not be reasonable.

The economy

Processors sell CPU time and communications bandwidth to jobs. They set the prices that are charged for their local resources independently of one another. The goal of a processor is to maximize revenue.

Jobs are allocated an initial amount of money (representing their priority), which they can spend on processing and migrating. If a job required μ CPU seconds to complete then it must buy μ/r_i seconds on some processor P_i in order to complete. It may migrate to a processor where CPU time is cheaper, but it must pay each time it crosses a link.

In order to make informed purchasing decisions, jobs need information about the prices of remote resources. These are advertised on *bulletin boards* maintained on adjacent processors; only entries for immediate neighbours are held. Each job attempts to purchase resources using information about prices, its remaining capital, and the resources it requires. This involves three stages:

1. It computes a budget set.
2. It computes a preference relation on the budget set.
3. It generates a bid for the preferred element of the budget set.

Example

Throughout the rest of this section we will refer to the following example. There are three processors arranged as in Figure 11.7, all with processing speed parameters equal to unity. The costs advertised in P_1's bulletin board are initially as given in Figure 11.7, but note that they are subject to change according to the laws of supply and demand.

There are two jobs in the system, both of them initially on P_1. They have the following properties:

351

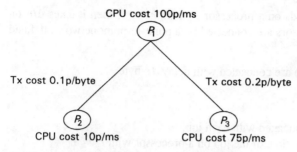

Figure 11.7 Example arrangements of processors.

J_1 $\mu = 30\,\text{ms}$
      $\text{ReqBC} = \text{RspBC} = 1000\,\text{bytes}$
      $\text{Capital} = \pounds 25$
J_2 $\mu = 10\,\text{ms}$
      $\text{ReqBC} = \text{RspBC} = 1000\,\text{bytes}$
      $\text{Capital} = \pounds 25$

Computing a budget set
A budget set contains the processor ids at which a job believes that it can afford service, given its needs and remaining funds. Three parts go towards making an estimated cost:

1. The cost of buying μ/r_i CPU seconds on processor P_i
2. The cost of crossing the link to reach P_i. This is clearly zero if the job is already at P_i
3. The cost of getting the result from P_i back to the originating processor.

(1) and (2) are easy to compute from the bulletin board. (3) is estimated on the basis of the costs over the path along which a job migrates as it executes. Each time a job crosses a link between two processors it sets aside money for its return trip. In the example, the costs for J_1 mean that both P_1 and P_3 are excluded from the budget set (being £30 and £26.50 respectively). However, P_2 can be seen to be in the set as follows:

1. $30\,\text{ms} \times \pounds 0.10/\text{ms} = \pounds 3.00$
2. $\text{ReqBC} \times \text{link price} = 1000 \times \pounds 0.001 = \pounds 1.00$
3. $\text{RspBC} \times \text{link price} = 1000 \times \pounds 0.001 = \pounds 1.00$

Total cost is £5.00, within the available budget. The budget sets for J_1 and J_2 are as follows:

- $B_1 = \{ (2, \pounds 5.00) \}$
- $B_2 = \{ (1, \pounds 1.00), (2, \pounds 3.00), (3, \pounds 11.50) \}$

Computing preferences
A job must choose the "best" element of its budget set; in order to do this it uses a *preference relation*. For example, this might be:

1. The job is to be done as cheaply as possible.

2. The job prefers the element of the budget set that represents the fastest service for it. This is calculated thus (assume that the job is at processor P_0 and is calculating service time following a move to P_i):

Service time $= \mu/r_i + (\text{ReqBC} \times d_{0i}) + (\text{RspBC} \times d_{i0})$

where d_{ij} is the delay per byte on the link between P_i and P_j. For example, if we assume 1 Mbit/s links in the example, the service time for J_2 at P_2 is:

$10\,\text{ms}/1 + (1000 \times 8 \times 10^{-6} + (1000 \times 8 \times 10^{-6}) = 26\,\text{ms}$

The service time for J_2 at P_1 is 10 ms, so J_2 would prefer P_1 on this basis.

3. A combination of the previous two approaches: for example, prefer P_i over P_j if:

$(C_m \times \text{COST}_i) + (C_t \times S_iT_i) < (C_m \times \text{COST}_i) + (C_t \times S_iT_i)$

where C_m and C_t are constants that determine the relative importance of money and service time.

Bidding

After computing its budget set and applying a preference relation, job J knows where it would like to be serviced. It then *bids* for the resources it needs. For example, if J_1 prefers P_2 it submits a bid for the link to P_2. When it reaches P_2 it then submits a bid for the processor. The bidding function for a job J is defined by two parameters C_J and δ_J. If J has M_J pounds remaining and the optimal element of its budget set is (i, S_i), then J's estimated surplus is $(M_J - S_i)$. For example, for J_1, the estimated surplus is £20. The price bid for a resource is the going rate defined in the bulletin board plus a fraction of the surplus. For example, the going rate for the link between P_1 and P_2 is £0.001 and J_1's surplus is £20. Thus J_1 bids the following for the link between P_1 and P_2:

£0.001 $\times$ ReqBC + £(25 – 5) $\times C_1$

When a resource becomes available there may be many bids for it. The processor chooses a winner by auction (see below). Then:

- if J's bid wins, it sets $C_J = C_J - \delta_J$
- otherwise, it sets $C_J = C_J + \delta_J$

C_J is kept within the range zero to one. The cost of the resource is set to be the price offered by the winner of the auction.

The purpose of the above rules is an attempt to resolve two contradictory goals: the desire to win the auction and the desire to spend as little as possible (since price information may be out of date). This can be seen to simulate the law of supply and demand. When competition is fierce, C_J increases, and when it is slack it decreases.

Auctions

There are two basic forms of auction:
- *Sealed bid*
  There is a single round of bidding and the highest bidder wins.
- *Dutch auction*
  There are multiple rounds of bidding which terminate when only one job remains.

Observations

The approach presented above cannot suffer from livelock, a state where a process spends almost all of its time migrating around the system in order to balance load and very little time actually executing. This is because processes have a limited amount of money, and each migration must be bought.

11.6 Summary

It is clear from the literature that there is an order:

process placement < load sharing < load balancing

As this order is traversed from left to right:
- There is an increase in the likely benefits.
- There is an increase in the fairness of the system.
- There is an increase in the complexity of implementation.
- There is an increase in the difficulty of analyzing the stability of the system.

(!) Reality checkpoint   All approaches are better than none, and it is a policy matter to decide whether the complexity of implementing a more dynamic system is worth the effort. There is a measure of unresolved controversy in the area within the literature; contradictory results have been obtained as a result of using different metrics and techniques for measuring effectiveness. Nevertheless, it is not unreasonable to suppose that a simple approach, perhaps utilizing only a single-load indicator variable, perhaps without information exchange between nodes, will give most of the benefits to be had.

Programmer-controlled migration of executing processes has advantages that are not dependent on the particular approach to load distribution chosen. For example, migration may allow data reduction to be performed on telemetry data.

11.7 Exercises

1. Consider a replicated multimedia file system. How would the multimedia aspects affect the choice of load-balancing techniques?
2. Fairness and stability might be related. How?

CHAPTER 12

Future lessons and challenges

12.1 Introduction

This chapter is the result of digesting a number of contributions to a lively debate on the lessons and challenges of distributed computing. The debate was initiated by A. Tanenbaum on the bulletin board comp.os.research.[1] It is intended to be read with a pinch of salt. Some of the structure of ideas emerging here could be regarded as the result of participatory design.

12.2 Definition

A *distributed system* is a collection of independent computers that do not share primary memory (i.e. not a shared-memory multiprocessor) but which act to the user like a single computer (single system image). By this definition, NFS, Andrew, the Sequent, and a lot of things are not distributed systems. Only a few such systems exist, and they are largely research prototypes.

12.3 Lessons and challenges

The following are generally accepted as true by researchers in distributed systems:

1. The client–server paradigm is a good one.
2. Microkernels are the way to go.
3. Unix can be successfully run as an application program.
4. RPC is a good idea to base your system on.
5. Atomic group communication (broadcast) is highly useful.
6. Caching at the fileserver is definitely worth doing.
7. Fileserver replication is an idea whose time has come.
8. Message passing is too primitive for application programmers to use.
9. Synchronous (blocking) communication is easier to use than asynchronous.
10. New languages are needed for writing distributed/parallel applications.
11. Distributed shared memory in one form or another is a convenient model.

---

1. From: ast@cs.vu.nl (Andy Tanenbaum) Subject: Have we learned anything in the last 20 years? Organization: Fac. Wiskunde and Informatica, Vrije Universiteit, Amsterdam.

Other lessons are still highly controversial:

1. Client caching is a good idea in a system where there are many more processors than users, and users do not have a "home" machine (e.g. hypercubes).
2. Atomic transactions are worth the overheads.
3. Causal ordering for group communication is good enough.
4. Threads should be managed by the kernel, not in user space.

Challenges include:

- *Microkernels are the way to go*
  For the system to work, the kernel has to be reliable. Putting the file system and other user services inside makes it harder to get right and less flexible. The performance loss is (at a guess) less than a factor of two. If you worry about factors of two, I humbly suggest you write all your code in assembler henceforth.
- *Synchronous (blocking) communication is easier to use than asynchronous*
  Starting a send, then going off to do something, followed by getting an interrupt when the send is done is a nightmare to program. If you must do something while waiting for the reply, put that code in another (synchronous) thread. The biggest problem in the computer industry is not slow machines, but hairy, unreliable software. Using asynchronous communication just makes the problem worse.
- *RPC is a good idea to base your system on.*
  Send/receive primitives make I/O your central paradigm. RPC makes procedure call, an abstraction mechanism, your central paradigm. Abstraction is a key tool for mastering complexity. We need all the help we can get. See Chapter 2.
- *Atomic group communication (broadcast or multicast) is highly useful*
  Not all communication is two-party. For replicated servers and many other applications, being able to send a (synchronous) message to everyone and know they all get it in the same order without loss makes programming easier and programs more reliable – a real win. See Chapter 8.
- *Distributed shared memory in one form or another is a convenient model*
  Even better than communicating synchronously is not communicating explicitly at all. Just let the programmer think there is shared memory, be it page-based, object-based, or some other. Let the system do the work. There is an obvious analogy with virtual memory. This can be reduced to a single theme: make it easier to build and use distributed systems.

12.4 Micro/nano/maxi kernels – how small is beautiful?

"Microkernel" is the term that has come into vogue to describe the ideal indispensable parts of the operating system, since most vendors' implementations of the Unix System grew beyond the elegant 64kbytes of Version 6 days. Because an operating system means different things to different people (does it include the file system, the scheduler, the communications code?), we will see many different views of what should be in a microkernel. Also, because of different amounts of expertise with hardware (e.g. MMU/context switch support, number of contexts supported), different implementors view the relative costs of "user space" and "kernel space" differently.

12.5 Blocking, synchronous and asynchronous interfaces – easy?

When programming in a functional, procedural or object-oriented language in common use (Miranda/Haskell/ML, Pascal/Modula/C, C++/Eiffel), the programmer only meets sequential single-thread-of-control gedanken-execution models. For distributed systems (read "real distributed systems", as opposed to network-split applications like trivial RPC-based ones), this is inadequate to provide the two things that DOS might bring us: failure transparency and parallelism. This part of the debate seems to circle around how much the system should do versus how much the "ordinary application programmer" will be able to cope with. As with microkernels, this area is highly subject to subjective experience.

12.6 Remote Procedure Call – latent potential?

RPC is either the saviour or the devil of distributed systems, depending on your perspective. It was certainly the tool of the 1980s. If the RPC returns information that is not needed immediately, there are two ways to get performance comparable to asynchronous communication:

1. restructure the program (values are returned by separate RPCs)
2. futures

Futures allow RPC to be used intuitively and the RPC to succeed immediately without violating the semantics of the program. Futures are very efficient with tag memory support. However, futures can also be transparently supported through classes (C++ or otherwise) on systems without hardware support.

12.7 Is atomic group communication useful?

Group communications is a necessary part of any distributed system by the original definition in Section 12.2. Atomic communication is needed for transactions and other things that require consistency. Do we need both together?

Transparent fault tolerance will be crucial. Most people over the history of programming have paid little or no attention to the possibility that computers can fail while their programs are executing. There's no reason to think that situation will change. But the cost of unhandled failure will rise dramatically as programs interact more frequently and in far more complex ways than they do now. Applications need to be made fault-tolerant, but it has to be done transparently. Transactions provide a semi-transparent mechanism in this regard, but transactions are applicable to only a small fraction of the applications that people use, even today. And they can impose a large performance degradation due to the hard global synchronization requirement at transaction completion.

12.8 Shared address spaces and distributed memory models

Distributed memory had early vogue pre-RPC, and is coming back on very reliable fast local networks. It isn't clear how it integrates with most safe modern programming techniques, but as a low-level structuring tool in low-latency situations, it may be very nice. Safe techniques are:

- user-level process locks at memory reference cost
- flexible memory segment control between groups of processes
- low-cost system call interface
- a fork that allows selective sharing of various resources including memory, file tables, locks, environment and notes
- two synchronization system calls to interface to the scheduler:
  - rendezvous – to provide a cheap synchronization primitive between processes in the same process group
  - sleep(0) – to reschedule the processor

12.9 Client–server paradigm

The client–server paradigm goes hand in hand with RPC. It also goes hand in hand with blocking and synchronous systems. However, it doesn't go with real distributed programs, since unless you seriously twist the structure of your algorithm, you gain nothing in fault tolerance or parallelism (fault tolerance is all dealt with by getting RPC out-of-band errors and recalling a server elsewhere, parallelism usually by a side-effect execution of a piece of code in a "server" through a change of roles for a future callback).

12.10 Unix – just another program?

Unix is a relatively popular operating system. For real distributed programs (as opposed to servers like Novell) a multi-tasking system of some kind is essential. So is some protection system (cf. threads and microkernels – how much?, how many levels?). There are now many applications ported to Unix, just as there are for MS-DOS. The debate here is whether we need to emulate the operating system or merely provide the system interface. For any real distributed applications (few) we probably need the system semantics. Most applications run on a single system, so the interface alone may be sufficient.

12.11 Is caching at the server good?

Caching anywhere is worthwhile, provided operations' semantics and failure modes are not compromised. This statement is like saying "good algorithms are worth using".

Caching all over the place is worth doing when the cost analysis says it is. But again this should be transparent to the programs that benefit from it.

12.12 Fileserver replication – how many, when?

Many fileserver systems introduced replicated filesystems around three years ago. Perhaps. Simple hardware solutions such as disk mirroring solve a lot of the reliability problems much more easily. Also, at least in a stable world, keeping your fileserver up is a better way to solve the problem.

Now consider optimistic vs. pessimistic replica consistency control. Pessimism says, "inconsistency is so intolerable that we are willing to take expensive measures (like obtaining remote locks) to prevent it from occurring". Optimism says, "inconsistent concurrent update is so rare in practice that it makes more sense to detect it and fix it up when it does occur than it does to go to great expense to prevent it". This sort of parallels deadlock detection vs. prevention. It seems that there is no right answer, but rather situations where one is best and situations where the other is best. So far, however, the conservative (pessimistic) approach (primarily inherited from the distributed database arena) has been most common.

12.13 Message passing – too hard for application programmers?

Message passing is the way most internal (incestuous) distributed programs like distributed routeing and clock synchronization algorithms are built. Because the consequences of sending a message are many (it may get there or not, and out of order with respect to any other messages from or to any other places, etc.), the programmer is then completely responsible for any eventualities – is this too much to ask?

12.14 Client caching – is it a good idea?

Client caching (e.g. in remote file systems) leads to potentially inconsistent views. In some systems (e.g. Unix) this is only statistically different from local file-system access (i.e. it happens more often in broken NFS implementations that mistakenly used client-side caches). In the event of unreliable networks, however, the inconsistency is offset by the higher availability and performance (e.g. AFS). In the B-ISDN networks of 2001, this will not be so much of an advantage. In most others, it is always undesirable.

12.15 Atomicity – useful, but too expensive?

Atomicity can be relatively expensive in terms of packets exchanged (and therefore network cost and latency) as well as in terms of programming complexity. Is it really worth it, or can we get by with yet another RPC mechanism most of the time?

12.16 Causal ordering in multi-party communication

By causal ordering we mean that if A says something to B and C and then B says something to C and A, then if the thing B says is as a result of the thing A said, C sees A's message and then B's. Otherwise, it may or may not, depending which way the network wind is blowing.

12.17 Threads and processes – kernel and user space

Threads are the virtual CPUs, and if they aren't properly encapsulated, poof!, there goes your cross-architectural application support!

The response to this statement depends a lot on how much migration threads are allowed. If you have a distributed shared-memory system on a homogeneous distributed system and you use thread migration as a load-balancing tool, you have a considerably different set of tradeoffs than if you have client/server distribution or heterogeneity. If some of the independent computers that make up the collection are shared-memory multiprocessors and threads are used to allow concurrent execution within a task running on those computers, the tradeoffs are different than if all of the independent computers are uniprocessors.

In the case of threads that do not migrate, it may be observed that many hardware implementations demand that preemptive scheduling occur on the supervisor side of the user/supervisor boundary – in what we normally refer to as "the kernel" – there must be some awareness of threads in "the kernel" to allow preemptive scheduling of competing tasks. Since hardware implementations often require that the cost of crossing the user/supervisor boundary is higher than the cost of a procedure call, efficiency dictates that many thread operations be implemented at the user level. However, such efficient implementations lead to the need to schedule threads at the user level, and so if threads are visible at the user level, then kernel scheduling and user-level scheduling of threads can compete, causing such undesirable behaviour as thread blocking and preemption of threads that are in critical regions.

The conclusion then is that efficiency concerns lead to a desire to place threads in the user address space, but that scheduling requirements require that the kernel have some knowledge of thread scheduling, at least for preemption. The answer is that the kernel and the user-level thread scheduler must cooperate to minimize the interference between the two levels of scheduling. The best way to accomplish this is currently being debated. One school of thought believes that kernel participation be minimized as much as possible, leaving most decisions to the user-level scheduler. The other says, "leave the kernel scheduler in place, but cause it to inform the user-level scheduler of certain operations, such as block, unblock and preemption".

Better: have a decent process model and avoid this process/thread dichotomy.

12.18 Thread versus process

Why are threads and processes different? Here are some reasons, both subjective and objective.

By their definition, threads do not have to be visible outside of a process. This allows (but does not require) thread creation and scheduling to be largely performed at user level. Some advantages of this are:

- Fewer kernel context swaps in most cases. Two hundred and fifty instructions for a null system call can swamp the cost of a fast context switch. Though a user-level scheduler has to call the kernel sometimes, experience has shown this to be much less frequent.
- Less checking of arguments. The kernel should not let a buggy or malicious client mess up its invariants, but it is the norm for a buggy client to have the ability to screw up its own libraries. Note that though it is the norm it can cause problems, and that is one reason why some of us are pushing for safe languages, where the features of the language that can screw up other facilities are isolated (e.g. mfree, pointer arithmetic, unchecked array dereferencing, passing addresses of objects outside the scope where the object is known to exist). This has been done with Modula-3 and we are working on doing this with C++.
- Fewer data structures shared between all processors. Since each process has its own ready queue the global ready queue is not accessed so much. (This advantage is not inherent but it is typical.)
- Allows for scheduling policy to more easily be adjusted on a per-process basis as much of the policy lives in a library.

The old disadvantages of user-level schedulers have been addressed a number of times, most completely by Anderson et al. in their work on scheduler activations. The problems they address include:

- page faults blocking the kernel thread being used by the user-level scheduler
- priorities not working between threads in different processes

They have also designed an RPC system that for many workloads works entirely at user level.

Subjective threads are a programming mechanism, like for loops or procedures. They make it easier to write programs that have certain attributes.

Processes are containers that are used to run a program on many OSs, in particular Unix. The user of a program should not have to care what particular implementation techniques were used in the implementation of the program. Processes act as firewalls between programs, allowing separate processes to fail independently from each other.

The Plan 9 model (Presotto & Wnterbottom 1993) solves the same problem that threads address with co-routines plus processes forked with the option to share nearly everything. Though the Plan 9 process model (or "variable weight processes") allows for a myriad of different types of processes sharing who knows what with who knows whom, the actual patterns of sharing are usually either of the thread variety (nearly everything) or of the normal process variety (nearly nothing), anything else is too confusing. With a good implementation threads can have the power of a process (independent blocking, ability to exploit multiprocessors) and, in general, the weight of a co-routine.

If process equals program then handling errors and debugging are much easier as the system knows the boundary of what should be grouped together and should be:

- killed when the program faults with a bad pointer reference or whatever
- written into the same core file
- manipulated with the debugger
- manipulated by a user with "ps" and "kill"

Threads inside processes allow this equation to hold much more uniformly. RPC and non-shared-memory (traditional) process groups can sometimes cause this equation to break down, but with much less frequency than it would in the Plan 9 model.

12.21 Log structured file systems (LFSs)

An LFS doesn't overwrite the old versions of blocks *anyway*, so it's trivial to implement tentative writes – you just commit all the outstanding writes by overwriting the superblock. An LFS is essentially an applicative data structure, where you make virtual (mostly shared-structure) copies of indexing structures.

The Butler Lampson "Hints" paper (Lampson 1981) mentions the well-known tactic of using logs for reliable store. The basic idea was to use two "superblocks" so that the one on disk always rooted a consistent file system. The active superblock was equipped with a pointer to an inode table (so inodes could be in any location on disk), to the free list, and to a "semi-free" list of blocks used by the old file system but not writable until sync. All writes were to free-blocks from the free list used by both the old and new file systems. Writing data to a block resulted in a copy and insertion of the old block onto the "semi-free" list. On a sync, the semi-free list was appended to the free list, and the newly saved superblock was marked as safe.

References

Ahuja, S. R., J. R. Ensor, D. N. Horn, 1988. Networking requirements of the rapport multimedia conferencing system. *Proc. INFOCOMM 1988*, 746–51.

Almes, G. T., A. P. Black, E. D. Lazowska, J. D. Noe 1985. The Eden system: a technical review. *IEEE Transactions on Software Engineering*, SE–11(1), 43–55.

Alonso, R. 1988. A process migration implementation for a Unix system. In *USENIX Winter Conference*, February.

APM 1989. *The ANSA reference manual*, release 1.1 edition. Cambridge: APM.

— 1992. *The ANSA Testbench Version 4.1 Manual*. Cambridge: APM.

— 1993. *ANSAware programmers manual*. Cambridge: APM.

Arango, M. et al.1992. Touring Machine: a software platform for distributed multimedia applications. *IFIP Upper Layer Protocols, Architectures and Applications, Vancouver, Canada*, June, 11.

Artsy, Y. & R. Finkel 1989. Designing a process migration facility. The Charlotte experience. *Computer*, 22(9).

Birman, K. P. 1991. *The process group approach to reliable distributed computing*. Technical Report, Cornell University, Ithaca, NY.

Birman, K. P. & T. A. Joseph 1987. Reliable communication in the presence of failures. *ACM Transactions Computer Systems* 5(1), 47–76.

Birrell, A. D. & B. J. Nelson 1984. Implementing remote procedure calls. *ACM Transactions Computer Systems* 2(1), 39–59.

Black, A., N. Hutchinson, E. Jul, H. Levy 1986. Object structure in the Emerald system. *Proceedings of OOPSLA 1986 – SIGPLAN Notices* 21(11).

Black, A., N. Hutchinson, E. Jul, H. Levy, L. Carter 1987. Distribution and abstract types in Emerald. *IEEE Transactions on Software Engineering* SE–13(1).

Bleazard, G. B. 1982. *Introducing teleconferencing*. London, UK: NCC Publications.

Bolognesi, T. & E. Brinksma 1987. Introduction to the ISO specification language LOTOS. *Computer Networks and ISDN Systems* 14, 25–59.

Budkowski, S. & P. Dembinski 1988. An introduction to Estelle; a specification language for distributed systems. *Computer Networks ISDN Systems* 14(1), 3–23.

Campbell, J. A. & M. P. d'Inverno 1989. Knowledge interchange protocols. *Proceedings of the First Workshop on Modelling an Autonomous Agent in a Multi-Agent World, MAAMAW 89*. ONERA.

Casavant, T. L. & J. G. Kuhl. A taxonomy of scheduling in general-purpose distributed computing systems. *IEEE Transactions on Software Engineering*, 14(2).

Casner, S. & S. Deering 1992. The first IETF audiocast. *ACM Computer Communications Review* 22(3), 92–97.

CCITT 1986. *X.ros0 or ISO/DP 9072/1*. Geneva: CCITT.

— 1995. *Specification of Abstract Syntax Notation One (ASN.1)*. ISO/DIS 8824.

Cheriton, D. R. 1984. The V kernel: a software base for distributed systems. *IEEE Software* 1(2), 19–42.

—1988. The V distributed system. *Communications of the ACM* 31(3), 314–33.

Cheriton, D. R., M. A. Malcolm, L. S. Melen, G. R. Sager 1979. Thoth, a portable real-time operating system. *Communications of the ACM* **22**(2).

Cheriton D. R. & W. Zwaenepoel 1983. The distributed V kernel and its performance for diskless workstations. *Proceedings of the Ninth Symposium on Operating System Principles – Operating Systems Review* **17**(5).

Chess, D. M. & M. F. Cowlishaw 1987. A large-scale computer conferencing system. *IBM Systems Journal* **26**(1), 138–53.

Clark D. D. & D. A. Wilson 1987. A comparison of commercial and military computer security policies. *Proceedings of the 1987 IEEE Symposium on Security and Privacy, April 27–29,* 184–94.

Clark, D. D. & D. L. Tennenhouse 1990. Architectural considerations for a new generation protocols. *SIGCOMM '90, September 1990, Computer Communication Review,* **20**(4), 200–208.

Crowcroft, J. & K. Paliwoda 1988. A multicast transport protocol. *Proceedings of the SIGCOMM 88 Symposium,* 247–56.

Crowley, T. 1990. MMConf: an infrastructure for building shared multimedia applications. *Proceedings of CSCW '90, Los Angeles, USA,* 329–42.

Department of Defense 1980. *Reference manual for the Ada progamming language.* Washington DC: DoD.

—1985. *Trusted computer system evaluation criteria orange book.* 5200.28-SDT. Washington DC: DoD.

Dickman, P. 1991. *Distributed object management in a non-small graph of autonomous networks with few failures.* PhD thesis, Computer laboratory, University of Cambridge.

Douglis, F. & J. Ousterhout 1991a. Process migration in the Sprite operating system. *Proceedings of the 7th International Conference on Distributed Computing Systems.*

—1991b. Transparent process migration – design alternatives and the Sprite implementation. *Software – Practice and Experience* **21**(8).

Drahota, A. & D. Hutcheson 1994. DAIS and its use at Hydro-Electric. *ANSAworks 94.* Cambridge: APM.

Eager, D. L., E. D. Lazowska, J. Zahorjan 1986. Adaptive load sharing in homogeneous distributed systems. *IEEE Transactions on Software Engineering* **12**(5).

—1988. The limited performance benefits of migrating active processes for load sharing. *ACM SIGMETRICS Conference on Measurements and Modelling of Computer Systems.*

Egido, C. 1988. Video conferencing as a technology to support group work: a review of its failure. *Bell Laboratories Technical Journal.*

Enslow, P. H. 1978. What is a distributed system? *Computer,* January, 13–21.

Feldmeier, D. 1993. A framework of architectural concepts for high speed communication systems. *IEEE Journal on Selected Areas of Communication.*

Ferguson, D., Y. Yemini, C. Nokolaou 1988. Microeconomic algorithms for load balancing in distributed computer systems. *Proceedings of the 8th International Conference on Distributed Computing Systems.*

Fitzgerald R. & R. F. Rashid 1986. The integration of virtual memory management and interprocess communication in Accent. *ACM Transactions on Computer Systems* **4**(2).

Floyd, S. & V. Jacobson 1993. On the synchronisation of periodic routing messages. *Proc. ACM SIGCOMM, 93 San Francisco.*

Floyd, S., V. Jacobson, C. G. Liu, S. McCanne, L. Zhang 1995. Reliable multicast framework for light-weight sessions and application framing. *SIGCOMM Symposium on Communications Architectures and Protocols,* Cambridge, Mass., September.

Forsdick, H. & T. Crowley 1989. *The BBN multi-media conferencing system.* BBN Technical Report 11, Bolt Beranek and Newman.

Freedman, D. 1991. Experience building a process migration subsystem for UNIX. *USENIX Winter Conference.*

Goscinski, A. 1991. Distributed operating systems: the logical design. Geneva: Addison-

Wesley.

Habert S. & L. Mosseri 1990. COOL: kernel support for object-oriented environments. *Proceedings of OOPSLA 1990 – SIGPLAN Notices* **25**(10).

Hać, A. & X-W. Jin 1987. Dynamic load balancing in a distributed system using a decentralized algorithm. *Proceedings of the 7th International Conference on Distributed Computing Systems.*

Hailes, S. M. V. 1991. The design and implementation of Troy, a distributed object-based language. PhD thesis, Computer laboratory, University of Cambridge.

Handley, M. J. & S. R. Wilbur 1992. Multimedia conferencing: from prototype to national pilot. *Proc. INET '91, Kobe.*

Herbert, A. 1994. An ANSA overview. *IEEE Network*, January, 18–23.

Herlihy, M. 1986. Quorum consensus replication method for abstract data types. *ACM Transactions on Computer Systems* **4**(1), 32–53.

Hiltz, S. R. & M. Turoff 1978. The network nation, human communication via computer. Reading, Mass.: Addison-Wesley.

Hoare, C. A. R. 1985. *Communicating sequential processes.* Englewood Cliffs, NJ: Prentice Hall.

Hunter, C. 1988. Process cloning: a system for duplicating UNIX processes. *USENIX Winter Conference.*

IBM 1988. SNA network management directions. *IBM System Journal* **27**(1).

IONA 1994a. *Orbix programmer's guide*, version 1.2. Dublin, Ireland: IONA Technologies.

— 1994b. *Orbix advanced programmer's guide*, version 1.2. Dublin, Ireland: IONA Technologies.

ISO 1989a. *LOTOS, a formal description technique based on the ordering of observational behavior*, ISO IS 8807. Geneva, Switz.: International Standards Organization.

— 1989b. *ESTELLE, a formal description technique based on an extended state transition model*, ISO IS 9074. Geneva, Switz.: International Standards Organization.

— 1995. *Open distributed processing.* ISO/IEC 10746.

ITU H.320 1992. Narrow-band visual telephone systems and terminal equipment. *ITU H series recommendations.* Geneva.

Jacobson, V. 1991a. Visual audio tool. *Unix Manual Page*, anonymous ftp from ftp.ee.lbl.gov:sun-vat.tar.Z.

—1991b. Tutorial on lightweight sessions to AARNet Annual Conference. http:// www.it.kth.se/ klemets/vatplay.html.

Jayant, N. 1990. High quality coding of telephone speech and wideband audio. *Conference Record of the International Conference on Communications (ICC)*, 927–31 (322.1.1–322.1.5).

Jul, E. 1989. Object mobility in a distributed object-oriented system. PhD thesis, Department of Electrical Engineering, University of Washington.

Jul, E., H. Levy, N. Hutchinson, A. Black 1987. *Fine grained mobility in the Emerald system.* Technical Report 87–02–03, University of Washington.

Kanakia, H. & D. R. Cheriton 1988. The VMP network adapter board (NAB): high-performance network communication for multiprocessors. *Proceedings of the SIGCOMM'88, Stanford, CA*, 175–87.

Kille, S. 1988. The QUIPU directory service. *Proceedings, Fourth International Symposium on Computer Message Systems*, 173–85.

Krueger, P. & M. Livny 1987. The diverse objectives of distributed scheduling policies. *Proceedings of the 7th International Conference on Distributed Computing Systems.*

—1988. A comparison of preemptive and non-preemptive load distributing. *Proceedings of the 8th International Conference on Distributed Computing Systems.*

Lam, K-Y. 1991. A new approach for improving system availability. PhD thesis, Computer laboratory, University of Cambridge.

Lamport, L. 1978. Time, clocks and the ordering of events in a distributed system. *Communica-

tions of the ACM **21**, 558–65.

Lazowska, E. D., H. M. Levy, G. T. Almes, M. J. Fischer, R. J. Fowler, S. C. Vestal 1981. The architecture of the Eden system. *Proceedings of the Eighth Symposium on Operating System Principles. Operating Systems Review* **15**(5), 1981.

Linguistic complexity and text comprehension, readability issues reconsidered 1988. New Jersey & London: Erlbaum.

Litzkow, M. 1987. Remote Unix. *USENIX Summer Conference.*

Litzkow, M. J., M. Livny, M. W. Mutka 1988. Condor – a hunter of idle workstations. *Proceedings of the 8th International Conference on Distributed Computing Systems*, 104–11.

Maguire, G. Q., Jr & J. M. Smith 1988. Process migration: effects on scientific computation. *SIGPLAN Notices* **23**(3).

Mandelberg, K. I. & V. S. Sunderam 1988. Process migration in UNIX networks. *USENIX Winter Conference.*

Meyer, B. 1988. *Object oriented software construction.* Englewood Cliffs, NJ: Prentice-Hall.

Mills, D. L. 1994. Improved algorithms for synchronizing computer network clocks. *SIGCOMM Symposium on COmmunications Architectures and Protocols*, London, UK, September, 317–27.

Milner, R. 1989. *Communication and concurrency.* Englewood Cliffs, NJ: Prentice Hall.

Mockapetris, P. V. 1985. *Domain names – implementation and specification.* RFC 1035 SRI-NIC. San Francisco, Cal.: SRI-NIC.

Mutka, M. W. & M. Livny 1987. Scheduling remote processing capacity in a workstations-processor bank computing system. *Proceedings of the 7th International Conference on Distributed Computing Systems.*

National Computer Security Center 1987. *Trusted network interpretation of the trusted computer system evaluation criteria.* NCSC-TG–005 Ver. 1.

National Foundation for Education Research 1989. *Legibility in childrens books: review of Research*, London: DoE.

Nicolaou, C. 1990. An architecture for real-time multimedia communication systems. *IEEE Journal on Selected Areas in Communication* **8**(3), 391–400.

Olivetti 1990. *The Pandora multimedia workstation.* Olivetti Research Labs Technical Report.

OMG 1993. *The common object request broker: architecutre and specification*, revision 1.2 (draft). OMG document number 93.12.43.

—1994. *Common object services specification.* OMG document number 94-1-1.

—1995a. *Common facilities architecture*, revision 4.0. OMG document number 95-1-2. In preparation.

—1995b. *Object models*, draft 0.3. OMG document number 95-1-13.

—1995c. *CORBAservices: common object services specification.* OMG document number 95-3-1.

—1995d. *CORBA 2.0/interoperability – universal networked objects.* OMG document number 95-3-10.

—1995e. *The common object request broker: architecture and specification*, revision 2.0.

Ousterhout, J. S. 1994. *Tcl and the TK toolkit.* Reading, Mass.: Addison-Wesley.

Palme, J. 1987. Distributed conferencing. *Computer Networks and ISDN Systems* **14**, 137–45.

Plummer, D. C. 1982. *An Ethernet address resolution protocol*, Internet document RFC-826. Los Angeles: Internet Society.

Postel, J. 1981. *Transmission control protocol – DARPA internet program protocol specification.* Internet document RFC-793. Los Angeles: Internet Society.

Postel, J. B. & J. K. Reynolds 1983. *Telnet protocol specification*, Internet document RFC-854. Los Angeles: Internet Society.

Powell, M. L. 1993. *Objects, references, identifiers and equality.* OMG document number 93.7.5.

Powell, M. L. & B. P. Miller 1983. Process migration in DEMOS/MP. *Proceedings of the Ninth Symposium on Operating System Principles. Operating Systems Review* **17**(5).

Presotto, D. & P. Winterbottom 1993. The organization of networks in Plan 9. *Proceedings of Usenix Winter Conference*, San Diego, Cal., January, 271–81.

Raj, R. K., E. Tempero, H. M. Levy, A. P. Black, N. C. Hutchinson, E. Jul 1991. Emerald: a general-purpose programming language. *Software – Practice and Experience* 21(1).

Rashid, R. F. & G. G. Robertson 1981. Accent: a communication oriented network operating system kernel. *Proceedings of the Eighth Symposium on Operating System Principles – Operating Systems Review* 15(5).

Rivest, R. L., A. Shamir, L. Adelman 1978. A method for obtaining digital signatures and public-key cryptosystems. *Communications of the ACM* 21(2), 120–26.

Saltzer, J. H., D. P. Reed, D. D. Clark 1986. End-to-end arguments in system design. *ACM Transactions on Computer Systems* 2(4), 277–88.

Sarin, S. & I. Grief 1985. Computer-based real-time conferencing systems. *IEEE Computer*, October, 33–45.

Schooler, E. 1993. Case study: multimedia conference control in a packet switched teleconferencing system. *Journal of Internetworking Research and Experience* 2(4), 99–120.

Searle J. R. 1975. A taxonomy of illocutionary acts. In *Language, mind and knowledge*, K. Gunderson (ed.). Minneapolis: University of Minnesota Press.

Shenker, S. & A. Weinrib 1989. The optimal control of heterogeneous queueing systems: a paradigm for load-sharing and routing. *IEEE Transactions on Computers* 38(12).

Shoch, J. F. & J. A. Hupp 1982. The Worm programs – early experience with a distributed computation. *Communications of the ACM* 25(3).

Smith, J. M. 1988. A survey of process migration mechanisms. *Operating Systems Review* 22(3).

Soley, R. M. (ed.) 1992. *Object management architecture guide*, revision 2.0, 2nd ed. OMG document number 92.11.1.

Solomon, M. H. & R. A. Finkel 1979. The Roscoe distributed operating system. *Proceedings of the Seventh Symposium on Operating System Principles. Operating Systems Review* 13(5).

Stallings, W. 1993. *SNMP, SNMPv2 and CMIP – the practical guide to network-management standards*. San Francisco, Cal.: Addison-Wesley.

Sun 1986. *Remote procedure call protocol specification*. Sun Microsystems Inc rfc1057/Part no. 800–1324–03, revision B.

—1995. *Hot Java home page*. Sun Microsystems. < URL:http://java.sun.com/ > .

Suzuki, T., H. Taniguchi, H. Takada 1986. *A real-time electronic conferencing system based on distributed Unix*. Tokyo, Japan: NTT Electrical Communications Laboratories.

Theimer, M. M., K. A. Lantz, D. R. Cheriton 1985. *Preemptable remote execution facilities for the V-system*. Technical Report STAN-CS-85–1087, Stanford University, California.

Turletti, I. T. & C. Huitema. Inria videoconferencing system. Unix Manual Page, anonymous ftp from avahi.inria.fr:/pub/videoconference 1992.

Unix Manual 1990. Make: maintain, update, and regenerate related programs and files. Unix Manual Page.

Waldspurger, C. A., T. Hogg, B. A. Huberman, J. O. Kephart, W. S. Stornetta 1992. Spawn – a distributed computational economy. *IEEE Transactions on Software Engineering* 18(2), 103–17.

Walker, B., G. Popek, R. English, C. Kline, G. Thiel 1983. The LOCUS distributed operating system. *Proceedings of the Ninth Symposium on Operating System Principles – Operating Systems Review* 17(5).

Wilbur, S. & B. Bacarisse 1987. Building distributed systems with remote procedure call. *IEE Software Engineering Journal* 2(5), 148–59.

Winograd, T. H. & F. Graves 1988. Computer systems and the design of organizational interaction. *ACM Transactions on Office Information Systems* 6(2), 153–72.

Wittie, L. D. & A. M. van Tilborg 1980. MICROS: a distributed operating system for MICRONET, a reconfigurable network computer. *IEEE Transactions on Computers* 29(12).

Xerox 1981. *Courier: the remote procedure call protocol*. XSIS 038112, Stamford, Conn.

X security, X11 Release 5 manual page. Cambridge, Mass: Massachusetts Institute of Technology.

Zayas, E. 1987. Attacking the process migration bottleneck. *Proceedings of the Eleventh Symposium on Operating System Principles – Operating Systems Review* 21(5).

Zhang, L. 1993. RSVP: a new resource ReSerVation Protocol. *IEEE Network* 9(5), 8–18.

Index